PREFACE

This Turkish dictionary, compiled for us by Fono of Istanbul, will be found an invaluable aid by the tourist or business visitor to Turkey. Compact, yet with over 21,000 headwords, it is similar to other pocket dictionaries in the world-famous Hugo series.

By using a double-column style of presentation, and by omitting to say if a word is a noun, verb, adjective etc., space is available for a great deal more definitions ... simple but complete.

The Turkish-English section has a guide to the pronunciation of Turkish vowels and consonants, and to the use of accents and other word markings. Read this carefully before using the dictionary.

A

abajur lamp-shade
abanmak lean over
abartmak exaggerate
abes useless, absurd
abide monument
abla elder sister
abluka blockade; **abluka etmek** blockade
abone subscriber / subscription
abuk sabuk nonsense
abur cubur unwholesome mixed food
acaba whether, I wonder
acayip strange, curious
acele haste, hurry, hasty
acemi novice, beginner, inexperienced
acente agent / agency
acı bitter, pain, grief, sorrow
acıklı tragic, touching, sad
acıkmak feel hungry
acılık bitterness
acımak feel pain, ache, hurt / feel pity, be sorry
acındırmak excite pity
acıtmak hurt, cause pain
acil urgent
aciz incapable, helpless, weak
aç hungry
açgözlü insatiable, covetous
açı angle
açık open / clear / vacant / light (colour)
açıkça openly, clearly
açıkgöz cunning, wiseguy (argo)
açık hava open air, outdoor
açıklama explanation
açıklamak, explain / make

public
açıklık opening, a space, gap
açıkoturum panel discussion
açık saçık indecent, immodestly dressed
açılış opening, beginning
açılmak be opened / recover (from faintness)
açlık hunger
açmak open, unfold / bloom (of a flower)
açmaz dilemma
ad name, reputation
ada island
adabımuaşeret rules of behaviour, manners
adak vow
adale muscle
adalet justice
adam man, person
adamak vow, devote
adamakıllı fully, thoroughly
adap rules, manners
adaptasyon adaptation
adaş namesake
aday candidate
Adem Adam
adet number, piece
âdet custom, habit
adeta almost / as usual
adım step, pace
adi ordinary, common / vulgar, mean
adil just
adilik commonness
adileşmek become common
adil judicial
adliye judicial, department of justice
adres address
af pardon, forgiving
afacan restless (boy)
afallamak be astonished, be stupefied
aferin bravo, well done
afet disaster, calamity / beauty
affetmek pardon, forgive, excuse, dismiss; **affedersiniz** I beg your pardon!
afiş poster, bill
afyon opium
afyonkeş opium addict
ağ net, web (spider)
ağa lord, master, big land owner
ağabey elder brother
ağaç tree / wood, wood-

en
ağaçkakan woodpecker
ağaçlık wooded place, grove
ağarmak become white, fade
ağartmak whiten, bleach
ağda thick syrup
ağıl pen, fold
ağır heavy / slow / offensive (words) / severe (illness)
ağırbaşlı grave, serious
ağır ceza criminal; **ağır ceza mahkemesi** criminal court
ağırlamak treat with respect, entertain
ağırlaşmak become heavier, more difficult, slower
ağırlık weight, heaviness, slowness, gravity
ağıt lament, wailing, mourning
ağız mouth, opening
ağızlık cigarette-holder
ağlamak weep, cry
ağlaşmak weep together, complain continually
ağlatmak cause to weep
agrandisman enlargement
ağrı pain, ache
ağrılı aching, painful
ağrımak ache, hurt; **başım ağrıyor** my head aches
ağrıtmak cause pain to, hurt
ağustos August
ağustosböceği cicada / chatterbox
ah sigh / Ah! Oh!
ahali inhabitants, people
ahbap friend
ahbaplık friendship
ahdetmek take a severe oath
ahenk accord, harmony
ahenkli harmonious
aheste slow, gentle
ahır stable
ahize telephone receiver
ahkam (pl. of **hüküm)** judgements, laws, rules
ahlak morals, character
ahlaksız immoral
ahmak fool, stupid
ahret the next world
ahşap wooden
ahtapot octopus
ahududu raspberry
ahval (pl. of **hal)** conditions, circumstances

aidat revenues
aile family, wife
ait concerning, belonging
ajan agent
ajans news agency
ak white
akabinde immediately following
akademi academy
akar (su) running
akaryakıt liquid fuel, fuel oil
akasya acacia
akbaba vulture
akciğer lungs
akçe coin, money (old)
Akdeniz The Mediterranean Sea
akıcı fluid / fluent
akıl intelligence, wisdom
akıllı clever
akılsız stupid
akım current
akın raid, rush
akıntı current
akıtmak make or let flow, pour, shed (tears)
akis opposite / reflection
akkor incandescent
aklamak whiten / whitewash / clear a character
aklıselim common sense
akli mental
akliyeci mental specialist
akmak flow
akordeon accordion
akort etmek tune
akraba relative
akran people of the same age, equals, peers
akreditif letter of credit
akrep scorpion / hour hand of a clock
akrobat acrobat
aksak lame, limping
aksamak limp, falter / be delayed
aksan accent
aksatmak hinder, delay
aksetmek reflect, echo
aksırık sneeze
aksırmak sneeze
aksi contrary, unlucky
aksilik perversity, misfortune
aksine on the contrary
aksitesir reaction
aksiyon share, stock
akşam evening
akşamleyin in the evening
akşam yemeği dinner
aktarma change (of train)
aktarmak trans-ship

aktif active, on the credit side
aktör actor
aktris actress
aktüalite actuality, newsreel
akupunktur acupuncture
akustik acoustics
akümülatör accumulator
akvaryum aquarium
akyuvar leucocyte
al red
ala speckled
âlâ excellent
alabalık trout
alabora capsize, overturn
alaca speckled, variegated
alacak credit, claim
alaçakaranlık dusk
alacaklı creditor
alafranga in the European style
alaimisema rainbow
alaka connexion; attachment / interest
alakadar connected, interested, concerned
alakalandırmak interest, arouse interest
alakalı connected, interested
alamet sign, mark, symbol
alan who takes or receives, purchaser
alan open space, square
alarm alarm
alaşağı etmek knock down
alaşım alloy, medley
alaturka Turkish style
alay troop, regiment
alay joke, mokery
albay colonel, captain (navy)
albeni charm
albüm album
albumin albumen
alçak low, vile
alçakgönüllü modest, humble
alçaklık lowness, meanness
alçalmak come down, descend / abase oneself, stoop
alçı plaster of Paris
aldanmak be deceived, be mistaken
aldatıcı deceptive
aldatmak deceive, cheat
aldırış etmemek pay no attention to
aldırmak pay attention

to / send someone to get
aldırmazlık indifference
alelacele in haste
alelade ordinary, usual
âlem world, everyone
alenen publicly, openly
aleni public, open
alerji allergy
alesta ready
alet tool, instrument
alev flame
alev almak catch fire
alevlenmek flare up, blaze
alevlendirmek inflame, stir up
alevli flaming
aleyh against
aleyhtar opponent
alfabe alphabet
algı perception
algılamak perceive
alıcı buyer, customer / receiver (telephone, wireless)
alık imbecile
alıkoymak keep, stop
alımlı attractive
alın forehead
alındı receipt
alıngan over-sensitive
alınmak take offense
alınyazısı destiny, fate
alış taking, buying
alışık accustomed to, used to, tame, familiaı
alışmak be accustomed, become familiar with, get used to
alıştırma exercise (gram)
alıştırmak accustom
alışveriş commerce, trade / shopping
ali high
alicenap generous
alim learned, scholar
alkış applause
alkışlamak applaud
alkol alcohol
alkolik alcoholic
Allah God
Allahaısmarladık good-bye
Allah aşkına for God's sake
allahlık imbecile, idiot
allak bullak turned upside-down
allık redness, rouge
almak take, get,„obtain / receive / buy / accept
Alman German
Almanca German
Almanya Germany

alo hello
Alp (dağları) the Alps
alt underside, bottom
altetmek overcome, defeat
altgeçit subway, underground passage
altı six
altıgen hexagon
altıncı sixth
altın gold, golden
altında under
altlık support, pad
altmış sixty
altmışıncı sixtieth
altüst upside down
altyapı foundation, basis
alüminyum aluminium
alyans wedding-ring
ama but
âmâ blind
amaç aim
amaçlamak intend, aim
amansız having no pity
amatör amateur
ambalaj packing, wrapping
ambar storehouse, hold (of a ship)
ambargo embargo
ambülans ambulance
amca (paternal) uncle
amcazade cousin, niece
amel action, deed / diarrhoea
amele worker, workman
ameli practical
ameliyat operation
ameliye operation, process
Amerika America
Amerikalı American
Amerikan American
amin amen
amir commanding / commander, chief
amiral admiral
amme the public, everyone
amonyak ammonia
amorti smallest prize in lottery
amortisman sinking fund
ampul electric light bulb
an moment, instant
ana mother / main, principal
anadil mother tongue
Anadolu Anatolia
Anadolulu Anatolian
anafor eddy / illicit gain
anaforcu parasite
anahtar key / electric switch

analiz analysis: **analiz etmek** analyse
analık motherhood,
ananas pineapple
anane tradition
ananevi traditional
anaokulu kindergarten
anarşi anarchy
anarşist anarchist
anatomi anatomy
anavatan motherland
anayasa constitution
anayol main road
anayurt motherland
ancak hardly, only, just, but, however
ançüez anchovy
andırmak bring to mind, bear a resemblance to
angajman engagement, undertaking
angarya forced labour
anı recollection, memoirs, memory
anılmak be mentioned
anımsamak recollect
anırmak bray
anıt monument
anıtkabir mausoleum
ani sudden, unexpected
aniden suddenly, instantly
anjin angina
anket general inquiry, questionnaire
anlam meaning
anlamak understand
anlamdaş synonymous
anlaşılır intelligible, clear
anlaşma agreement
anlaşmak understand one another / come to an agreement
anlaşmazlık misunderstanding, disagreement
anlaşmak misunderstanding
anlatmak explain, tell, narrate
anlayış understanding
anmak mention, celebrate, commemorate
anne mother
anneanne grandmother (mother's mother)
anonim joint-stock, anonymous
anormal abnormal
ansızın suddenly
ansiklopedi encyclopedia
ant oath; **ant içmek** take an oath;
anten antenna, aerial

arabulucu mediator
Arabistan Arabia
aracı medium, go-between
araç means, tool, vehicle
aradabir now and then
araklamak steal (argo)
aralamak leave ajar
aralık space / interval (in place or time)
aralık December
aramak seek, look for, search
aranağme refrain
Arap Arab
arapsabunu soft soap
arapsaçı mess, complicated
arasıra now and then
araştırma research, investigation
araştırmak research, investigate
araz symptom
arazi land, estate
ardısıra following, behind
ardiye warehouse
argo slang
arı bee
arı clean, pure
arı kovanı beehive
arıza accident, incident, defect
arızalı broken, uneven, defective
arızi accidental, casual
arife eve
aritmetik arithmetic
Arjantin Argentina
ark irrigation canal
arka back, reverse side
arkadaş companion, friend
arkasında behind, at the back
arkeoloji archaeology
arlanmak be ashamed
arlanmaz shamelss
arma armorial bearings, coat of arms
armağan present, gift
armatör shipowner
armonika harmonica
armut pear
Arnavutluk Albania
arpa barley
arpacık sty / foresight of a gun
arsa building land, lot
arsız impudent
arşiv archives
artezyen artesian well
artı plus
artık left, remaining, what

is left
artık any more, no more
artırma act of increasing / economising / auction
artırmak increase / economise
artış increase
artist actor / actress
artmak increase, multiply, remain over
arya aria
arz the earth
arz representation, petition
arz etmek present, submit
arzu wish, desire
arzu etmek wish, desire
arzuhal written petition
arzulamak desire, long for
as ace
asabi nervous
asabileşmek become nervous
asabiyeci neurologist
asal (sayı) prime number
asalak parasite
asalet nobility of birth
asaleten acting as principal, not as a representative
asansör lift, elevator
asap nerve
asayiş order and security
asfalt asphalt
asgari minimum
asıl origin, root, source, foundation, main
asılı hanging, suspended
asılmak be hung or suspended, be hanged / insist
asılsız untrue, groundless
asır century
asi rebel
asil principal / noble
asilik rebellion
asillik nobility
asilzade noble, nobleman
asistan assistant
asit acid
asker soldier
askeri military
askerlik military service
askı hanger / suspenders
asla never
aslan lion
aslen originally, essentially
asil fundamental, essential
asma suspended / vine; **asma köprü** suspension

bridge
asmak hang, suspend
aspirin aspirin
asri modern, up-to-date
astar lining
asteğmen second lieutenant
astragan astrakhan
astronomi astronomy
astronot astronaut
assubay noncommissioned officer
asude tranquil
Asya Asia
aş cooked food, meal
aşağı down, lower
aşağılamak lower, degrade
aşağılık lowness / vulgar; **aşağılık duygusu** inferiority complex
aşama degree, rank / stage, step
aşçı cook
aşı inoculation
aşık in love / lover
aşılamak grafting, inoculate
aşındırmak wear out (by friction)
aşınmak be worn away (by friction)
aşırı excessive, extreme
aşırmak steal, pinch
aşikâr clear, evident
aşina acquaintance
aşiret tribe
aşk love, passion
aşkın over, above
aşmak pass the limit, exceed
aşure mixed sweet dish
at horse
ata father, ancestor
ataç clip
ataerkil patriarchal
atak reckless, daring
atalet idleness, inertia
atamak appoint
atardamar artery
atasözü proverb
ataşe attaché
atelye workshop, studio
ateş fire / fever
ateşböceği fire-fly
ateşçi fireman
ateşkes cease-fire
ateşli burning, passionate, having a temperature
atfetmek attribute
atıcı marksman / braggart (argo)
atılgan dashing, bold

atılım attempt
atılmak be thrown / attack
atış firing
atışmak quarrel
atıştırmak gobble food
atik quick, alert
atkı scarf, shawl
atlamak jump over / omit, skip
Atlantik Atlantic
atlas atlas
atlatmak have a narrow escape / put off
atlet athlete / vest
atletizm athletics
atlı horseman, rider
atlıkarınca merry-go-round
atmaca sparrowhawk
atmak throw
atmosfer atmosphere
atom atom
atölye workshop, workplace, atelier
av hunting, fishing / prey
avadanlık tool kit
avam the common people
avanak fool
avans advance
avantaj advantage
avantüriye adventurous
avare vagabond / good-for-nothing
avcı hunter
avcılık hunting, shooting
avdet return; **avdet etmek** return
avize chandelier
avlamak hunt
avlu courtyard
avrat wife
Avrupa Europe
Avrupalı European
avuç palm of the hand
avuç dolusu handful
avukat lawyer
avunmak console
avurt cheek-pouch
Avustralya Australia
Avusturya Austria
avutmak console, distract
ay month / moon / crescent
ayak foot / step
ayakkabı shoe
ayaklanmak rebel, revolt
ayaktakımı mob, rabble
ayaktopu football
ayak üstü standing / in a hurry
ayakyolu water-closet
ayanbeyan very clear

ayar carat, accuracy, standard, regulating
ayarlamak regulate
ayarlı regulated, adjusted
ayartmak lead astray
ayaz frost
ayazma sacred spring
aybaşı first day of a month / menstrual period
ayçiçeği sunflower
aydın enlightened, cultured
aydınlatmak enlighten
aydınlık light, daylight
aygır stallion
aygıt tool, instrument
ayı bear
ayık sober
ayıklamak clean, select
ayılmak recover from drunkness or a faint
ayıp shame, disgrace
ayıplamak find fault with, censure
ayırım act of separating, distinction
ayırım differing, distinguish,
ayırmak part / separate / distinguish, set apart
ayırt etmek distinguish
ayırtman examiner
ay ışığı moonlight
ayin rite
aykırı crosswise, perverse, contrary to
aylak unemployed
aylık monthly / monthly salary
ayna mirror, looking-glass
aynasız unpleasant / policeman (argo)
aynen without any change
aynı identical, the same
ayran buttermilk
ayrı apart alone, separately
ayrıca in addition
ayrıcalık privilege
ayrılık separation
ayrılmak depart, leave
ayrıntı details
ayva quince
ayyaş alcoholic, drunkard
az little, few, insufficient, seldom
aza member
azade free
azalık membership
azaltmak diminish,

decrease
azamet greatness
azami maximum
azap pain, torture; **azap çekmek** suffer
azar reproach, scolding
azar azar little by little
azarlamak scold, reproach
azat liberation, release
azdırmak spoil, make worse, rouse
azgın furious, mad
azıcık a little
azık food
azılı violent, dangerous
azımsamak belittle, find too little
azınlık minority
azıtmak become unreasonable, go too far
azil dismissal
azim resolution, determination, will power
azimli resolute, determined
aziz dear, saint
azizlik joke, teasing, practical joke
azletmek dismiss
azmak go astray, become mad
azman monstrous
azmetmek intend, be determined
azot nitrogen
Azrail the angel of death

B

baba father
babalık paternity
babaanne grandmother (father's mother)
baca chimney, funnel (of a ship)
bacak leg / (card) knave
bacanak brother-in-law
bacı elder sister
badana whitewash
badem almond
bademcik tonsil
badem ezmesi almond paste
bagaj luggage
bağ tie, bandage, connection, lace
bağ vineyard
bağdaşma being in

harmony
bağdaşmak get on well with one another
bağımlı dependant
bağımsız independant
bağıntı relation
bağırış shouting, yelling
bağırmak shout, yell
bağırsak intestine
bağış gift, donation
bağışık immune
bağışlamak give gratis, donate / forgive, pardon
bağlaç conjunction
bağlamak tie, bind, fasten
bağlantı connection
bağlı bound, tied / dependent on, connected with
bağlılık devotion
bağnaz fanatical
bahadır brave, gallant
bahane pretext, excuse
bahar spring / spice
baharat spices
bahçe garden
bahçıvan gardener
bahis subject, bet
bahriye navy
bahriyeli sailor
bahsetmek mention
bahşetmek give, grant
bahşiş tip
baht luck
bahtiyar lucky, happy
bakan minister
bakanlar kurulu council of ministers, cabinet
bakanlık ministry
bakıcı attendant / nurse
bakım glance, attention, care, maintenance
bakımsız neglected, disorderly
bakınmak look around
bakır copper
bakış look
baki kalmak remain over, survive
bakir virgin, untouched
bakire virgin (girl)
bakiye remainder
bakkal grocer
bakla broad-bean
baklava Turkish sweet pastry
baklava biçimi lozenge-shaped
bakliyat legumes, peas and beans
bakmak look at, look after

bakraç bucket
bakteri microbe, bacterium
bal honey
balarısı honey-bee
balata brake lining
balayı honeymoon
balçık wet clay, sticking mud
baldır calf of the leg
baldız wife's sister
bale ballet
balgam phlegm
balık fish
balıkadam skindiver
balıkçı fisherman
balıkyağı fish-oil, cod liver oil
baliğ olmak amount to
balina whale
Balkanlar the Balkans
balkon balcony
ballandırmak praise enthusiastically
balmumu wax
balo ball
balon balloon
balta axe
baltalamak sabotage
baltalayıcı saboteur
balya bale
balyoz sledge-hammer
bambaşka quite different
bambu bamboo
bamya okra
bana me, to me
bandaj bandage
bandıra flag
bandırmak dip into a fluid
bando musical band
bank bench
banka bank; **banker** banker
bankacı bank-official
banknot banknote
banliyö suburb
bant tape / ribbon
banyo bath
bar drinking bar, low cabaret
baraj dam
baraka hut, shed
barbar barbarian
barbunya red mullet / a kind of bean
bardak glass
barem official rate of salaries
barınak lodging
barındırmak give shelter to, put one up
barınmak take refuge or shelter

barış peace
barışık at peace, reconciled
barışmak make it up, become reconciled
barışsever peace-maker, peaceful, pacifist
bari at least
barikat barricade
bariz prominent, clear
barmen bartender, barman
baro the bar (legal)
barometre barometer
barut gunpowder
baruthane powder factory
basamak step
basık pressed down, low
basılı printed
basım printing
basımevi printing house
basın press, newspapers
basınç pressure
basil bacillus
basiret perception, foresight
basit simple
basitleştirmek simplify
basketbol basketball
baskı press / restraint, oppression
baskın raid, sudden attack / superior
basküi bascule
basma (kumaş) calico
basmak press / print / attack suddenly
basmakalıp conventional
bastırmak repress, overwhelm, extinguish
bastıbacak short legged
baston walking stick
basur haemorrhoids
baş head / beginning / leader, chief
başabaş equal, equally
baş ağrısı headache
başak ear of grain, spike
başarı success, achievement
başarılı successful
başarmak succeed in, accomplish
başbakan prime minister
başbaşa face to face, tête-à-tète
başbuğ leader
başçavuş sergeant-major
baş dönmesi giddlness
baş etmek cope with
başıboş vagaband, free, uncontrolled
başka other, another, different, other than

başkalaşmak grow different, change
baş kaldırmak rebel
başkan president, chairman
başkası someone else
başkent capital (city)
başkomutan commander in-chief
başlamak begin
başlangıç beginning
başlıbaşına in itself
başlıca principal, chief
başlık cap, headcovering / title
başöğretmen headmaster
başörtüsü kerchief
başparmak thumb
başsağlığı condolence
başsavcı attorney-general
başta on top, ahead, leading
baştanbaşa entirely, thoroughly
başvurmak apply to
başucu head (of a bed)
başyazı editorial
batak quagmire, bog, marsh
batakçı fraudulent, swindler
batakhane gambling den
bataklık marsh, swamp
batarya battery
batı the west, west
batık sunk
batıl false, unsound, superstitious
batırmak submerge, sink / ruin / thrust into
batış sinking, decline / setting (of the sun)
batmak sink / set / prick
battal cancelled / large and clumsy
battaniye blanket
bavul trunk (traveller's), suitcase
bay Mister (Mr.), gentleman
bayağı common, ordinary
bayan lady, Mrs, Miss
bayat stale, not fresh
baygın fainted, unconscious
bayılmak faint, swoon
bayır slope
bayi seller, retailer
baykuş owl
bayrak flag
bayram feast-day, holiday
baytar veterinary surgeon
bazan sometimes

bazı some, certain
bebek baby / doll
becerikli skillful
becermek do something with success, be able to, manage to
bedava for nothing, free
bedbaht unfortunate, unhappy
bedbin pessimistic
beddua curse
bedel substitute price / in exchange for
beden trunk, body
bedenen physically
bedeni bodily
bedesten old bazaar, market
beğeni good taste
beğenmek like
behemahal in any case, at all costs
beher to each, for each
bej light brown
bekâr bachelor
bekâret virginity
bekçi watchman, sentry
bekleme salonu waiting room
beklemek wait / expect
bekletmek keep waiting
bel waist
bel spade (tool)
bela trouble, calamity
belalı troublesome
Belçika Belgium
belde town, country
belediye municipality
belediye reisi mayor
beleş gratis, free
belge document, certificate
belgesel documentary
belirgin clear, evident
belirlemek determine
belirli certain, definite
belirmek appear, loom
belirsiz indistinct, uncertain
belirti mark, sign
belirtmek state, point out, make clear
belkemiği backbone
belki perhaps, maybe
bellek mind, memory
bellemek learn by heart, memorize
belli known, evident
bembeyaz extremely white, snow white
ben I
ben mole
bence in my opinion, as for me

bencil egoistic, selfish
benek spot on the skin
beni me
benim my, mine
benimki mine
benimsemek pretend to own, claim
beniz colour of the face
benli having moles
benlik egoism, pride, selfishness
bent dam / paragraph
benzemek look like, resemble
benzer resembling, alike
benzetmek make an imitation or copy of / see a resemblance / make resemble / compare to / mistake somebody for
benzin benzine, petrol, gasoline
beraat acquittal
beraat etmek be acquitted
beraber together
berat patent
berbat bad, ruined, worse
berber barber, hair-dresser
bere beret / bruise
bereket abundance
bereketli fruitful, fertile
berelemek bruise, batter
beri since / here
berrak clear, limpid
bertaraf etmek get rid of
besili well nourished
besin food
beslemek feed, nourish
besleyici nutritious
beste tune, musical composition
besteci composer
bestelemek compose music
beş five
beşer mankind
beşeri human
beşeriyet humanity
beşgen pentagon, fivesided
beşik cradle
beşinci fifth
beter worse
beton concrete
bey gentleman
beyan declaration, expression
beyanat discourse, speech
beyanname manifesto, declaration

beyaz white
beyazımsı whitish
beyazperde screen (movie)
beyefendi sir, esquire
beygir horse, hack horse
beygirgücü horse power
beyhude vain, in vain
beyin brain
beyinsiz brainless
beyit couplet
beylik conventional; belonging to the government, government property
beynelmilel international
bez cloth / gland
bezdirmek plague
bezelye pea
bezgin tired of
bezik bezigue
bezir linseed oil
bezmek get tired of
bıçak knife
bıçaklamak stab
bıçkı log saw, sawyer's saw
bıkmak get tired of, be sick of
bıldırcın quail
bırakmak release, let, leave
bıyık moustache, whisker
biber pepper
biberon feeding bottle
bibliyografi bibliography
biblo bibelot, small ornament
biçare without help, wretched, unfortunate
biçerdöğer cutter and thresher
biçilmek be cut out, be clipped, be sawn, be reaped
biçim form, shape, sort, manner
biçimli decent, well proportioned
biçimsiz untidy, unsuitable; ill-shaped
biçki tailoring
biçmek cut out, divide
bidon oil drum, can, tin
biftek beefsteak
bigudi hair curler
bihaber unaware
bılakis on the contrary
bilanço balance sheet
bilardo billiards
bildik known, acquaintance
bildirge report
bildiri communiqué

bildirmek notify, inform
bile even
bilek wrist
bilemek sharpen
bileşik compound
bileşim mixture
bilet ticket
biletçi conductor
bileyici knife grinder, sharpener
bilezik bracelet
bilgi knowledge
bilgiç pedant
bilgili learned
bilgin learned man, scientist
bilgisayar computer
bilhassa especially
bilim science
bilimsel scientific
bilinç the conscious
bilinçaltı subconscious
bilinçli conscious
bilirkişi expert
billur crystal
bilmece riddle, cross-word
bilmek know
bilmukabele in return, the same to you
bilye marble / bearing ball
bin thousand
bina building
binbaşı major
bindirmek cause to mount / to collide with
binek used for riding
binici rider
binmek mount, ride / get on
bir one / a, an
bira beer, ale
birahane beerhouse, pub
birader brother
biraz a little, some
birbiri each other, one another
birçok a lot of, many
bir daha once more, again
birden altogether, at a time / suddenly
birdenbire suddenly
birdirbir leapfrog
birebir most efficacious
birey individual
bireysel individual
biri, birisi, one of them, someone
biricik unique
birikim accumulation
birikinti accumulation, heap

birikmek assemble, accumulate
biriktirmek collect, save up (money)
birim unit
birinci first
birisi bak **biri**
birkaç some, a few
birleşik united
birleşmek unite
birleştirmek join, unite, meet
birlik union, association, unit (mil.)
birörnek same pattern
birtakım some, certain
birtürlü never, by no means, in no way
bisiklet bicycle
bismillah in the name of God
bisküvi biscuit
bit louse
bitap exhausted, very tired
bitaraf neutral, impartial
bitek fertile
biteviye monotonous
bitik exhausted
bitim ending
bitirmek finish, complete
bitişik adjoining, next to
bitişmek join, adhere
bitkin exhausted
bitki vegetation, plant
bitkisel plant like, vegetal
bitli lousy
bitmek finish, come to an end / grow
biyografi biography
biyoloji biology
biz we
bizar sick of, wearied
bizi, bize us
bizim our
bizimki ours
bizzat in person, personally
blok block, group
bloknot pad
blöf bluff
blucin jeans
bluz blouse
boa boa
bobin bobbin
bocalamak stumble, falter
bodrum underground chamber, cellar, basement
bodur short
boğa bull
boğaz throat, mountain

pass, strait
Boğaziçi the Bosphorus
boğazlamak strangle
boğazlı gluttonous, having appetite
boğmaca (öksürüğü) whooping cough
boğmak strangle / suffocate / drown
boğucu suffocating
boğuk hoarse (voice)
boğulmak be choked, be drowned
boğum node, knot
boğuntu oppression, suffocation / cheating (argo)
boğuşmak fight, struggle
bohça bundle
bok dung, excrement
boks, boxing
boksör boxer
bol wide, loose / abundant
bolluk wideness / abundance
bomba bomb
bombalamak bomb
bombardıman bombardment
bomboş completely empty
boncuk bead
bonfile sirloin steak
bono bond, bill
bonservis certificate of good service
bora tempest
borazan trumpet, bugle
borç debt, loan
borçlanmak get into debt
borçlu indebted, debtor
bordo claret red
bordro payroll
bornoz bathrobe, burnous
borsa stock exchange
boru pipe, tube
bostan melon garden
boş empty, vain, useless, unoccupied, free
boşal(t)mak empty, pour out
boşama divorce
boşanmak break, be divorced
boşboğaz garrulous, indiscreet
boşluk emptiness / space / hollowness / gap / vacuum
bot boot, dinghy
botanik botany
boy length, height
boya dye, paint
boyacı dyer, shoeshine

boyamak dye, paint
boykot etmek boycott
boylam longitude
boynuz horn
boyun neck
boyuna lengthwise / continually
boyun atkısı scarf
boyunbağı necktie
boyunca along
boyunduruk yoke
boyut dimension
boz grey
bozgun defeat
bozguncu anarchist
bozkır steppe, barren land
bozmak spoil, destroy
bozuk out of order, broken, spoilt
bozuk para small change
bozulmak go wrong, be upset, go bad
bozuşmak become estranged
böbrek kidney
böbürlenmek boast
böcek insect, bug
böğürmek bellow, moo
böğürtlen blackberry
bölen divisor
bölge district, zone
bölmek divide
bölü divided by
bölük squadron (mil.)
bölüm portion, chapter, part
bölünen dividened
bölüş(tür)mek divide up, share out
bön silly , naive
börek pie, pastry
börülce kidney-bean
böyle such, so, thus
böylece so, thus, like this
branda hammock, canvas
branş branch
bravo bravo!
Brezilya Brazil
briç bridge
briket briquette
brlyantin brilliantine
bronşit bronchitis
broş brooch
broşür brochure
brüt gross, total
bu this, **bunlar** these
bucak corner / small town, sub-district
buçuk half
budak knot in timber
budala silly, fool
budamak trim, prune
buğday wheat

buğu steam, vapour
buğulanmak fog up, steam up
bugün today
bugünkü today's
buhar steam, vapour
buhran crisis
buket bouquet
bulamaç thick soup
bulamak smear
bulanık turbid, cloudy
bulanmak become cloudy or turbid / turn (stomach)
bulantı nausea
bulaşıcı contagious, infectious
bulaşık soiled, dirty / contagious / dirty plates
bulaşmak be smeared / have to do with
Bulgar Bulgarian;
Bulgaristan Bulgaria
bulgu a finding
bulgur cracked wheat
bulmaca riddle, puzzle, crossword
bulmak find, invent
buluğ puberty
bulunmak be found, be present
buluş invention, discovery
buluşmak meet
bulut cloud; **bulutlu** cloudy
bulvar boulevard, avenue
bunak in one's second childhood, senile
bunalım crisis, depression
bunalmak be stupefied, be suffocated
bunamak enter one's dotage
bunca so much, so long, so many, all these, this much
bunlar these
burada here, this place
burası this place
burç tower / constellation
burçak vetch
burgu corkscrew, gimlet
burjuva bourgeois
burkulmak be twisted, twist
burma spiral
burmak twist, wring
burs scholarship
buruk acrid, sour
burun nose, beak

burun deliği nostril
buruşmak be wrinkled
buruşturmak crease, wrinkle
buruşuk wrinkled
buse kiss
but the buttocks, leg of meat
buut dimension
buyurmak order
buyurun come in, help yourself
buz ice
buzağı calf (year old)
buzdolabı refrigerator
buzhane ice-house
buzlu iced
buzlu cam frosted glass
buzul glacier
bücür short, squat
büfe buffet, snack bar
büklüm twist, curl
bükmek twist, bend, spin
bükülmek be twisted
bülbül nightingale
bülten bulletin
bünye structure
büro office
bürünmek be wrapped in, surrounded
büsbütün altogether, quite entirely
bütçe budget
bütün whole, entire, complete, wholly, the whole
bütünleme (sınavı) make up examination
bütünlemek complete
büyü spell
büyük great, big large
büyükanne grandmother
büyükbaba grandfather
büyükelçi ambassador
büyülemek bewitch, charm, fascinate
büyüteç magnifying glass
büyütmek bring up, grow / exaggerate
büzmek constrict
büzülmek contract, shrink

C

caba free, gratis
cacık chopped cucumber in buttermilk
cadde main street
cadı witch, hag
cahil ignorant, inexpe-

rienced, uneducated
cahillik ignorance
caiz permitted, possible
caka ostentation, showing off
cam glass, pane, window
cambaz acrobat
camcı glazier
camekan shopwindow
cami mosque
camia assembly of people
can soul, life
canan sweetheart
canavar monster, wild beast
cana yakın pleasant
candan sincere
canciğer very close, intimate
cani criminal
cankurtaran ambulance, life-saving
canlanmak come to life, become active
canlı lively, active
cansiperane self sacrificing
can sıkıcı boring
can sıkıntısı boredom
cansız lifeless, weak
cari current, valid
casus spy
caymak swerve, deviate, change one's mind, give up
caz jazz
cazibe attraction, charm
cazibeli attractive
cazip attracting
cebir force / algebra (math)
cebren by force
ced ancestor
cefa ill-treatment, torment
cehalet ignorance
cehennem hell
ceket jacket, coat
cellat executioner
celp etmek attract / summon
celse sitting, session
cemaat community, group
ceman in all, as a total
cemiyet society, association
cenaze funeral
cengaver warlike
cenk war, battle
cennet heaven
centilmen gentleman / polite
cenup the south

cep pocket, purse
cephane ammunition
cep harçlığı pocket money
cephe front
cerahat pus
cerbezeli loquacious, talkative
cereme penalty
cereyan current, draught
cerrah surgeon
cesaret boldness, courage
ceset corpse
cesur bold, daring, courageous
cetvel tabulated form, list / ruler
cevaben in reply
cevap answer, reply
cevaplandırmak answer
cevher substance, mineral, ore
ceviz walnut; **Hindistan cevizi** coconut
ceylan gazelle
ceza punishment, fine
cezaevi prison, jail
cezalandırmak punish
cezir ebb tide
cezp attraction
cezp etmek attract
cezve coffee-pot
cılız delicate, thin, weak
cılk rotten
cımbız tweezers
cıngar fight, quarrel (argo)
cırlak shrill (voice)
cırlamak screech
cıva mercury
cıvata bolt
cıvık sticky, wet
cıvıldamak twitter, chirp
cıvıl cıvıl twittering
cıvıltı twittering
cızbız grilled meat
cızırdamak sizzle, creak
cibiliyet nature
cibinlik mosquito net
cici (childish) pretty, nice
cidar wall
cidden seriously, indeed
ciddi serious
ciddiyet seriousness
ciğer liver, lungs
cihan world, universe
cihangir world conqueror
cihaz apparatus, equipment
cihet side, direction
cila polish, luster
cilt skin / binding (of a book) / volume

ciltlemek bind (a book)
cilve coquetry
cilveli coquettish
cimri miser, stingy
cin demon
cinai criminal
cinayet crime, murder
cingöz shrewd
cinnet madness
cins kind, sort, sex
cinsel sexual
cinsi sexual
cirit javelin
ciro endorsement
cisim body, material, object
civar environments, neighbourhood
civciv chick
civcivli full of movement, rush hour
coğrafi geographical
coğrafya geography
cop truncheon
coşku zeal, enthusiasm
coşkun overflowing
coşmak overflow
cömert generous
cuma Friday
cumartesi Saturday
cumba bay window
cumhurbaşkanı president of the republic
cumhuriyet republic
cunta junta
curcuna noisy confusion
cüce dwarf
cümbüş merry-making, entertainment, orgy
cümle sentence, whole
cümlecik clause
cümleten all together
cüret boldness
cüretkar bold
cürüm crime, fault, sin, guilt
cüsse body, bigness
cüsseli huge
cüzam leprosy
cüzamlı leprous
cüzdan wallet, portfolio, purse
cüzi trifling, small

Ç

çaba effort
çabalamak strive,

struggle, try to
çabuk quick
çabucak quickly
çadır tent
çağ time, age, period, era
çağdaş contemporary
çağdışı out of date, behind the times
çağırmak call / invite
çağırtmak send for
çağla green almond
çağlamak burble, murmur
çağlayan waterfall, cascade, cataract
çağrı invitation, call
çağrışım association
çakal jackal, coyote
çakı pocket knife
çakıl pebble
çakıllık pebbly place
çakır bluish grey
çakırkeyf tipsy, tight
çakışmak fit into one another
çakmak nail, strike
çakmak lighter
çakmaktaşı flint
çalar saat alarm clock
çalgı musical instrument
çalı bush, shrub
çalışkan hard-working, industrious
çalışmak work, study
çalıştırmak set to work, employ
çalkalamak rinse
çalkalanmak be agitated / (of a ship) roll / (of the sea) become rough
çalkantı agitaion, a shaking
çalmak knock (on a door) / ring (a bell) / steal / play (musical instrument)
çam fir, pine
çamaşır underclothing, linen, underwear / washing, laundry
çamaşırhane laundry
çamlık pinewood(s)
çamur mud
çamurlu muddy
çamurluk mud-guard, wing
çan bell
çanak pot
çanta bag, briefcase
çap diameter
çapa hoe, mattock
çapaçul untidy
çapak crust rount the

eyes
çapaklanmak become gummy
çapalamak hoe
çapkın vagabond, rascal
çapraşık complicated, entangled
çapraz crossing, crosswise, intersecting
çar tsar
çarçabuk very quickly
çarçur waste, squandering
çardak trellis, arbour
çare remedy, means
çaresiz irremediable, inevitable, helpless
çarık peasant's sandal
çark wheel
çarkçı engineer, mechanic
çarmıha germek crucify
çarpan multiplier
çarpı multiplication sign
çarpık crooked, awry
çarpılmak be crooked, meet with divine punishment
çarpıntı palpitation
çarpışma collision, conflict, fight
çarpışmak strike one another, fight, collide
çarpma blow
çarpmak strike, bump, multiply (math.)
çarşaf sheet (of a bed)
çarşamba Wednesday
çarşı market, bazaar
çatal fork
çatı framework, skeleton, roof; **çatı katı** attic
çatık frowning
çatırdamak make a chattering or clattering sound, crackle
çatırtı crackle, snap
çatışma fight
çatışmak collide, conflict, fight
çatlak crack, cracked
çatlamak crack, split
çatlatmak crack, split
çatmak fit together, build, meet / challenge
çavdar rye
çavuş sergeant
çay tea
çay tea party
çay stream, river
çaydanlık teapot
çayhane tea-shop, tea-house
çayır meadow, pasture

çayırkuşu lark
çaylak kite (bird)
çehre face, countenance
Çek Czech
çek cheque
çekecek shoehorn
çekememek envy
çeki measure of weight (about 500 lb)
çekici attractive
çekiç hammer
çekidüzen vermek put in order, tidy up
çekiliş drawing
çekilmek be pulled / withdraw / retire
çekilmez unendurabel, unbearable
çekim conjugation (gram.)
çekimser abstainer
çekingen timid, shy
çekinmek refrain from, hesitate
çekirdek pip / nucleus / seed
çekirge grasshopper, locust
çekiş drawing, traction
çekişmek struggle, quarrel
çekiştirmek criticize, gossip / pull
çekmece drawer
çekmek pull, draw, drag / attract / suffer / bear / take after
Çekoslovak Czechoslovak
çektirmek suffer
çelenk wreath
çelik steel
çelimsiz lean, shapeless
çelişik contradictory
çelişki contradiction
çelişme contradiction
çelme trip with the foot
çelmek trip up / divert
çeltik rice-field
çember hoop, ring of wood or metal
çene jaw, chin
çene çalmak chatter
çenebaz chatter-box
çene kemiği jaw-bone
çengel hook
çengelliiğne safetypin
çengi public dancing girl
çentik notch, nick
çepçevre all around
çerçeve frame
çerez appetizer
çergi gipsy's tent
çeribaşı gipsy leader
çeşit sort, variety

çeşitkenar unequal sided (geom.)
çeşitli various
çeşme fountain
çeşni taste, flavour
çete band, gang
çetin hard, difficult
çetrefil complicated
çevik quick, agile
çeviri translation
çevirmek turn, translate
çevre circuit, surroundings, circles
çevrelemek surround
çevrilmek be turned, revolve, be surrounded
çeyiz bride's trousseau
çeyrek quarter
çıban boil
çığ avalanche
çığır way, era
çığlık cry, scream
çıkagelmek appear suddenly, turn up
çıkar profit, advantage, own good
çıkarma landing (mil.)
çıkarmak take out, extract, remove, produce
çıkar yol right way out
çıkık dislocated, projecting
çıkıntı projection
çıkış exit, start
çıkın small bundle
çıkışmak suffice / scold
çıkma exit
çıkmak come or go out, appear, set forth, ascend
çıkmaz (sokak) blind alley
çıkrık reel, spining wheel
çılbır poached eggs and yogurt
çıldırmak go mad
çıldırtmak make mad, enrage
çılgın mad, insane, crazy
çınar plane-tree
çıngar quarrel, dispute
çıngırak small bell
çınlamak give out a ringing sound
çıplak naked, bare, nude
çırak apprentice
çırçıplak stark naked
çırpı twig
çırpınmak struggle
çırpıntı flutter
çırpıştırmak scribble hastily

çıta long narrow strip of wood
çıtçıt press-button
çıtırdamak crackle
çıtı pıtı dainty, delicate
çıtkırıldım effeminate, fragile
çıtlatmak drop a hint
çıyan centipede
çızıktırmak scribble
çiçek flower / smallpox
çiçek aşısı vaccination
çiçekçi florist
çiçekli in bloom, decorated with flowers
çiçeklik vase, flower stand, flower bed
çift pair, couple, double
çiftçi farmer
çifte paired, double / double-barrelled gun
çiftleşmek mate (of animals)
çiftlik farm
çiğ dew
çiğ raw, uncooked, crude
çiğdem crocus, meadow saffron
çiğnemek chew / trample on, run over
çikolata chocolate
çiklet chewing gum
çil bright, freckled
çile hank (of wool etc.)
çile suffering
çilek strawberry; **ağaç çileği** raspberry
çilekeş suffering
çilingir locksmith
çilli freckled
çim turf
çimdik pinch
çimen grass, meadow, lawn
çimento cement
Çin China; **Çinli** Chinese
çingene gipsy
çini porcelain, chinaware
çini mürekkebi İndia ink
çinko zinc
çirkef dirty water / ill-bred
çirkin ugly
çiroz dried sprat
çiselemek drizzle
çiş urine, pee
çit fence of brush wood, hedge
çitilemek rub while washing
çitlembik terebinth berry
çivi nail
çividi indigo blue
çivilemek nail

çivit indigo
çizelge list, table
çizgi line, scratch, stripe
çizik line, scratch
çizme top-boot
çizmek draw
çoban shepherd
çoban köpeği sheepdog
çobanyıldızı the planet Venus
çocuk infant, child
çocuk düşürmek abortion
çocukça childish
çocukluk childhood
çoğalmak increase
çoğu most
çoğul plural
çoğunluk majority, **salt çoğunluk** absolute majority
çok much, many, very, a lot of
çokça a good deal
çok görmek deny, withold
çokluk abundance
çolak one-armed
çoluk çocuk wife and children, family, household, swarm of children
çomak stick
çorak barren, waste
çorap stocking, sock
çorba soup
çökelek residue (chem.)
çökmek kneel / collapse, fall down / cave in
çöküntü depression / bend
çöl desert, wilderness
çömelmek squat down on one's heels
çömez apprentice
çömlek earthenware pot
çöp rubbish, litter
çöpçatan go-between
çöpçü dustman, street sweeper
çöplük rubbish-heap
çörek round cake, bun
çözmek untie, solve (a problem)
çözük loose untied, solved
çözülmek melt, thaw (ice)
çözüm solution
çözümlemek analyse
çözüntü breaking up
çubuk twig, rod, pipe
çuha thick cloth
çukur ditch, hollow, cavity, pit
çullanmak fall upon
çulluk woodcock

çuval sack
çuvaldız packing needle
çünkü because
çürük rotten / bruise
çürümek rot, decay
çüş whoa

D

-da, -de, -te, -ta in, on, at, too, also
dadanmak acquire a taste, develop the habit
dadı nurse
dağ mountain
dağcı mountaineer
dağılmak scatter, be spread
dağınık scattered, untidy
dağıtım distribution
dağıtmak scatter, distribute
dağlamak brand, scorch
dağlı mountaineer
dağlıç stump tailed sheep
dağlık mountainous
daha more
dahi also, too
dahi genius
dahil included, including / interior
dahili internal, inner
dahiliye ministry of the interior, clinic for internal diseases
dahiyane of genius
daima always, continuously
daimi constant, permanent
dair about, concerning
daire circle / department / apartment, flat
dairevi circular
dakik minute, punctual
dakika minute
daktilo typewriter / typist
dal branch
dalak spleen
dalaşmak quarrel
dalavere trick, intrigue
daldırmak plunge, dip
dalga wave, undulation
dalgacı lazy, idle
dalgakıran breakwater
dalgalanmak wave, float
dalgalı rough (sea) / undulating, wavy

dalgıç diver
dalgın absent-minded
dalgınlık distraction, reverie
dalkavuk sycophant, flatterer
dalmak plunge, dive
dalyan fish-pond
dam roof, stable
dama the game of draughts, checkers
damacana demijohn
damak palate
damalı checkered
damar vein, seam
damat son-in-law, bridegroom
damga stamp, mark
damgalamak mark with a stamp
damgalı stamped, marked
damga pulu revenue stamp
damıtmak distill
damızlık stallion, animal kept for breeding
damla drop
damlalık dropper
damlamak drip
damlatmak pour out drop by drop
damping dumping
-dan, -den from, than
dana calf **dana eti** veal
dangalak idiotic, fool
danışıklı planned, contrived
danışma consultation / information
danışmak consult
danışman counsellor, adviser
Danıştay supreme court
Danimarka Denmark
Danimarkalı Dane, Danish
dans dance
dans etmek dance
dansöz woman dancer
dantel lacework
dar narrow, tight
dara tare
darağacı gallows
daralmak become narrow or tight, shrink
darbe blow, stroke
dargın offended, cross
darı millet
darılmak scold / get cross
darlaş(tır)mak tighten
darlık narrowness / poverty
darmadağın in utter confusion

darphane mint (money)
darülaceze poorhouse
darüşşafaka school for orphans
dava lawsuit / trial (law) / problem, matter, **dava etmek** sue
davacı claimant, plaintiff
davalı contested, defendant
davar cattle, live-stock
davavekili attorney
davet invitation,
davetiye (card of) invitation
davetli guest, invited
davranış behaviour, attitude
davranmak prepare for action, behave
davul drum, **davulcu** drummer
dayak prop, support / beating
dayak atmak give a thrashing, beat
dayamak prop up, support / lean / rest
dayanıklı lasting, strong
dayanıksız not lasting, weak
dayanışma solidarity
support
dayanmak lean / resist / last / rely
dayatmak persist, insist
dayı uncle (on the mother's side)
dazlak bald
de, da and / also, too
debdebe display, **debdebeli** magnificent, pompous
debelenmek struggle and kick
debriyaj clutch pedal
dede grandfather
dedektif detective
dedikodu gossip
defa time
defaten all at once
defetmek drive away, expel, get rid of
defile fashion show
defin burial
define buried treasure
defne bay-tree, laurel
defnetmek bury
defolmak go away
defter note-book, register
defterdar chief finance officer of a province
değer value, price
değerlendirmek appreci-

ate, make more valuable
değerli valuable, worthy
değersiz worthless
değil not
değin until
değinmek mention, refer
değirmen mill
değişik different, varied, changed
değişiklik variation, alteration, change
değişim alteration
değişken changeable / variable
değişmek change
değiştirmek change, alter / exchange
değme few, rarely, hardly any
değmek touch / be worth
değnek stick
deha genius
dehşet terror
dehliz corridor
dejenere degenerate
dejenere olmak degenerate
dekametre ten metres
dekan faculty dean
dekor decoration, scene
dekolte low-cut (dress), low-necked
delalet guidance, sign
delege delegate
deli mad, crazy
delik hole
delikanlı young man
delil proof
delilik madness
delinmek burst, become worn, have a hole
delirmek go mad
delmek pierce
delta delta
demagoji demagogy
demec statement, speech
demek say
demet bunch
demin just now
demir iron / anchor
demir atmak anchor
demirbaş permanent, inventory
demirci blacksmith
demirlemek anchor (ship)
demirli at anchor
demirperde iron curtain
demiryolu railway
demlemek steep, stew (tea)
demode out of fashion
demokrasi democracy
demokrat democrat

den, dan, ten, tan from, than
deneme trial, test
denemek try, test
denetim inspection
denetlemek control, censure
deney test, experiment
deneysel experimental
denge balance
dengelemek balance
dengeli balanced
deniz sea
denizaltı submarine
denizaşırı overseas
denizci seaman, sailor
denizkızı mermaid
denk bale / equal
denklem equation
denli degree
densiz lacking in manners
deplasman changing place, touring
depo depot, store
depozito deposit
deprem earthquake
depreş(tir)mek move, stir
derbeder vagabond, careless
dere stream, brook
derebeyi despot
derebeylik feudalism
derece step, degree, grade / thermometer
dereotu dill
dergi magazine, periodical
derhal at once
deri skin, hide / leather
derin deep, profound
derinlik depth
derlemek collect, compile
derli toplu tidy, tidied up, in good order
derman strength / remedy
dermansız feeble
derme çatma jerry-built
dernek association
ders lesson, lecture; **ders çalışmak** study
dershane classroom
dert trouble, complaint
dertleşmek have a heart to heart talk
dertli sorrowful
dertsiz free from sorrow, care-free
deruhte etmek undertake
derviş dervish
derya sea
desen design, pattern
desilitre deciliter
desimal decimal

desimetre decimeter
despot despot
destan legend
deste packet, bundle
destek prop, support
desteklemek prop, support
deşmek pierce
dev giant
deva medicine, remedy
devalüasyon devaluation
devam continuation
devam etmek continue / attend (a course or lessons)
devamlı continuous
devaynası magnifying mirror
deve camel
devekuşu ostrich
deveran circulation
devinmek move
devir rotation, tour, period, era
devirmek overturn
devlet state, government
devralmak take over
devran times
devre period, cycle, circuit
devren by transfer, subletting
devretmek revolve, transfer
devrialem round the world, world-tour
devrilmek be overturned
devrim evolution, revolution
devriye patrol
devşirme irregular (troops), picked up
deyim expression, term, idiom
deyiş saying, term
dezenfekte disinfection
dırdır grumbling, nag
dırıltı complaints, grumbling
dış outer, exterior, outside
dışarı abroad, out
dışarısı outside
dışbükey convex (lens)
dışişleri foreign affairs
dışkı dirt, dung
didiklemek pick to pieces / search
didinmek toil, use effort, strive
didişmek quarrel
difteri diphtheria
diğer other, another, next

dik perpendicular, upright, steep
dik başlı obstinate
dikdörtgen rectangle
diken thorn
dikenli thorny; prickly
dikenli tel barbed wire
dikey vertical
dikili sewn / planted
dikim act of sewing / planting
dikiş sewing / seam
dikiz peeping
dikizlemek peep
dik kafalı obstinate
dikkat attention, care
dikkat etmek pay attention
dikkatle carefully
dikkatli attentive, careful
dikkatsiz inattentive, careless
diklenmek stand up to
dikmek sew / plant
diktatör dictator
dikte etmek dictate
dil tongue / language
dilber charming, darling
dilbilgisi grammar
dilci linguist
dilek wish, desire
dilekçe petition
dilemek wish for
dilenci beggar
dilenmek beg
dilim slice
dilmek cut into slices
dilsiz dumb
dimağ brain, mind
dimdik upright
din religion
dinamik dynamics, dynamic, energetic
dinamit dynamite
dinamo dynamo
dinç vigorous
dindar religious, pious
dingil axle
dini religious
dinlemek listen to, pay attention to, obey
dinlenmek rest
dinleyiciler audience
dinmek cease, stop
dinsiz without religion, atheist
dip bottom
dipçik butt of a rifle
diploma diploma
diplomasi diplomacy
diplomat diplomat
dipsiz bottomless
dir, dır, tir, tır is; **dirler** are

dirayet ability
direk pole, post / mast
direksiyon steering wheel
direktif order, directive
direktör manager, director
direnç resistance
direniş resistance, active opposition
direnmek resist
diretmek insist on
diri alive
dirilmek come to life
diriltmek bring to life
dirlik peace, comfortable living
dirsek elbow, bend
disiplin discipline
disk discus
disko disco
dispanser dispensary
diş tooth
diş ağrısı toothache
dişbudak ash-tree
dişçi dentist
dişeti gums
diş fırçası toothbrush
dişi female
dişlemek set teeth in
dişli gear
diş macunu toothpaste
divan council of state / divan, sofa
divanıharp court martial
diyafram diaphragm
diyagram diagram
diyalekt dialect
diyalog dialogue
diyanet religious affairs
diyar country
diyez (müzik) sharp
diz knee
dizanteri dysentery
dizdize knee to knee
dize line (poetry)
dizel diesel
dizgi typesetting
dizgin bridle, rein
dizi line, row / series
dizili in a line, arranged
dizkapağı knee-cap
dizmek arrange in a row
dobra dobra bluntly
doçent assistant professor
doğa nature
doğal natural
doğan falcon
doğma birth
doğmak be born, rise (sun, moon or stars)
doğrama chopping / woodwork, joinery
doğramak cut into pieces,

cut up, chop
doğru true, right / straight / honest / straight line (geom.)
doğruca directly
doğrulamak confirm
doğrulmak become straight / rise up / make for
doğrultmak put straight or right
doğrultu direction, extension
doğruluk straightness, truth, honesty
doğrusu in fact
doğu the east
doğum birth
doğumevi maternity home
doğum yeri (tarihi) place (date) of birth
doğurmak give birth to
doğuş birth
doksan ninety
doktor doctor
doktrin doctrine
doktora degree of doctorate
doku tissue
dokuma weaving, woven textile
dokumacı weaver
dokumak weave
dokunaklı touching, moving
dokunmak touch, affect
dokunulmazlık immunity
dokuz nine
dokuzuncu ninth
dolamak wind round, encircle
dolambaç curve, bend
dolambaçlı winding
dolandırıcı swindler
dolandırmak cheat, swindle
dolanmak go about (round), surround
dolap cupboard / water-wheel / trick
dolar dollar
dolaşım circulation
dolaşmak go round, walk about, make a tour / become tangled
dolay surroundings, suburb
dolayı on account of, because of
dolayısıyla indirectly, as result of, because of
dolaylı indirect
doldurmak fill, stuff, load

(a gun)
dolgu the filling (of a tooth)
dolgun full, filled, plump
dolma (yemek) stuffed vegetables
dolmak fill, become full
dolmakalem (fountain) pen
dolmuş shared taxi
dolu full, loaded / hail
doludizgin at full speed
dolunay full moon
domates tomato
domuz swine, pig
don frost
don panties; underpants
donanma navy
donatım equipment, ordnance
dondurma ice-cream
donmak freeze
donuk frozen
doruk summit
dost friend
dosya file
doymak to have had enough, be satisfied
doz dose
dökme cast metal, cast iron
dökmek pour, spill / cast (metal) / shed (tears)
dökülmek be poured, fall out, be spilled
dökümhane foundry
döküntü debris / remnants / skin eruption
döl generation, offspring
döndürmek turn
dönek untrustworthy, changeable
dönem period, era, term
dönemeç bend
dönence tropic
dönmek turn, turn back, return, change
dönüm acre
dönüm new direction, turning point
dönüş turn, return, coming back
dönüşlü (fiil) reflexive verb
dönüşmek change into
dönüşüm transformation
dördüncü fourth
dört four
dörtgen quadrangle
dörtköşe square
dörtnal gallop
dörtyol ağzı four crossroads

döşek bed, mattress
döşeme furniture / floor / upholstery
döşemek lay, cover with, furnish
döven threshing-machine
döviz foreign currency
dövme wrought (copper etc.) / tattoo
dövmek beat
dövünmek beat oneself
dövüşmek fight, quarrel
drahoma dowry
dram drama
dua prayer
duba pontoon
dublaj dubbing
duble double
duçar afflicted
dudak lip
duhuliye entrance fee
dul widow, widower
duman smoke, fume
dumanlı smoky, misty
dur stop
durak a stop
duraklama standstill
duraklamak hesitate, come to a stop
durdurmak stop
durgun calm, stagnant
durmak stop, cease, remain
duru limpid
durulamak rinse
durulmak become clear and limpid / become calm
durum position, condition, state
duruşma sitting of a court, trial
duş shower, showerbath
dut mulberry
duvak veil (bride)
duvar wall
duy electric socket
duyarlık sensibility
duygu sensation, feeling
duygulanmak be moved, be affected
duygulu sensitive
duygusuz insensitive
duymak hear / feel
duyu sense
duyurmak announce, divulge
duyuru announcement
düdük whistle
düdüklü tencere pressure cooker
düello duel
düğme button
düğmelemek button up

düğüm knot
düğün wedding
dükkân shop
dülger carpenter
dümdüz flat, level
dümen rudder
dün yesterday
dünkü of yesterday
dünür fathers of a husband and his wife
dünya world, the earth
dünyevi worldly
düpedüz flat, level / boldly, openly
dürbün field-glasses, binoculars
dürtmek prod
dürüst straight, honest
düstur principle, formula
düş dream
düşey vertical
düşkün fallen, poor / addicted to
düşlemek dream
düşman enemy
düşmanlık enmity
düşmek fall
düşsel imaginary
düşünce thought
düşünmek think of, ponder over
düşünür thinker
düşürmek drop, cause to fall / abort
düz flat, level
düzelmek be put in order, be improved, grow better
düzeltmek make smooth, put in order, correct, improve
düzen order, regularity, harmony
düzenbaz tricky, cheat, trickster
düzenlemek arrange, put in order, prepare
düzenli in order, orderly, regular
düzensiz in disorder, untidy, irregular
düzensizlik disorder, untidiness
düzey plane / stage, level
düzgün smooth, in (good) order, orderly
düzine dozen
düzlem plane (geom.)
düzlük smoothness, flatness / flat ground
düzme false, made-up
düztaban flat-footed
düzyazı prose

E

ebat dimension
ebe midwife
ebedi eternal, everlasting
ebediyen eternally, for ever
ebediyet eternity
ebeveyn parents
ebru marbled
ecdat ancestors
ece queen
ecel the appointed hour of death
ecnebi foreign, foreigner
ecza drugs, chemicals
eczacı chemist
eczane pharmacy, chemist's
eda payment, performing / manner, air, affection
edalı having airs
edat preposition
edebi literary
edebiyat literature
edep decency, decorum
edepli polite, with good manners
edepsiz impolite, ill mannered, impertinent
edevat tools
edilgen (fiil) passive (verb)
edilmek be done, be made
edinmek get, procure, obtain
edip man of letters
editör publisher
efektif cash, ready money
efendi master, sir
efendim what? I beg your pardon?
efkar ideas / anxiety
efkarlanmak become worried
efrat members, individuals
efsane fable, myth, legend
Ege Aegean; **Ege Denizi** the Aegean sea
egemen sovereign, ruling
egoist selfish, egoist
egzersiz exercise
egzoz exhaust-pipe
eğe file

eğelemek file
eğer if
eğik slanting, leaning
eğilim inclination
eğilmek bend, bow
eğim slope
eğitici educational
eğitim teaching, education, training
eğitimci educator
eğitsel educational
eğlence entertainment, fun
eğlenceli enjoyable, amusing, entertaining
eğlendirmek amuse
eğlenmek enjoy / stop
eğmek bend
eğreti borrowed, temporary
eğri crooked, bent
eğril(t)mek twist, bend
ehemmiyet importance
ehil efficient, qualified
ehli tame
ehliyet qualification / driving licence
ehliyetname certificate, licence
ehram pyramid
ehven easy, cheap
ejder dragon, monster
ek joint, addition
ekâbir great persons
ekalliyet minority
ekili planted, cultivated
ekim sowing
ekim October
ekin crops
ekip team, group
eklem articulation, joint
eklemek join, add
ekli attached
ekmek bread / sow
ekmekçi baker
ekonomi economy
ekonomik economy
ekran screen
eksantrik eccentric, queer
eksen axis
ekseriya generally
ekseriyet majority
ekseriyetle generally
eksi minus
eksik deficient, incomplete, missing
eksiksiz complete
eksilmek become less, decrease
eksiltmek reduce
eksiltme putting up to tender
eksiz seamless, one

piece
eksper expert
ekspres express
ekstra the very best, extra
ekşi sour
ekvator equator
el hand / people, people outside one's family
ela light-brown
el açmak beg
elalem everybody, the strangers
el arabası hand-cart, wheelbarrow
elastiki elastic
elbet decidedly, certainly
elbirliği cooperation
elbise clothes, dress, a suit
elçi envoy, **büyük elçi** ambassador
el değirmeni coffee grinder
eldiven glove
elebaşı chief, ringleader
elek sieve
elektrik electricity
elektrikçi electrician
elektrikli electric
elektronik electronics
elem sorrow, pain
eleman element / personnel
eleme (sınav) preliminary (examination)
elemek sift, sieve / eliminate, select
elenmek be defeated, be beaten, be eliminated
eleştiri criticism
eleştirmek criticize
eleştirmen critic
eli açık generous
elim painful
elişi hand-made
elle by hand
ellemek handle, touch (by hands)
elli fifty
ellinci fiftieth
elma apple
elmas diamond
elveda farewell, good-bye
elverişli suitable, convenient, sufficient
elvermek suffice
elyaf fibres
el yazısı manuscript, handwriting
elzem most necessary
emanet entrusted (thing), left luggage

emanet etmek entrust
emaneten for safekeeping
emare sign, token
emaye enamelled
emek labour, effort
emekçi labourer, worker
emeklemek try to walk (a baby), walk on all fours
emekli retired, pensioner
emel desire
emin safe, sure, trustworthy
emir order, command
emirname decree
emlak real estate
emmek suck
emniyet safety, security / confidence
emniyetli trustworthy, reliable
emperyalizm imperialism
emretmek order, command
emsal similars, precedents
emsalsiz peerless, matchless, unequalled
emtia goods
emzik nipple, spout
emzirmek suckle
en width, breadth
en most
enayi fool
encik puppy, kitten
endam body, figure
ender rare
endişe anxiety
endüksiyon induction
endüstri industry
enerji energy, power
enerjik energetic
enfarktüs infarctus
enfes delightful, choicest
enfiye snuff
enflasyon inflation
enfraruj infra red
engebe roughness (of land)
engebeli uneven (ground)
engel obstacle
engellemek hinder, stop, prevent
engerek adder (snake)
engin vast
enginar artichoke
enişte husband of a sister or aunt
enjeksiyon injection
enkaz debris
enlem latitude
enli wide, broad
ense nape

enselemek seize, arrest
enstitü institute
entari loose robe, dress
entelektüel intellectual
enteresan interesting
enternasyonal international
entrika intrigue
epeyce pretty, fairly
er man / private (soldier)
erat soldiers
erdem virtue
er geç sooner or later
ergenlik pimples / coming of age, maturity
ergin mature, ripe
erguvan Judas tree
erik plum
eril masculine
erimek melt, thaw
erişmek arrive, attain
eritmek melt
eriyik solution, dissolved
erkân high officials
erkek man, male
erken early
erkenci early riser
ermek reach, attain
Ermeni Armenian
Ermenistan Armenia
eroin heroin
ertelemek delay, postpone
ertesi next, following
erzak provisions, food
esans essence, perfume
esaret slavery, captivity
esas principle, basic
esasen essentially, in principle
esaslı fundamental, true
esef regret
esen healthy, well
eser sign, trace / work (of art)
esinlenmek be inspired
esinti breeze
esir captive, slave
esirgemek spare, protect / withold, deny
ski old, ancient
eskici dealer in old clothes
eskimek be worn out
eskiz sketch, draft
eskitmek wear out
eskrim fencing
esmek blow
esmer brunette, dark
esnaf tradesman
esnasında during, while
esnek elastic
esnemek yawn

espri wit
esrar secrets / hashish
esrarengiz mysterious
esrarkeş hashish addict
estağfurullah not at all
estetik aesthetics
eş mate, fellow, husband or wife
eşanlamlı synonymous
eşarp scarf
eşcinsel homosexual
eşdeğer equivalence
eşek donkey, ass
eşelemek stir up
eşik threshold
eşinmek scratch and paw the soil
eşit equal
eşkenar üçgen equilateral triangle
eşkiya brigand
eşmek dig
eşofman tracksuit
eşraf notables
eşşiz peerless
eşya things, goods
et meat, flesh
etajer stand, dresser
etap stage
etek skirt
eteklik skirt
etiket label, tag
etken (fiil) active (verb)
etki effect, influence
etkili effectual
etli plump, fleshy
etmek make, do / be worth, amount to
etraf sides, surroundings
etraflı fully
ettirgen (fiil) causative (verb)
etüd study
ev house, home
ev idaresi housekeeping
ev kadını housewife
evcil domesticated, domestic
evcimen homelover
evermek marry off
evet yes
evham apprehensions
evlat children, child
evladiyelik heirloom
evlatlık adopted child
evlenme marriage
evlenmek marry
evli married
evlilik marriage
evliya saint
evrak documents, papers
evren universe
evrenbilim cosmology
evrensel universal

evrim evolution
evsaf qualities
evvel before / ago / first
evvela firstly, first
evvelce previously, formerly
evvelki former
eyalet province
eyer saddle
eylem action / operation / verb
eylül September
eyvah alas
eyvallah thanks / goodbye
ezan call for prayer (from a minaret)
ezber by heart
ezberlemek learn by heart, memorize
ezeli eternal
ezgi melody
ezik crushed
ezilmek be crushed
eziyet torture, trouble, torment
eziyet etmek torture, give trouble
eziyetli painful
ezmek crush

F

faal active
faaliyet activity
fabrika factory
fabrikatör manufacturer
facia tragedy
fahiş excessive
fahişe harlot, whore, prostitute
fahri honorary
faik superior
fail agent, subject (gram.)
faiz interest
fakat but
fakir poor
fakülte faculty
fal fortune
falan so and so, such and such
falcı fortune - teller
falso error, blunder

familya family
fani mortal
fanila flannel
fantezi fancy, fantasy
fanus glass jar
far headlight
faraş dust-pan
faraza supposing that
farazi hypothetical
faraziye hypothesis
fare mouse, rat
fark difference
fark etmek distinguish, differ, notice
farklı different
farksız same, equal, alike
farz obligatory / supposition
farz etmek suppose
Fas Morocco
fasıl chapter, section
fasıla interval, interruption, **fasıla vermek** interrupt
fasılasız continuous
fasikül fascicle
fasulye bean
fatih conqueror
fatura invoice, bill
faul foul
favori whiskers / favourite
fayans faience, tiles
fayda use, advantage
faydacılık pragmatism (phil.)
faydalanmak make use
faydasız useless
fazilet merit, virtue
faziletli virtuous
fazla remainder, excessive, more than, too much
fazlalaşmak increase
fecaat calamity
feci tragic, painful
feda sacrifice
fedai patriot / bodyguard / sacrificing
fedakar self-sacrificing
federasyon federation
felaket disaster
felaketzede victim (of a disaster), injured
felç paralysis
felek the firmament, fortune, fate
felsefe philosophy
felsefi philosophical
fen science
fena bad
fenalaşmak become worse, become unwell

fenalık badness, harm
fener lantern, lighthouse
fenni scientific
fer lustre, brightness
feragat abandonment, self-sacrifice
ferah spacious, cheerful
ferahlamak become spacious, become cheerful
ferden individually
ferdi individual
feribot ferry-boat
ferman command, imperial edict
fermuar zip fastaner
fersah league, 5 km.
fersiz without radiance
fert individual, person
feryat cry, scream
feryat etmek cry out
fesat corruption, malice
feshetmek abolish, dissolve, cancel, annul
fesih abolition, cancellation
fesleğen sweet basil
festival festival
fethetmek conquer
fetih conquest
fettan alluring, seducer
feveran uproar
fevkalade extraordinary
feza space
fıçı barrel
fıkırdak flirtatious, coquettish
fıkırdamak make a bubbling sound / flirt, chuckle
fıkra article / joke
fındık hazelnut
fırça brush
fırıldak weathercock.
fırın oven
fırıncı baker
fırlamak fly out, rush
fırlatmak hurl
fırsat opportunity, chance
fırsatçı opportunist
fırtına storm: **fırtınalı** stormy
fısıldamak whisper
fısıltı whisper
fıskiye jet (of water)
fıstık pea-nut, pistachio nut
fışırtı rustling noise
fışkı dung
fışkırmak gush out, (of a plant) spring up
fıtık hernia
fidan young plant

fidanlık nursery garden
fide seedling
fidye ransom
figan wail
fihrist index, list
fiil action, verb
fikir idea, opinion
fikri intellectual
fikstür fixtures
fil elephant
filan so and so, such and such
fildişi ivory
file net
fileto fillet
filhakika in truth, in fact
filika ship's boat
filinta carbine, flint
Filistin Palestine
Filistinli Palestinian
filiz young shoot
filizi bright green
filizlenmek sprout
film film
filo fleet
filozof philosopher
filotilla filotilla
filtre filter
Fin Finnish
final final
fincan cup
fingirdek coquettish
Finlandiya Finland,
Finlandiyalı Finn
fino pet-dog
firar desertion, escape
firar etmek escape, desert
firari fugitive
fire loss of weight by evaporation
firkete hairpin
firma (commercial) firm
fiske flick
fiskos whispering
fiş counter / plug (electric)
fişek cartridge
fişlemek classify
fitil fuse / wick
fitillemek light the fuse of (a mine or a bomb)
fitlemek instigate
fitne seduction / mischief-maker, instigator
fitre alms given at the close of Ramazan
fiyaka showing-off **fiyaka yapmak** show off
fiyasko fiasco
fiyat price
fizik physics
fizikötesi metaphysics
flama signal flag
floresan fluorescent

floş floss
flört flirt / (girl) boy friend
flüt flute
fob (commercial) free on board
fobi phobia
fok (balığı) seal
fokurdamak bubble, boil up
fol nest-egg
folklor folklore.
folluk sitting-box
fonetik phonetics
fonksiyon function
fora out! open!
forma form, part (16 pages) of a book
formalite formality
formül formula
formüler formulary
fors personal flag / influence
forum forum
forvet forward
fosfor phosphorus
fosil fossil
fotin boot
foto photo
fotoğraf photograph
fotoğrafçı photographer,
fotojenik photogenic
fotokopi photocopy
foya falsehood, lie
fötr şapka felt hat
francala fine white bread
Fransa France
Fransız French
Fransızca French
frekans frequency
fren brake
frengi syphilis
frenlemek step on the brakes, stop
fresk fresco, wall painting
frikik free-kick
friksiyon friction
fuar fair, exposition
fuaye foyer
fuhuş prostituion
fukara poor
fukaralık poverty
fulya jonquil
fundalık thicket
furgon luggage-van
furya rush, boom
futbol football, soccer
futbolcu footboll player
fuzuli excessive, super. fluous, unnecessary
fütursuz indifferent
füze missile

G

gabardin gabardine
gaddar cruel
gaf blunder
gafil inattentive, unwary
gaflet inattention
gaga beak
gagalamak peck
gaile anxiety, worry
gaip absent, lost, loss
gala gala, opening night
galeri gallery
galeta biscuit, dry bread
galeyan effervescing, rage
galiba probably
galibiyet victory
galip victorious; **galip gelmek** win, surpass
galvanize galvanized
gam anxiety, grief
gamlı grieved
gammaz tell-tale, informer
gammazlamak tell tales about, inform against
gamsız carefree
gamze dimple
gangren gangrene
gangster gangster
ganimet booty
gar station
garaj garage
garanti guarantee
garaz spite, grudge
gardiyan guardian
gardrop wardrobe
gargara gargle
garip stranger, strange
garipsemek find strange, feel a stranger
gark etmek overwhelm
gark olmak be submerged, be covered or overwhelmed
garnizon garrison
garnitür garnish
garp the west
garson waiter
gaseyan vomiting, **gaseyan etmek** vomit
gasp wrongful seizure
gasp etmek seize by force
gavur non-moslem
gaye aim
gayet extremely

gayret zeal, energy; **gayret vermek** encourage
gayret etmek endeavour
gayretli energetic
gayri other, other than
gayri ihtiyari involuntary
gayri meşru illegitimate, illegal
gayri muntazam irregular, disorderly
gayritabii unnatural, abnormal
gaz gas
gaza holy war
gazaplanmak become infuriated
gazel lyric poem
gazete newspaper
gazeteci journalist / newspaper seller
gazi veteran of a war
gazino beerhouse, restaurant with show
gazlamak step on the gas, accelerate
gazoz fizzy lemonade or gingerbeer
gebe pregnant
gebermek die (contemptuously)
gece night, by night
gece baskını night raid, night-attack
gececi night-worker
gecekondu squatter's house, shanty, slum area
gecelemek spend or pass the night
geceleyin at night
gecelik night-gown
gece yarısı midnight
gecikme delay
gecikmek be late
geciktirmek cause to be late, delay
geç late, **geç kalmak** be late
geçe past (o'clock)
geçen last, past
geçer current, saleable
geçerli valid, validity, **geçerli oy** valid vote
geçici temporary / infectious
geçilmez impassable
geçim compatibility / living
geçim derdi the struggle to earn one's living
geçimli affable
geçimsiz unable to get on with others, bad tempered

geçinmek live (on), get on well with others
geçirmek make or let pass / go through / see off
geçiş transition
geçişli transitive
geçişsiz intransitive
geciştirmek get over
geçit passage
geçkin overripe, aged
geçmek pass by, pass, pass through
geçmez not current / incurable / non-infectious, **su geçmez** impermeable, water-proof
geçmiş past
gedik breach, notch, gap
gedikli notched / regular (mil)
geğirmek belch
gelberi iron rake
gelecek future, next
gelenek tradition
geleneksel traditional
gelengeçen passer-by
gelgeç fanciful, flighty, temporary
gelgit the tides
gelin bride / daughter-in-law
gelince as for; **bana gelince** as for me
gelincik poppy / weasel
gelinlik wedding-dress
gelir income
geliş the act or manner of coming, arrival
gelişigüzel at random, haphazard
gelişim progress
gelişme development
gelişmek grow up, develop
geliştirmek develop, improve
gelmek come, arrive
gem bit (of a horse)
gemi ship, **gemici** sailor
genç young, young man
gençlik youth
gene again, still
genel general
genelev brothel
genelge circular, notice
genel af amnesty
genelkurmay general staff
genellikle usually, generally
general general
geniş wide, ample
genişlemek widen, extend

geniz nasal passages
gensoru general questioning, interpellation
geometri geometry
gerçek real, true / truth
gerçekleşmek become true, materialize
gerçekleştirmek realize, carry out
gerçekten really
gerçi although
gerdan neck
gerdanlık necklace
gerdek nuptial chamber
gereç tool, instrument
gereğince as required
gerek necessary, need
gerekçe reason
gerekli necessary
gerekmek be necessary
gereksinim need
gereksinmek feel the necessity
gerektirmek necessitate
gergedan rhinoceros
gergef embroiderer's frame
gergin stretched, strained
gerginlik tension
geri back, backwards, rear
geri almak take back
geri dönmek turn back, return
gerici reactionary
geri kalmak remain behind
geri koymak put back, postpone
gerilemek recede, remain behind, move back, retreat
gerili stretched
gerilik backwardness
gerilim tension
gerilla guerilla
gerinmek stretch oneself
geri vermek give back
geriye backwards
germek stretch, tighten
getirmek bring
gevelemek mumble
geveze talkative
geviş chewing the cud
gevrek friable, brittle
gevremek become dry and crisp
gevşek loose, slack
gevşemek become loose
gevşetmek loosen
geyik deer
gez backsight of a gun
gezegen planet
gezgin traveller

gezginci (esnaf) peddler
gezi trip, journey
gezici travelling
gezinmek stroll
gezinti walk, outing
gezmek walk about, go about, travel
gıcık coughing fit
gıcır gıcır brand new
gıcırdamak creak, squeak
gıcırdatmak make creak, gnash
gıcırtı a creaking noise
gıda food, nourishment
gıdaklamak cackle
gıdalı nutritious
gıdıklamak tickle
gına (getirmek) be tired of, be sick of
gıpta admiration, **gıpta etmek** envy (without ill-will)
gırtlak windpipe
gırtlaklamak strangle
gıyaben in the absence of / know by name
gibi like, as
gider expenditure
giderek gradually
gidermek remove, satisfy
gidiş departure / conduct / gait
gidişat the course of events / goings on
gidişgeliş return (ticket)
girdap whirlpool
girgin pushing, not shy, bold
girift intricate
girinti recess
girintili having recesses
giriş entrance, entry / introduction
girişim enterprise, attempt
girişken pushing, enterprising
girişmek set about, start, meddle
Girit Crete
girizgâh introduction
girmek enter, go into / penetrate
gişe ticket-window, box office
gitmek go, go away
gittikçe gradually
giydirmek put on, dress
giyecek clothing
giyinmek dress oneself
giymek wear, put on
giysi clothing

gizlemek hide, conceal
gizli hidden, secret
gizlice in secret
glikoz glucose
gliserin glycerine
gocuk sheepskin cloak
gocunmak be offended
gol goal
golf golf
gonca bud
gondol gondola
gonk gong
goril gorilla
gotik gothic
göbek navel / belly / centre
göbeklenmek grow a belly
göç migration; **göç etmek** migrate
göçebe nomad
göçmek change one's abode / fall in
göçmen immigrant
göğüs breast, chest, bosom
göğüslemek breast, stand up against
göğüslük breastplate, apron
gök sky, heavens
gökdelen skyscraper
gökgürültüsü thunder
gökkubbe universe
gökkuşağı rainbow
göktaşı meteor
gökyüzü firmament, sky
göl lake
gölge shadow, shade
gömlek shirt
gömme encrusted, built-in
gömmek bury
gömülmek be buried, sink deeply
gömülü buried.
göndermek send
gönül heart, feelings
gönüllü willing / volunteer
gönülsüz unwilling
gönye square (instrument)
göre according to, by
görenek tradition, custom
görev duty, work
görevli official, employee / on duty
görevlendirmek entrust, charge
görgü experience / breeding, manners
görgülü well-bred
görkemli majestic, splendid

görme seeing / sight; **sonradan görme** upstrat
görmek see
görmezlikten gelmek pretend not to see
görmemiş unmannerly
görücü a person sent to inspect a prospective bride
görümce husband's sister
görünmek appear, seem
görünmez invisible
görüntü image
görünüm appearance
görünür apparent, visible
görünüş appearance
görüş point of view, seeing, sight
görüşme interview, talk
görüşmek meet and talk
gösterge indicator
gösteri show
gösteriş ostentation, display
gösterişli imposing, showy
göstermek show, indicate
göt bottom, bottocks
götürmek take to
götürü in a lump sum
gövde body, trunk
göz eye; **gözalıcı** striking
gözaltı house arrest
gözbebeği apple (of the eye) / favourite
gözcü watchman, sentinel / oculist
gözdağı intimidation
gözde favourite
gözetlemek observe, peep, watch
gözetmek look after, take care
gözkapağı eye-lid
göz kırpmak wink
göz kulak olmak look after, take care of
gözlem observation
gözlemek watch for, keep an eye on
gözlük spectacles, glasses
göz yaşı tears
grafik graphic
gram gram
gramer grammar
gramofon gramophone
granit granite
gravür engraving
grev strike
greyfrut grape fruit
gri grey
grip influenza, flu

grizu pit gas, firedamp
grup group
gudde gland
gurbet being away from home
gurultu rumbling noise
gurup sunset
gurur pride
gururlu proud, conceited
gübre dung, fertiliser
gücenmek be offended
güç difficult, hard / strength, force
güçbela with great difficulty
güçlenmek be strengthened, become strong
güçleşmek become difficult, get harder
güçlü strong
güçlük difficulty
güçsüz weak, **işsiz güçsüz** without a job
güderi chamois leather, buck-skin
güdük tailless
güdümlü controlled, guided
güfte the words of a song, lyrics
güğüm copper jug
gül rose
güldürmek make laugh, amuse
güldürü comedy
güldürücü amusing
güle güle good-bye
güler smiling
güler yüzlü cheerful
gülle cannon-ball, bar-shot
gülmek laugh, **güle güle** good-bye
gülmez sullen
gülsuyu rose-water
gülümsemek smile
gülünç ridiculous
gülüşmek laugh together
gülyağı attar of roses
gümbürdemek thunder
gümbürtü loud noise, uproar
gümrük customs
gümrükçü customs officer
gümüş silver, **gümüş kaplama** silver plated
gün day
günah sin
günahsız blameless, without sin, innocent
günaşırı every other day
günaydın good morning
güncel actual

günbatışı sunset
gündelik daily wages / daily
gündelikçi day labourer
gündem agenda
gündoğuşu sunrise
gündüz daytime, by day
gündüzün in the day time
günebakan sunflower
güneş sun
güneşlenmek sun-bathe
güneşli sunny
güney south
günlük daily
güpegündüz in broad daylight
günübirlik for the day
gür abundant, dense
gürbüz sturdy, healthy
Gürcü Georgian
Gürcistan Georgia
güreş wrestling
güreşçi wrestler
gürgen hornbeam, beech
gürlemek make a loud noise; **gök gürlemek** thunder
gürlük abundance
güruh group, mob
gürüldemek thunder
gürültü noise, uproar
gürültülü noisy
gütmek pasture, nurse / have in mind
güve clothes-moth
güveç earthenware pot
güven confidence; **güven oyu** vote of confidence
güvence guarantee
güvenlik security, **güvenlik konseyi** security council
güvenmek trust (in), rely (on)
güvercin pigeon
güverte deck
güvey bridegroom
güya as if, as though
güz autumn
güzel beautiful, pretty, fine, nice
güzellik beauty
güzergâh route
güzide choice

H

haber information news
haberdar aware
haberci messenger

haberleşmek correspond
Habeşistan Abyssinia
habis wicked, wretched, malignant
hac pilgrimage to Mecca
hacet necessity, need
hacı pilgrim
hacim volume, size
haciz distraint
hacmen in volume, in size
haczetmek distrain
haç cross
Haçlı (seferleri) Crusaders
had limit, degree
hademe servant, janitor
hadi go on! come on! let us
hadis narrative, religious tradition of the Prophet
hadise event, accident
hafız one who has commited the Koran to memory
hafıza memory
hafif light, easy, slight
hafiye detective
hafiflemek lose weight
hafriyat excavations
hafta week
haftalık weekly / weekly wages
haham rabbi
hain traitor, ungrateful
haiz possesing
hak engraving
hak God / right, justice, **Cenabı Hak** God
hakan sultan
hakaret insult; **hakaret etmek** insult
hakem arbitrator, referee
hak etmek deserve
hakikat truth, reality
hakikaten really
hakikatli faithful
hakikatsiz unfaithful
hakiki true, real
hakim dominating / judge
hakimiyet domination, rule, sovereignty
hakir despicable; **hakir görmek** despise
hakkaniyet justice
hakkında about, concerning
hakkıyla rightfully
haklamak finish, beat (argo)
haklı right, fair
haksız wrong, unjust
haksızlık injustice
hal condition, situation /

the present time/ case
hal solution
hal market place
hala aunt
hâlâ still
halat rope
halayık female servant
halazade cousin, niece
halbuki whereas, however
halef successor
halen now, at present
halı carpet
Haliç the Golden Horn
halife substitute, Caliph
halihazırda at present
halis pure, sincere, sincerely
halita mixture, alloy
haliyle naturally
halk people, nation
halka ring, circle
halkoyu public vote, referendum
hallaç cotton-carder
halletmek solve
halsiz exhausted, weak
halt dung, dirt
halter weight lifting
halterci weight lifter
haltetmek mix / do something stupid
ham unripe, raw **ham madde** raw material
hamak hammock
hamal porter
hamaliye porterage
hamam public-bath, bathroom
hamarat industrious
hamdolsun thank God
hami protector
hamil bearing, bearer
hamile pregnant
hamiş marginal note, postscript
hamiyetli philanthropic
hamlaşmak grow stiff
hamle attack, dash, effort
hamletmek attribute
hamlık unripeness
hammadde raw material
hamsi sprat
hamule cargo, load
hamur dough / half baked
han khan
han inn, commercial building
hançer dagger
hançere larynx
hane house, subdivision
hanedan dynasty
hanende singer (woman)

hangar hangar, shed
hangi which
hanım lady
hanımeli honeysuckle
hani where
hantal clumsy
hap pill
hapis imprisonment, prison, imprisoned
hapishane prison
hapsetmek imprison
hapşırmak sneeze
hara stud farm
harabe a ruin
haraç tribute
haraçmezat selling by auction
haram forbidden by religion
harami thief
harap ruined, devastated, **harap olmak** be devastated; **harap etmek** destroy
hararet heat, temperature
hararetle warmly / keenly, with enthusiasm
hararetli warm / excited
harbetmek go to war. make war
harbiye war academy
harcamak spend, expend
harcıalem in common use
harcırah travelling expenses
harç expenditure, expenses
harç mortar
harçlık pocket-money
hardal mustard
hareket movement, act / departure
hareketli active, mobile
hareketsiz motionless
harem women's apartments (old use)
harf letter
harfi tarif the definite article
harfiyen word for word, literally
harıl harıl assiduously
haricen externally
harici external, foreign
hariciye vekaleti ministry of foreign affairs; **hariciye vekili** minister of foreign affairs
hariç the outside / abroad / external / excluded / except
harika wonder, marvellous

harikulade extraordinary
haris greedy, avaricious
harita map
harlı burning
harman operation of threshing grain, threshingfloor / blend (tea, tobacco)
harmanlamak blend (tea, tobacco)
harman yeri threshing-floor
harp war
has special, peculiar to / pure
hasar damage, loss
hasat harvest
hasbıhal private and friendly chat
haset envy, jealousy; **haset etmek** envy
haset jealous, envious
hasıl resulting, produced; **hasıl olmak** result; **hasıl etmek** produce
hasılat revenues, products
hasılı to sum up, in short
hasım enemy, opponent
hasır rush mat, straw mat
hasis stingy, miserly
hasmane hostile
haspa a pleasant girl
hasret longing, **hasretini çekmek** long for
hasretmek restrict, devote
hassas sensitive, careful
hassasiyet sensitivity, care
hassaten particularly
hasta sick, ill
hastabakıcı hospital attendant, nurse
hastalanmak become sick
hastalık illness
hastane hospital
haşa God forbid!
haşarat insects
haşarı naughty
haşere insect
haşhaş poppy
haşır neşir be in close contact with
haşin violent, rude
haşlama boiled, stewed
haşlamak boil, scald / scold
haşmet majesty
haşmetli majestic
hat line
hata mistake, fault

hatalı erroneous
hatır memory, thought / sake; **hatırı için** for the sake of
hatıra memory
hatırat memories, memoirs
hatırlamak remember, recall
hatırlatmak remind
hatırlı influential, esteemed
hatırşinas courteous, affable, considerate
hatip preacher, orator
hatmetmek conclude, complete
hatta even
hattat calligrapher (old)
hatun woman (old)
hava air, weather
havaalanı airfield
havacı aviator, **havacılık** aviation
havadan for nothing
havadar airy
havadis news
havafişeği rocket
havagazı coal-gas
havai aerial / skyblue (colour); **havai meşrep** frivolous
havaiyat trifles
havalanmak be aired, fly
havale assignment, referring, remittance, **havale etmek** transfer
havaleli bulky
havalename order for payment
havali environs, neighbourhood
havalimanı airport
havan mortar
havasız airless
havayolu airline
havlamak bark
havlu towel
havra synagogue
havsala comprehension
havuç carrot
havuz pond, dock
Havva Eve
havya soldering-iron
havyar caviare
hay hey!, alas!
haya shame
hayal image / fancy, imagination / day dream **hayal etmek** imagine
hayalet phantom, ghost
hayali like a spectre,

hardly perceptible / imaginary
hayalperest castle builder, dreamer
hayasız shameless
hayat life, living
hayati vital
hayatiyet vitality
haydi come! come on!
haydut brigand, outlaw
hayhay certainly
hayhuy confusion, tumult
hayıflanmak regret, lament
hayır good, profit, charity
hayır no
hayırdua a blessing
hayırlı good, blessed
hayırsız useless, good for nothing
haykırış a shouting, yell
haykırmak shout, scream
haylaz idle, lazy
hayli very, pretty
hayran admiring,
hayranlık admiration
hayret amazement
hayret etmek be surprised at
haysiyet dignity, honour
haysiyetli honourable
haysiyetsiz mean, devoid of honour
hayvan animal
hayvanat animals
hayvanat bahçesi zoo
hayvani animal-like, of animals
hayvansal animal-like, bestial
haz pleasure, enjoyment
hazan autumn
hazım digestion, **hazımsızlık** indigestion
hazır ready / present (not absent) / readymade; **hazır etmek** prepare, have ready
hazırcevap witty
hazırlamak prepare
hazırlık preparation
hazırol attention (mil)
hazin sad
hazine treasure, treasury
haznedar treasurer
haziran June
hazne tank, cistern
hazret excellency
hazzetmek like, be fond of
heba etmek waste, spoil
hece syllable
hecelemek spell by

syllables
hedef target, aim
hediye gift, present
hekim doctor, physician
hektar hectare
hela closet
helak destruction
helal lawful, legitimate
helal etmek give up a legitimate claim to another
hele at least, especially
helecan excitement, agitation
helezon spiral
helikopter helicopter
helva sweetmeat, halva
hem and also, both and
hemcins of the same kind
hemen at once, just now, nearly, immediately
hemen hemen almost
hemfikir of the same opinion
hemşeri citizen
hemşire sister, nurse
hendek ditch, trench
hengame uproar, tumult, chaos
henüz yet, still, just, now
hep all, wholly, always
hepsi all, all of it
her every, each
hercai inconstant
hercümerç disordered, mass
hergele untrained horse / rough, coarse fellow
her gün every day
herhalde in any case
herhangi whoever, whatever
herif fellow
herkes everyone
her kim whoever
her nasıl in whatever way, however
her nasılsa somehow
her ne whatever
her nedense for some reason or other
her ne kadar however much
her nerede wherever
her ne vakit whenever
her neyse whatever it be, anyhow
her vakit always
her yerde everywhere
her zaman always
hesabi economical, thrifty
hesap counting,

calculation, account, bill, arithmetic
hesapçı miserly
hesaplamak calculate
hesaplı well-considered, economical
hesapsız countless / without reflection
hevenk bunches hung up
heves desire, zeal, eagerness
heveslendirmek awake desire
heveslenmek desire
hevesli desirous, eager
hey hello, look here
heybe saddle-bag
heybet awe, majesty
heybetli majestic
heyecan excitement
heyecanlanmak get excited
heyelan landslide
heyet committee, delegation, board
heyhat alas!
heykel statue
heykeltraş sculptor
hezeyan delirium
hezimet complete defeat
hıçkırık sob, hiccough
hıçkırmak sob
hıfzıssıhha hygiene
hımbıl slow
hınç rancour, grudge, revenge
hınzır foul fellow
hır row, quarrel
hırçın ill-tempered
hırdavat ironmongery, hardware
hırdavatçı ironmonger, hardware dealer
hırgür quarrel
hırıldamak growl
hıristiyan Christian
hırka woollen jacket
hırlamak growl
hırpalamak mistreat
hırpani ruffled, untidy, shabby
hırs greed, anger
hırsız thief
hırsızlık theft
hırslanmak get angry
hırslı angry, desirous
hısım relative, **hısımlık** relationship
hışım indignation
hışırtı rustling sound
hıyar cucumber
hız speed
hızar big saw, saw mill
hızlandırmak speed up, accelerate

hızlanmak gain speed
hızlı swift; fast
hibe gift
hicab shame
hiciv satire
hicran separation / bitterness of heart
hicret emigration
hicvetmek satirize
hiç no, nothing, not at all, never
hiddet fury, violence
hiddetlenmek get angry
hiddetli angry
hidrojen hydrogen
hikâye story
hikâyeci short-story writer, narrator
hilal crescent
Hilaliahmer the Red Crescent
hile trick
hilebaz deceitful, cheat
hilekârlık deceit, trickery
hileli false, fraudulent
hilesiz genuine
hilkat creation
himaye protection, defence; **himaye etmek** protect
himmet effort, zeal / benevolence; **himmet etmek** take trouble
hindi turkey
Hindistan India
hindistancevizi coconut
hinoğlu scoundrel
Hintli Indian
hintyağı castor-oil
hipermetrop far-sighted
hipotenüs hypotenuse
hipotez hypothesis
his sense, perception, feeling
hisar fortress
hisli sensitive
hisse share
hissedar shareholder
hisseli belonging to various people
hissetmek feel
hissi sensible, sentimental
hissiyat sensations, feelings
hissiz unfeeling
hitaben addressing
hitabet oratory
hitam conclusion; **hitam bulmak** come to an end
hitap address; **hitap etmek** address
hiyanet treachery

hiza line, level
hizmet service, duty
hizmetçi servant, maid
hizmetkâr servant
hoca moslem priest / teacher (old)
hohlamak breathe upon
hokka inkpot
hokkabaz juggler
hol hall
Hollanda Holland;
Hollandalı Dutchman
homurdanmak grumble
homurtulu grumbling
hoparlör loudspeaker
hoplamak jump up and down
hoppa volatile
hor contemptible
horlamak snore / ill-treat
horoz cock, rooster
hortlak ghost
hortum hose-pipe
hostes air hostess
hoş pleasant, charming
hoşaf stewed dry fruit
hoşbeş chat
hoşça pleasantly, nicely
hoşça kalın good-bye
hoşgörmek tolerate
hoşgörü tolerance
hoşlanmak like, be fond of
hoşluk pleasantness
hoşnut pleased, contented, satisfied
hoşsohbet good company
hovarda open handed, rake, playboy
hoyrat coarse and clumsy, awkward
hödük bumpkin
höpürdetmek drink noisily
hörgüç hump of a camel
hububat cereals
hudut limits, frontier, boundary, border
hukuk rights, law
hukuki legal, juridical
hulya day-dream
humma fever
hunhar bloodthirsty
huni funnel
hurafe superstition
hurda scrap metal
hurdacı second-hand metal dealer
hurdahaş in fragments, in pieces
huri beautiful girl
hurma date (fruit)
hurufat letters, type
husule gelmek be ac-

complished, occur
husumet enmity
husus particularity, matter, point
hususi special, private, personel
hususiyet speciality, peculiarity
huşu deep reverence, awe
huy habit, humour
huy etmek, huy edinmek form the habit of doing
huylanmak get into bad habits, become touchy
huylu tempered; **iyi huylu** good-tempered
huzme ray, bundle
huzur presence / quiet, peace of mind
huzurlu comfortable, tranquil
huzursuz uneasy, troubled, fidgety
hücre cell
hücum attack, assult
hükmen in accordance with rules, judicially
hükmetmek give a decision, order
hükmi judicial, nominal
hüküm rule, command, judgement, decision / sovereignty, rule / influence
hükümdar monarch
hükümet government
hükümlü convict, condemned
hükümran ruler, sovereign
hükümsüz no longer in force / null, invalid
hüner skill, talent
hünerli skilful, talented
hüngür hüngür (sob) violently, bitterly
hünkâr sultan
hür free
hürmet respect
hürmeten out of respect
hürmetkâr respectful
hürmetli respectable
hürmetsiz disrespectful
hürriyet freedom, liberty
hüsnühal good conduct, decency
hüsnüniyet good intention, good will
hüsnükabul friendly reception, cordial welcome
hüsran disappointment
hüviyet identity; **hüviyet**

cüzdanı identity card

hüzün sadness, melancholy
hüzünlü sad

I

ıhlamur linden-tree
ıkınmak make a great physical effort
ılıca hot spring
ılık lukewarm, tepid
ılımlı moderate
ılındırmak, ılıştırmak make tepid, make warm
Irak Iraq
ırak distant, far
ıraksak divergent, concave (lens)
ırgalamak shake, move / interest, concern
ırgat labourer, workman / capstan
ırk race; **ırkçılık** racialism
ırkçı racist
ırmak river, brook
ırz honour, chastity
ısı heat
ısınmak get warm
ısırgan (otu) nettle
ısırmak bite
ısıtmak heat
ıska miss, **ıska geçmek** miss (the ball)
ıskala musical scale
ıskarta discard; **ıskartaya çıkarmak** discard
ıskat throwing down / alms given on behalf of the dead
ıslah improvement, reform / **ıslah etmek** improve, reform
ıslahat improvements, reforms
ıslahane reformatory
ıslak wet
ıslanmak become wet, get wet
ıslatmak wet
ıslık whistle
ısmarlama ordered, made to order
ısmarlamak order
ıspanak spinach
ıspazmoz spasm
ısrar insistence; **ısrar etmek** insist
ıssız lonely, deserted

ıstakoz lobster
ıstampa stamping pad
ıstavroz cross
ıstırap trouble, anxiety
ışık light
ışıl ışıl sparkling
ışıldak searchlight
ışıldamak shine, sparkle
ışıltılı flash, shining
ışın gleam, flash
ıtır rose-geranium
ıvır zıvır trifles
ızbandut huge terrifying man
ızgara gridiron, grill

İ

iade giving back, return; **iade etmek** give back, restore
iadeli taahhütlü return registered (letter)
iane donation, assistance, contribution
iaşe subsistence
ibadet prayer, worship
ibare sentence, clause
ibaret consisting of
ibate lodging; **iaşe ibate** board and lodging
ibik comb (of a cock etc), crest
iblis satan, devil
ibra discharge / clarify
İbrani Hebrew
İbranice Hebrew language
ibraz presentation
ibraz etmek show, present, produce
ibre needle of an instrument
ibret example, warning, **ibret almak** take warning
ibrik kettle, ewer
ibrişim silk thread
icabet acceptance; **icabet etmek** accept (an invitation)
icap a requiring; **icabında** in case of need
icap etmek require, be necessary
icar letting, rent
icat invention
icat etmek invent
icra execution, performance; **icra etmek** perform, execute

icra court-bailiff / performing
iç inside, interior
içbükey concave (lens)
içecek drink, beverage
içerde inside
içeri in
içerik content(s)
içerlek secluded, inside
içerlemek be angry
içermek contain, include
içgüdü instinct
iç içe one within the other
için for, in order to
için için secretly
içindekiler contents
içişleri interior affairs
içki drink
içkili (restaurant) licensed to sell alcoholic drinks / drunk
içlenmek be affected
içli sensitive
içlidışlı very intimate
içme drinking / spring of mineral water
içmek drink; **sigara, tütün içmek** smoke
içmeler the hot springs
iç sıkıntısı boredom
içten sincere
içtima assembly, meeting
içtimai social
içtüzük statute
içyağı suet
içyüz inside of a matter, the real truth
idam execution
idame upkeep; **idame etmek** preserve, continue
idare management, direction; **idare etmek** administer, manage / economise, suffice
idareci manager, administrator
idareli economical
idarehane office, administration
idaresiz wasteful, who manages badly
idareten administratively, temporarily
idari administrative
iddia claim / bet; **iddia etmek** claim
iddiacı obstinate, betting
iddialı disputed, conflicting
iddianame (the) formal charge, indictment
ideal ideal
idman physical exercise,

sport
idrak perception, intelligence, reaching; **idrak etmek** comprehend
idrar urine
ifa performance, fulfilment / **ifa etmek** execute, fulfil
ifade expression, statement (court) **ifade etmek** express, declare
iffet chastity; **iffetli** chaste
iflas bankruptcy; **iflaş etmek** go bankrupt
ifrat excess, overdoing
ifrit demon
ifşa divulgation; **ifşa etmek** divulge, reveal
ifşaat revelations
iftar the breaking of a fast
iftihar pride; **iftihar etmek** be proud of
iftira slander **iftira etmek** slander
iğfal deception, seduction; **iğfal etmek** seduce
iğne needle, pin / injection / **iğne deliği** the eye of a needle
iğnelemek prick / pin / speak sarcastically
iğnelik needlecase
iğrenç disgusting, loathsome
iğrenmek be disgusted
ihale handing over, transfer, adjudication
ihanet treason
ihbar notification; **ihbar etmek** inform, denounce
ihbarname notification
ihdas etmek produce, create, establish
ihlal a spoiling; **ihlal etmek** infringe
ihmal negligence
ihmal etmek neglect
ihmalkâr negligent
ihracat exports; **ihracatçı** exporter
ihraç exportation / expulsion; **ihraç etmek** export / expel
ihsan grant
ihtar warning, a reminding; **ihtar etmek** remind, warn
ihtilaf disagreement
ihtilaflı controversial
ihtilal revolution
ihtimal probability.

probable, probably
ihtimam care; **ihtimam etmek** take pains, look after
ihtira invention; **ihtira beratı** patent
ihtiras passion, ambition, lust
ihtisas specialization
ihtişam magnificence
ihtiva etmek contain
ihtiyaç necessity, want, need
ihtiyar old person / aged, old
ihtiyari optional
ihtiyarlamak grow old
ihtiyat precaution, reserve
ihtiyaten by way of precaution, as a reserve
ihtiyatlı prudent
ihtiyatsız imprudent
ihya bringing to life
ikame setting up; **ikame etmek** set up
ikamet residence; **ikamet etmek** stay, live
ikametgâh place of residence
ikaz warning; **ikaz etmek** warn
iken while, when, as
iki two; **ikisi** both of them
ikilem dilemma
ikilik disunion
ikinci second
ikindi afternoon
ikişer two each
ikiyüzlü two-faced
ikiz twins
iklim climate
ikmal completion, make up; **ikmal etmek** complete, supply; **ikmale kalmak** fail in an exam
ikmal sınavı make-up exam
ikna etmek convince
ikrah disgust, loathing; **ikrah etmek** loathe
ikram gift, showing honour or hospitality; **ikram etmek** show honour to / offer, serve / discount
ikramiye bonus, prize
iksir elixir
iktidar ability, power / party in power
iktidarlı capable; **iktidarsız** incapable

iktisadi economical
iktisat economy, economics
iktisatçı economist
il province, county
ilaç remedy, medicine
ilaçlamak spray a chemical, disinfect
ilah god
ilahe goddess
ilahi hymn
ilahi divine
ilahiyat theology
ilam sentence, judicial decree
ilan advertisement, declaration
ilancılık advertising
ilave addition, supplement; **ilave etmek** add
ilaveten in addition (to)
ilçe county
ile with, by means of
ilelebet forever
ileri advanced / forward / future / fast (a clock) / the forward part
ilerici reformer
ileride in front / in future / beyond
ileri gelen important person
ileri gelmek result
ilerlemek advance, progress
ilerletmek make progress, advance
iletişim communication
iletki protractor
iletken conductor (elec)
iletmek send, carry off
ilgi interest; **ilgili** interested, connected with
ilgilenmek be interested in, look after
ilgili concerning, about, connected with
ilginç interesting
ilham inspiration
ilham etmek inspire
ilik marrow, loop
iliklemek button up
ilikli buttoned up
ilim science
ilişik relation, connection connected, related / attached
ilişiksiz free
ilişki tie, connection
ilişkin pertaining to
ilişmek interfere with / sit down for a moment
iliştirmek attach

ilk first
ilkbahar spring
ilkçağ ancient times
ilke element, principle
ilkel primitive
ilkin first
ilkokul primary school
ilköğretim primary education
ilkönce first of all
illallah (etmek) be sick of
ille especially
illet disease / cause
illetli ill, diseased
ilmi scientific
ilmühaber certificate
iltica etmek take refuge
iltifat compliments; **iltifat etmek** compliment
iltihak joining; **iltihak etmek** join, annex
iltihap inflammation
iltimas favouritism; **iltimas etmek** show favouritism
ima sign, hint, allusion
ima etmek hint, allude
imal manufacture, making; **imal etmek** manufacture, make, produce
imalat production
imalathane factory
imalı allusive
imam religious leader
iman belief, faith
imansız atheist, cruel
imar improvement by cultivating or building, restoration
imbik still, retort
imdat help
imece work done for the community by a whole village
imge image
imha destruction; **imha etmek** destroy
imkân possibility
imkânsız impossible
imla orthography, spelling
imparator emperor
imparatoriçe empress
imrenmek envy, covet
imtihan examination, test; **imtihan etmek** examine
imtiyaz privilege
imtiyazlı privileged
imza signature; **imza etmek** sign
imzalamak sign

in den
inanç belief / confidence
inandırmak persuade
inanılır credible
inanılmaz incredible
inanış belief
inanmak believe
inat obstinacy; **inat etmek** persist
inatçı obstinate
ince thin, slender, delicate, fine
incelemek examine minutely
incelik delicacy, refinement
incelmek become thin
inceltmek make slender or thin
inci pearl
incik shin
incil Gospel, Bible
incinmek be hurt, be offended
incir fig
inciraǧacı fig-tree
incitici hurting
incitmek hurt, offend
indirgemek reduce
indirim reduction, discount
indirimli reduced (price)
indirme descent, unloading, taking down, reducing
indirmek lower, cause to descend; **denize indirmek** launch
inek cow
infaz execution of an order; **infaz etmek** carry out
infilak explosion; **infilak etmek** burst, explode
İngiliz English, Englisman, Englishwoman
İngilizce English, in English
İngiltere England
inhisar monopoly
inildemek moan
inisyatif initiative
iniş descent, slope
inkâr denial; **inkâr etmek** deny
inkılap revolution
inkıta interruption; **inkıtaa uğramak** be interrupted
inkisar breaking, curse; **inkisarı hayal** disappointment; **inkisar etmek** curse
inkişaf development; **inkişaf etmek** develop

inlemek moan, groan
inletmek cause to moan, oppress
inme apoplexy
inmek descend, alight, fall / come down, get off
inmeli paralysed
insaf reasonable **insaf etmek** act with justice
insaflı just, reasonable
insafsız unjust, without a conscience, cruel
insan human being, man, human
insani human
insaniyet love of humanity, kindness, humanity
insanlık humanity / benevolence
insanüstü superhuman
inşa construction; **inşa etmek** construct, build
inşaat building-site
inşallah I hope
intiba impression
intibak adaptation, adjustment; **intibak etmek** conform, adapt oneself
intihar suicide; **intihar etmek** commit suicide
intikal transfer from one place to another, transfer of property, transmission, going over; **intikal etmek** move, pass to another subject
intikam revenge; **intikam almak** take revenge
intikamcı vindictive
intisap attachment; **intisap etmek** join
intizam regularity, order
intizamsız irregular, disordered
intizar expectation; **intizar etmek** await
inzibat discipline / military police
inzibati disciplinary
inziva seclusion; **inzivaya çekilmek** retire into seclusion
ip string, rope, cord
ipek silk
ipekböceği silkworm
iplik thread
ipnotizma etmek hypnotize
ipotek mortgage

ipsiz vagabond
iptal annulment; **iptal etmek** annul, cancel
iptidai primitive
iptila addiction
ipucu clue
irade will, will-power
irade dışı unwillingly, involuntary
irat income, revenue
iri big, large
irkilmek be startled
irsi hereditary
irsiyet heredity
irtibat connexion, tie
irtica reaction, fanaticism
irtifa height, altitude
is soot
İsa Jesus
isabet hitting the mark
ise if
ishal diarrhoea
isilik heat-spots
isim name, noun; **özel isim** proper noun
isimfiil gerund
iskambil playing card
iskân setting; **iskân etmek** settle
iskandil sounding-lead
İskandinav Scandinavian
iskele pier, wharf / scaffolding
iskelet skeleton
iskemle chair
iskonto discount
İslam İslam
İslamiyet religion of İslam
islenmek become black with soot
islim steam
ismen by name
isnat imputation, attribution; **isnat etmek** impute, ascribe
İspanya Spain
İspanyol Spanish
ispat proof; **ispat etmek** prove
ispirto spirit, alcohol
israf wasteful expenditure; **israf etmek** waste
İsrail İsrael
istakoz lobster
istampa stamp pad
istasyon station
istavrit horse mackerel, scad
istek wish, longing
isteka billiards cue
istekli desirous, eager

isteksiz reluctant
istem volition / demand
istemek want, ask for, require
isterik hysterical
istiap capacity; **istiap haddi** maximum capacity
istibdat despotism
istida petition
istidat aptitude, talent; **istidatlı** talented
istif stowage; **istif etmek** pack, stow
istifa resignation; **istifa etmek** resign
istifade profit, advantage; **istifade etmek** benefit, profit; **istifadeli** advantageous
istifaname letter of resignation
istifçilik hoarding (for profit)
istifham interrogation
istifra vomiting; **istifra etmek** vomit
istihbar etmek get information
istihbarat news, information, **istihbarat servisi** intelligence service
istihkak ration
istihkâm fortification, military engineering
istihlak consumption, using up; **istihlak etmek** consume, use up
istihsal producing, production
istihsal etmek produce, obtain
istihza irony, sarcasm; **istihza etmek** ridicule
istikamet direction
istikbal future
istiklal independence
istikrar stability; **istikrarlı** settled, stabilized
istikraz loan
istila invasion: **istila etmek** invade
istim steam
istimlak expropriation; **istimlak etmek** expropriate
istinaden based on
istinat support; **istinat etmek** lean
istirahat rest, **istirahat etmek** rest
istirham petition, asking a favour; **istirham etmek** beg

istiridye oyster
istismar etmek exploit
istisnai exception; **istisna etmek** except, exclude
istisnal exceptional
istişare consultation
İsveç Sweden
İsveçli Swedish, Swede
İsviçre Switzerland
İsviçreli Swiss
isyan rebellion; **isyan etmek** rebel
isyankâr rebellious
iş work, action, business, occupation, profession, affair, job
işaret sign, signal, mark
işbaşı foreman / hour at which work begins
işbirliği cooperation
işbu this
işçi workman, labourer
işgal occupation; **işgal etmek** occupy
işgüç occupation, employment
işgünü weekday **workday**
işgüzar officious, busybody
işitilmek be heard
işitmek hear
işkembe tripe
işkence torture
işkillenmek be suspicious
işkilli suspicious
işlek working easily / busy (street)
işlem procedure, operation, effect
işleme handwork, embroidery
işlemek work, function / ply (a ship or vehicle) commit (a crime)
işlemeli embroidered
işletme the working (of a railway or a mine etc.). the running (of a hotel etc), management
işletmek run, operate / administer
işportacı peddler
işsiz unemployed; **işsizlik** unemployment
iştah appetite
iştahlı desirous, hungry
iştahsız without appetite
işte look, here
iştigal work, occupation
iştirak participation; **iştirak etmek** participate in, take part in
işve coquetry
işvebaz coquettish

işveren employer
it dog (in contempt)
itaat obedience; **itaat etmek** obey; itaatli obedient; **itaatsiz** disobedient
İtalya Italy
İtalyan Italian
İtalyanca Italian
itelemek push, move, stir
itfaiye fire brigade
itfaiyeci fireman
ithaf dedication; **ithaf etmek** dedicate
ithal importing; **ithal etmek** import
ithalat imports
itham accusation; **itham etmek** accuse
itibar esteem, regard, prestige; **itibar etmek** esteem
itibaren starting from
itibari theoretical, nominal
itibarlı esteemed, having credit
itibarsız discredited
itidal moderation
itikat belief, creed; **itikat etmek** believe in
itimat confidence; **itimat etmek** rely on, have confidence in; **itimat telkin etmek** inspire confidence
itimatname letter of credentials
itimatsızlık mistrust
itina care, attention;
itina etmek pay attention
itiraf confession; **itiraf etmek** confess, admit
itiraz objection; **itiraz etmek** object
itişmek push one another
itiyat habit
itmek push
ittifak harmony, alliance, agreement
ittihat union, unison
ivedi in a hurry
ivme acceleration
iyelik possession; **iyelik zamiri** possessive pronoun
iyi good, well
iyice thoroughly
iyileşmek get better
iyimser optimist
iyilik goodness, kindness
iyot iodine

iz footprint, trace, track
izafi relative
izah explanation; **izah etmek** explain
izahat explanations
izahname manifesto
izale removing; **izale etmek** remove
izbe basement, den
izci (boy) ·scout
izhidam crowd, rush
izdivaç marriage
izdüşüm projection
izhar etmek manifest
izin permission, leave; **izinli** on leave
izinsiz without permission; **izinsiz kalmak** be kept in
İzlanda Iceland
izlemek trace footmarks, trace, follow
izlenim impression; **izle-nimcilik** impressionism
izmarit cigarette stub
izolasyon isolation, insulation
izalatör insulator
izzetinefis self respect
izzetli honourable

J

jaluzi venetian blind
jambon ham
jandarma gendarme
jant rim (of a wheel)
Japon Japan, Japanese
Japonca Japanese
Japonya Japan
jarse jersey cloth
jartiyer suspender belt
jelatin gelatine
jeneratör generator
jeoloji geology
jest gesture
jeton slot piece (coin)
jilet razor blade
jimnastik gymnastics
judo judo
jurnal report
jurnalci informer, denouncer
Jupiter the planet Jupiter
jüri jury
jüpon under petticoat, slip

outine
kabız constipation
kabil possible
kabile tribe
kabiliyet capability, skill
kabiliyetli skilful, efficient

K

kaan khan
kaba large but light, spongy / coarse, vulgar, rude
kabaca coarsely, roughly
kabadayı bully
kabahat fault / offence; **kabahatlı** guilty; **kabahatsız** innocent
kabak pumpkin, gourd, marrow / bald, bare
kabakulak mumps
kabalaşmak become coarse, rude or vulgar
kabalık coarseness, rudeness
kabara hop-nail
kabarcık bubble / pimple, blister
kabarık swollen, swelling
kabarmak swell, blister
kabartma embossed, raised in relief
kabartmak cause to swell
kabataslak roughly, in

kabine cabinet, small room
kabir grave, tomb
kablo cable
kabotaj coasting trade
kabristan cemetery
kabuk bark, skin, shell, crust
kabuklanmak form a crust or skin
kabul acceptance / reception / consent, **kabul etmek** accept / receive / consent
kabullenmek appropriate, own
kaburga rib / frame of a ship
kâbus nightmare
kabza handle, butt (knife, gun)
kabzımal middleman, wholesale dealer
kaç how many, how much, **kaça** what is the

price, **birkaç** a few, some
kaçak fugitive, deserter / smuggled
kaçakçı smuggler
kaçamak flight, evasion, subterfuge, furtive
kaçık crazy
kaçıncı what number in order
kaçınılmaz inevitable
kaçınmak avoid, abstain, spare
kaçırmak make or let escape / miss (a train etc.) / lose / kidnap / go mad
kaçışmak disperse, flee, become panic-stricken
kaçmak flee, run away, escape, desert
kadar as much (many) as, as ... as / about, around / till, until
kadastro land survey, cadastre
kadayıf sweet pastry
kadeh glass, cup, goblet
kadem foot
kademe step, degree
kademli lucky, auspicious
kader destiny, fate
kadercilik fatalism
kadı Moslem judge
kadın woman
kadırga galley
kadife velvet
kadim old, ancient
kadir capable, powerful
kadir worth, value
kadirşinas appreciative
kadran face of a clock, dial
kadro staff, roll
kafa head, intelligence
kafadar intimate friend
kafasız stupid
kafatası skull
kafes cage, lattice
kafeslemek cheat
kafeterya cafeteria
kâfi enough, sufficient
kafile convoy, caravan
kâfir unbeliever
kafiye rhyme; **kafiyeli** rhyming
kâğıt paper
kâğıt sepeti wastepaper basket
kağnı two wheeled ox-car
kâhin soothsayer
kahır anxiety, distress

kahırlanmak be grieved distressed
kahkaha laughter
kahpe prostitute / cheat
kahraman hero
kahretmek overpower / be distressed
kahrolsun damn him, damn
kahvaltı breakfast
kahve coffee
kahveci keeper of a coffee-house
kahvehane cafe
kahverengi brown
kâhya steward, bailiff, housekeeper, butler / car park attendant
kaide base, rule
kâinat universe
kakao cocoa
kakma repoussé, repoussé work
kaktüs cactus
kâkül lock of hair
kalabalık crowd, throng, crowded; **kalabalık etmek** be in the way
kalafat caulking
kalafatlamak caulk / hide defects
kalakalmak stand petrified
kalas beam, plank
kalay tin
kalaycı tinsmith
kalaylamak tin, plate with tin / abuse, swear
kalaylı tin plated
kalben sincerely
kalbetmek transform, convert
kalbur sieve, riddle, screen
kalburlamak sieve
kalburüstü selected, distinguished
kalça hip
kaldıraç lever, crank
kaldırım pavement
kaldırmak raise, lift, remove, abolish
kale fortrees, castle / goal
kaleci goal keeper
kalem pen, pencil
kalemtıraş pencil sharpener
kalemucu nib
kalender a man without worldly ambition, bohemian

kalfa master builder, qualified workman, foreman
kalıcı permanent, lasting
kalın thick
kalın kafalı thickheaded
kalıntı remnant, remainder
kalıp mould, form, model
kalıplamak make in a mould
kalıtım heredity
kalite quality
kalkan shield / turbot
kalkınma recovery, progress
kalkınmak recover, make progress, develop
kalkışmak attempt
kalkmak rise, get up, start, stand up
kallavi huge, weighty
kalleş unreliable, backstabbing
kalmak remain, be left, stay
kalori calory
kalorifer central heating
kalp heart
kalp false
kalpazan false-coiner, counterfeiter
kalpsiz cruel, rude
kalsiyum calcium
kaltak saddle / harlot
kalyon galleon
kama wedge, dagger
kamara (ship's) cabin
kamarot (ship's) steward
kamaşmak be dazzled
kamaştırmak dazzle
kambiyo foreign exchange
kambur hunchback
kamçı whip
kamçılamak whip
kamelya camelia
kamer moon
kameriye arbour
kamış cane, reed
kâmilen entirely
kamineto spirit-lamp
kamp camp
kampana bell
kampanya campaign
kamu all, the whole public
kamulaştırmak nationalize
kamuflaj camouflage
kamuoyu public vote, referendum
kamyon lorry, truck
kamyonet small truck,

van
kan blood; **kan davası** blood-feud
kanaat conviction, opinion, contentment
kanaatkâr contented, satisfied with little
Kanada Canada
Kanadalı Canadian
kanal canal
kanamak bleed
kanarya canary
kanat wing
kanatlanmak take to wings
kanatlı winged, folded
kanatlamak make bleed
kanca hook
kancık bitch / treacherous
kançıbanı boil
kandırıcı convincing
kandırmak cheat, persuade
kandil oil lamp
kanepe sofa, couch, settee
kanaviçe canvas
kangal coil
kangren gangrene
kanguru kangaroo
kanı belief, thought
kanıksamak be satiated
kanırmak force back, bend
kanıt proof, evidence
kanıtlamak prove
kanlı bloody
kanmak be persuaded
kanser cancer
kansız anaemic, **kansızlık** anaemia
kantar weighing machine
kantin canteen, snack bar
kanun law, statue
kanunen legally
kanuni legal; **gayrikanuni** illegal
kanyak cognac
kap cover, vessel, dish
kapak cover, lid
kapaklanmak fall on one's face, capsize
kapaklı provided with a lid / concealed
kapalı shut, closed
kapalıçarşı covered market, arcade
kapamak shut, close, cover up
kapan trap
kapanık overcast, dark / shy
kapanmak be shut or

closed / be cloudy
kaparo earnest money, deposit
kapasite capacity
kapatma kept mistress
kapatmak shut, close
kapı door, gate
kapıcı doorkeeper, porter
kapılanmak secure a situation
kapılmak be deceived, be seized, be carried away
kapış manner of seizing, looting
kapışmak snatch a thing together, fight
kapital capital
kapitalizm capitalism
kapkacak pots and pans, utensils
kapkara exceedingly black
kaplama coating, covering / crowning, plating (tooth) / covered, plated
kaplamak plate, surround, comprise
kaplan tiger
kaplı covered, plated / bound (book)
kaplıca thermal, hot springs
kaplumbağa tortoise
kapmak snatch, seize
kaporta bonnet, hood
kapris fancy, caprice
kapsam scope, radius / extension
kapsamak cover, include
kapsül capsule
kaptan captain (sea)
kapuska cabbage stew
kaput military cloak
kar snow; **kar yağmak** snow
kâr profit, gain
kara black
kara land, shore
karaağaç elm
karabatak cormorant
karabiber black pepper
karaborsa blackmarket
karaca roe deer
karaciğer liver
Karadeniz the Black Sea
karafatma cockroach
karagöz black-eyed / blackbream (fish)
Karagöz Turkish puppet show
kara haber news of death

karahumma typhus
karakalem pencil drawing
karakaş black eye-browed
karakol police station, patrol
karakter character
karalama writing exercise, scribbling
karalamak scribble, write in a copy book
karaltı a figure in the dark
karambol collision
karamsar pessimistic.
karanfil pink (flower), carnation
karanlık darkness, dark
karantina quarantine
karar decision; **karar vermek** decide
karargâh headquarters
karartamak estimate with the eye
kararlarında about
kararlaşmak be decided
kararlaştırmak decide
kararlı decided, settled
kararmak darken, become black or dark
kararname decree
kararsız changeable, hesitating, unstable
karasevda melancholy
kara suları territorial waters
karatavuk blackbird
karaturp horse-radish
karavana mess-tin
karayağız dark-complextioned
karayazı evil fate
karayel north-west wind
karbon carbon
karbonat carbonate
karbüratör carburettor
kardeş brother, sister
kardeşçe brotherly
kardeşlik brotherhood
kare square
karekök square root
kareli checkered, check
kâr etmek profit
karga crow, raven
kargaburun curved forceps
kargacık burgacık scrawl, unintelligible (writing)
kargaşa confusion, disorder
kargaşalık confusion, tumult

kârgir built of brick or stone
kargı pike
karı wife, woman; **karı koca** husband and wife
karın belly, stomach
karın ağrısı stomach ache / nuisance
karınca ant
karıncalanmak have pins and needles
karış span
karışık mixed, confused, complex
karışıklık confusion, disorder
karışım mixture
karışlamak measure by the span
karışmak mix with, interfere, meddle
karıştırıcı causing confusion, misleading / mixer
karıştırmak mix, confuse, mingle
karides shrimp
karikatür cartoon, caricature
karlı covered with snow
kârlı profitable, advantageous
karma composite, mixed
karmakarışık in disorder
karnabahar cauliflower
karne ticket, (report) card
karoser body of a car
karpit calcium carbide
karpuz water-melon
kârsız unprofitable
karşı opposite
karşı karşıya face to face
karşılamak go to meet, meet (a need), welcome
karşılanmak be met
karşılaşmak confront one another, meet
karşılaştırmak cause to meet / compare
karşılık equivalent / reply
karşılıklı corresponding, done in return, facing one another, mutual
karşın in spite of
karşıt contrary, opposite, counter
kart old
kart card
kartal eagle
kartlaşmak become old
karton cardboard
kartopu snowball

kartpostal postcard
kartvizit carte-de-visite, visiting card
karyola bed
kas muscle
kasa chest, safe / cash desk
kasaba small town
kasadar cashier
kasap / butcher's
kasaplık trade of a butcher / fit for slaughter
kasatura sword, bayonet
kasavet sorrow, anxiety
kâse bowl
kasık groin
kasılmak be stretched, diminish, restrain / be conceited
kasım November
kasımpatı chrysanthemum
kasıntı tightness
kasırga whirlwind
kaskatı very hard, petrified
kasket cap
kasmak stretch tight
kasnak rim, drum
kast, kasıt intention
kasten intentionally, on purpose, deliberately
kastetmek intend, mean
kasti premeditated, intentional
kasvet depression
kaş eyebrow; **kaş çatmak** frown
kaşağı currycomb
kaşağılamak curry
kaşar a kind of chsese
kaşarlanmak become hardened and experienced
kaşe cachet, pill
kaşık spoon
kaşımak scratch
kaşınmak scratch oneself, itch
kaşıntı itching
kâşif discoverer
kaşkol scarf
kat fold, layer, coating / storey (of a building), flat, floor
katakulli cheating
katalog catalogue
katar string (of camels etc.), train
kategori category
katetmek cut, / travel over
katı hard, dry
katık anything eaten with bread

katılaşmak become hard
katılık hardness
katılmak be mixed, join others, contribute
katır mule
katırtırnağı sweet broom
katışık mixed
katışmak join in
kati definite
katil murderer
katileşmek become definite
kâtip clerk, secretary
katiyet definiteness
katiyen definitely (no)
katkı addition
katlamak fold, pleat
katlanmak bend, fold / undergo, suffer
katletmek kill
katliam massacre
katma addition, added
katma değer vergisi value added tax
katmak add, mix
katot cathode
Katolik Catholic
katran tar; **katranlı** tarred
katsayı coefficient
kauçuk rubber
kav tinder
kavaf dealer in shoes
kavak poplar
kaval pipe (musical instrument)
kavalye male partner
kavanoz jar
kavga quarrel, fight; **kavga etmek** quarrel, fight
kavgacı quarrelsome
kavim tribe
kavis bow, arc, curve
kavram notion, concept
kavramak seize, understand
kavruk scorched, dried up, weak, parched
kavrulmak be roasted, be scorched, parch
kavrulmuş roasted
kavşak junction, crossroads
kavun melon
kavurmak fry, roast, scorch
kavurma dried (or fried) meat
kavuşmak come together, join, meet
kavuşturmak bring together, join
kaya rock
kayabalığı black gobby

kayak ski
kayatuzu rock-salt
kaybetmek lose
kaybolmak be lost, get lost
kaydetmek enrol, register
kaydırmak cause to slip
kaydile provided
kaydiye registration
kaydolmak be enrolled
kaygan slippery, gliding
kaygı anxiety
kaygılı anxious
kaygısız carefree, without anxiety
kayık boat
kayıkhane boathouse
kayın beech (tree)
kayınbirader brother-in-law
kayınpeder father-in-law
kayınvalide mother-in- law
kayıp lost, missing
kayırıcı protector
kayırmak protect
kayısı apricot
kayış strap, belt
kayıt restriction / enrolment, registration, recording
kayıtlı restricted, registered
kayıtsız unregistered / indifferent
kaymak cream
kaymak slip, slide, glide
kaymakam governor of a town
kaymaklı creamy
kaynak spring (of water), fountain, / source
kaynak welding
kaynama boiling, welding
kaynamak boil
kaynana mother-in-law
kaynarca hot springs
kaynaştırmak cause to unite
kaynata father-in-law
kaynatmak boil
kaypak slippery, unreliable
kaz goose
kaza accident / borough, county, district
kazaen by accident
kazai judicial
kazak pullover / despotic husband
kazan cauldron, boiler
kazancı boiler-maker
kazanmak earn, win
kazanç gain, profit
kazançlı profitable

kazara by chance
kazazede wrecked, met with accident or misfortune
kazı excavation
kazık stake
kazıkçı swindler, trickster
kazıklamak overcharge
kazımak scratch, scrape, eradicate
kazıntı scrapings, erasure
kazma act of digging / mattock, pick axe
kazmak dig, excavate
kebap roast meat
kebir great, grand
keççap ketchup
keçe felt
keçeleşmek become matted
keçi goat
keçiboynuzu carob bean
keder grief
kederlenmek be sorrowful
kederli sorrowful, grieving
kedi cat
kefal ǵrey mullet
kefalet bail, security,
kefaletle bırakmak release on bail
kefaletname written guarantee
kefaret atonement, penance
kefe scale (of a balance)
kefen shroud
kefenlemek wrap in a shroud
kefere unbelievers
kefil surety, bail, guarantor; **kefil olmak** stand as surety
kehanet soothsaying, foretelling; **kehanet etmek** predict the future
kek cake
kekelemek stammer, stutter
kekeme stammering
kekik thyme
keklik patridge
kekre acrid, sour
kel bald, bare
kelam word, speech
kelebek butterfly
kelek unripe melon
kelepçe handcuffs; **kelepçeli** handcuffed
kelepir bargain
keleş nice, handsome / bald
kelime word

kelle head / sheep's head / loaf
kellifelli well-dressed
kellik baldness
kem evil, bad
kemal perfection, worth, maturity
keman violin
kemancı violinist
kement lasso
kemer belt / arch
kemik bone
kemikli bony
kemirici corrosive, gnawing
kemirmek gnaw / corrode
kemiyet quantity, number
kem küm etmek hu n and haw
kenar edge, border / corner / out of the way; **kenar mahalle** slum area
kendi self; **kendim** myself
kendi himself (herself, itself); **kendi kendine** (all) by himself; all alone
kendi halinde inoffensive
kendir hemp
kene tick
kenef closet (vulgar)
kenet clamp
kenetlenmek clamp together
kenevir hemp
kent town, city
kentsoylu bourgeois
kep cap
kepaze contemptible, vile, shameless
kepçe ladle, skimmer
kepek bran / dandruff, scurf
kepenk shop shutter, trapdoor
keramet miracle
kerata shoehorn (old) / scoundrel
kere times
kereste timber, lumber, timber-work
kereviz celery
kerhane brothel
kerim generous
kerime daughter
kerkenez hawk
kermes festival, fair
kerpeten pincers
kerpiç sun-dried brick
kerte mark, degree, point, notch
kertenkele lizard
kertik notch, notched

kertmek notch, scratch
kervan caravan
kervansaray caravanserai
kesafet density, thickness
kesat dullness, inactivity (in a market)
kesbetmek gain, acqurie
kese purse, small bag, hair glove, pouch
kesekâğıdı paper bag
keselemek rub the body with a hairglove
keser adze
kesif dense, thick
kesik cut, broken
kesilmek be cut, cease, be cut off / be coagulated (milk)
kesim slaughter (of an animal) / cut, shape / division
kesin definite, certain
kesinleşmek become final or decisive
kesinti cutting, chip / deduction
kesir fragment, fraction
kesirli fractional (number)
kesişmek intersect
keski bill-hook, chisel
keskin sharp, severe
kesme cut
kesmek cut, cut off / interrupt / diminish
kesmeşeker lump (sugar)
kestane chestnut
kestirme snooze / short cut
kestirmek cause to cut, cause to cease / have a snooze
keşfetmek discover
keşide drawing (in a lottery)
keşif discovery, reconnaissance; **keşif kolu** reconnoitring patrol
keşiş monk, hermit
keşişhane monastery
keşişleme southwest wind
keşke would that, I wish
keşmekeş great confusion, disorder
keten linen, flax
ketentohumu linseed
ketum reticent, keeping a secret, discreet
kevgir colander, skimmer
kevser abundance / a river in paradise
keyfi arbitrary

keyfiyet condition, circumstance
keyif bodily and mental condition / merriment, pleasure, joy
keyiflenmek become gay
keyifli merry, happy
keyifsiz gloomy, not cheerful, unwell
kez time(s)
keza also
kezzap nitric acid
kıble direction, direction of Mecca
Kıbrıs Cyprus
Kıbrıslı Cypriot
kıç hind part, behind / stern (of a ship) / bottom, buttocks
kıdem seniority
kıdemli senior
kıdemsiz junior
kıkırdak cartilage
kıl hair, made of hair, bristle
kılavuz guide, pilot
kılcal capillary; **kılcal damar** capillary vessel
kılçık fishbone
kılıbık henpecked
kılıç sword
kılıçbalığı swordfish
kılıf case, sheath
kılık shape, appearance
kılıksız deformed, badly dressed, shabby
kıllanmak become hairy
kıllı hairy
kılmak do, perform
kımılda(n)mak move
kın sheath
kına henna; **kınalı** dyed with henna
kınamak reproach, blame
kınnap yarn, string
kıpırdamak move slightly
kıpırdatmak cause to move
kıpır kıpır fidgety, restless
kıpırtı slight movement
kıpıştırmak wink
kıpkırmızı very red
Kıpti gipsy
kır the country, wilderness
kır grey
kıraat reading
kıraathane oriental coffeehouse
kıraç sterile, barren
kırağı frost
kıran destructive epidemic

kırat carat, quality
kırbaç whip
kırçıl sprinkled with grey
kırgın offended, dispirited, upset
kırıcı rude
kırık broken, break, fracture
kırıkçı bone-setter
kırıklık state of being broken, physical weariness
kırılma refraction
kırılmak break, be broken / be hurt
kırım massacre / fold
kırıntı crumb
kırışık wrinkle, crease
kırışmak become wrinkled, crease
kırıtış coquetry
kırıtmak behave in a coquettish manner
kırk forty
kırkayak centipede
kırkıncı fortieth
kırkmak shear, clip
kırlangıç swallow
kırlaşmak become grey
kırma fold, crease / half-breed
kırmak break, fold / offend / discount, lower (prices)
kırmalı pleated
kırmızı red
kırmızımtrak reddish
kırmızıötesi infra-red
kırpık clipped
kırpıntı clippings
kırpmak clip, trim, shear / wink (eyes)
kırtasiye stationery
kırtasiyecilik bureaucracy
kısa short
kısaca shortly, in short
kısalmak become short, shrink
kısas retaliation
kısık squeezed up / hoarse (voice)
kısılmak be squeezed / become hoarse
kısım part, portion, sort, section
kısıntı restriction, cut
kısır barren, sterile; **kısırlık** sterility
kısıtlama restriction
kısıtlı restricted
kıskaç pincers, pliers
kıskanç jealous, envious
kıskanmak envy

kıskıvrak tightly bound
kısmak reduce, cut / lower (voice) / pinch
kısmen partly
kısmet share, lot, luck
kısmetli lucky
kısmi partial
kısrak mare
kıssa story (with a moral)
kıstırmak pinch / catch by driving into a narrow place
kış winter
kışın in winter
kışkırtmak frighten away, incite, excite, provoke
kışla barracks
kışlamak pass the winter
kışlık suitable for the winter
kıt little, few, scarce, rare, scanty
kıta continent / detachment / stanza
kıtırdatmak make a crunching sound
kıt kanaat in scarcity, hardly enough
kıtlaşmak become scarce
kıtlık scarcity, famine
kıvam the right state, the right moment
kıvanç delight, pride
kıvılcım spark
kıvır kıvır wriggling, writhing
kıvırcık curly, crisp
kıvırmak curl, coil, twist / succeed
kıvır zıvır trifling, nonsense
kıvrak supple, brisk, dexterous, agile, lively
kıvranmak writhe, wriggle
kıvrık folded, twisted, coiled
kıvrılmak be twisted
kıvrım twist, curl, fold
kıvrıntı coil, turn, twist
kıyafet appearance of a person, aspect, attire
kıyafetsiz ill-looking
kıyak elegant, good (argo)
kıyamet the end of the world, doomsday
kıyas comparison; **kıyas etmek** compare
kıyasen by comparison, compared with
kıyasi regular
kıyı edge, shore
kıyım act of mincing /

massacre
kıyma mincemeat, minced
kıymak mince / slaughter / not to spare
kıymalı with mincemeat
kıymet value, price
kıymetlendirmek increase the value of
kıymetlenmek appreciate, become valuable
kıymetli valuable, precious
kıymık splinter
kız girl / daughter / virgin
kızak sledge, slide
kızamık measles
kızan youth, lad
kızartma roasted food / roasting
kızarmak turn red / roast, fry / blush
kızdırmak heat / annoy, enrage
kızgın hot / angry
kızıl red / scarlet fever
Kızılay Red Crescent
kızılcık cornelian cherry
kızıl derili (red) İndian
Kızılhaç (the) Red Crescent
kızışmak get excited, increase in fury
kız kardeş sister
kızlık virginity
kızmak get hot, / get angry
ki that
kibar noble, distinguished, gentle
kibir pride, contempt, conceit
kibirli proud, haughty, conceited
kibrit match
kifayet sufficiency, capacity
kil clay
kiler store-room, pantry
kilim woven matting
kilise church
kilit lock, latch
kilitlemek lock
kilitlenmek be locked
kilitli locked
kilogram kilogramme
kilometre kilometre
kilovat kilowatt
kim who
kimi some
kimin whose
kimlik certificate of birth, identity
kimse someone, anyone,

nobody
kimsesiz without relations or friends
kimya chemistry
kimyager chemist
kimyevi chemical
kimyon cummin
kin grudge; **kin tutmak** cherish a grudge
kinaye allusion
kinayeli allusive
kinci vindictive
kinin quinine
kip mood, mode,
kir dirt
kira rent, hire
kiracı tenant, lodger
kiralamak rent, hire, let
kiralık to let, for hire
kiraz cherry
kireç lime
kireçlenme calcification
kireçli containing lime / whitewashed
kireçtaşı limestone
kiremit tile
kiriş bowstring, rafter
kirlenmek become dirty
kirletmek make dirty, soil, defame
kirli dirty, soiled
kirpi hedgehog
kirpik eyelash
kişi person
kişilik personality
kişnemek neigh, whinny
kitabe inscription, epitaph
kitabevi bookstore
kitabi bookish
kitap book
kitapçı bookseller
kitapsız pagan, atheist
klasik classic
klasör file
klavye keyboard
klik cilique
klinik clinic
klişe cliché
klor chlorine
klorofil chlorophyl
koalisyon coalition
kobay guinea-pig
koca old / large / husband
kocakarı old woman
kocamak grow old
kocaman huge
kocasız unmarried, widow
koç ram
koçan corncob, stump, heart (of a vegetable)
kodaman large, notable, magnate
kodes prison

kof hollow, rotten / ignorant / weak
koğuş dormitory, ward
kok coke
koklamak smell, sniff
koklaşmak smell one another
kokmak smell, stink
kokmuş rotten
kokteyl cocktail
koku smell, scent, odour
kokulu perfumed, odorous
kokutmak make smell, give out a smell
kol arm / wing (of an army) / handle
kola starch
kolay easy
kolayca easily
kolaylamak have nearly finished
kolaylaşmak become easy
kolaylık easiness, comfort, facility
kolcu watchman
koldaş companion
kol düğmesi cuff-link
kolej private high school
koleksiyon collection
kolera cholera
koli parcel
kol kola arm in arm
kollamak keep under observation, protect
kollektif collective
kollektif şirket joint stock company
kolon column
kolonya Cologne water, eau de Cologne
kolordu army corps
kol saati wrist watch
koltuk armpit / armchair
koltuk altı armpit
koltuk değneği crutch
kolye necklace
koma coma
komando commando
kombinezon combination, arrangement / petticoat, slip
komedi comedy
komik comical, comedian
komiser commissary
komisyon commission
komisyoncu commission agent, broker
komite committee
kompartıman compartment
kompas compass

komple full, complete
kompliman compliment
komplo intrigue, plot
kompozisyon composition
kompozitör composer
komposto stewed fruit, compote
komprime tablet
kompütür computer
komşu neighbour
komuta command, order
komutan commander
komünist communist
komünizm communism
konak halting-place / mansion
konaklamak stay for the night (on a journey)
konca bud
kondansatör condenser
kondisyon physical fitness / condition
konfeksiyon ready made clothes
kondüktör conductor
konferans lecture
konfor comfort
kongre congress
koni cone
konmak alight / settle, camp
konser concert
konservatuar conservatoire
konserve tinned food
konsolos consul
konsoloshane consulate
konsültasyon medical consultation
konşimento bill of lading
kont count, earl
kontak contact, short-circuit
kontenjan quota
kontes countess
kontluk county
kontrat contract
kontratak counter-attack
kontrol check, control; **kontrol etmek** control, check up
kontrplak plywood
konu subject, topic
konuk guest
konu komşu neighbours
konuksever hospitable
konum position
konuşkan talkative
konuşmak converse, talk, speak, chat
konut residence, house
konyak brandy
kooperatif cooperative
koparmak pluck, pick,

break off, take by force
kopça hook and eye
kopmak break in two, snap, break off
kopuk broken off / penniless, vagabond
kopya copy / cheating
kopyacı who copies / who cheats (at exams)
kor red-hot cinder
koramiral vice admiral
kordela ribbon
kordiplomatik the diplomatic corps
kordon cord, cordon
korgeneral lieutenant general
koridor corridor
korkak cowardly, coward
korkmak be afraid (of)
korku fear, danger
korkulu frightening, dangerous; **korkulu rüya** nightmare
korkuluk scarecrow / banister
korkunç terrible, fearful, dreadful
korkusuz fearless
korkutmak frighten
korna (motor car), horn
korniş cornice
koro chorus
korsan pirate
korse corset
koru small wood, grove
korucu forest watchman
koruk unripe grape
korumak defend, watch over, protect
korunmak defend oneself
koruyucu protector
koskoca enormous
kostüm costume, suit
koşma ballad
koşmak run / harness (horse)
koşu race
koşucu runner
koşul condition, circumstances
koşum harness
koşuşmak run about
kot (blue) jeans
kota quota
kotra cutter
kova bucket
kovalamaca game of "catch"
kovalamak pursue, chase
kovan hive / cartridge case
kovmak drive away, repel,

expel
kovuk hollow, cavity
kovuşturma investigation, law-suit, prosecution
koy small bay, inlet
koymak put
koyu thick, dense / dark
koyulmak be put / begin, set out (off)
koyultmak render dense, thicken
koyun sheep
koyuneti mutton
koyuvermek let go, allow
koz trump
koza silk cocoon
kozalak cypress cone
kozmopolit cosmopolitan
kozmetik cosmetics
köçek dancing-boy
köfte meat ball
köhne old, worn
kök root, base, origin
köken origin
köklemek uproot
kökleşmek take root
köklü rooted
köknar scotch pine, fir
köle slave
kömür coal, charcoal
kömürcü coal dealer
kömürlük coal-hole
kömür ocağı coal-mine
köpek dog
köpekbalığı shark
köpekdişi canine tooth, eye tooth
köpeklik baseness, malice
köprü bridge
köprücük collar bone
köpük froth, foam
köpürmek foam, lather / become furious
kör blind / blunt (knife)
körbağırsak appendix
kör döğüşü confusion
kördüğüm knot that can't be undone, deadlock
körebe blindman's buff
körfez gulf
körkörüne blindly
körkütük blind drunk
körlenmek become blunt
körletmek blind / blunt
körpe fresh, tender, young and fresh,
körük bellows
körüklemek fan with bellows / incite
körüklenmek incite, encourage, agitate
köse with little or no beard

kösele stout leather for soles
köstebek mole
köstek watch-chain, hobble, lock-chain
köşe corner, angle
köşe başı street corner
köşebent angle-iron
köşegen diameter, diagonal
köşk villa
kötek a beating
kötü bad
kötümser pessimist
kötülemek slander, discredit
kötüleşmek become bad, grow worse
kötülük badness, harm, malice
kötürüm paralysed, crippled
kötüye kullanmak misuse, abuse
köy village, hamlet
köylü peasant, villager
köz embers
kral king
kraliçe queen
kramp cramp
krater crater
kravat tie
kredi credit
krem cream, custard
krema cream, custard
kreş crèche
kriko jack
kristal crystal
kritik critical / critique
kriz crisis / fit, attack
krizantem chrysanthemum
kroki sketch
krom chromium
kronometre chronometer
kruvazör cruiser
kuaför hairdresser
kubbe dome, cupola
kucak embrace / lap / armful
kucaklamak embrace / surround
kucaklaşmak embrace each other
kudret power, strength, wealth
kudretli powerful, capable
kudretsiz powerless, feable
kudurmak go mad
kudurmuş mad
kudurtmak infuriate
kuduz hydrophobia,

rabies
Kudüs Jerusalem
kuğu swan
kukla puppet
kukuleta hood
kul slave, creature
kulaç fathom
kulak ear; **kulak asmak** pay attention
kulaklık headphones
kulakmemesi earlobe
kule tower
kulis back stage, wings
kullanış use, application
kullanışlı handy
kullanmak use, employ, drive (a car)
kulluk slavery
kulp handle
kulplu having a handle
kuluçka broody hen; **kuluçka devri** incubation period
kulübe hut, shed
kulüp club
kum sand
kuma fellow wife in a polygamous household
kumanda command; **kumanda etmek** command
kumandan commander
kumanya ship's provisions, portable rations
kumar gambling
kumar oynamak gamble
kumarbaz gambler
kumarhane gambling house
kumaş cloth, tissue, texture
kumbara moneybox / bomb
kumpanya company, firm
kumral reddish yellow
kumru turtle-dove
kum saati hour-glass
kumsal sandy place, the sands
kundak bundle of rags, swaddling clothes
kundaklamak swaddle / set fire to, sabotage
kundura shoe
kunduracı shoemaker
kunduz beaver
kupa cup / heart (cards)
kupon coupon
kur rate of exchange / courting
kur'a lot; **kur'a çekmek** draw lots

kurabiye cake, bun
kurak dry, arid
kuraklık drought
kural rule
kuram theory
Kuran the Koran
kurbağa frog, toad
kurbağalama frogwise
kurban sacrifice, offering, victim; **kurban kesmek** kill as a sacrifice; **kurban olmak** sacrifice oneself, be a victim
kurbanlık animal destined for sacrifice
kurcalamak scratch, irritate, meddle with
kurdele ribbon
kurgu winding (watch / winding key / montage
kurgubilim science fiction
kurmak set up, establish, organize, plan / set (trap) / wind (clock)
kurmay staff (military), **Genel Kurmay Başkanı** Chief of the General Staff
kurna marble basin (bath)
kurnaz cunning, shrewd
kurs course
kursak crop (of a bird) / stomach
kurşun lead / bullet
kurşuni lead-coloured, grey
kurşunkalem pencil
kurt wolf
kurt worm, maggot (fruit)
kurtarıcı saviour / breakdown lorry
kurtarmak save, rescue
kurtlanmak become maggoty / become impatient
kurtlu maggoty / fidgety
kurtulmak escape, be saved, get rid of
kurtuluş liberation, escape, freedom
kuru dry, dried, withered
kurucu founder
kurul committee, council
kurulamak wipe, dry
kurultay assembly, congress
kurulu set up
kuruluk dryness
kuruluş being founded, establishment, organ-

ization
kurum institution / soot
kurum pose, conceit
kurumak dry up
kurumlanmak give oneself airs, show off
kurumlu conceited
kuruntu strange fancy, suspicion, illusion
kuruntulu anxious, neurasthenic
kurusıkı blank shot / empty threat
kuruş kouroush, piastre
kurutma kağıdı blotting-paper
kurutmak dry
kusmak vomit
kusur defect, fault
kusurlu defective, faulty
kusursuz without defect, innocent
kuş bird
kuşak girdle / supporting beam / generation
kuşanmak put on a girdle, dress
kuşatmak surround
kuşbaşı in small pieces (meat), in big flakes (snow)
kuşbaz bird-fancier
kuşbeyinli idiot
kuşe (kağıdı) heavily glazed paper
kuşetli (vagon) sleeping-car, couchette
kuşkonmaz asparagus
kuşku suspicion
kuşkulanmak get suspicious
kuşpalazı diphtheria
kuştüyü feather-bed
kuşüzümü dried currants
kuşyemi bird-seed
kutlamak celebrate, congratulate
kutsal sacred, divine
kutu box, case
kutup pole
kutupyıldızı pole star
kuvvet strength, force, power
kuvvetlenmek become strong
kuvvetli strong, powerful
kuvvetsiz weak, feeble
kuyruk tail / queue (of people)
kuyruk acısı rancour
kuyrukluyıldız comet
kuytu dark, hidden, remote spot

kuyu well, pit
kuyumcu goldsmith; jeweller
kuzen cousin
kuzey north
kuzu lamb
küçücük tiny
küçük small, little / young / minor, petty
küçükdil the uvula
küçüklük smallness / childhood / meanness
küçülmek become small, wane / stoop
küçültmek make small, diminish / humiliate
küçültücü humiliating
küçümsemek belittle
küf mould; **küf tutmak** become mouldy
küfe large basket
küfelik dead-drunk
küfretmek swear
küfür cursing, swearing, curse
küfürbaz swearing, curser
küheylan pure-bred Arab horse
kükremek roar, become wild and raging
kükürt sulphur
kül ash / the whole
külçe metal ingot
külfet trouble, inconvenience, pain
külfetli troublesome / expensive
külhanbeyi rowdy
küllenmek be turned to ashes, be forgotten
külliyetli plenty of.
külot drawers, panties
külrengi ash-coloured
kültür culture
külüstür shabby, old
küme heap, mass, pile / league
kümes poultry-house, coop
künde hobble, trap
künk water-pipe
künye personal data
küp jar / cube
küpe ear-ring
küpeşte gunwale
kürdan toothpick
küre globe, sphere
kürek shovel, oar (of a boat)
kürek kemiği shoulder-blade
küremek shovel up
kürk fur, fur-coat

kürsü pulpit, chair
kürtaj abortion
küskün offended, sulky, upset
küsmek be offended, be sulky
küspe residue of crushed seeds, oilcake
küstah insolent; **küstahlık** insolence
küsur fractions
küt blunt
kütle heap, mass, bulk
kütük log, block
kütüphane library
kütürdemek give out o crackling sound
küvet bath-tub, basin

L

labirent labyrinth
laboratuar laboratory
lacivert navy blue
laçka slack, play (in machinery)
lades wishingbone
laf word, talk
lafazan talkative
lafebesi talkative, chatterbox
lafetmek speak / gossip / chat
lağım sewer, underground tunnel, drain
lağımcı sewerman
lağvetmek abrogate, cancel, annul
lahana cabbage
lahit tomb
lahmacun meat pizza
lahza instant, moment
laik secular
lakap family name, nick name, surname
lakayt indifferent
lake lacquer
lakerda salted tunny
lakin but, nevertheless
lakırdı words, talk
laklak idle talk
lale tulip
lalettayin any, at random
lamba lamp
lanet curse / peevish

lanetleme act of cursing, accursed
lanetlemek curse, damn
lapa rice-pudding
lapa lapa (snow) in large flakes
lapacı languid, flabby
lastik rubber, tyre
lastikli elastic
laterna barrel-organ
latif fine, pleasant, elegant subtle
latife joke
Latin Latin
Latince Latin
laubali too familiar, careless, offhand
lav lava
lavabo washbasin
lavanta lavender water
layık deserving, worthy
lazım necessary, requisite; **lazım olmak** be necessary
lazımlık chamber pot
leblebi roasted chick peas
leğen bowl, basin
Leh Pole, Polish
lehçe dialect
lehim solder
lehimlemek solder
Lehistan Poland
lehte in one's favour, for
leke stain, mark; **leke çıkarmak** remove a stain
lekelemek stain, cast aspersions on
lekeli stained / dishonoured; **lekeli humma** typhus fever
lekesiz spotless
lenger copper dish
leş carcass
levazım materials, munitions, provisions
levent well set-up lad
levha signboard, plate
levrek bass (fish)
leylak lilac
leylek stork
leyli boarder (at a school)
leziz delicious, relishing
lezzet taste, pleasure, **lezzet duymak** enjoy the taste of, find pleasure in
lezzetli delicious, tasty
lezzetsiz tasteless, insipid
liberal liberal

liberalizm liberalism
Libya Libya
lider leader
lif fibre
lig league, union
liman harbour, port
limoni touchy
limonluk greenhouse
likör liqueur
limon lemon
limit limit
limontuzu salt of lemon
linç lynch
linyit lignite
lira lira, pound
liret İtalian lira
lirik lyric, lyrical
lisan language, tongue
lisaniyat philology, linguistics
lisans licence
lise lycée, high school
liste list
litre litre
liyakat suitability
lobut cudgel
loca box (at a theatre)
lodos southwest wind
logaritma logarithm
lohusa woman after childbirth, in childbed
lokal local, offical
casino, canteen
lokanta restaurant
lokavt lock-out
lokma morsel, a mouthful / piece / fritter (pastry)
lokomotif locomotive
lokum Turkish delight
lop hard-boiled (egg)
lord lord
lostra shoe polish
losyon lotion, Eau de Cologne
loş dark, gloomy
Lübnan Lebanon
lüfer bluefish
lügat dictionary
lügatçe glossary, vocabulary
lüks luxury, luxurious
lüle curl, fold
lületaşı please
lütfen please / kindly / as a favour
lütfetmek have the kindness, do the favour
lütuf kindness, favour
lütufkâr kind, gracious
lüzum necessity, need
lüzumlu necessary, useful
lüzumsuz unnecessary

M

maada besides, except, but
maaile the whole family
maalesef unfortunately
maalmemnuniye with pleasure
maamafih nevertheless, however
maarif education
maaş monthly salary
maateessüf with regret
maazallah God preserve us, God forbid
mabet temple
Macar Hungarian
Macaristan Hungary
macera adventure
maceraperest adventurer
macun paste, cement
maç match
maça spade (cards)
madalya medal
madalyon locket
madam madam, Mrs.
madde matter, substance, material / item
maddeci materialist
maddeten materially, physically
maddi material, physical
maddiyat materialism
madem while, since, as, now that
maden mine, mineral; **maden kömürü** coal; **maden suyu** mineral water
madeni mineral, metallic
madik trick
madrabaz cheat, impostor
mafsal joint
magazin magazine
magnetik magnetic
magnezyum magnesium
mağara cave
mağaza shop, storehouse
mağdur unjustly treated
mağlubiyet defeat
mağlup defeated
mağrur proud
mahal place, spot
mahalle quarter, district, parish
mahalleli neighbours
mahalli local
maharet skill

maharetli skillful
mahçubiyet shame
mahçup ashamed
mahdum son
mahdut limited
mahfaza case
mahfuz protected, kept
mahir skillful, able
mahiyet reality, character, essence
mahkeme court
mahkûm sentenced, subject, prisoner, convict
mahkûmiyet sentence
mahluk creature
mahlukat creatures
mahmur sleepy, dreamy
mahmuz spur
mahmuzlamak spur
mahpus prisoner
mahrem prohibited, secret, confidential
mahremiyet secrecy
mahrum deprived
mahrumiyet being deprived; **mahrumiyete katlanmak** do without
mahsuben to the account of, on account
mahsul product, crop
mahsuldar productive, fertile
mahsup counted
mahsur confined, cut off
mahsus special, peculiar / on purpose
mahşer great crowd
mahvetmek destroy
mahvolmak be destroyed
mahya illumination between two minarets
mahzen cellar, vault
mahzun sad, gloomy
mahzur objection, inconvenience
maiyet suite, retinue
majiskül capital letter
makale article
makam post, rank, office
makamlar the authorities
makara pulley, reel, spool
makarna macaroni
makas scissors,shears, points (of a railway)
makasçı pointsman
makat the behind, anus
makbul accepted, liked, esteemed
makbuz receipt
maket sketch
maki brushwood, bush
makine machine, engine

makineli tüfek machine-gun
makinist mechanic, engine driver
maksat aim, purpose, intention
maktu fixed price
maktul killed, slain
makul reasonable
makyaj make-up
makyaj yapmak put on make up
mal property, goods
mala trowel
malak buffalo calf
malarya malaria
maletmek take possession of, attribute to
mali financial
malik owning, possesing; **malik olmak** have, possess
malikâne large estate
maliye finance / ministry of finance
maliyeci financier
maliyet cost; **maliyet fiyatı** cost-price
mal olmak cost
mal sahibi proprietor
Malta Malta
maltaeriği loquat
malzeme material
mama food (baby)
mamafih nevertheless, however
mamul made, manufactured
mana meaning, sense
manalı significant
manasız senseless, absurd
manastır monastery
manav fruiterer, fruitseller, greengrocer
mancınık catapult
manda buffalo
manda dominion, mandate
mandal latch, clip
mandalina tangerine
mandallamak latch, clip
mandıra dairy farm
mandolin mandolin
manen in sense, morally
manevi moral, spiritual, immaterial
maneviyat morale
manevra manoeuvre
manga squad
mangal brazier
manganez manganese
mani preventing, obstacle

mânia obstacle
manifatura drapery
manifaturacı draper
manikür manicure
manivela lever
mankafa stupid
manken mannequin
manolya magnolia
mansiyon honourable mention
manşet headline
mantar mushroom / cork
mantık logic
mantıki logical
manto overcoat
manyak insane, madman
manyetizma magnetism
manzara view, scene
manzum written in rhyme, in verse
manzume series / poem
marangoz cabinet maker, carpenter
maraton marathon race
maraz disease, illness, evil
margarin margarine
marifet skill, talent, means
marifetli skillful
mariz sick(ly) / beating
marka mark, brand, make
Marmara the Marmara Sea
marmelat marmalade
marş march
marşandiz goods (freight) train
mart March
martaval nonsense, lies
martı sea gull
martin martini rifle
maruf known, well known
marul lettuce
maruz exposed to, open
maruzat matters submitted, petition
masa table
masatenisi table tennis, ping-pong
masaj massage
masal tale
maskara buffoon, laughingstock / eye paint
maskaralık buffoonery
maskelemek mask, camouflage
maskeli masked
masmavi very blue
mason freemason
masör masseur
masöz masseuse
masraf expense

masraflı expensive
mastar infinitive (dilbilgisi)
masum innocent
maşa pincers, tongs
maşallah God save him! How fine!
maşrapa metal drinking cup, mug
mat without lustre / checkmate
matara tin waterbottle, soldier's flask
matbaa printing-office, printing-works
matbaacı printer
matbua printed matter
matbuat the press
matem mourning; **matem tutmak** mourn
matematik mathematics
matemli mourning
materyalist materialist
mat etmek checkmate / overcome
matine matinee
matkap drill, auger
maval untrue story
mavi blue
mavimsi bluish
mavna barge, lighter
mavzer mauser, rifle
maya ferment, yeast, origin
mayalamak ferment
mayasıl chilblain
maydanoz parsley
mayhoş slightly acid, sourish
mayın mine (explosive)
mayıs May
mayıs fresh cow dung
mayi liquid
maymun monkey, ape; **maymun iştahlı** capricious
maymuncuk picklock, pass-key
mayna down sails; **mayna etmek** cease work
mayo bathing-suit
mayonez mayonnaise
maytap fire woks
mazbata official report, protocol, minutes
mazbut well-built, solid / neat, decent
mazeret excuse, apology
mazgal loop-hole
mazhar olmak attain, be gifted, have the honour of
mazi past, bygone
mazlum victim of cruelty,

inoffensive
mazot crude oil, fuel oil
mazur excused, excusable; **mazur görmek** excuse
meblağ sum, amount
mebus deputy, member of parliament
mecal power
mecalsiz powerless
mecazi figurative, metaphorical
mecbur compelled
mecburen compulsorily
mecburi obligatory, compulsory
mecburiyet obligation
meclis assembly, council; **Millet Meclisi** National Assembly
mecmu assembled, total
mecmua magazine, periodical
mecnun madly in love
mecra watercourse, canal, drainage
meçhul unknown
meddah public story teller
medeni civilized, civil
medeniyet civilization
medet help, aid
medrese Moslem theological school
medyum medium
medyun indebted, obliged
mefhum concept, idea
mefruşat furniture
meftun madly in love with, admiring, fascinated
megafon megaphone
megaloman megalomaniac
meğer but, yet
meğerse actually, in fact
Mehmetçik the Turkish "Tommy"
mehtap moonlight
mehter ancient military band
mekân place, abode
mekanik mechanics, mechanical
mekanizma mechanism
mekik shuttle
mektep (old) school; **ana mektebi** kindergarten
mektup letter, note
mektuplaşmak correspond by letter, exchange letters

melal gloom, melancholy
melankoli melancholy
melek angel
meleke proficiency, skill
melemek bleat
melez half-breed, hybrid
melodi melody
melodram melodrama
meltem breeze
melül low-spirited, sad
melun accursed
memba spring, source
meme breast, teat, nipple, tumour (med.)
memeli mammals (zool.)
memleket country, motherland, hometown
memleketli fellow countryman, compatriot
memnun pleased, glad
memnun etmek please
memnuniyet pleasure
memnuniyetle with pleasure
memur official, employee / charged with
memuriyet government job, civil service, post
men prohibition
menderes winding river
mendil handkerchief
mendirek breakwater
menekşe violet
menenjit menengitis
menetmek forbid
menfaat advantage, profit, benefit
menfaatperest selfish
menfez air-hole, opening
menfi negative, perverse
menfilik negation
menfur loathed, detestable
mengene vice, clamp
meni semen, sperm
menkul movables
mensucat textiles
mensup connected with, member
menşe place of origin, source; **menşeli** exported from, of origin
menteşe hinge
menzil halting-place / range (of a gun)
mera pasture
merak curiosity / anxiety / hobby
meraklanmak be anxious, have an interest in
meraklı curious, fond of, interested in

meraksız free from anxiety, uninterested, care-free
meram intention
meram etmek intend
merasim ceremony
mercan coral
mercek lens (optic)
merci source to which a thing is referred
mercimek lentil
merdane roller-pin
merdiven ladder, stairs
meret damned
merhaba hello!, hi!
merhabalaşmak greet one another
merhale stage
merhamet mercy, pity
merhem ointment
merhum deceased, the late
meridyen meridian
Merih (the planet) Mars
merinos merino
meriyet being in force
merkep donkey
merkez centre
merkezi central
merkeziyet centralization
merkezkaç centrifugal
Merkür Mercury
mermer marble
mermi projectile, bullet
merserize cotton thread
mersi thank you
mersin myrtle (bot); sturgeon (fish)
mersiye elegy
mert manly, brave
mertçe bravely
mertebe degree, rank
mertlik courage
mesafe distance, range
mesai efforts, work
mesai saatleri working hours
mesaj message
mesamat pores
mesane bladder
mescit small mosque
mesela for instance, for example
mesele problem, question
mesire excursion spot, promenade
mesken dwelling
meskün inhabited
meslek career, profession
mesleki professional
mesleksiz without a career
meslektaş colleague, of the same profession

mesnet place of support, fulcrum
mest drunk
mest edici intoxicating, fascinating
mesul responsible
mesuliyet responsibility
mesuliyetli involving responsibility
mesut happy
meşakkat hardship, toil
meşale torch
meşe oak
meşe odunu oak wood
meşgale business, occupation
meşgul busy, occupied
meşguliyet occupation, vocation
meşhur famous
meşin leather
meşrep character; **hafif meşrep** frivolous
meşru legal, legitimate
meşrubat drinks
meşruiyet legitimacy
meşruti constitutional
meşrutiyet constitutional government
meşum ill-omened, sinister, fatal
met flow of the tide, tide
meta goods, merchandise
metabolizme metabolism
metafizik metaphysics
metanet firmness
metazori by force and threats
meteliksiz penniless
meteor meteor
methetmek praise
methiye eulogy
metin text
metin firm, strong
metot method
metre metre
metres mistress, concubine
metro subway, undergorund train
metruk abandoned, deserted
mevcudiyet existence, presence
mevcut existing, present
mevduat deposits, investments
mevki place, situation
mevkuf arrested
Mevla God
mevsim season
mevsimlik seasonal, for spring and autumn

mevsimsiz unseasonable, out-of-place
mevzi place, position
mevzii local, regional
mevzu subject, topic
mevzuat the laws, rules
mevzubahis in question
mey wine
meydan square, space
meyhane wine shop, bar, pub
meymenetsiz disagreeable (person), inauspicious
meyve fruit
mezar grave
mezarlık cemetery, graveyard
mezartaşı tombstone
mezat auction sale
mezbaha slaughterhouse
meze apetizer
mezbele refuse heap
meziyet virtue
mezun graduate, graduated / on leave, free
mıh nail
mıhlamak nail
mıknatıs magnet
mıknatisiyet magnetism
mıncıklamak squeeze and squash
mıntıka district, zone, region
mırıldanmak mutter
mırıltı muttering
mırın kırın (etmek) grumble, be reluctant
Mısır Egypt
mısır maize
Mısırlı Egyptian
mısra line (of poetry)
mışıl mışıl sound asleep
mıymıntı slack, lazy
mızıkçı one who does not obey the rules of a game, spoil-sport, spoil-game
mızıklanmak spoil a game by not obeying the rules
mızmız hesitant, difficult to please
mızrak lance, spear
mızrap plectrum
miat fixed time, validity
mide stomach
midesiz having bad taste
midilli pony
midye mussel
miğfer helmet
migren migraine
mihenk touchstone
mihmandar host, guide

mihnet trouble
mihrace maharajah
mihrak focus
mihrap niche
mihver pivot, axle, axis
mika mica
mikrofon microphone
mikrop microbe
mikroskop microscope
miktar quantity, amount
mikyas scale, standard
mil mile
mil pivot, axle / clay
miladi dating from the birth of Christ, B.C., A.D.
milat birth of Christ
miligram milligram
milimetre millimetre
milis militia
militan militant
millet nation, people
milletlerarası international
milletvekili deputy, member of parliament
milli national
millileştirmek nationalize
milliyet nationality
milliyetçi nationalist
milyar milliard, billion
milyon million
milyoner millionaire
mimar architect
mimari architectural
mimber pulpit in a mosqùe
mimik mimic
mimlemek mark down, blacklist
mimli marked off, suspect
mimoza mimosa
minare minaret
minder mattress, cushion
mine enamel
minibüs minibus
minik small
minimini tiny
minimum minimum
minkale protractor
minnet obligation; **minnet etmek** ask a favour, be obliged
minnettar grateful, obliged
mintan shirt (old)
minyatür miniature
minyon dainty, tiny
miras inheritance
mirasçı inheritor, heir
mirasyedi spendthrift, extravagant
mis musk; **mis gibi** sweet

scented, delicious
misafir guest, visitor
misafirhane public guest house for travellers
misafirlik visit
misafirperver hospitable; **misafirperverlik** hospitality
misal model, example
misilleme retaliation
misilli similar, like
misina gut, fishing line
misket musket, marble
miskin lazy, abject
miskinlik abjectness
misli ...times as much, ...times as many
misyoner missionary
miting public meeting
mitoloji mythology
mitralyöz machine-gun
miyavlamak mew
miyop short-sighted
mizaç temperament
mizah humour, joke
mizahi humorous
mizan balance
mizanpaj layout
mobilya furniture
moda fashion
model model, pattern
modern modern
mola rest
molekül molecule
molla theological student
moloz rough stones, rubble
monarşi monarchy
monolog monologue
monoton monotonous
montaj fitting, assembling
mor purple
morarmak become bruised
morfin morphine
morg mortuary, morgue
morina codfish
mors morse (code)
moruk old man
mostra pattern, sample, specimen
motif motive, pattern
motor motor, engine
motosiklet motorcycle
mozaik mosaic work
möble furniture
möbleli furnished
mösyö Mr.
muadil equivalent
muaf exempt, pardoned / immune (to an illness)
muafiyet exemption / immunity

muallak suspended, in suspense
muallim teacher (old)
muamele treatment, conduct, procedure
muamele etmek treat
muamma enigma
muasır contemporary
muaşeret social intercourse; **adabı muaşeret** rules of social behaviour, etiquette
muattal disused
muavin assistant
muayene inspection, examination; **muayene etmek** inspect, examine
muayenehane surgery, consulting room
muayyen definite
muazzam great, enormous
mubah lawful, permissible
mubayaa purchase, wholesale buying
mucibince as necessary, according to
mucip rendering necessary, causing, motive
mucit inventor
mucize miracle
mucizevi miraculous
mucur gravel (for roads)
muço cabin-boy
mudi depositor
mufassal detailed
muflon thick lining attached to overcoats
mugalata misleading argument, fallacy
muğlak obscure, complex
muhabbet affection, friendly chat
muhabere correspondence
muhabere etmek correspond
muhabir correspondent
muhaceret emigration
muhacir emigrant, refugee
muhafaza protection, conservation, guarding
muhafazakâr conservative
muhafız guard
muhakeme trial, judgement; **muhakeme etmek** judge
muhakkak certain, without doubt

muhalefet opposition; **muhalefet etmek** oppose
muhalif opposing, contrary
muharebe war, battle
muharip warrior, combatant
muharrik causing to move, impelling
muharrir writer, author
muhasara siege; **muhasara etmek** besiege
muhasebat accounts
muhasebe book-keeping
muhasebeci accountant, book-keeper
muhatap one addressed in speech
muhayyel imaginary
muhayyer optional, on approval; **muhayyer almak** buy on trial
muhayyile imagination
muhbir informer
muhit surroundings
muhrip destroyer
muhtaç in want, in need of; **muhtaç olmak** be in need of
muhtar free to choose, autonomous / headman, alderman, village leader
muhtariyet autonomy
muhtasar shortened, abridged
muhtelif various
muhtemel probable
muhterem respected, honoured
muhteşem magnificent
muhteva contents
muhteviyat contents
muhtıra note, memorandum, agenda
mukabele confronting, reply
mukabil in return
mukaddeme preface, introduction
mukadder predestined, fated
mukadderat destiny, fate
mukaddes sacred, holy
mukaddesat sacred things
mukavele contract
mukavelename written agreement
mukavemet resistance
mukavim resisting, lasting
mukavva cardboard

mukayese comparison; **mukayese etmek** compare
muktedir capable, able
mum wax, candle
mumya mummy
mumyalamak embalm
munhasıran exclusively
munis sociable, lovable
muntazam regular, orderly, in order
muntazaman regularly
muntazır who waits expenctantly
munzam additional, extra
murahhas delegate
murakabe control
murakıp controller
murat wish, intention
murdar dirty
musademe collision, encounter; **musademe etmek** collide with, encounter
musadere confiscation; **musadere etmek** confiscate
musahhih proof reader
musalla taşı stone on which the coffin is placed during the funeral service
musallat worrying, molesting
Musevi Jewish, Jew
musibet calamity, evil
musiki music
musikişinas musician
muska charm, amulet
musluk tap
mustarip suffering, ailing
muşamba tarpaulin, linoleum / mackintosh
muşmula mediar
muşta fist (iron ring)
mutaassıp fanatical
mutabakat concordance, agreement
mutabık agreeing
mutat customary, usual, habitual, custom, habit **bermutat** as usual
muteber esteemed, valid, notable
mutedil moderate
mutemet reliable / intendant
mutena select
mutfak kitchen
mutlak absolute, absolutely
mutlaka absolutely

mutlakiyet autocracy
mutlu happy / lucky
mutluluk happiness
muvafakat consent; **muvafakat etmek** consent
muvaffak successful; **muvaffak olmak** succeed
muvaffakiyet success
muvaffakiyetsizlik failure
muvafık agreeable, suitable, fitting
muvakkat temporary
muvakkaten temporarily
muvazene balance, stability
muvazeneli balanced
muvazzaf regular (army), executive
muz banana
muzaffer victorious
muzır harmful, mischief maker
muzip teasing, practical joker
mübadele exchange
mübadil exchanged
mübalağa exaggeration; **mübalağa etmek** exaggerate
mübalağalı exaggerated
mübarek blessed, sacred
mübaşir usher
mübrem urgent, inevitable
mücadele struggle
mücahit who fights for an ideal
mücbir compelling
müceddet new, brand new
mücellit bookbinder
mücevherat jewellery
mücrim guilty, criminal
mücver croquette
müdafaa defence, pleading
müdafaa vekaleti the ministry of defence
müdafi defender
müdahale interference; **müdahale etmek** interfere, intervene
müdavim regular visitor, frequenting
müddet period, time
müdrik comprehending
müdür director, manager
müdüriyet directorate, head office, management
müebbeden eternally
müebbet eternal, for life
müellif author
müessese establishment,

institution
müessif regrettable
müessir effective, impressive
müeyyide sanction
müezzin muezzin
müfettiş inspector
müflis bankrupt, penniless, broke
müfredat details, particulars / curriculum (schools)
müfreze detachment
müftü senior Moslem priest
mühendis engineer
mühim important
mühimmat ammunition
mühlet term, delay
mühür seal
mühürlemek stamp with a seal
mühürlü sealed
müjde good news
müjdeci who brings good news
mükâfat reward, prize
mükâleme conversation
mükellef charged, taxed / pompous, grand
mükellefiyet obligation, liability
mükemmel complete, perfect, excellent, splendid
mükemmelen perfectly
mükerrer repeated
mükerreren repeatedly
mülahaza consideration, reflection
mülakat interview
mülayim mild, gentle, soft
mülk property
mülki belonging to the state, civil
mülkiye civil service
mülkiyet ownership
mülteci refugee
mültefit courteous
mümbit fertile
mümessil representative
mümeyyiz assistant examiner
mümin believer in Islam
mümkün possible; **mümkün olduğu kadar** as far as possible
mümtaz distinguished
münakaşa giving of a contract to the lowest bidder, Dutch auction
münakaşa dispute; **münakaşa etmek** dispute

münasebet relation, connection
münasebetli reasonable, suitable
münasebetsiz absurd
münasip suitable, proper
münavebe alternation
münavebeyle alternately, in turns
münazara discussion, debate
münbit fertile
münderecat contents (of a book), index
müneccim astrologer
münekkit critic
münevver educated, educated person
münferit isolated, separated
münhal vacant
münzevi living alone, recluse, secluded
müphem vague
müphemiyet vagueness
müptela addicted to, having a passion
müptezel abundant / common
müracaat application, reference; **müracaat etmek** refer to, consult, apply
mürebbi tutor
mürebbiye governess
müreffeh prosperous, well off
mürekkep ink / compound, composed
mürekkepbalığı cuttlefish
mürettebat crew (of a ship)
mürettip compositor (printing)
mürit disciple
mürşit who shows the right way, inspirer
mürteci reactionary, fanatic
müruruzaman prescription, lapse of time
mürüvvet generosity / family feast (for a marriage etc.)
müsaade permission
müsaade etmek permit, allow, let
müsabaka competition, race
müsademe collision
müsadere confiscation
müsait favourable, convenient
müsamaha tolerance

müsamahakâr tolerant
müsamere entertainment (school)
müsavi equal
müsekkin quieting, sedative
müshil purgative
Müslim Moslem
Müslüman Moslem
Müslümanlık Islam, Mohammedanism
müspet positive
müsrif spendthrift
müstacel urgent
müstahak deserving; **müstahak olmak** be deserving
müstahdem employee
müstahkem fortified
müstahsil producer
müstahzar prepared
müstakbel future, would-be
müstakil independent, apart
müstakilen solely, alone
müstamel used
müstehcen obscene
müstehlik consumer
müstehzi mocking, sarcastic, ironical
müstemleke colony
müstenkif who abstains
müsterih at ease, relieved
müstesna exceptional
müsteşar under secretary
müstevli invading
müsvedde draft, rough copy
müşahede a seeing, observation; **müşahede etmek** see, witness, observe
müşahhas concrete, identified
müşavir adviser
müşerref honoured; **müşerref olmak** be honoured
müşfik tender, kind
müşkül difficult, difficulty
müşkülat difficulties
müşkülpesent fastidious, difficult to please
müştemilat outbuildings, premises
müşterek common, joint, in common
müştereken jointly
müşteri customer
mütalaa a studying,

remark, opinion, study
mütareke armistice
müteaddit numerous, several
müteahhit who undertakes, contractor
müteakiben successively, following it, then
müteakip successive, next
mütebaki remaining, remainder
mütebessim smiling
mütecanis homogeneous
mütecaviz exceeding, aggressor
mütecessis inquisitive
müteessir grieved, affected, hurt
mütefekkir thinker
müteferrik separated, various, miscellaneous
mütehakkim despotic
mütehammil enduring
müteharrik moving
mütehassıs specialist
mütekait retired on a pension, pensioner, veteran
mütekâmil perfect, developed
mütemadi continuous
mütemadiyen continuously
mütemayil inclined
mütemmim completing
mütenasip symmetrical, proportioned
mütercim translator, interpreter
mütereddit hesitating
müteşebbis enterprising
müteşekkil formed
müteşekkir thankful, obliged, grateful
mütevazı modest
mütevekkil resigned, trusting in God
mütevellit caused, because of
müthiş terrible
müttefik allied, ally / agreeing
müttefikan unanimously, in agreement
müvekkil client (of a lawyer)
müvezzi news-vendor, postman
müyesser olmak be granted (by God)
müzakere discussion, negotiation / oral exam
müzayede auction

müze museum
müziç annoying
müzik music
müzikal musical
müzisyen musician
müzmin chronic

N

naaş corpse
nabız pulse
naçar helpless, reluctantly compelled
naçiz humble, trifling
nadan ignorant, impertinent
nadide rare
nadim regretful, repentant; **nadim olmak** regret, repent
nadir rare, unusual
nafaka maintenance money, alimony
nafıa public works
nafile useless, in vain
nağme tune, song; **ara nağmesi** intermezzo, interlude
nahak unjust; **nahak yere** unjustly
nahiye region, district, ward
nahoş unpleasant
nail who obtains; **nail olmak** obtain, attain
nakarat refrain
nakavt knock-out
nakden in cash
nakdi cash
nakış design embroidery; **nakış işlemek** embroider
nakil transport, transfer / translation
nâkil transporting, conductor
nakit cash, money
naklen by transfer
nakletmek transport, transfer, move
nakliyat transport
nakliye transport expenses
nakşetmek engrave

nal horseshoe
nalbant shoeing smith
nalbur ironmonger, hardware dealer
nalça iron heel or tip on a boot
nalın clogs
nallamak shoe
nam name, reputation
namağlup unconquered, undefeated
namahrem not related or intimate
namaz Moslem ritual worship; **namaz kılmak** perform the ritual prayer
name letter
namert unmanly, cowardly
namertçe cowardly
namına in the name of, on behalf of; **...namında** by the name of...
namlı noted, famous / infamous / notorious
namlu barrel (of a gun)
namus honour
namuslu honest
namussuz dishonest
namüsait unfavourable
namütenahi unending, infinite
namzet candidate
nane mint, peppermint; **naneşekeri** peppermint drop
nankör ungrateful
nar pomegranate
nara cry, shout; **nara atmak** yell
narenciye orange family, citrus fruits
nargile hubble-bubble
narh fixed price
narin slender, delicate, slim
narkoz narcosis
nasıl how
nasılsa somehow
nasır corn (med)
nasırlaşmak become calloused
nasırlı with corns
nasihat advice; **nasihat etmek** advise
nasip lot, share, destiny
naşir publisher
natüralizm naturalism
natürmort still life
navlun freight
naylon nylon
naz coyness, mincing
nazar look / the evil eye

nazaran according to, compared with
nazari theoretical
nazariyatçı theorist
nazariye theory
nazarlık charm against the evil eye
nazenin delicately beautiful
nazım who arranges, regulator
nazır overlooking, facing / minister (old)
nazik delicate, elegant, kind, gentle
nazlanmak feign reluctance, simper
nazlı coy /reluctant
ne what / whatever
nebat plant, vegetation
nebati vegetable, botanical
nebze bit, portion
neci of what trade
nedamet regret, remorse, repentance
neden why / reason, cause
nedense for some reason or other, however
nedime maid of honour
nefaset exquisiteness, beauty
nefer private soldier
nefes breath
nefes almak breathe
nefes darlığı asthma
nefis self, soul
nefis excellent, delicious
nefret disgust, hate, hatred
nefret etmek detest, hate, abhor
neft naphtha
nefti of dark brownish green colour
neftyağı naphtha oil
negatif negative
nehir river
ne kadar how much; **ne kadar olsa** after all
nekahet convalescence
nem moisture, dampness
nemlenmek become damp
nemli damp, humid
nemrut cruel, proud
nere what place
nerede where
nerede ise before long, soon
nereden where from
nergis narcissus
nesil generation

nesir prose
nesne thing, object / direct object **(dilbilgisi)**
neşe gaiety, joy
neşelendirmek grow merry; make gay, cheer up
neşelenmek grow merry, be revived
neşeli merry, gay
neşesiz in bad humour, dull, cheerless
neşir spreading, broadcast, a publishing, publication
neşretmek spread about, publish
neşriyat publications
neşter lancet
net net, clear
netameli sinister
netice consequence, result, conclusion
nevale food; **nevale düzmek** provide food
nevazil cold in the head
nevi sort, kind
nevri dönmek become moody or angry
ney flute
nezaket delicacy, refinement, kindness;
nezaketli refined
nezaret view / superintendence, administration
nezih pure in character
nezle cold in the head, cold
nışadır ammonia
nice how, many a...
nicelik state, quantity
niçin why, what for
nida cry, exclamation
nihai final
nihale table mat
nihayet end; **nihayet bulmak** come to an end; **nihayet vermek** put an end to
nihayet at last
nihayetsiz. endless, infinite
nikâh marriage; **nikâh kıymak** perform the ceremony of marriage
nikâhlı betrothed, married, wedded
nikâhsız unmarried, not wedded
nikel nickel; **nikelaj** nickel plating
nikotin nicotine
Nil the Nile

nilüfer water-lily, lotus
nimet comfort, blessing, favour / food
nine granny
ninni lullaby
nirengi triangulation
nisaiye gynaecology
nisan April
nispet proportion, relation, ration, comparison
nispeten relatively
nişan sign, mark, target
nişancı marksman
nişangâh target, butt
nişanlamak sign, aim at / engage to
nişanlanmak become engaged to
nişanlı engaged to be married, fiancée, fiancé
nişasta starch
nitekim as a matter of fact, just as
nitelemek modify, qualify; **niteleme sıfatı** qualifying adjective
nitelik quality, qualification
nitrat nitrate
nitrojen nitrogen
niyaz entreaty; **niyaz etmek** entreat
niye why
niyet intention, purpose, gim
niyetli intending, intended, who has resolved to fast
nizam order, law, system; **nizama koymak** put in order
nizami legal, regular
nizamlı in order, regular
nizamname regulation
nizamsız in disorder, irregular
nobran discourteous
Noel Christmas
nohut chickpea
noksan deficient, defective, missing
noksanlık deficiency
nokta point, dot, spot / full stop, period
noktalı virgül semicolon
normal normal
Norveç Norway
Norveçli Norwegian
not note, mark **not etmek** write down
nota note, music score
noter notary

nöbet turn (of duty etc.) / watch / fit (of fever); **nöbetleşe** in turn
nöbetçi watchman, sentry, on duty
nötr neutral, neuter
nötron neutron
Nuh Noah
numara number, marks
numaralı numbered
numune sample, pattern, example, model
nur light (heavenly)
nurani luminous, shining
nutuk speech, discourse, **nutku tutulmak** be confused and silent
nüans nuance, shade
nüfus population / people, person; **nüfus cüzdanı** identity card
nüfuz penetration, influence **nüfuz etmek** penetrate
nüfuzlu influential
nüksetmek relapse
nükte witty remark
nüktedan witty person
nümayiş demonstration, manifestation
nümune bak; **numune**
nümunelik pattern, sample (free)
nüsha coppy / issue
nüve nucleus

O

o he, she, it, that
oba nomad tent
objektif objective
obur gluttonous
ocak January
ocak furnace, hearth, fire place, quarry, mine
od fire
oda room
odacı servant in an office
odak focus
odalık concubine (old)
odun firewood, log
oduncu wood-cutter
odunluk wood-shed
ofis office
oflamak say "ugh", sigh
ofsayd offside
oğlak kid / capricorn
oğlan boy

oğul son / swarm of bees
oje nail polish
ok arrow / pole (of a carriage)
okaliptüs eucalyptus
okçu bowman, archer
okkalı heavy
oklava rolling-pin
oksijen oxygen
oksit oxide
okşamak caress, stroke
okşayış caress, patting
okul school
okumak read / study / sing
okumuş educated, learned
okunaklı legible
okur reader
okutmak cause to read or learn / educate / sell (argo)
okuyucu reader / singer
okyanus ocean
olabilir possible, may be
olacak which will happen, inevitable
olagelmek happen frequently
olağan that commonly happens, possible, ordinary
olağanüstü extraordinary
olan being, becoming
olanak possibility
olanaksız impossible, improbable
olanca existing, fully, to the utmost
olarak being, as
olası probable
olasılık probability
olay event
oldukça rather, fairly
oldurmak cause to become, cause to ripen
olgu event, fact
olgun ripe, mature
olgunlaşmak become ripe, develop, mature
olimpiyat olympic
olmadık without precedent, unusual
olmak be, exist / become, happen / fit, suit / ripen
olmamış unripe, raw
olmaz impossible
olmuş ripe, completed, that has happened
olta fishing line
oluk gutter pipe, spout
oluklu channelled,

grooved
olumlu affirmative, positive
olumsuz negative
olur possible, it may be, all right
oluş genesis / event
oluşmak take form
oluşum formation, progress
omlet omelette
omurga backbone / keel
omurgalılar vertebrate
omurilik medulla, spinal marrow
omuz shoulder
omuz silkmek shrug
omuzlamak give a shoulder to, shoulder
on ten
ona to him, to her, to it
onar ten each
onamak approve
onarmak repair, restore
onarım repairing, restoration
onay approval
onaylamak ratify
onbaşı corporal
onca according to him, in his opinion
onda bir one tenth; **ondalık** ten percent, decimal
ondüle curled, curly
onikiparmak bağırsağı duodenum
onlar they
onun his, her, its
onuncu tenth
onur dignity, honour
onunki his, hers
onurlu proud
onurlandırmak honour, do honour
onursal honorary
opera opera
operasyon operation
operatör surgeon
operet operetta
optik optics, optical
ora that place
orada there
oradan from there
orak sickle, reaping hook, scythe
oralı of that place
oran proportion
oranlı proportioned, symmetrical
oransız badly proportioned, unsymmetrical
orantı proportion
oraya there
ordinaryüs (full) professor

ordino certificate of ownership
ordu army
ordugâh military camp
org (music) organ
organ organ
organik organic
organizma organism
orgeneral full general
orijinal original
orkestra orchestra
orkide orchid
orman forest, wood
ormancılık forestry
ormanlık woodland
orospu whore
orta middle, centre, central
ortaç participle
ortaçağ middle ages
ortada in the middle
Orta Doğu Middle East
ortaelçi minister in an embassy
orta halli middle-class, well-to-do
ortak partner; **ortak olmak** be a partner
ortaklaşa in common
ortaklık partnership
ortalama average
ortalamak divide in the middle
ortalık the world around
ortam circumstances, situation, condition
orta malı common to all, common property
ortanca middle, middling
ortaokul secondary school
ortaoyunu old Turkish theatrical show
ortodoks orthodox
oruç fasting, fast; **oruç tutmak** fast
oruçlu fasting
Osmanlı Ottoman
Osmanlıca the Ottoman Turkish language
osurmak fart
ot grass
otalamak poison
otağ tent (king's)
otel hotel
otlak pasture, meadow
otlamak graze
otluk pasture
oto motor-car, car
otobüs bus
otomasyon automation
otomatik automatic
otomobil car
otonomi autonomy
otopark car park

otorite authority
otostop hitchhiking
oturak seat / chamber pot / seated
oturaklı solid (man) / well settled
oturmak sit, dwell, settle, live, run aground
oturtmak cause to sit, place
oturum sitting (of a court etc); **açık oturum** panel discussion
otuz thirty
otuzar thirty each
otuzuncu thirtieth
ova plain
ovalamak rub, massage
ovmak rub
ovuşturmak rub
oy vote / voting; **oy vermek** vote for
oya embroidery on the edges of a garment, crochet-work
oyalamak put one off to gain time, distract / amuse (to distract)
oyalanmak loiter, waste time
oyalı pinked, embroidered on the edge
oylamak vote / put to a vote
oyma decoration by hollowing out, carving, engraving
oymak excavate, engrave, carve
oymalı carved, engraved
oynak playful, mobile, unstable, flirtatious
oynaklık mobility, friskiness, frivolity
oynak yeri articulation
oynamak play, move, dance
oynaş sweetheart
oynaşmak play with one another
oynatmak move / cause to play or dance / go mad
oysaki yet, whereas
oyuk hollowed out, hollow part, cave
oyun play, dance, game
oyunbozan spoilsport, kill-joy
oyuncak toy, plaything
oyuncu player, actor, dancer
ozan poet, minstrel
ozon ozone

Ö

öbek heap, group
öbek öbek heaps of, scattered
öbür the other
öbür gün the day after tomorrow
öç revenge; **öç almak** take revenge
öd gall, bile
ödemek pay
ödemeler payments
ödemeli cash on delivery
ödenek compensation, payment, funds
ödeşmek pay one another, settle accounts
ödev duty, work
ödlek cowardly
ödül reward, prize
ödün compensation
ödünç loan; **ödünç almak** borrow; **ödünç vermek** lend
öfke anger, rage, fury
öfkelenmek get angry
öfkeli angry
öğe element
öğle noon; **öğleden sonra** afternoon
öğleyin at noon
öğrenci student, pupil, learner
öğrenim education
öğrenmek learn
öğretici teaching, educational, instructive
öğretim teaching, instruction
öğretmek teach, instruct
öğretmen teacher
öğün meal
öğünmek boast
öğürmek bellow, belch
öğüş praise
öğüt advice
öğütmek grind
öğütücü that grinds, molar (tooth)
ökçe heel (of shoes)
ökçeli having heels; **yüksek ökçeli** high-heeled
ökse birdlime, trap
öksürmek cough
öksürük a cough
öksüz orphan
öküz ox
ölçmek measure

ölçü measure, limit
ölçüm the measure of a thing, scale
ölçüsüz unmeasured, unmeasurable, excessive
öldüresiye to death, ruthlessly
öldürmek kill, murder
öldürücü fatal, deadly, mortal
ölgün faded, withered
ölmek die
ölmez immortal, undying, eternal
ölmüş dead
ölü dead, lifeless, corpse
ölücü mortal
ölüm death
ölümlü mortal
ölümsüz immortal
ömür life
ön front / the future
ön ayak olmak lead
önce first; **ilkönce** first of all, before
önceden beforehand
önceleri at (in) the beginning
öncelik priority
öncü vanguard
önder leader; **önderlik** leadership
önek prefix
önem importance
önemli important
önemsemek feel the importance of
önerge proposal
öneri suggestion, proposal
önermek propose, suggest
öngörmek keep in mind
öngörü foresight, sagacity
önlem precaution, preventive measures
önlemek prevent, stop
önlük apron
önseçim preliminary, primary election
önsezi presentiment
önsöz preface
öntakı prefix
önüsıra before him
önyargı prejudice
öpmek kiss
öpücük kiss
öpüşmek kiss one another
ördek duck
örf common usage, custom, tradition

örfi customary; **örfi idare** martial law
örgü plait (hair), knitting (wool)
örgüt organization, association
örme plaiting, knitting, plaited
örmek plait, knit, darn (socks)
örneğin for example
örnek example, specimen, sample, pattern
örs anvil
örtbas hushing up; **örtbas etmek** hush up, suppress
örtmek cover, conceal, shut, close
örtü cover
örtücü covering
örtülü covered, shut
örtüsüz uncovered, open
örücü darner
örülü plaited, knitted
örümcek spider
örümcek ağı cobweb
öte the further side, beyond, further
öteberi various things, this and that
ötedenberi for a long time
öteki the other
öte yanda on the other side
öte yandan on the other hand
ötmek sing (of birds), resound
öttürmek make sound or ring
ötürü on account of, because of
ötüş singing
övgü praise, flattering
övmek praise
övünç boasting
öykü story, fable
öyle so, such, like that
öyleyse if so
öylece in that manner, thus
öz self / essence, kernel / genuine, real
özbeöz real, true, genuine
özdeş identical
özdeyiş maxim, epigram
özel private, special
özellik characteristics, peculiarity
özellikle especially
özen care, pains
özenmek take pains, try

hard / desire to have the same
özenti aping, mocking, imitation
özerk autonomous
özet summary
özetlemek sum up, summarize, abridge
özge different from the others, unique
özgü exclusive, peculiar
özgül specific
özgür free
özgürlük freedom
özlem longing, desire
özlemek miss, long for
özleyiş longing
özlü sappy, pulpy
özlük nature / personal, individual
özne subject
özsu juice, sap
özümleme digestion
özür defect / excuse; **özür dilemek** ask for pardon, apologize
özürlü defective / having an excuse
özveri renunciation, selfdenial

P

pabuç shoe
pabuççu shoemaker
paça sheep's trotters / lower part of the trouser leg
paçavra rag
padişah ruler, sultan
pafta each part of a large map, sectional map
paha price; **paha biçilmez** priceless, invaluable
pahacı who sells at a high price
pahalanmak become dear, go up, increase
pahalı expensive, dear
pak clean, pure
paket packet, parcel
paketlemek pack up
pakt pact
pala scimitar
palabıyık who has large curved moustaches

palamut bonito / acorn
palanga tackle
palas palace, big hotel
palaska cartridge belt
palavra boast, brag
palavracı braggart, boasting
palazlanmak grow plump
paldır küldür with great noise, headlong
palet palette
palmiye palmtree
palto overcoat
palyaço harlequin, clown
pamuk cotton
pamuklu of cotton
panayır fair
pancar beet
pandispanya sponge cake
panjur Venetian blinds, shutter
pandomim pantomime
panik panic
pankart big poster, billboard
pano painter's panel
pansiyon boardinghouse
pansiyoner boarder, lodger
pansuman dressing for a wound
panter panther
pantolon trousers
panzehir antidote
Papa the Pope
papağan parrot
papara dish of bread and broth / scolding
papatya camomile, daisy
papaz priest / king (cards)
papyon bow-tie
para money; **para etmek** have value
parabol parabola; **parabolik** parabolic
parafe etmek sign initial
parafin paraffin wax
paragraf paragraph
paralamak cut to pieces, tear up
paralanmak be broken or cut to pieces / become rich
paralel parallel
paralelkenar parallelogram
paralı rich, wealthy
paramparça all in bits **paramparça etmek** tear to pieces
parantez paranthesis
parasız penniless / free

paraşüt parachute
paratoner lightning rod
paravana folding screen
parazit parasite / atmospherics (radio)
parça piece, bit; **bir parça** a little
parçalamak break or cut into pieces
parça parça all in pieces
pardesü overcoat
pardon pardon
parfüm perfume
parıldamak gleam, glitter, shine
parıltı glitter, gleam, flash
park park
parke parquet (floor)
parlak bright, brilliant, shining
parlaklık brilliance
parlamak shine
parlamento parliament
parlatmak cause to shine
parmak finger, thumb, toe; **parmak izi** finger print
parmaklık railing, balustrade
parola password
pars leopard
parsa money collected from spectators
parsel plot of land
parşömen parchment
parter parterre
parti party
partizan partisan
pas rust
pas pass (football)
pasaj passage / arcade with shops
pasaklı dirty, slovenly, untidy
pasaport passport
pasif passive
paskalya Easter
paslanmak become rusty
paso pass
paspas doormat
pasta sweet, cake, pastry
pastane pastryshop
pastel pastel
pastil pastille
pastırma dried salt meat
pastörize pasteurised
paşa general (old)
pataklamak beat
patates potato
patavatsız tactless
paten skate

patent patent, licence
patırdamak make a knocking noise
patırtı noise, row
patırtılı noisy, rowdy
patik baby's shoes
patika path, track
patinaj skating, sliding
patiska cambric
patlak burst, torn open
patlama explosion
patlamak burst, explode
patlatmak cause to burst or explode
patlayıcı explosive
patlıcan aubergine, eggplant
Patrik Patriarch
patron employer, boss, pattern (tailoring)
pavurya hermit crab
pavyon night club / pavilion
payda denominator
paydaş partner
paydos break, rest; **paydos etmek** cease work
paye grade, rank, degree
payitaht capital
paylamak scold
paylaşmak share
pazar bazaar, market
pazar Sunday
pazarlama marketing
pazarlık bargaining, deal; **pazarlık etmek** bargain
pazartesi Monday
pazen cotton flannel
pazı biceps
peçe veil
peçete napkin
pedagoji pedagogy
pedal pedal
peder father
pederşahi patriarchal
pedikür pedicure
pehlivan wrestler
pejmürde shabby
pek hard, firm
pek very
pekala all right
peki, pekiyi very good, all right
pekiştirme stiffening / intensive (dilbilgisi)
pekiştirmek become hard, intensify, consolidate
peklik constipation
pekmez boiled grapejuice, molasses
pelerin pelerine, hood
pelikan pelican
pelte jelly

peltek stammering
pelteklik stammer, lisp
pelür onionskin (paper)
pembe rosy, pink
pencere window
pençe paw, claw
pençelemek grasp
pençeleşmek struggle
penguen penguin
penisilin penicillin
pens pincers, tongs
perakende retail
perakendeci retailer
perçem tuft of hair
perçin rivet, clenching
perdah polish, gloss, finishing shave
perdahlamak polish
perde curtain, screen / act (of a play)
perende somersault; **perende atmak** turn a somersault
pergel pair of compasses
perhiz diet
peri fairy
perili haunted
periskop periscope
perişan scattered, in disorder, in confusion, wretched; **perişan etmek** scatter; ruin
permi permit
peron platform
personel personnel, staff
perspektif perspective
perşembe Thursday
pertavsız mognifying glass
peruka wig
pervane propeller
pervasız fearless
pervaz fringe, border
pes low, bass; **pes etmek** submit, give in
pespaye common, vulgar
pestil fruit pulp pressed into thin layers
peşin first, paid in advance, cash, in advance
peşinci seller for cash
peşinen in advance
peşisıra following him (her, it)
peşkeş gift
peşkir napkin, towel
peşrev overture, prelude
peştamal bath-towel
petek honeycomb
petrol petroleum
pey deposit, bid
peyda produced, born; **peyda olmak** appear

peyderpey in succession, step by step
peygamber prophet
peyk satellite / follower
peynir cheese
peyzaj landscape
pezevenk pimp
pıhtı coagulated liquid, clot
pıhtılaşmak become coagulated
pılı pırtı old rubbish, bag and baggage
pınar spring, fountain
pırasa leek
pırıldamak gleam, glitter
pırıltı gleam
pırlanta brilliant
pırtık torn, ragged
pısırık shy, diffident, timid
pıtırdamak make a tapping sound
pıtırtı tapping sound
piç bastard
pide flat bread
pijama pyjamas
pik cast iron
pikap pick-up
pike diving (aeroplane) / quiting
piknik picnic
pil electric battery
pilaki stew with oil and onions
pilav rice (cooked)
piliç chicken
pilot pilot
pineklemek slumber, doze
pingpong ping-pong
pinti miserly, stingy
pipo pipe
pir old man, patron saint
piramit pyramid
pire flea
pirelenmek smell a rat, get suspicious
pirinç rice / brass
pirzola grilled chop, cutlet
pis dirty, impure
pisboğaz greedy
pisi pisine uselessly, for nothing
pislemek dirty, soil
pist running track / runway
piston piston
pişik inflamed sore, blister
pişirmek cook
pişkin well cooked / experienced

pişman regretful, sorry, repentant
pişman olmak regret
pişmanlık regret
pişmek be cooked / be experienced, be matured
pişmemiş uncooked / inexperienced
piyade infantry
piyango lottery
piyano piano
piyanist pianist
piyasa public place, current price, market
piyaz salad of boiled beans / flattery
piyes play (theatre)
plaj beach
plak plate, disk, record
plaka licence plate
plan plan; **arka plan** background; **ön plan** foreground
planör glider
planya carpenter's plane
plastik plastic
platform platform
platin platinum
platonik platonic
plazma plasma
plonjon diving head first
poğaça kind of lardy cake, flat pastry
pohpohlamak flatter
poker poker (game)
polemik polemic
poliçe bill of exchange, insurance policy, draft
poligon range, polygon
poliklinik clinic for outpatients
polis policeman / police
politika politics, policy
politikacı politician
Polonya Poland
pomat pomade
pompa pump
ponpon powder puff
popüler popular
porselen porcelain, chinaware
porsiyon portion
porsuk badger
porsuk withered
portakal orange
portatif portable
Portekiz Portugal
portmanto coat stand
portre portrait
posa dregs, sediment
post skin, hide
posta the post, mail, postal service

postacı postman
postane post-office
postal heavy army shoe
posta pulu postage stamp
pot fold, crease
pot kırmak make a blunder
pota small crucible
potansiyel potential
potasyum potassium
potin half boot
potur knee-beeches
poyraz north-east wind
poz pose, exposure
pörsük withered, wrinkled
pösteki sheepskin
pranga fetters attached to the legs of criminals, chain
pratik practical, useful / practice
prens prince
prenses princess
prensip principle
pres press, pressure
prestij prestige
prevantoryum hospital for weak persons
prim premium
priz wall-socket
prizma prism
problem problem
profesör professor
profesyonel professional
profil profile
program programme
proje project, scheme
projeksiyon projection
projektör projector, searchlight
propaganda propaganda
protein protein
protesto protest; **protesto etmek** protest
protokol protocol
prova trial, printer's proof / fitting, rehearsal; **prova etmek** try on
psikoloji psychology
puan point
pudra face powder
pudriyer compact
puf circular cushion
puflamak blow, puff
pul stamp / thin round disk / scale (of fish)
pulluk plough
punto size of type
pupa stern (of a ship), following wind, poop
puro cigar
puslanmak become misty
puslu hazy, misty

pusu ambush; **pusu kurmak** lay an ambush
pusula note, list
pusula compass
put idol, cross
putperest idolater, pagan
putrel iron beam
püflemek blow out, puff
püf noktası delicate and vital spot
püre mash
pürüz roughness, difficulty
pürüzlenmek become rough
pürüzlü rough, shaggy, uneven
pürüzsüz smooth, even
püskül tassel
püskürmek blow out water, spray, scatter
püskürtmek drive away, scatter

R

rabıta tie, connection
rabıtalı in good order regular, mannerly
radar radar
radde degree, extent
radyatör radiator
radyo radio, wireless
radyoaktif radio-active
radyatör radiator
radyum radium
raf shelf
rafadan lightly boiled (egg)
rafineri refinery
rağbet desire, demand / popularity
rağbette in demand, liked
rağmen in spite of
rahat rest, ease, comfort / comfortable, easy; **rahat etmek** be at ease, make oneself comfortable
rahatlık ease, comfort
rahatsız uneasy, ill, uncomfortable; **rahatsızlık** uneasiness, disturb **rahatsız etmek** disturb
rahibe nun
rahim womb
rahip monk
rahmet blessing, mercy / rain

rahmetli the deceased
rakam figure, number
raket tennis-racket
rakı raki
rakım altitude above sea-level
rakipsiz unrivalled
rakkas pendulum
raks dance, dancing
raksetmek dance
ralanti idling
rali rally
ramazan the month of Moslem fast, Ramadan
ram etmek cause to yield
rampa incline, loading platform, boarding
randevu rendezvous; date, appointment; **randevuevi** brothel
randıman yield, output, efficiency
randımanlı productive
ranza bunk
rapor report
raportör reporter
raptetmek bind, fasten, attach
raptiye drawing pin, fastener, clip
rasat observation
rasathane observatory
rasgele by chance, at random
rast gelmek come across, meet by chance / cause to succeed
raspa scraper, rasp
rastlamak meet by chance, encounter, run into
raunt round (boxing)
ray rail
rayiç current, current value
rayiha smell, odour
razı consenting, willing; **razı etmek** satisfy, persuade
reaksiyon reaction
realist realistic
realite reality
reçel jam
reçete recipe, prescription
reçine resin
reddetmek reject, repel, refuse
refah comfort, luxury
refakat etmek accompany
referandum referendum
refik companion, husband
refika wife

refleks reflex
reflektör reflector
reform reform
regülatör regulator, adjuster
rehavet slackness, lethargy, lassitude
rehber guide, guidebook
rehberlik guiding; **rehberlik etmek** guide
rehin pawn, pledge; **rehine koymak** pawn
rehine object given as pledge, hostage
reis head, chief
reisicumhur president of a republic
rejim regime / diet
rejisör director
rekabet rivalry, competition
rekolte harvest
rekor record
rekortmen record-breaker, record holder
rektör rector
Ren the Rhine
rencide etmek hurt, offend
rençber farm-hand
rende grater, plane
rendelemek plane, grate
rengârenk multicoloured
renk colour
renkli coloured
renksiz colourless, pale
repertuar repertoire, repertory
resim drawing, picture, photography; **resim çekmek** take a photograph
resimli illustrated
resmen officially
resmi official, formal
resmigeçit parade
resmiyet formality
ressam painter, artist
restoran restaurant
resul prophet, envoy
reşit of full age, over 18 years old
ret repelling, rejecting, refutation
retuş retouch
reva proper; **reva görmek** deem proper
revaçta in demand, current
revan olmak go, set out
revani sweet with semolina
reverans bow, courtesy
revir small hospital,

infirmary, clinic
revizyon revision, checking
revolver revolver, pistol
revü show, revue
rey vote; **reye koymak** put to the vote
rezalet vileness, scandalous behaviour; **rezalet çıkarmak** cause a scandal
rezil vile, disgraced; **rezil etmek** disgrace, **rezil olmak** be disgraced
rezistans resistance (elec.)
rıhtım quay, wharf, docks, waterfront
rıza consent
riayet respect, esteem
riayet etmek pay attention to
riayetkâr respectful
rica request; **rica etmek** request, ask
rica etmek retreat
rimel cosmetic for the eyelashes, mascara
ringa herring
ritim rhythm
riya hypocrisy
riyakâr hypocritical
riyakârlık hypocrisy
riyaset presidency
riyazi mathematical
riziko risk
robdöşambır dressing gown
Rodos Rhodes
roka rocket (for salad)
roket rocket
rol role, part (theatre)
roman novel; **romancı** novelist
romantik romantic
Romanya Rumania
Romanyalı Rumanian
romatizma rheumatism
romatizmalı rheumatic
rop robe
rosto roast meat
rota ship's course, route
rotatif rotative, rotatory
rozet rosette, badge
römorkör tugboat
Rönesans Renaissance
röntgen X-ray
röportaj reportage, interview
rötar delay, retard
rövanş revenge, return
rugan patent leather
ruh spirit, soul
ruhani spiritual

ruhbilim psycology
ruhi psychological
ruhiyat psychology
ruhsal spiritual
ruhsat permission, leave, licence
ruhsatlı authorized
ruhsatname permit, licence
ruhsuz lifeless, spritless, dull
ruj lipstick
rulet roulette
Rum Greek
Rumca Greek
rumi Gregorian (calendar)
rumuz signs, symbols
Rus Russian
Rusça Russian
Rusya Russia
rutubet dampness
rutubetli damp
rüya dream; **rüya görmek** have a dream
rüküş badly dressed, shabby
rüsum duties, taxes
rüşt coming of age
rüşvet bribe
rütbe degree, rank
rüzgâr wind

S

saadet happiness
saat hour, watch, clock
saatçi watch-maker
sabah morning / in the morning
sabahki this morning's
sabahlamak sit up all night
sabahları every morning
sabahleyin in the morning
sabahlık woman's morning dress, dressing gown
saban plough
sabık former, previous
sabıka former conviction
sabıkalı previously convicted, notorious
sabır patience
sabırlı patient
sabırsız impatient
sabırsızlanmak grow impatient
sabit fixed, stationary,

firm
sabotaj sabotage
sabretmek be patient
sabun soap
sabunlamak soap, lather
sabunlu soapy, lathered
sac sheet-iron
sacayağı trivet
saç hair
saçak fringe / eaves of a house
saçaklı fringed / untidy
saçılmak be scattered
saçlı having hair
saçma nonsense / act of scattering / small shot
saçmak scatter, sprinkle
saçmalamak talk non-sense
sada echo, sound
sadaka alms, charity
sadakat fidelity, loyalty
sadakatli faithful
sade mere, simple, unmixed, plain, simply, just
sadece merely, simply
sadeleştirmek simplify
sadet point or object in view, scope
sadelik simplicity
sadık faithful
sadist sadist
sadme collision, shock
sadrazam grand vizier
saf row, line
saf pure, simple
safa peace, pleasure; **safa geldiniz** welcome
safdil simple-hearted
safha phase
safi clear, net
saflık simplicity
safra ballast
safra bile, gall (bio.)
safsata sophistry, non-sense
sağ alive
sağ right-hand
sağaçık outside right
sağanak downpour, shower
sağcı right wing sympathizer, conservative
sağdıç best man
sağduyu common sense
sağır deaf
sağırlık deafness
sağiç inside right
sağlam sound, healthy, strong
sağlamak secure, ensure
sağlamlaştırmak become

firm, be fortified
sağlamlık soundness, firmness, health
sağlıcak good health
sağlık life, good health, all is well; **sağlık bakanlığı** ministry of health; **sağlık olsun** never mind; **sağlığınıza** to your health
sağmak milk
sağrı rump
saha open space, field
sahan copper food dish
sahanlık platform (of a tram)
sahi true, correct
sahici real
sahiden really
sahife page
sahip possessing, owner, possessor
sahipsiz with no owner, abandoned
sahne scene, stage
sahra desert, wilderness
sahte false, counterfeit
sahtekâr fraud, forger, imposter; **sahtekârlık** forgery
sair other
saka water-carrier
sakakuşu goldfinch
sakal beard, whiskers
sakallı bearded
sakar clumsy, butter fingered
sakarin saccharine
sakat disabled, invalid, broken / defect
sakatlamak damage, cripple
sakatlık infirmity, defect
sakın beware! take care!
sakınca objection, dawback, harm
sakınma avoidance of risks
sakınmak be cautious, guard oneself from, protect, deny
sâkıt fallen, aborted, null
sakız chewing-gum
saki cupbearer
sakil ugly, sluggish
sakin quiet / inhabitant
saklamak hide, keep
saklambaç hide-and-seek
saklanmak hide, be kept
saklı hidden, preserved
saksafon saxophone
saksağan magpie
saksı flower-pot
sal raft

salâh improvement, goodness
salahiyet authority, right
salahiyetli authorized,. compatent
salak silly, idiot
salam salami
salamura brine, pickle / pickled
salaş thatched booth
salata salad / lettuce
salatalık cucumber
salavat prayers
salça sauce, gravy
saldırgan aggressive
saldırı attack, aggression
saldırma act of attacking / large knife
saldırmak attack, hurl oneself, pounce
saldırmazlık non-aggression
salep salep, orchis
salgı secretion (bio.)
salgın contegious, epidemic
salhane slaughterhouse
salı Tuesday
salık vermek recommend
salıncak swing
salınmak sway, oscillate
salıvermek let go, set free, release
salim free from suffering, safe, free from
salimen safely and soundly
salip cross
salkım bunch of grapes
salkım saçak hanging about untidily, falling down
salkımsögüt weeping-willow
sallamak swing, rock, shake / put off
sallandırmak swing, hang / delay
sallanmak swing, rock, oscillate, shake
sallapati careless, without reflection
salmak let go, send / attack
salmastra gasket
salon hall
salt simple, sole, absolute
saltanat sovereignty, rule / splendour
saltanatlı royal, pompous
salya saliva
salyangoz snail
saman straw

samanlık straw-rick, barn
samanyolu the milky way
samimi sincere, intimate
samimiyet sincerity
san reputation
sana (to) you
sanat trade / art / skill
sanatçı artist
sanatkârlık skill, profession of art
sanatlı artistic, skilful
sanatoryum sanatorium
sanayi industry
sanayileşmek industrialize
sancak flag, standard / starboard
sancaktar standardbearer
sancı ache, pain
sancı(lan)mak ache
sandal rowing-boat
sandal sandal
sandalye chair
sandık chest, box
sandviç sandwich
sanı opinion, thought
sanık suspected, accused
saniye second
sanki as if, as though
sanlı well-known
sanmak think, suppose
sansar marten, pole-cat
sansür censorship
santimetre centimetre
santral central
santrifüj centrifugal
santrfor centre-forward
sap stem, handle / stalk
sapa off the road, out of the way
sapan sling, catapult / plough
sapık pervert / perverted
sapıtmak cause to deviate / go mad
saplantı fixed idea in the mind
saplı having a handle / sticking into a thing
sapmak swerve, deviate, turn off
sapsarı very yellow
sapsız without a handle
saptamak fix, establish
sara epileptic fit
saraç leather-worker, saddler
sarahat clearness
sararmak turn yellow or pale
saray palace, court

sardalye sardine
sardunya geranium
sarf expenditure, use
sarfetmek spend
sarfınazar putting aside
sarfiyat expenses
sargı bandage
sarhoş drunk
sarı yellow, pale
sarıca yellowish
sarık turban
sarıklı wearing a turban
sarılı coloured yellow / wound, surrounded
sarılık yellowness / jaundice
sarılmak be wound, clasp, be surrounded, embrace
sarımsak garlic
sarımtırak yellowish
sarınmak wrap oneself in
sarışın fair-haired, blonde
sâri contagious
sarih clear, explicit
sarkaç pendulum
sarkık hanging loosely, flabby, slack
sarkıntı molestation
sarkıntılık molestation to women; **sarkıntılık etmek** molest
sarkıt stalactite
sarkıtmak hang, suspend
sarkmak hang down, lean out
sarma act of winding, embrace
sarmak wind or wrap round, surround, interest
sarmaşdolaş in a close embrace
sarmaşık ivy
sarnıç cistern
sarp steep, hard
sarplaşmak become steep
sarraf money-changer
sarsak palsied, shaky
sarsıntı shaking, earthquake
sarsmak shake
sataşmak seek a quarrel
sathi superficial
satıcı salesman, seller
satıh surface, face
satılık on sale, for sale
satılmış sold
satın alıcı purchaser
satın almak buy
satır line; **satırbaşı** paragraph
satır large knife, chopper

satış sale
satmak sell
satranç chess
savaş war, struggle, fight, battle
savaşmak fight
savcı public prosecutor
savma sending away, dismissal
savmak get rid of, drive away, get over
savruk clumsy, untidy
savsaklamak delay without reason
savul out of the way!
savulmak stand aside
savunma bakanlığı ministry of defence
savunmak defend
savurmak throw into the air, blow about
savuşmak slip away
savuşturmak avoid
sayaç meter, counter
saydam transparent
sayesinde thanks to
sayfa page
sayfiye villages near a large town, resort
saygı respect
saygıdeğer estimable
saygılı respectful
saygın respected
saygısız disrespectful, impertinent
saygısızlık disrespect
sayı number
sayıklama delirium, talking in one's sleep
sayılı counted / rare
sayılmak be counted / be esteemed
sayım census
sayın esteemed, dear
sayısız innumerable
sayıştay court of accounts
saymak count, regard, esteem, respect
sayman financial officer
saz rush, reed
saz musical instrument
sazan carp (fish)
sebat firmness, constancy
sebatkar persistent
sebatsız unstable, fickle
sebep cause, reason
sebepsiz without a reason
sebil free distribution of water
sebze vegetable

seccade prayer rug
secde prostration in Moslem worship
seçici who chooses, selector
seçim choice, election
seçkin select, chosen
seçme choosing, choice, election
seçmece allowing the purchaser to choose
seçmek choose, select
seçmen voter
seda voice / echo
sedef mother-of-pearl
sedye stretcher
sefahat dissipation, debauch
sefalet poverty, misery
sefaret embassy
sefarethane embassy
sefer time / journey / state of war, military expedition
seferber mobilized for war
seferberlik mobilization
seferi pertaining to travel or state of war
sefertası travelling food box, lunch-box
sefil poor, miserable
sefir ambassador
segman segment, packing ring
seğirmek twitch nervously (eye)
seğirtmek run, rush
seher early morning, dawn
sehpa tripod, gallows
sehven by mistake
sekiz eight
sekizer eight each
sekizinci eighth
sekmek hop
sekreter secretary
seks sex
seksek hopscotch
seksen eighty
sekseninci eightieth
seksi sexy
seksoloji sexology
sekte stoppage, interruption, stroke
sektör sector
sel flood, torrent
selahiyet authority, right
selahiyetli authorized, competent
selam salutation, greeting **selam söylemek** give one's regards to;

selam vermek greet, salute
selamet safety, successful result, security
selametlemek see off
selamlamak greet, salute
selamlaşmak greet each other
sele flat basket
selef predecessor
selim safe, sound; **aklıselim** common sense
selvi cypress
selüloz cellulose
sema sky, heaven
semaver samovar
semavi celestial, divine
sembol symbol
semer packsaddle
semere fruit, result
seminer seminary
semirmek grow fat
semirtmek fatten
semiz fat, fleshy, wellfed
semizotu purslane
sempati sympathy
semt region, neighbourhood, quarter
sen you
senaryo scenario
senato senate
senatör senator
sendelemek stagger
sendika syndicate, trade union
sene year
senet document, receipt, written proof, bond
senfoni symphony
seni you (object)
senin your, yours
seninki yours
senlibenli very intimate
senkronik synchronized
sentetik synthetic
sentez synthesis
sepet basket
sepetlemek get rid of (a tiresome person)
ser head, chief
ser, sera greenhouse
serap mirage
serapa entirely, from head to foot, thoroughly
serbest free
serbestçe freely
serbesti liberty
serbestlik freedom
serçe sparrow
serçe parmak little finger
serdar commander (old)
serdengeçti self sacrificing soldier

serdümen quartermaster
serencam event, adventure
sereserpe free and unrestrained, spreading out
sergi exhibition, display
sergilemek exhibit, display
sergüzeşt adventure
serhat frontier
seri quick, fast, swift
seri series, set
serilmek lie spread on the ground
serin cool, chilly
serinlemek become cool
serkeş rebellious, unruly
serlevha title, heading, head-line
sermaye capital, first cost, cost-price
sermayedar capitalist
sermek spread out, lay, spread over / neglect
sermürettip chief compositor
serpelemek drizzle
serpilmek fall as if sprinkled / grow (a child)
serpinti drizzle
serpiştirmek sprinkle, drizzle
serpme sprinkling / castnet
serpmek sprinkle, scatter by hand
sersem stunned / foolish
sersemlemek be stunned / become silly, become giddy
serseri vagabond, tramp, vagrant
sert hard / severe
sertifika certificate
sertleşmek become hard, become severe (stiff)
serum serum
serüven adventure
servet wealth, riches
servi cypress
servis service
ses sound / voice
seslenmek call out
sesli having a voice, sound (film); **sesli harf** vowel
sessiz quiet, silent; **sessiz harf** consonant
sessizlik silence
set dam, dyke
sevap good deed
sevda love, passion

sevdalı in love
sevdazede stricken with love
sevgi love, affection
sevgili beloved, darling
sevici lesbian
sevimli lovable, affable
sevimsiz unattractive
sevinç joy, delight
sevindirmek give pleasure, please
sevinmek be pleased, rejoice
sevişmek love each other, make love
seviye level, rank, standard
sevk dispatch; **sevk ve idare** management, administration
sevk etmek send, drive, lead, dispatch
sevkitabii instinct
sevkiyat dispatch (of troops)
sevmek love, like
seyahat journey, travelling
seyir movement, progress / show, spectácle / on looking
seyirci spectator
seyis groom, stableman
seylap flood, torrent
seyrek wide, apart, infrequent, rare
seyrekleşmek become infrequent
seyreklik openness, interval, rarity
seyretmek look at, watch / go along, progress
seyrüsefer traffic
seyyah traveller
seyyal fluid
seyyar portable, travelling
seyyare planet
sezgi perception, intuition
sezgicilik intuitionism
sezi feeling
sezinlemek feel, perceive
sezmek perceive, feel
sezon season
sıcacık pleasantly hot
sıcak hot / heat
sıcakkanlı warm hearted, friendly
sıçan rat, mouse
sıçmak excrete, shit
sıçrama jumping
sıçramak jump, spring
sıçrayış jumping

sıfat quality / adjective (dilbilgisi)
sıfır zero, nought
sığ shallow
sığınak shelter, refuge
sığınmak shelter, take shelter
sığıntı one who takes refuge, sponger
sığır ox, cow, cattle
sığırcık starling
sığırtmaç herdsman, cowboy, cowman
sığışmak fit into a confined space with difficulty, squeeze
sığlık shallowness
sığmak go in, be contained by
sıhhat health, correctness
sıhhi hygienic
sıhhiye health department
sık dense, thick / close / frequent / frequently
sıkı tight, severe
sıkıcı boring
sıkı fıkı intimate
sıkılgan shy, timid
sıkılmak be pressed, be bored, be uneasy, be in straits
sıkıntı financial difficulty, annoyance, boredom
sıkışık closely pressed together
sıkışmak be closely pressed against one another, be in straits
sıkıştırmak press, squeeze, force
sıkıyönetim martial law
sıklaşmak be frequent / be close together
sıklaştırmak bring close together, render frequent
sıklet weight
sıklık frequency, closeness
sıkma squeezing
sıkmak squeeze, tighten, press / annoy
sık sık often, frequently
sıla going home
sımsıkı very tight
sınai industrial
sınamak try doing
sınav examination
sınıf class, category
sınıflamak classify
sınıfta kalmak fail in class, fail to pass

sınır frontier, boundary
sınırlamak limit, restrict
sınırlı limited, restricted
sıpa baby donkey
sır glaze, silvering
sır secret, mystery
sıra row, rank, order, turn
sıradağ mountain chain
sıralamak arrange in a row
sıralı in row, in due order
sırasız out of order / improper
sırça glass
sırdaş confidant, sharer of a secret
sırf pure, sheer
sırık pole; **sırıkla atlama** pole-jump
sırılsıklam very wet, drenched, soaking wet
sırt back
sırtlamak take on one's back
sırtlan hyena
sıska thin, weak, lean
sıtma malaria, fever
sıva plaster; **sıvalı** plastered
sıvamak plaster
sıvanmak be plastered with, be coated over
sıvazlamak caress, stroke
sıvı liquid
sıvık semi-fluid
sıvışmak steal away
sıvışık sticky, gooey
sıyanet protection; **sıyanet etmek** protect
sıyga mood, mode (dilbilgisi)
sıygaya çekmek ask endless questions, question somebody
sıyırmak tear off, strip off
sıyrık scratch, skinned
sıyrılmak be peeled, be scraped off, sneak away
sızdırmak cause to ooze out, squeeze (money) out of
sızı pain, ache
sızıltı complaint
sızıntı oozing, leakage
sızlamak suffer sharp pain, ache
sızlanmak moan with pain, lament, complain, whining

sızmak ooze, leake / pass out
sicil register, record
sicilli registered
sicim string, twine
sidik urine
sifon siphon
siftah first sale; **siftah etmek** make the first sale of the day, begin
sigara cigarette
sigorta insurance
sigortalı insured
sihir magic
sihirbaz magician
sihirlemek bewitch
sihirli magic
silah weapon, arms
silahla(n)mak arm
silahlı armed
silahsızlanma disarmament
silahlı kuvvetler armed forces
silecek windshield wiper
silgi duster, rubber
silik rubbed out, indistinct
silindir cylinder
silinmek be erased, be scraped, be rubbed
silinti wipings, erasure
silkelemek shake off
silkinmek shake oneself
silkinti shake, shake off
silkmek shake (out)
sille slap
silme brimful
silmek wipe, clean, erase
silo silo
silsile chain, series; **silsilei meratip** hierarch
siluet silhouette
sim silver
simetri symmetry; **simetrik** symmetrical
sima face
simge symbol
simit lifebuoy / round cake with sesame
simsar middleman, commission agent
simsiyah jet black, pitch black
sinarit (balığı) tunny fish
sincap squirrel
sindirim digestion
sindirmek digest, assimilate / terrify
sine bosom, breast
sinek fly / club (cards)
sinekkaydı very smooth

(shave)
sinema cinema
sini round metal tray (old)
sinir sinew, nerve
sinirlenmek become irritated (nervous)
sinirli nervous, irritable
sinmek subside, be absorbed, be cowed
sinsi stealthy, sneaking, insidious
sinyal signal
sipahi cavalry soldier
sipariş order, commission
siper shield, trench, shelter
siperlenmek take shelter
sirayet contagion, infection, **sirayet etmek** spread, infect
sirk circus
sirke vinegar
sirküler circular
sis fog, mist
sislenmek become foggy
sisli foggy, misty, hazy
sistem system
sistire carpenter's scraper
sitayiş eulogy, praise
sitem reproach
sitemkâr reproaching
sivil civilian / naked (argo)
sivilce pimple
sivri sharp- pointed
sivrilmek become prominent
sivriltmek make pointed
sivrisinek mosquito
siyah black
siyasal bilgiler political sciences
siyaset policy, politics
siyaseten politically
siyasi political, diplomatic
siyatik sciatica
siz you
...siz without
sizin your, yours
sizinki yours
skandal scandal
skeç sketch
ski skiing, ski
slogan slogan
smokin dinner-jacket
soba stove
sodyum sodium
sofa hall
sofra dining-table; **sofra bezi** table cloth
softa a man too religious,

bigot
sofu religious, pious
soğan onion
soğancık spinal cord
soğuk cold / cold weather / frigid / unfriendly
soğuk almak catch a chill (cold)
soğukça somewhat cold, rather cold
soğukkanlı cool-headed, cold-blooded
soğukluk coldness / chilliness of manner / dessert
soğumak become cold / cease to care for, cool, be alienated
soğutmak cool, alienate
sohbet friendly chat
sokak road, street, lane
sokak kapısı front door
sokmak thrust into, insert
sokulgan quick to make friends, affable
sokulmak insinuate oneself
sokuşturmak push secretly into a thing, cram, force into
sol left
sol (müzik) sol
solaçık outside left
solcu leftist, socialist
soliç inside left
solist soloist
solgun pale, faded, withered
sollamak pass a vehicle
solmak fade, wither
solmaz unfading
solucan earthworm
soluk breath, breathing, panting
soluk faded
soluksoluğa panting, in a hurry
solumak pant, breathe heavily
solungaç gills
solunum respiration
som solid
somun loaf / nut (of a bolt)
somurtkan sulky, frowning
somurtmak sulk, pout
somut concrete
somya spring mattress
son the end, result, last, final, latest
sonbahar autumn, fall

sondaj test bore, drilling
sonek suffix
sonra afterwards, later, after
sonraki coming after, following, latter
sonsuz endless, eternal, infinite
sonuç end, result
sonuncu last, final
sopa thick stick / beating, **sopa atmak** give a beating to
sorgu interrogation, cross-examination
sormak ask, inquire
soru question
sorumlu responsible
sorumsuz irresponsible
sorun problem, matter, question
soruşturmak ask for information, investigate
sosis sausage
sosyal social
sosyalist socialist
sosyalizm socialism
sosyete the upper class / society
sosyoloji sociology
Sovyetler Birliği the Soviet Union
soy family, ancestors, race
soyadı surname
soyaçekim heredity
soygun pillage, robbery
soyguncu plunderer, pillager, robber
soylu of good family
soymak strip, undress / rob
soysuz degenerate
soysuzlaşmak degenerate
soytarı clown, buffoon
soyunmak undress (oneself)
soyut abstract
söğüş boiled (meat etc)
söğüt willow
sökmek tear down, dismantle, undo
sökük unstitched
sökülmek be unstitched / give (argo)
sökün etmek burst in suddenly in a crowd, crop up
sömestir semester
sömürmek exploit, devour
söndürmek extinguish, put out
sönmek go out (fire), be extinguished

sönük extinguished
sövmek curse, swear
söylemek tell, say
söyleniş pronunciation
söylenmek grumble / to be said
söylenti rumour, gossip
söyleşi talk, chatter with friends
söyletmek cause to tell
söylev speech
söyleyiş manner of speaking
söz word, speech, promise, **söz atmak** make an improper remark to
sözbirliği agreement
sözcü spokesman
sözcük word
sözde as though, supposing that, so called, would be
söz etmek mention
sözgelişi course of a conversation, for example
söz kesimi agreement to marry
söz konusu subject mentioned, matter in hand
sözleşmek agree together
sözleşme contract, agreement
sözlü in word, oral / future fiancée
sözlük dictionary
sözügeçen aforesaid
sperma sperm
spiker announcer
spor sports; **sporcu** athlete, sportsman
sportmen sportsman
stadyum stadium
staj training
stajyer trainee
standard standard
statik static
statü rules
steno stenography
step steppe (geo)
stepne spare tyre
sterilize sterilized
stok stock, invention
stratejik strategic
striptiz strip-tease
stüdyo studio
su water / juice (fruit)
sual question, inquiry
suare evening party
suaygırı hippopotamus
subay officer
su bendi reservoir, dam
su birikintisi puddle,

pool
sucu water-seller
sucuk sausage
suç fault, crime, guilt
suçiçeği chicken pox
suçlamak accuse
suçlu guilty
suçsuz innocent
suçüstü red-handed
sudan insignificant
sudolabı water wheel
su dökmek make water / urinate
suflör prompter
sugeçirmez waterproof
sui... (suffix) evil...
suiistimal misuse; **suiistimal etmek** misuse
suikast criminal attempt
suiniyet evil intention
sukesimi waterline
sukut fall, lapse; **hayal sukutu** disappointment
sulak watery
sulamak irrigate, water
sulanmak become watery / hang on (argo), display sexual interest in
sulh peace
sulhen peaceably
sultan ruler
sulu watery / importunate
suluboya water colour
sumen blotter
sundurma open shed
suni artificial
sunmak offer, present
sunturlu severe, boisterous (swearing etc.)
sunucu compére
supap valve
sur city wall, ramparts
surat face; **surat asmak** frown, make a long face
suratsız sulky, frowning, ugly
sure chapter of the Koran
suret form, shape, copy
sureta in appearance
Suriye Syria
Suriyeli Syrian
sus shut up, hush
susam sesame
susamak be thirsty, be longing for
suskun silent
susmak be silent
sus payı hush money
susta durmak stand on (its) hind legs
sustalı switchblade

susturmak silence
susturucu silencer
susuz waterless, arid, thirsty
sutyen brassiere, bra
sübjektif subjective, influenced by personal feelings
sübyan boys (old)
süet suede leather
süfli low, common, shabby
süklüm püklüm in a crestfallen manner, sheepish
sükse success, hit
sükun quiet, calm
sükunet quiet, calm
sükut silence; **sükut etmek** be silent
sülale family, dynasty
sülüğen red lead
sülük leech
sülün pheasant
sümbül hyacinth
sümkürmek expel mucus from the nose, blow one's nose
sümsük uncouth, stupid
sümük mucus, snot
sümüklü snotty
sümüklüböcek snail
sünepe slovenly
sünger sponge
süngertaşı pumice-stone
süngü bayonet
sünnet circumcision; **sünnet etmek** circumcise
sünnetli circumcised
süprüntü rubbish
süpürge broom, sweeper
süpürmek sweep
sürahi decanter, pitcher
sürat speed; **süratle** quickly
süratli quick, fast, swift
sürçmek stumble
sürçü lisan slip of the tongue
süre period, duration
süreç process
sürekli prolonged, steady
süreksiz transitory
sürfe caterpillar, larva
sürgit unending
sürgü bolt (of a door)
sürgün exiled / shoot
sürme bolt, drawer / eyesalve
sürmek drive away, drive (a car etc.) / exile / push along / rub on / sell /spend (life etc.) /

go on, continue
sürmelemek bolt (a door)
sürmeli bolted / tinged with eyesalve
sürpriz surprise
sürtmek rub one thing against another / wander about aimlessly, loiter
sürtük (woman) gadabout
sürtünmek rub oneself against, creep / seek a quarrel
sürü herd, flock, crowd
sürücü driver
sürüklemek drag along
sürüklenmek drag oneself, be dragged along, trail
sürükleyici fascinating, exciting
sürüm demand, sale
sürümlü in great demand
sürünceme delay
süründürmek bring into utter misery, make crawl
sürüngen reptile
sürünmek grovel, crawl / live in misery
süs ornament, toilette
süslemek adorn
süslenmek adorn oneself, dress up
süslü ornamented, decorated
süt milk
sütanne foster mother, wet-nurse
sütbeyaz milk-tooth
sütbeyaz milk-white
sütçü milkman, dairyman
sütdişi milk-tooth
süthane dairy
sütkardeş foster-brother, foster-sister
süt kuzusu sucking lamb, baby
sütlaç rice-pudding
sütliman dead calm
sütlü milky
sütnine foster mother, wet-nurse
sütsüz without milk / ignoble
sütun column, pillar, column (in a newspaper etc.)
sütübozuk base, mean, without character
sütyen brassiere
süvari cavalryman, rider / captain (navy)

captain (in the navy)
süveter sweater
süzgeç filter
süzgün languid
süzme filtered, oozed, strained
süzmek strain, filter / look attentively
süzülmek be strained, be filtered / slip away / waste away

Ş

şadırvan fountain for ablutions
şafak twilight, dawn
şaft shaft
şah Shah
şahadet witnessing, testimony; **şahadet parmağı** index finger; **şahadet getirmek** pronounce the Moslem creed
şahadetname diploma, certificate
şahane magnificent
şahdamarı artery, aorta
şaheser masterpiece
şahıs person; **şahsa mahsus** personal
şahlanmak rear up (horse) / fly into a passion
şahıslandırmak personify
şahika summit
şahin falcon
şahit witness
şahitlik testimony
şahmerdan battering ram
şahsen personally, in person, for one
şahsi personal, private
şahsiyet personality
şair poet
şairane poetical
şaka fun, joke
şakadan teasingly, in joke
şakak temple (face)
şakalaşmak joke with one another, tease
şakımak sing (of a bird)
şakırdamak rattle, jingle
şakırtı clatter, rattle
şaki criminal, brigand, bandit
şaklaban clown, jester

şaklamak make a loud cracking noise
şaklatmak crack (a whip)
şakrak joyful, merry
şakramak twitter
şakşak applause / flattery
şakşakçı toady, flatterer
şakul plummet
şakuli perpendicular
şal shawl
şalgam turnip
şalter switch board
şalvar baggy trousers
şamandıra buoy
şamar slap
şamata noise, uproar
şamdan candlestick
şamfıstığı pistachio
şamil including, comprising
şampanya champagne
şampiyon champion
şampuan shampoo
şan fame
şangırdamak jingle
şanlı glorious, famous
şans luck
şanslı lucky
şantaj blackmail
şantiye building site
şantör male singer
şantöz female singer
şanjman gear, shift
şap alum
şapırda(t)mak make a smacking noise with the lips, splash
şapka hat; **şapkacı** hatter
şaplak smacking on the face
şaplatmak make a smacking noise (with lips or hands), slap
şapşal slovenly
şarampol stockade
şarap wine
şarapnel shrapnel
şarj charge
şarıldamak flow with a splashing noise
şarıltı splashing noise
şarjör automatic gun drum
şark the east
şarkiyat orientalism
şarkı song; **şarkı söylemek** sing
şarkıcı singer
şarküteri delicatessen
şarlatan charlatan
şarpi sharpie

şart condition / necessary
şarti conditional
şartname list of conditions
şasi chassis
şaşaa splendour
şaşaalı sparkling, resplendid
şaşalamak be bewildered
şaşı cross-eyed
şaşılacak surprising
şaşılık squint
şaşırmak be surprised, be confused, become bewildered
şaşırtma misleading, confusing, puzzling
şaşırtmak confuse, mislead, embarrass
şaşkın bewildered, stupid
şaşkınlık bewilderment
şaşmak go astray / be surprised
şat flat bottomed boat, lighter
şatafat luxury
şatafatlı pompous, luxurious
şato castle
şayak serge
şayan worthy
şayet if
şayi divulged
şayia rumour
şebboy wallflower
şebek long-tailed monkey, baboon
şebeke net, network / band (of robbers) / university student's transportation pass
şebnem dew
şecere genealogical tree
şef chief, leader
şefaat intercession
şeffaf transparent
şef garson head waiter
şefkat compassion
şefkatli compassionate
şefkatsiz unkind, cruel
şeftali peach
şehadet death in battle
şehir city; **hemşehri** fellow citizen
şehirdışı suburb
şehirlerarası long-distance (call)
şehit martyr; **şehitlik** martyrdom
şehla slight squinting
şehriye vermicelli
şehvani sensual, lustful
şehvet sensuality, lust

şehvetli voluptuous
şehzade prince
şeker sugar, a sweet; **şeker hastalığı** diabetes; **şeker kamışı** sugar cane
şekerleme candied fruit / dose (sleep)
şekil form, shape, figure / manner, way
şekillendirmek form, give a shape
şeklen in form
şelale waterfall, cataract
şema sketch, plan
şempanze chimpanzee
şemsiye umbrella
şen cheerful, merry
şenlendirmek enliven, cheer up
şenlenmek become cheerful
şenlik cheerfulness, public rejoicing, festival
şer harm, wickedness
şerait conditions
şer'an in accordance with Moslem law
şerbet sherbet
şerbetli immune, bewitched against (snakebites etc.)
şeref honour
şerefiye tax on increase in land value
şereflendirmek acquire honour, be honoured
şerefli honoured, esteemed
şerh explanation, commentary
şeriat the religious law
şerik partner, accomplice
şerir bad, wicked
şerit ribbon, tape
şevk eagerness, zeal
şevkli eager, zealous
şey thing; **bir şey** something; **bir şey değil** it is nothing, not at all
şeyh head of a religious order, sheikh
şeytan satan, devil
şeytani diabolical
şeytanlık devilry
şezlong chaise longue, deck chair
şık one of the many alternatives, choice
şık smart; **şıklık** smartness
şıkırdamak rattle, jingle, clink
şıllık loose woman,

whore
şımarık spoilt
şımarmak be spoilt, get above oneself
şımartmak spoil
şıngırdamak clink
şıngirtı the noise of breaking glass, clicking
şıp noise of a drop falling / easily, at once
şıppadak at once
şıpsevdi quick to fall in love
şıra grape juice
şırıltı splashing sound of water, ripple
şırınga syringe
şiddet violence, intensity, severity, hardness
şiddetli violent, severe, intense
şifa healing; **şifa bulmak** recover health
şifahen orally
şifahi oral
şifoniyer dresser
şifre code, cipher; **şifreli** in cipher
şiir poetry, poem
şikâyet complaint; **şikâyet etmek** complain
şike rigged game for money
şilep cargo boat, cargo liner
Şili Chile
şilte mattress
şimal the north
şimali northern
şimdi now, the present, meanwhile
şimdiki of today, of the present time
şimşek lightning
şimşir box wood (tree)
şirin sweet, charming; **şirinlik** sweetness
şirket company
şirret troublesome, shrew, evil-disposed
şiryan artery
şiş spit, skewer / knit-tingneedle / meat on a skewer
şiş swelling / swollen
şişe bottle, flask
şişirmek cause to swell / exaggerate / do hastily and carelessly
şiş kebabı roasted meat on a spit
şişkin swollen, puffed up

şişkinlik swelling
şişlemek stab (argo)
şişman fat, stout, plump
şişmanlatmak fatten, cause to get fat
şişmek swell, grow fat
şive style, accent
şizofreni schizophrenia
şofben hot-water boiler
şoför driver
şok shock
şom evil
şom ağızlı who always predicts misfortune
şort shorts
şose causeway
şoson galoshes, high boots
şöhret fame, reputation
şöhret bulmak become famous
şöhretli famous, well-known, celebrated
şölen feast
şömine fireplace, furnace
şövale easel (painter's)
şövalye knight
şöyle so, thus, such
şöyle böyle so-so
şöylece in this manner, thus
şu that
şua ray of light, beam
şubat February
şube branch, section
şuh lively, coquettish
şu kadar (that) this much
şule flame, gleam
şura that place; **şurada** there
şûra council; **şûrayıdevlet** council of state
şuracıkta right here
şurası that place
şurup syrup, fruit-juice
şut shoot, shot
şuur comprehension, mind, conscience
şuurlu conscious, intelligent
şuursuz unconscious / mindless
şükran gratitude
şükretmek be thankful
şükür thanks to God
şümul including, comprising; **şümulü olmak** cover
şümullü comprehensive, extensive
şüphe doubt, suspicion, **şüphe etmek** doubt,

suspect
şüphecilik scepticism
şüphelenmek have a suspicion, suspect
şüpheli doubtful
şüphesiz doubtless, sure, certainly
şüphesiz of course
şürekâ partners
şüyu publicly talked, publicity

T

ta even until, even as far as
taaccüp wonder, astonishment; **taaccüp etmek** be astonished
taahhüt undertaking (to do a thing); **taahhüt etmek** undertake, guarantee
taahhütlü registered (letter)
taahhütname contract
taalluk connection, attachment
taallukat relations
taam food, meal
taammüden intentionally
taammüt premeditation
taarruz attack, assault; **taarruz etmek** attack, assail
taassup fanaticism
taba tobacco green
tababet science of medicine
tabak plate, dish
tabaka layer, sheet, class, fold
tabaka tobacco box
tabakhane tanyard, tannery
tabaklamak leather dressing
taban sole (of the foot or shoe)
tabana kuvvet fleeing fast
tabanca pistol, revolver
tabansız cowardly
tabela table (list), sign, sign-board
tabetmek print
tabi dependent, subject; **tabi olmak** be dependent on, be subject to
tabi printer, publisher

tabiat nature / habit
tabiatüstü supernatural
tabii natural, naturally, of course
tabiyet nationality
tabib doctor, physician
tabir expression; **tabir olmak** express in words / interpret (a dream)
tabiye tactics
tabla tray, ash-tray, flat disk
tabldot table d'hote, fixed price menu
tablet tablet
tablo picture, tableau
tabu taboo
tabur battalion
taburcu recovered, discharged from hospital
tabure stool, footstool
tabut coffin
tabya fort, bastion
tacir merchant, trader
taciz bothering; **taciz etmek** annoy
taç crown
taçyapraklı gamopetalus
tadım taste
tadımlık for tasting
tadil adjustment, modification, alteration; **tadil etmek** adjust, alter
tadilat modifications
taflan cherry laurel
tafra pride, conceit, showing off
tafsilat details, particulars; **tafsilat vermek** explain in detail
tafsilatlı detailed
tafta taffeta
tahakkuk realization, proving to be true
tahakkuk etmek prove true, come true
tahakküm oppression, dictatorship; **tahakküm etmek** oppress, dominate
tahammül endurance, patience; **tahammül etmek** endure, put up with
tahammülsüz impatient, intolerant
tahammür fermentation **tahammür etmek** ferment
taharri investigation
tahavvül change, transformation; **tahavvül etmek** change

tahayyül imagination; **tahayyül etmek** imagine
tahdidat limitations
tahdit limitation; **tahdit etmek** limit, define, restrict
tahfif assuagement; **tahfif etmek** lighten, mitigate, relieve
tahıl cereals, grain
tahin sesame oil
tahkik verification; **tahkik etmek** verify, ascertain, investigate
tahkikat investigations, inquiry
tahkim fortifying; **tahkim etmek** fortify
tahkir insult; **tahkir etmek** insult, scorn
tahlil analysis; **tahlil etmek** analyse
tahlisiye salvage
tahliye emptying, unloading discharge; **tahliye etmek** empty, discharge
tahmil loading; **tahmil etmek** load
tahmin estimate, guess; **tahmin etmek** estimate
tahminen approximately, at a guess
tahmini approximate
tahribat destructions
tahrif falsification, corruption; **tahrif etmek** falsify, distort
tahrik moving, incitement; **tahrik etmek** move, excite, incite, provoke, stimulate
tahrip destruction; **tahrip etmek** destroy
tahripkâr destructive
tahrir writing, essay
tahrirat documents, official letters
tahriri written
tahriş irritation; **tahriş etmek** irritate
tahsil collection (of taxes) / education, study; **ilk tahsil** elementary education
tahsilat collection of revenues
tahsildar tax-collector
tahsis assignment; **tahsis etmek** assign (to a purpose or person), allocate
tahsisat money devoted to a special purpose, allowance, allocation

taht throne; **tahta geçmek** succeed to the throne
tahta wood, wooden
tahtakurusu bed-bug
tahtaperde wooden partition
tahterevalli see-saw
tahvil transforming, converting; **tahvil etmek** convert, **tahvilat** bond
tak arch
taka small wooden freight boat, barge
takaddüm precedence; **takaddüm etmek** precede
takas exchange of goods
takat power
takatsız powerless
takaza taunting
takbih blame; **takbih etmek** blame, disapprove, reproach
takdim presentation, offer **takdim etmek** present, introduce / offer
takdir fate, appreciation; **takdir etmek** appreciate, praise
takdirname letter of commendation
takdiri supposed
takdirkâr praising
takdis şanctification; **takdis etmek** sanctify
takı case ending
takılmak be affixed / catch, be tangled up / tease, deride
takım a set of things, suit (of clothes), team
takım yıldız constellation
takınmak attach to oneself, wear / affect
takıntı connection, affair
takırdamak make a tapping noise
takıştırmak wear as an ornament, dress up
takızafer triumphal arch
takibat legal proceedings, prosecution
takip pursuit; **takip etmek** follow, pursue
takke skullcap
takla somersault; **takla atmak** turn a somersault
taklit imitation, caunterfeit; **taklitçi** imitator,

mimic
takma act of attaching, attached / false (teeth etc.)
takmak affix, attach, put on
takoz wooden wedge, cleat
takriben approximately, about
takribi approximate
takrir statement, report / notification of transference of real property
taksa postage due
taksi taxi cab
taksim dividing, division, partition; **taksim etmek** divide up, share out
taksimat divisions
taksimetre taximeter
taksirat fault, sin, misdeed, destiny
taksit instalment
taksitle by instalments
taktik tactics
takunya clog
takvim calendar
takviye reinforcement; **takviye etmek** reinforce
talan pillage, sack
talaş sawdust, wood shavings
talebe student, pupil
talep request, demand; **talep etmek** request, ask for
talepname written request, petition
tali following, secondary, subordinate
talih luck
talihli lucky
talihsiz unlucky
talik suspension; **talik etmek** suspend, put off
talim practice, drill; **talim etmek** practise, drill
talimat instructions, directions
talimatname book of instructions, regulations
talip applicant, who requests; **talip olmak** demand
talk talc
taltif gratifying, favour; **taltif etmek** gratify, recompense
tam complete, perfect, completely, exactly
tamaen out of greed
tamah greed, stinginess

tamahkâr greedy, stingy, avid
tamam complete, ready, right, that's right
tamamen completely
tamamlamak complete, terminate
tambur oriental guitar, lute
tamir repair, restoration; **tamir etmek** repair
tamirat repairs
tamlama compound word
tampon wad, bumber
tamsayı absolute number
tan the dawn
tandır oven in the earth
tane grain, piece, a single thing, pip
tanelemek separate into grains, granulate
taneli having grains
tango tango
tanıdık acquaintance
tanık witness
tanımak recognize / acknowledge
tanımlamak define
tanınmak become known
tanınmış well known
tanış an acquaintance
tanışmak make acquaintance with one another, meet
tanıştırmak introduce, present
tanıt proof
tanıtıcı introductory, explanotary
tanıtmak introduce (persons), make known
tanjant tangent
tank tank
tanker tanker
Tanrı God
tanrılık divinity
tansiyon blood pressure, tension
tantana pomp, display; **tantanalı** magnificent, pompous
tanyeli morning breeze
tanyeri dawn
tanzifat street-sweeping
tanzim putting into order; **tanzim etmek** put into order, organize, arrange
tanzimat reforms
tapa fuse
tapınak temple
tapmak worship
tapon discarded, outcast
taptaze very fresh

tapu title deeds, real property registration
taraça terrace
taraf side, direction, party
tarafeyn the two sides
tarafgir partisan, partial; **tarafgirlik** partisanship
tarafsız neutral, impartial
taraftar partisan, in favour of, supporter
tarak comb, rake
taraklı broad-footed
tarama salt mass (fish)
taramak comb, rake
taranmak comb one's hair, be raked
tarassut watching, watch, observation; **tarassut etmek** watch, observe, lie in wait
tarçın cinnamon
tard expulsion
tardetmek expel, degrade
tarh imposition (of taxes), subtraction
tarh flower-bed
tarhana dried curds flour soup
tarhetmek subtract
tarım agriculture
tarımsal agricultural
tarif description; **tarif etmek** describe
tarife tariff, rate / recipe
tarih history / date; **tarih atmak** put the date
tarihçi historian
tarihi historical
tarihli dated
tarihsiz undated
tarikat religious order
tarla field
tarlakuşu lark
tartaklamak ill-treat, shake, assault
tartı weight
tartılmak be weighed
tartışmak discuss, debate, argue
tartmak weigh / estimate
tarumar scattered; **tarumar etmek** make a mess of
tarz manner, style, method
tarziye apology; **tarziye vermek** make an apology, apologise
tas bowl
tasa grief, anxiety
tasalanmak worry, become anxious
tasalı anxious, grieved

tasallut aggression; **tasallut etmek** behave aggressively towards
tasarı draft law, bill / scheme, plan
tasarlamak plan, draft, design
tasarruf possession / saving
tasasız free from care, care free
tasavvuf mysticism
tasavvur imagination, idea; **tasavvur etmek** imagine
tasdik confirmation, approval; **tasdik etmek** confirm, certify, approve
tasdikli certified
tasdikname letter of ratification, certificate
tasfiye clarifying, refining, elimination; **tasfiye etmek** clean, eliminate, refine
tasfiyehane refinery
tashih correction; **tashih etmek** correct
taslak draft, sketch
taslamak pretend
tasma collar (of a dog)
tasnif classification; **tasnif etmek** classify
tasrif inflection, conjugation; **tasrif etmek** decline, conjugate (dilbilgisi)
tastamam complete
tasvip approval; **tasvip etmek** approve
tasvir description / portrait; **tasvir etmek** describe
taş stone, rock
taşçı stonemason
taşım coming to the boil
taşımacılık transportation
taşımak carry, transport
taşınmak move to another place, move house
taşınmaz real, immovable
taşırmak cause to overflow, boil over
taşıt vehicle
taşıyıcı porter
taşkın overflowing
taşkınlık insolence
taşkömürü coal
taşlama satiric poem
taşlamak stone
taşlı stony, rocky
taşlık stony place, stone

courtyard / paved
taşmak overflow, boil over
taşocağı stone quarry
taşra the provinces, the country
taşralı provincial
taşyürekli stony-hearted
tat taste, flavour / pleasure, delight
Tatar Tartar
tatarcık sandfly
tatbik application; **tatbik etmek** apply
tatbikat applications, exercises; **tatbikatta** in practice
tatbiki practical, applied
tatil holiday, suspension of work; **tatil etmek** suspend, take a holiday
tatlandırmak sweeten
tatlanmak sweeten
tatlı sweet
tatlılık sweetness, kinαness
tatmak taste, experience
tatmin reassurance, satisfaction; **tatmin etmek** satisfy, compensate
tatminkâr satisfying
tatsız tasteless, insipid
tatsızlık unpleasantness
tav anneal / well-nourished, (prime) condition / trick; **tavına getirmek** bring to the best condition
tava frying pan
tavan ceiling
tavassut intervention; **tavassut etmek** intervene, mediate
tavır manner, attitude
taviz compensation, concession; **taviz vermek** make a concession
tavla backgammon
tavla stable
tavlamak temper / deceive
tavsamak cool down, decline
tavsiye recommendation; **tavsiye etmek** recommend; **tavsiye mektubu** letter of recommendation
tavşan hare; **ada tavşanı** rabbit
tavuk hen
tavus peacock
tay colt
tayfa crew / band
tayfun typhoon

tayın ration
tayin appointment; **tayin etmek** appoint, fix, decide
Tayland Thailand
tayyare aeroplane
tayyör woman's tailor-made costume
taze fresh, recent, young
tazelemek renew, refresh
tazelenmek become fresh, be renewed
tazı greyhound
taziye condolence
taziz honouring the memory of (a person); **taziz etmek** honour the memory of
tazmin indemnification; **tazmin etmek** indemnify
tazminat indemnities
tazyik pressure, opression, compression
tazyik etmek press, oppress
T.C. Turkish Republic
teamül custom, tradition
teati exchange; **teati etmek** exchange
tebaa subjects
tebahhur etmek evaporate
tebarüz etmek become manifest; **tebarüz ettirmek** show clearly, point out
tebdil change; **tebdil etmek** change
tebeddül alteration; **tebeddül etmek** alter
tebelleş pestering
teberru charitable gift, contribution, donation
tebessüm smile; **tebessüm etmek** smile
tebeşir chalk
tebliğ delivering, transmitting, giving notice; **tebliğ etmek** deliver a message, notify
tebligat communications, reports, notifications
tebrik congratulation; **tebrik etmek** congratulate
tecavüz transgressing, attacking; **tecavüz etmek** transgress, attack, assault, rape
tecavüzi aggressive, offensive
tecelli destiny; **tecelli etmek** appear
tecessüm personification;

tecessüm etmek be personified; **tecessüm ettirmek** personify
tecessüs curiosity
tecil postponement
tecil etmek postpone, defer
tecim commerce
tecrit separating, isolating; **tecrit etmek** isolate
tecrübe trial, experience; **tecrübe etmek** try, experience
tecrübeli experienced
tecrübesiz inexperienced
tecrübi experimental
tecziye etmek punish
teçhiz etmek equip
teçhizat equipment
tedai association, procuring
tedarik etmek provide, obtain, prepare
tedarikli prepared
tedavi cure, medical treatment
tedavül circulation, currency; **tedavül etmek** circulate
tedbir precaution, measure
tedbirli provident, cautious
tedbirsiz improvident, imprudent
tedhiş terror, terrifying
tedhişçi terrorist
tedirgin etmek give no peace, cause to go to another place, annoy
tediye payment; **tediye etmek** pay
tedricen gradually
tedrici gradual
tedris teaching; **tedris etmek** teach
tedrisat course of lessons; education
teessüf regret; **teessüf etmek** regret
teessür grief, emotion
teessüs being founded
tef tambourine
tefeci usurer
tefekkür reflection; **tefek-kür etmek** meditate
teferruat details / accessories
tefessüh decomposition; **tefessüh etmek** decompose, decay
tefrik distinction; **tefrik etmek** distinguish

tefrika discord / a serial story in a newspaper
tefriş furnishing (a room); **tefriş etmek** furnish
teftiş inspection; **teftiş etmek** inspect
teğet tangent
teğmen lieutenant
tehdit threat; **tehdit etmek** threaten
tehevvür sudden burst of anger, fury; **tehevvür etmek** burst into anger
tehir delay; **tehir etmek** defer, delay, postpone, put off
tehirli delayed, late
tehlike danger
tehlikeli dangerous
tehlikesiz without danger, safe
tek single, sole / unique, unrivaled / odd (number)
tekabül meeting, correspondence
tekâmül progress, development; **tekâmül etmek** develop, advance, make progress
tekaüt retired, pensioned
tekbaşına all by oneself
tekbir say "God is most great"
tekdir scolding, reprimand; **tekdir etmek** scold, reprove
teke he-goat
tekel monopoly
teker teker one by one
tekerlek wheel, tyre / circular
tekerleme rigmarole
tekerlemek roll
tekerrür repetition; **tekerrür etmek** be repeated
tekil singular (gram.)
tekin olmayan haunted
tekir spotted, tabby
tekit confirmation, repetition (of a message, etc.) **tekit etmek** confirm, repeat (a message)
tekke dervish monastery
teklif proposal, offer; **teklif etmek** propose, offer; suggest
teklifsiz without ceremony, familiar
tekme kick
tekmelemek kick
tekmil all; **tekmil etmek** complete, finish, make up

tekne trough, hull, vessel
teknik technique
teknik okul technical school
teknisyen technician, mechanic
teknoloji technology
tekrar repetition, again; **tekrar etmek** repeat
tekrarlamak repeat
teksir multiplication;
teksir multiplication; **teksir etmek** multiply, duplicate
tek tük here and there, one or two
tekzip contradiction, denial; **tekzip etmek** contradict, deny
tel wire, cable
tela horsehair stiffening
telaffuz pronunciation; **teleffuz etmek** pronounce
telafi etmek compensate, make up for
telakki regarding, considering, view; **telakki etmek** regard, consider
telaş confusion, flurry; **telaş etmek** be confused, be alarmed
telaşlı confused, upset, excited
telaşsız calm, composed
teldolap food safe
telef ruin, destruction; **telef etmek** ruin, destroy, kill; **telef olmak** be destroyed, be ruined, perish
telefat casualties
teleferik cable lift
telefon telephone
telefon rehberi telephone directory
teleks teleprinter, telex
teleskop telescope
televizyon television
telgraf telegram, telegraph
telif reconciling, compilation; **telif etmek** reconcile, write; **telif hakkı** copyright
telkin suggestion, inspiration; **telkin etmek** suggest, inspire
tellak bath attendant
tellal town-crier, middleman
telli wired
tel örgü barbed wire, wirework

telsiz without wire, wireless
telve coffee grounds
temas contact; **temas etmek** touch, make contact with
temaşa looking on, watch, scene; **temaşa etmek** look on
temayül inclination, tendency; **temayül etmek** have a tendency to
temayüz etmek be distinguished
tembel lazy, idle
tembih warning
tembih etmek warn, excite
temdit prolongation; **temdit etmek** prolong, extend
temel foundation, base; **temel atmak** lay the foundation
temelleşmek become firmly established, settle down permanently
temelli permanent, for good
temelsiz without foundation
temeltaşı foundation stone
temenna oriental salute
temenni wish; **temenni etmek** wish
temerküz concentration; **temerküz etmek** be concentrated; **temerküz kampı** concentration camp
temettü profit, gain
temin assurance; **temin etmek** assure / obtain
teminat security, deposit, guarantee
temiz clean; **temize çekmek** make a (clean) fair copy
temizlemek clean
temizleyici cleaner, cleanser
temizlik cleanness
temkin self possession, dignity
temkinli calm, composed
temmuz July
tempo time, pace
temrin exercise (dilbilgisi)
temsil comparing / performance / representation; **temsil etmek**

represent / perform
temsilci representative, agent
temsilen representing
temyiz etmek appeal; **temyiz mahkemesi** court of appeal
ten flesh, skin
tenasül generation, reproduction
tenasüp proportion
tenbih waking, warning; **tenbih etmek** warn, excite
tencere saucepan
teneffüs breathing / pause for rest; **teneffüs etmek** breathe
teneffüshane place for resting (school recreation)
teneke tin, a tin
teneşir the bench on which the corpse is washed
tenezzüh excursion, promenade
tenezzül coming down, condescension; **...e tenezzül etmek** deign to, stoop
tenha solitary, lonely
tenhalaşmak become deserted
tenis tennis
tenkit criticism; **tenkit etmek** criticize
tensip approval; **tensip etmek** approve
tente awning, canvas
tentene lace
tentürdiyot tincture of iodine
tenvir illumination; **tenvir etmek** illuminate, make clear, enlighten
tenvirat lighting
tenzil reduction, subtraction; **tenzil etmek** reduce, subtract
tenzilat reduction
tenzilat yapmak make a reduction in price
tenzilatlı reduced in price
teorem theorem
teori theory
tepe hill, top
tepecik little hill
tepeleme full to the brim
tepelemek thrash unmercifully, overcome
tepetaklak head foremost, head over heels

tepeüstü upside-down, head first, headlong
tepinmek stamp
tepişmek kick one another
tepki reaction
tepkili jet
tepmek kick, recoil
tepsi tray
ter sweat, perspiration
terakki progress; **terakki etmek** make progress, advance
terane melody / same old story
teras terrace
terazi pair of scales
terbiye training, good manners; **terbiye etmek** train, teach manners, educate
terbiyeci pedagogue, trainer
terbiyeli good-mannered, polite
terbiyesiz ill-mannered, impolite
tercih preference, **tercih etmek** prefer
tercihan preferably
tercüman interpreter, translator
tercüme translation
tercümeihal biography
tereddüt hesitation; **tereddüt etmek** hesitate
tereke heritage
terennüm etmek sing
tereotu dill
tereyağı butter
terfi promotion; **terfi etmek** be promoted
tergal tergal
terhis discharge; **terhis etmek** discharge from the army; **terhis olmak** be discharged
terilen terylene
terim term
terk abandonment
terketmek abandon, leave, desert
terkip composition, structure, phrase
terlemek sweat, perspire
terlik slipper
termik thermic
terminal terminal
termometre thermometer
termos thermos
ters reverse, opposite, contrary; **ters gelmek** to be in the wrong way
tersane dockyard

tersine in the reverse way, on the contrary
terslemek answer harshly, scold
terslik contrariness, sulkiness
ters yön opposite direction
tersyüz etmek turn inside out
tertemiz very clean
tertibat arrangements, installations
tertip arrangement, order, composition; **tertip etmek** arrange, prepare, organize
tertipli well-organized, tidy
tertipsiz badly planned, untidy
terzi tailor, dressmaker
tesadüf meeting by chance, coincidence; **tesadüf etmek** meet by chance, encounter
tesadüfen by chance
tesadüf chance
tesanüt mutual support
tesbit fixing, establishing, **tesbit etmek** establish, fix
tescil registration; **tescil etmek** register
teselli consolation; **teselli etmek** console
tesellüm taking receipt
teselsül continuous succession
teshin heating; **teshin etmek** heat
teshir fascination; **teshir etmek** fascinate, charm
tesir effect; **tesir etmek** affect, influence
tesirli impressive, moving
tesis foundation; **tesis etmek** found, establish
tesisat establishment, installations
tesit celebration; **tesit etmek** celebrate
teskere litter, stretcher
teskin etmek pacify, calm
teslim handing over, delivery, surrender
teslim etmek deliver
teslimiyet submission
tespih string of beads
test test
testere saw
testi pitcher
tesviye making level,

smoothing; **tesviye etmek** level, smooth
tesviyeci planer
teşbih simile, allegory
teşçi etmek encourage
teşebbüs enterprise
teşebbüs etmek try, attempt
teşekkül etmek be formed
teşekkür giving thanks; **teşekkür etmek** thank
teşerrüf etmek feel honoured, have the honour of
teşhir making public, exhibiting; **teşhir etmek** make public, expose to the public, exhibit, display
teşhis diagnosis, recognition of a person; **teşhis etmek** identify, diagnose
teşkil formation; **teşkil etmek** form, constitute
teşkilat organization
teşkilatçı organizer
teşri legislation
teşrif visit; **teşrif etmek** come, honour (by one's presence)
teşrifat ceremonies, protocol
teşrifatçı master of ceremonies
teşrii legislative; **teşrii masuniyet** parliamentary inviolability
teşriki mesai cooperation
teşvik encouragement; **teşvik etmek** encourage; **teşvik edici** encouraging
teşyi seeing off; **teşyi etmek** see off
tetanos tetanus
tetik trigger / quick
tetkik close examination; **tetkik etmek** examine closely
tetkikat investigation
tevakkuf stopping
tevarüs inheriting; **tevarüs etmek** inherit
tevatür hearsay
tevazu modesty
tevcih turning towards; **tevcih etmek** turn towards, direct towards, confer, address
tevdi etmek entrust
tevdiat deposits (in a

bank)
teveccüh favour; **teveccüh etmek** turn one's attention to, favour
tevekkeli without reason, no wonder
tevekkül putting one's trust in God; **tevekkül etmek** resign oneself
tevellüt birth; **tevellüt etmek** be born, spring from
tevellütlü born in
tevessül etmek attempt, resort, take steps / stoop
tevil forced interpretation, evasion; **tevil etmek** put a forced construction on, try to evade
tevkif arrest; **tevkif etmek** arrest, stop
tevkifhane house of detention
Tevrat The old Testament
tevsi enlargement; **tevsi etmek** enlarge
tevsik etmek prove, confirm
tevzi distribution; **tevzi etmek** distribute
teyel tacking, basting
teyellemek tack, baste
teyit confirmation; **teyit etmek** confirm
teyp tape recorder
teyze aunt
tez quickly
tez thesis
tezahürat demonstration / cheering, applause
tezat contrast
tezcanlı hustling, hasting
tezek dried dung (used as fuel
tezelden without delay
tezgâh work-bench, counter, stall
tezgâhtar shop assistant salesman
tezkere note / soldier's discharge papers / licence
tezlik speed, haste
tezyinat adornments, decoration
tezyini decorative
tıbben medically
tıbbi medical
tıbbiye medical faculty (school)
tıbbiyeli medical

student
tığ crochet-needle
tık tık ticking noise
tıka basa brimful; **tıka basa doldurmak** fill to the brim
tıkaç plug, gag
tıkalı plugged, blocked
tıkamak plug, gag, choke, stop up, block
tıkanık choked, blocked
tıkanıklık choking, suffocation; **tıkanmak** be suffocated, be blocked
tıkınmak eat in haste
tıkırdamak make a clicking or rattling noise
tıkırtı clicking or rattling sound
tıkışmak cram together
tıkıştırmak cram into a small place / eat hastily
tıkız fleshy, hard
tıklım tıklım brimful, crowded
tıkmak thrust into, cram into
tıknaz plumpish
tılsım talisman, spell
tımar grooming; **tımar etmek** groom
tımarhane lunatic asylum
tıngırtı clicking noise
tınlamak tinkle
tınmamak pretend not to hear, take no notice
tıp medical science, medicine
tıpa plug, cork
tıpatıp exactly
tıpırtı sound of drops or light footsteps
tıpış tıpış (gitmek) patter, toddle
tıpkı exactly the same
tırabzan banister
tıraş (sakal) shaving; **tıraş etmek** shave; **tıraş olmak** shave; **saç tıraşı** haircut
tıraşçı boring talker
tıraşlı clean-shaven
tırıs canter; **tırıs gitmek** canter
tırmalamak scratch
tırmanmak climb
tırmık rake
tırmalamak scratch
tırnak finger-nail
tırnaklamak scratch with the nails
tırpan scythe

tırtıkçı pickpocket
tırtıklamak rob (argo)
tırtıklı uneven, jagged
tırtıl caterpillar, milling
tırtıllı having a milled edge
tıslamak hiss like a goose
tıynet character
tıynetsiz of low character
ticaret trade, commerce
ticarethane firm
ticari commercial
tifo typhoid fever
tiftik mohair
tifüs typhus
tik mannerism, tic
tiksinmek loathe, detest
tiksinti disgust, loathing
tilki fox
timsah crocodile, alligator
timsal symbol
tinsel spiritual
tip type
tipi blizzard, snowstorm
tipik typical
tiraj circulation
tirbuşon corkscrew
tire sewing cotton
tire dash, hyphen, (-) sign
tiryaki addicted (to cigarettes, coffee, etc.), addict
titiz peevish, fastidious, particular
titrek trembling, shaking
titreme trembling
titremek tremble, shake, quiver
titreşim vibration
tiyatro theatre
tiz high-pitched
tohum seed, sperm
tohumluk suitable for seed
tok satiated, full; **karnım tok** I am not hungry / I am not interested
toka buckle / shaking hands
tokalaşmak shake hands with
tokat slap; **tokat atmak** slap, smack
tokgözlü not covetous
tokluk satiety
tokmak mallet
tokuşmak butt one another, collide
toksin toxin
tokuşturmak cause to collide / clink (glasses)

tolga helmet
tomar roll (of paper etc), scroll
tombala lotto
tombalak plump, round
tombul plump
tomruk log
tomurcuk bud
ton ton / tone / shade
tonaj tonnage
tonga trap; **tongaya basmak** be deceived (argo)
tonilato tonnage
top ball / cannon-ball / roll (of paper etc.)
top cannon, **top atmak** fire a gun / go bankrupt (argo)
topaç top (plaything)
topak roundish lump
topal cripple, lame
topallamak limp
topallık lameness
toparlak round
toparlamak pack up, sum up
toparlanmak pull oneself together
topatan kind of melon
topçu artilleryman, artillery
tophane gun factory
toplam total, addition
toplamak gather, collect, sum up, add
toplanmak assemble, come together, regain one's health
toplantı assembly, gathering, meeting
toplardamar vein
toplaşmak gather together
toplu compact, tidy, plump, collective
topluiğne pin
topluluk society, association, group
toplum society, community
toplumbilim sociology
toplusözleşme social (or collective) contract
toprak ground, earth, soil, earthen
toptan wholesale
toptancı wholesaler
topu topu in all
topuk heel, ankle
topuz knob, knot, mace
topyekün total
torba bag, pouch
torik bonito fish

torna lathe; **tornacı** turner
tornavida screwdriver
tornistan etmek go astern
torpil torpedo
torpillemek torpedo
tortu deposit, sediment, dregs
tortulu having sediment
torun grandchild
tos a blow with the head; **tos vurmak** butt (with head or horns)
tost toast, toasted bread
toy inexperienced
toyluk inexperience
toz dust, powder; **toz almak** dust
tozlanmak become dusty
tozlu dusty
tozluk gaiter
tozutmak raise a dust
töhmet suspicion, guilt, offence
tökezlemek stumble
tömbeki Persian tobacco
töre customs, traditions
tören celebration, ceremony
törpü rasp, file
törpülemek rasp, file
tövbe repentance; **tövbe etmek** repent
tövbekâr penitent, repentant
trafik traffic
trahom trachoma
trajedi tragedy
traktör tractor
Trakya Thrace
trampa exchange
trampet drum
tramvay tram-car
transatlantik ocean-liner
transformatör transformer
transfer transfer
transit transit
trapez trapeze, tightrope
tren train
tretuvar pavement, sidewalk
tribün tribune
triko knitted, knitwear
troleybüs trolley-bus
trombon trombone
tropikal tropical
tröst trust
trup troupe
tufan rainstorm, flood, deluge
tufeyli parasite
tugay brigade
tuğamiral rear-admiral

tuğgeneral brigadier general
tuğla brick
tuhaf curious, funny
tuhafiye millinery, drapery; **tuhafiyeci** milliner, draper
tuhaflık strangeness
tul length, longitude
tuluat sudden ideas, improvisations
tulum skin made into a bag, overalls
tulumba pump
tumturaklı bombastic
Tuna (nehri) the Danube
tunç bronze
tundura tundra
tur tour
tura heads (coin)
turfanda early fruit or vegetables
turist tourist
turizm tourism
turna crane (bird), garfish
turne tour
turnike turnstile
turnuva tournament
turp radish
turşu pickle
turta cake, tart
turuncu orange
turunç Seville orange
tuş key (of a piano etc.) / touch (wrestling)
tutam small handful, pinch
tutamak handle
tutanak minutes of a meeting
tutar total, sum
tutarlı acceptable, admissible
tutarsız inconsequent
tutkal glue
tutkallamak glue
tutku passion, zeal
tutkun seized, in love, captive
tutkunluk passion, love
tutmak hold, keep, stop / hire / take root
tutsak prisoner
tutturmak cause to hold, insist on
tutucu conservative
tutuk paralysed, slow
tutuklamak arrest
tutuklu arrested
tutukluk shyness, slowness, detention
tutulmak be held / fall in love with / be hired /

tutulmak be held / fali in love with 1 be hired / be ill with
tutum manner, conduct / economy
tutumlu economical, thrifty
tutunmak hold on, take a hold, cling to
tutuşmak catch fire / begin to quarrel
tutuşturmak set fire to, set ablaze
tutya zinc
tuval panel, easel
tuvalet toilet, lavatory / evening dress
tuz salt
tuzak trap; **tuzak kurmak** lay a trap
tuzla salt-mine
tuzlama salted
tuzlu salt, salty, salted / expensive
tuzluk salt-cellar
tuzruhu hydrochloric acid
tuzsuz unsalted, insipid
tüccar merchant
tüfek rifle, gun
tükenmek be exhausted, come to an end
tükenmez inexhaustible, endless; **tükenmez kalem** ball-point pen
tüketici consumer
tüketim consumption
tüketmek exhaust, use up
tükürmek spit
tükürük spittle
tül tulle
tülbent muslin
tüm the whole
tümamiral vice-admiral
tümdengelim deduction
tümen division, great number
tümevarım induction
tümgeneral major-general
tümleç object, complement
tümör tumour
tümsek small mound
tünek perch
tüp tube
tür sort, kind
türbe tomb, mausoleum
türbedar keeper of tomb
türbin turbine
türedi upstart
türetmek derive / produce, invent

türev derivative
Türk Turk, Turkish
Türkçe Turkish
Türkistan Turkestan
Türkiyat Turkology
Türkiye Turkey
Türkiye Cumhuriyeti the Turkish Republic
Türkleşmek become a Turk
Türkoloji Turkology
türkü folk-song; **türkü söylemek** sing folk-songs
türlü sort, kind, various / dish of various vegetables / mixed
tütmek smoke (of a chimney etc.), give out smoke
tütsü incense, fumigation
tütsülemek fumigate; **kafayı tütsülemek** become drunk
tütün tobacco; **tütüncü** tobacconist
tüy feather, hair
tüykalem quill
tüylenmek grow feathers / be rich (argo)
tüysüz unfeathered / young
tüzelkişi juristic person
tüzük regulation, rules

U

ucube strange thing, very ugly
ucuz cheap
ucuzlamak become cheap
ucuzluk cheapness, sale
uç tip, top, point, end
uçak aeroplane, airplane
uçaksavar anti-aircraft
uçarı dissolute
uçkur belt (underwear)
uçlu pointed
uçmak fly / evaporate / fade away
uçsuz without a point **uçsuz bucaksız** endless, vast
uçucu flying / evaporating
uçuk blain on the lip
uçuklamak break out in

pimples
uçurmak cause to fly / exaggerate
uçurtma kite
uçurum precipice, chasm
uçuş flight
uçuşmak fly together, fly about
ufacık tiny
ufak small
ufak tefek small, of no account
ufala(n)mak berak into pieces, crumble
ufki horizontal
ufuk horizon
uğrak place through which one passes, site
uğramak stop at (a place), call at / suffer, experience
uğraş work, dealing, occupation
uğraşmak struggle, strive, strive hard, try to
uğraştırmak cause to struggle, cause annoyance to
uğratmak cause to stop at / bring to / cause
uğruna for the sake of
uğuldamak hum, buzz
uğultu humming noise
uğur good luck
uğurlamak see someone off
uğurlu lucky
uğursuz inauspicious, bringing bad luck
uğursuzluk ill-omen
uhrevi pertaining to the next world, spiritual
ukala wiseacre, pedant
ukalalık pretence of being clever, pedantry
ulak courier
ulama liaison, linking
ulaşım communication, transport
ulaşmak reach, arrive
ulaştırma communication, transport
ulaştırma bakanlığı ministry of transport and communications
ulaştırmak cause to reach, transport
ulu great, great man
ululuk greatness
ulumak howl
uluorta openly, without reserve

ulus nation
ulusal national
uluslararası international
ulvi high, sublime
umacı ogre (for children)
ummadık unexpected
ummak hope, expect, anticipate
umman ocean
umulmak be expected
umum general, all, the public
umumiyetle in general, generally
umursamak consider important
umut hope
un flour
unlu prepared with flour, sprinkled with flour
unsur element
unutkan forgetful
unutmak forget
unvan title, name
ur tumour
uranyum uranium
urgan rope
us mind, reason; **usa vurmak** reason
usanç boredom, disgust
usandırıcı boring, tedious
usandırmak bore
usanmak become bored, become sick of, be tired of
usare sap, juice
usavurmak reason
uskumru mackerel
uskur screw, propeller
uslandırmak make sensible, reform, improve
uslanmak become well-behaved
uslu sensible, well-behaved, docile
usta master, master workman, foreman / skilled
ustabaşı head foreman
ustalık proficiency / mastery
ustalıklı cleverly made, masterly
ustura razor
usturuplu right, good
usul system, method, manner
usul, usulca gently, slowly, quietly
usulsüz unmethodical, contrary to the rules
uşak boy / male servant
ut lute

utanç shame, bashfulness
utandırmak make ashamed, cause to blush, put to shame
utangaç shy, timid
utanış being ashamed
utanmak be ashamed, be shy
utanmaz shameless, impudent; **utanmazlık** impudence
uyak rhyme
uyandırmak waken, stir, wake
uyanık awake / bright, smart
uyanmak wake up
uyarı warning
uyarlama adaptation
uyarlamak adapt
uyarmak wake somebody up, arouse, warn
uydu satellite
uydurma invented, made up
uydurmak make fit, adapt / invent, make up
uygar civilized
uygarlık civilization
uygulama application, practice
uygun favourable, fitting, proper
uygunluk appropriateness, suitability
uygunsuz unsuitable, disagreeable
uyku sleep
uykucu fond of sleep
uykusuz sleepless; **uykusuzluk** sleeplessness, insomnia
uymak conform, fit, adapt oneself, suit, yield
uyruk subject, citizen; **yabancı uyruklu** foreigner
uysal easy-going, docile
uyuklamak doze
uyum harmony
uyumak sleep
uyuntu lazy, idle
uyurgezer sleep-walker
uyuşmak become numb
uyuşmak come to an understanding, agree
uyuşmazlık difference, disagreement
uyuşturmak benumb, deaden
uyuşturucu that deadens; **uyuşturucu ilaç** nar-

cotic
uyuşuk numbed, lazy;
uyuşukluk numbness, laziness
uyutmak send to sleep / deceive (argo)
uyutucu soporific
uyuz itch, mange / itchy, mangy
uzak far off, distant
Uzakdoğu Far East
uzaklaşmak go away, become remote
uzaklaştırmak dismiss, send away, expel (from school)
uzaklık distance
uzamak grow long, extend / be prolonged
uzanmak stretch oneself out, lie down
uzatmak lengthen / extend, stretch / pass, hand / prolong
uzay space
uz gören sagacious
uzlaşma agreement
uzlaşmak come to an agreement, compromise
uzman specialist, expert
uzun long, tall
uzunçalar long play
uzunluk length
uzuv organ
uzvi organic
uzviyet organism

Ü

ücra remote, out of the way
ücret pay, wage, fee, price, cost
ücretli receiving pay, paid
ücretsiz unpaid, free
üç three
üçer three each
üçgen triangle
üçkâğıtçı swindler
üçköşeli triangular
üçüncü third
üçüz triplets
üflemek blow out, blow
üfürükçü sorcerer
üleşmek share
üleştirmek share out, distribute
ülke country, realm
ülkü ideal

ülkücü idealist
ülser ulcer
ültimatom ultimatum
ültraviyole ultraviolet
ümit hope; **ümit etmek** hope, expect
ümitlendirmek make hopeful, fill with hope
ümitlenmek be hopeful
ümitsiz hopeless
ümitvar hopeful
ümmet community (of the same religion)
ümmi illiterate
ün fame; **ün salmak** become famous
üniforma uniform
üniversite university
ünlem cry, shout / exclamation
ünlem işareti exclamation mark
ünlemek cry out
ünlü famous / vowel
ünsiyet familiarity; **ünsiyet peyda etmek** be familiar with
Ürdün Jordan
üreğen productive, prolific
üre urea
üremek multiply, increase
üremi uremia
üreteç generator
üretici producer
üretim production
üretmek breed, produce
ürkek timid, skittish; **ürkeklik** timidity
ürkmek startle with fear, become skittish
ürkütmek startle, frighten
ürpermek make the hair stand on end, bristle up
ürümek howl
ürün product
üryani eriği thin skinned plum
üs base
üslûp style (of writing)
üst upper or outside surface, the top of a thing, upper / upper rank (army) / on
üstat master
üstbaş dress, clothing
üstçavuş sergeant-major
üstderi epidermis
üste in addition
üstelemek dwell on a thing, insist / recur (illness)
üstelik furthermore, be-

sides
üstsubay senior officer
üsttaraf remainder, upper part
üstte on top
üstteğmen first lieutenant
üstübeç white lead
üstün superior; **üstün gelmek** surpass
üstünde on, over, above
üstünkörü carelessly
üstünlük superiority
üstüpü oakum
üstüste one on top of the other
üşengen slothful, lazy
üşenmek be too lazy to do something
üşmek flock to a place
üşümek feel cold, catch cold, be cold
üşüşmek crowd together, flock
üşütmek catch cold
üşütük nutty
ütü iron
ütücü ironer
ütülü ironed, pressed
üvey ana stepmother
üvey baba stepfather
üvey çocuk stepchild
üvey kardeş stepbrother (sister)
üvey kız stepdaughter
üvey oğul stepson
üye member
üzengi stirrup
üzere just about to, on the point of
üzeri upper or outer surface of a thing, on
üzerine on to, upon, about
üzgün sad, worried
üzmek worry, tire
üzücü sad, saddening
üzülmek be sorry or worried
üzüm grape
üzüm suyu grapejuice
üzüntü anxiety, worry
üzüntülü painful, grieved
üzüntüsüz carefree

V

vaat promise
vaat etmek promise
vade fixed date, permit-

ted term
vadeli (hesap) time deposit
vadeli satış time sale
vadesiz (hesap) demand deposit
vadi valley
vaftiz baptism; **vaftiz etmek** baptize
vagon car, railway waggon
vah vah what a pity, how sad
vaha oasis
vahamet gravity
vahim grave, dangerous
vahşet savageness, terror
vahşi wild, savage
vahşilik wildness, brutality
vahşiyane savagely
vaız sermon
vaiz preacher
vaka event, case
vakar dignity
vakfetmek devote
vakıa event, fact
vakıa it is true that, the fact is
vakıf pious foundation
vakıf aware; **vakıf olmak** be aware of
vaki happening, true, reality
vakit time
vakitli done at the right time, in time
vakitsiz untimely, out of season
vakitli vakitsiz at all sorts of times
vaktihal financial circumstances
vaktile in the past, once
vakum vacuum
vakur dignified
valf valve
vali governor (of a province)
valide mother
valiz suitcase
vallahi by God!
vals waltz
vampir vampire
vantilatör ventilator, fan
vanilya vanilla
vantuz cupping-glass
vapur ship, boat
var there is / have
varaka note, document
vardiya watch / shift
var etmek create
varılmak be reached

varış arrival
...vari (suffix) like..
varidat income
varil small cask, barrel
varis heir
varit which happens, admissible
variyet wealth, income
variyetli wealthy, well off
varlık existence, presence / wealth
varlıklı wealthy, well off
varmak arrive, reach / attain / end in
var olmak exist
var oluşçuluk existentialism
varoş suburb
varta danger, peril
varsayım hypothesis, assumption
varsaymak asume, suppose
varsın let it (be), let him (come)
varyete variety show
vasat average, mediocre
vasati average
vasıf quality
vasıflandırmak qualify, classify
vasıl olmak arrive
vasıta means / vehicle
vasıtasız direct
vasi guardian, trustee
vasiyet will
vasiyetname written will
vat watt
vatan motherland, (one's) country
vatandaş compatriot
vatani pertaining to one's native land
vatanperver patriot; **vatanperverlik** patriotism
vatman tram-driver
vaveyla cry of lament
vay! oh! ow!
vazelin vaseline
vazgeçmek give up
vazife duty, task
vazifeşinas dutiful
vaziyet position, situation
vazo vase
ve and; **vesaire** et cetera, and so an
veba plague
vebal sin
vecibe obligation
veciz terse, laconic
vecize terse saying, epigram
vect ecstasy

veda farewell, leave taking; **veda etmek** say farewell to
vedalaşmak bid each other farewell
vefa fidelity, faithfulness
vefakar faithful
vefasız faithless
vefat death; **vefat etmek** die, pass away
vehim foreboding, groundless fear, illusion
vehmetmek surmise, have the illusion that
vekâlet representation / ministry / power of attorney
vekâlet etmek represent, be attorney for, act for
vekâleten as representative, by proxy
vekâletname power of attorney
vekil agent, deputy / minister of state; **vekil etmek** appoint as one's representative
vekilharç steward, butler
velakin but still, but yet
velev ki even if
velhasıl in short
veli guardian (of a child) / saint
veliaht heir to the throne
velinimet benefactor
Venüs Venus
velvele outcry
veranda porch, veranda
veraset inheritance
verecek dept
verem tuberculosis
veremli consumptive
veresiye on credit
verev oblique, on the bias
vergi tax / gift; **Allah vergisi** gift of God
vergilendirmek tax
verici transmitter
veri datum
verim production, output
verimli productive, profitable, fertile
verimsiz unfruitful
veriştirmek utter abuse, scold, reprove
vermek give
vermut vermouth
vernik varnish
vesait means, transportation

vesika document
vesile means, opportunity, pretext
vestiyer cloak-room
vesvese secret fear, scruple
veteriner veterinary surgeon
veto veto
veya or
veyahut or
vezin metre (poetry), weighing
vezir vizier
vezne pay-office, cash desk
veznedar cashier
vıcık sticky, viscid
vınlamak buzz, hum
vır vır etmek nag, grumble
vız buzz; **vız gelmek** be a matter of indifference (argo)
vızıldamak buzz, hum
vızıltı buzzing noise
vızır vızır with a whitz, very quickly
vicdan conscience
vicdani pertaining to conscience
vicdanlı conscientious
vicdansız unjust, unscrupulous
vida screw
vidalamak screw
vidalı screwed
video video player
vilayet province
villa villa
vinç crane
vira continuously
viraj curve (of a road)
viran devastated, ruined
virane ruin
viranelik place of ruins
virgül comma
virtüöz virtuoso
virüs virus
viski whisky
vişne morello cherry
vitamin vitamin
vites gear
vites değiştirmek shift (change) gear
vitrin shop-window
viyaklamak squawk
viyolonsel violoncello
vize visa
vizite doctor's fee / rounds (by a doctor)
vizon mink
volan flywheel
voleybol volleyball
volkan volcano

volkanik volcanic
volt volt
volta turn round
voltaj voltage
votka vodka
v.s. (abbrev, for **ve saire)** et cetera (etc.)
vuku occurence; **vuku bulmak** happen, occur
vukuat incidents
vukuf knowledge, information, notion
vurdumduymaz insensitive, blockhead
vurgu stress
vurgun booty, profeteering; **vurgun vurmak** make a successful speculation
vurguncu speculator
vurmak strike, hit
vurulmak be struck, be madly in love with
vuruş blow
vuruşmak fight
vuslat lovers union
vuzuh clearness
vücut body, existence
vücutça bodily
vüsat spaciousness, capacity

Y

ya! You don't say! Really! oh!
ya... ya either.... or
yaba wooden fork (hay)
yaban wilderness
yabancı stranger, foreigner, foreign, unknown
yabani untamed, wild
yad etmek recollect, commemorate
yadigâr souvenir
yadırgamak find strange or odd
yadsımak deny, reject
yafta label
yağ oil, fat, grease
yağcı maker or seller of oil or butter / flatterer (argo)
yağdanlık oil-can
yağdırmak rain down, pour out
yağdoku fat tissue

yağhane oil-factory
yağış rain
yağışlı rainy
yağız darkish brown
yağlamak grease, oil / flatter (sl.)
yağlanmak be greased, become dirty with grease / get fat
yağlı fat, greasy, oily
yağlıboya point
yağlıkapı rich employer
yağlıkuyruk a rich windfall, profitable customer
yağma booty; **yağma etmek** plunder
yağmacı plunderer
yağmak rain; **dolu yağmak** hail
yağmur rain
yağmurlu rainy
yağmurluk raincoat
yağsız skim (milk or cheese)
yahni meat stewed with onions
yahu you fellow, oh God
Yahudi Jew, Jewish
Yahudice Hebrew
yahut or
yaka collar / side
yakacak fuel
yakalamak seize, catch, get hold of
yakamoz phosphorescence in the sea
yakapaça by force
yakarış begging
yakarmak beg
yakı plaster, cautery
yakıcı burning, caustic
yakılmak be burnt
yakın near, nearby place / soon
Yakın Doğu Near East
yakın çağ modern age
yakında near by, in the near future, recently, soon
yakınlaşmak approach
yakınlık nearness
yakınmak complain
yakınsak convergent
yakışık convenience
yakışıklı handsome
yakışıksız unsuitable, ugly
yakışmak be suitable, be proper, look well
yakıştırmak expect of / make up
yakıt fuel

yaklaşılmak be approached
yaklaşık more or less, about, approximately
yaklaşmak approach
yakmak burn
yakut ruby
yalak drinking-basin, trough
yalama licking, abrasion
yalamak lick
yalan lie, false
yalancı liar, false
yalancıdolma stuffed vegetables with olive oil
yalancılık mendacity
yalanlamak deny
yalanmak lick oneself
yalçın bare, steep
yaldız gilding
yaldızlamak gild
yaldızlı gilt
yalı shore / waterside residence
yalın single, bare
yalınayak barefooted
yalın hal nominative case (dilbilgisi)
yalınkat single-fold
yalıtkan insulating
yalnız alone, only
yalnızlık loneliness
yalpa the rolling of a ship
yaltakçı flatterer
yaltaklanmak fawn, cringe
yalvarıcı entreating
yalvarış entreaty, begging
yalvarmak entreat, beg
yama patch; **yama vurmak** put on a patch, patch up
yamaç slope of a hill
yamak apprentice, assistant
yamalamak patch
yamalı patched
yamamak patch / impose on
yaman strong, capable, smart
yamanmak be patched on / install oneself, hang on
yampiri sideways
yamrı yumru uneven and lumpy, deformed
yamuk trapezoid (geom.)
yamyam cannibal
yamyassı quite flat

yan side, flank, direction
yana towards, in favour of, on the side of
yanak cheek
yanardağ volcano
yanaşık adjacent, compact
yanaşılmak be approached
yanaşma approaching / casual labourer, hireling
yanaşmak draw near, come alongside / seem willing
yan çizmek sneak off
yandan from the side
yandaş supporter
yan gelmek take one's ease
yangın fire
yanıbaşında by the side of
yanık burnt / touching, moving
yanılgı error, mistake
yanılmak make a mistake, be mistaken
yanılmaz unfailing, infallible
yanıltıcı misleading
yanıltmak cause to make a mistake, mislead
yanısıra by the side of, in addition to
yanıt answer
yanıtlamak answer
yani namely, that is
yankesici pickpocket
yankı echo
yanlış error, wrong
yanlışlık mistake, error
yanmak burn / feel grieved
yanpiri leaning to one side, crooked
yansıma reflection
yansımak reflect
yan yana side by side
yapağı wool in the fleece, fleece of wool
yapayalnız absolutely alone, all by oneself
yapı building, structure
yapıcı maker, builder
yapılış method of construction (doing)
yapılmış made
yapım construction / production
yapımcı producer
yapısal structural
yapıt building, work
yapışık stuck on

yapışkan sticky, adhesive / hanger on
yapışmak stick to, adhere
yapıştırmak stick on, attach
yapıt work (of art)
yapma act of doing or making / false
yapmacık artificial, false
yapmak do, make
yaprak leaf, sheet of paper
yaprak dökümü the fall of leaves
yapraklanmak come into leaf
yapraksız leafless
yaptırım sanction
yar precipice (geog.)
yâr lover, friend
yara wound, cut, sore
Yarabbi My God
Yaradan Creator
yaradılış creation, nature
yaralamak wound
yaralı wounded
yaramak be serviceable, be of use
yaramaz unserviceable, good-for-nothing, naughty
yaranmak curry favour
yarar serviceable, useful, use, gain
yararlanmak make use of
yararlı useful, profitable
yararlık usefulness, capability / heroism
yararsız useless
yarasa bat
yaraşmak become, fit, match
yaratıcı creative
yaratık creature
yaratmak create
yarbay lieutenant - colonel, (navy) commander
yarda yard (of measure)
yardakçı accomplice
yardım help, aid; **yardım etmek** help
yardımcı helper, assistant
yardımcı fiil auxiliary verb (dilbilgisi)
yardımlaşmak help one another
yardımsever helpful, benevolent, charitable
yarenlik friendly conversation, chat
yargı judgement

yargıç judge
yargılamak judge
Yargıtay Supreme Court of Appeal
yarı half
yarıçap diameter
yarık split, cracked, crack
yarılamak be half way through
yarılmak be split
yarım half
yarımküre hemisphere
yarımada peninsula
yarım yamalak incompletely, improperly
yarın tomorrow
yarı saydam semi-transparent
yarış race, competition; **yarış etmek** compete, race
yarışma competition
yarışmacı competitor
yarışmak race, compete
yarı yarıya dividing equally, fifty-fifty
yarı yolda half-way
yarma act of splitting, cleft / boorish fellow
yarmak split, cleave
yas mourning; **yas tutmak** be in mourning
yasa law
yasak prohibition, forbidden, prohibited
yasama legislation
yasemin jasmine
yaslamak support
yaslanmak lean against, recline
yaslı in mourning
yassı flat
yassılaşmak become flat
yassıltmak flatten
yassılık flatness
yastık pillow, pad
yaş wet, moisture / tears
yaş age
yaşa long live!
yaşam life, living
yaşama living
yaşamak live
yaşantı way of life, living
yaşarmak become wet (for the eyes)
yaşatmak keep alive
yaşayış life, living
yaşıt of the same age
yaşlanmak become wet (of the eyes)
yaşlanmak grow old
yaşlı wet, suffused with tears

yaşlı aged, old
yaşlık wetness
yaşlılık old age
yat yacht
yatağan yataghan, curved sword
yatak bed / bearing
yatakhane dormitory
yataklık being a receiver of stolen goods
yataklı vagon wagon-lit, sleeping-car
yatak odası bedroom
yatalak bedridden
yatay horizontal
yatık leaning to one side
yatılı okul boarding school
yatırım investment; **yatırım yapmak** invest
yatırmak lay down, deposit
yatışmak calm down
yatıştırmak calm, soothe
yatkın laid down, that has lain too long / willing, able
yatmak lie down, go to bed
yavan tasteless, insipid; **yavanlık** insipidity
yavaş slow, slowly
yavaşça slowly
yavaşlatmak slow down, slacken
yavaşlamak slow down, reduce the speed
yavru the young, nestling
yavrukurt junior scout
yavrulamak bring forth young
yavuklu engaged to marry
yay bow, spring
yaya on foot. pedestrian
yaya kaldırımı pavement
yayan on foot
yaygara clamour
yaygaracı noisy, noisy fellow, cry baby
yaygı cloth spread out
yaygın diffused, wide-spread, common
yayık churn
yayımcı publisher
yayımlamak publish
yayınevi publishing house
yayla high plateau, highland
yaylı having springs
yaylım ateşi volley, salvo
yaymak spread, disperse / extend

yayvan broad
yaz summer
yazar writer, author
yazgı destiny, fate
yazı writing / article / handwriting / destiny
yazı tahtası blackboard
yazı makinesi typewriter
yazıcı clerk, secretary
yazıhane office
yazık a pity, a shame, what a shame!
yazılı written, inscribed, registered
yazım spelling
yazın in summer
yazın literature
yazış manner of writing
yazışmak correspond
yazıt inscription
yazlamak pass the summer (in a place)
yazlık suitable for the summer / summer clothing / summer resort
yazma act of writing / hand printed kerchief / written / writing
yazmak write
yedek spare, reserve; **yedek parça** spare part; **yedek subay** reserve officer
yedi seven
yedinci seventh
yedirmek cause to eat, feed
yedişer seven each
yediveren ever blooming plant
yegâne unique, sole
yeğ better
yeğen nephew, niece
yeğlemek prefer
yeğ tutmak prefer
yeis despair
yek one; **yekdiğer** one another
yeknesak uniform, homogeneous, monotonous; **yeknesaklık** uniformity, monotony
yekpare in a single piece
yekten all at once
yekûn total
yekvücut unified
yel wind
yel değirmeni windmill
yele mane
yelek waistcoat
yelken sail; **yelken açmak** hoist sails
yelkenli fitted with sails, sailing-boat

yelkovan minute-hand of a watch
yellemek fan
yelpaze fan
yelpazelenmek fan oneself
yeltenmek attempt to do something beyond one's power or rights, try in vain
yem food for animals, bait
yemek food, a meal
yemekhane dining hall
yemeklik serving as food
yemin oath; **yemin etmek** swear
yeminli bound by oath
yemiş fruit
yemyeşil very green
yen sleeve
yenge the wife of one's brother or uncle
yengeç crab
yengeç burcu tropic of cancer
yeni new, recent, recently; **yeniden** over again, from the beginning
yeni baştan over again, all over
yeniçeri janissary
yeniden anew, once again
yenik defeated, beaten; **yenik düşmek** be defeated
yenik eaten, gnawed, nibbled; **(bit) yeniği** something fishy
yenilemek renew
yenilgi defeat
yenilik newness, novelty
yenilmek be overcome, lose (at a game)
yenir edible
yenişmek try to beat one another
yenmek be eaten
yenmek overcome, conquer, win
yepyeni brand new
yer ground, place, space
yeraltı underground
yerbilim geology
yerçekimi gravity, gravitation
yerel local
yerelması Jerusalem artichoke
yer etmek make a mark, leave an impression

yergi backbiting, disparagament, satire
yerinde appropriate, right
yerinmek bemoan, regret
yerkabuğu the earth's crust
yerleşmek settle down
yerleştirmek put into place, arrange in proper order / put into employment / deploy
yerli native, local
yermek loathe, criticize, blame
yersiz homeless / out of place, irrelevant
yeryüzü the face of the earth, the world
yeşermek bloom
yeşil green
yeşilimtrak greenish
yeşillenmek become green
yeşilli mixed with green
yeşillik greenness / meadow / salad
yeşim (taşı) jasper
yetenek ability, talent
yetenekli talented, capable
yeter sufficient, enough
yeterli sufficient
yetim orphan
yetimhane orphanage
yetinmek be contented
yetişkin grown up
yetişmek reach / suffice / grow up, mature / catch
yetişmiş mature, grown up
yetiştirici breeder
yetiştirmek cause to reach / bring up / educate / breed
yetki authority
yetkili competent, qualified, authorized
yetmek suffice, be enough
yetmiş seventy
yetmişer seventy each
yetmişinci seventieth
yevmiye daily pay, wage
yezit impious, vile fellow
yığılı heaped, piled up
yığılmak be heaped up, crowd together, collapse
yığın heap, pile
yığınak heap, mass
yığıntı accumulation, heap
yığmak pile up
yıkama act of washing;

yıkama makinası washing machine
yıkamak wash
yıkanmak wash (oneself)
yıkıcı destructive
yıkık fallen down
yıkılmak be demolished, fall down
yıkım ruin, calamity
yıkıntı ruin(s)
yıkmak pull down, demolish
yıl year
yılan snake
yılanbalığı eel
yılankavi spiral, coiling
yılbaşı new year's day, new year's eve
yıldırım lightning
yıldırmak frighten, daunt, terrify
yıldız star
yıldızçiçeği dahlia
yıldönümü anniversary
yılgın cowed, subdued, daunted
yılışık sticky, shameless
yılışmak grin unpleasantly, importune
yıllanmış old, aged, very old
yıllık year-book, annual / a year's salary
yılmak dread
yılmaz undaunted, fearless
yıpranmak wear out, be worn
yıpratıcı exhausting, toilsome
yıpratmak wear out
yırtıcı (hayvan) beast of prey
yırtık torn, rent
yırtınmak shriek in desperation, be fearfully perturbed
yırtmaç slit
yırtmak tear, rend
yiğit brave, courageous / young man
yiğitlik heroism
yine again, still
yinelemek repeat
yirmi twenty
yirminci twentieth
yirmişer twenty each
yitik lost
yitirmek lose
yitmek be lost
yiv groove, rifling (of a gun)
yiyecek food
yiyici taker of bribes,

bribee
yo! oh no!
yobaz fanatic
yobazlık fanaticism
yoga yoga
yoğun thick, dense
yoğunluk density
yoğurmak knead
yoğurt yoghurt
yok non-existent / absent / no / there is not
yok etmek annihilate
yoklama inspection, examination, roll-call
yoklamak feel with the fingers, examine / try / visit
yokluk absence, lack
yoksa or, if not, otherwise
yoksul poor, possesing nothing, destitute
yoksulluk destitution, poverty
yoksun deprived, lacking
yokuş rise, slope, rising
yokuş aşağı downhill; **yokuş yukarı** uphill
yok yere uselessly, in vain
yol road / way, method / stripe
yolcu traveller, passenger
yolculuk travelling, travel, journey; **yolculuk etmek** travel
yoldaş fellow traveller, comrade, companion
yolharcı travelling expenses
yol kesici highwayman, bandit
yollama act of sending, forwarding
yollamak send, dispatch, forward
yollanmak be sent off, set off
yollu striped / fast / by way of / loose
yolmak pluck
yolsuz roadless / contrary to law
yolsuzluk impropriety, irregularity, misuse, abuse, embezzlement
yoluk plucked
yonca clover
yonga chip
yonmak cut, chip into shape
yontmak chip into shape /

sharpen / exploit
yontulmamış not chipped, rough / uneducated, unmannerly
yordam technique, method
yorgan quilt
yorgun tired
yorgunluk fatigue
yormak tire / comment
yortu Christian feast
yorucu fatiguing, wearisome, tiring
yorulmak be tired
yorum commentary, interpretation, anticipation
yorumlamak comment on, interpret
yosma coquette, loose woman
yosun moss; **deniz yosunu** seaweed
yosunlu mossy
yoz boorish, uncouth / degenerate
yozlaşmak grow wild, degenerate
yön direction
yönelmek head towards
yöneltmek direct
yönetici administrator
yönetmek manage, direct, control; **yönetim** management; **yönetim kurulu** board of directors
yönetmelik governing statute, regulations
yönetmen director
yöntem method, way
yöre side, environment, neighbourhood
yöresel regional, local
yörük nomad
yörünge course orbit
yudum mouthful
yufka thin, week / thin layer of dough
Yugoslav Yugoslav
Yugoslavya Yugoslavia
yuhalamak boo, hoot
yukarda above, overhead
yukardan from above
yukarı high, above, upwards, upper part
yulaf oats
yular halter
yumak ball (of wool etc.), yarn
yummak shut, close (eye)
yumru round
yumruk fist / blow
yumruklamak hit with the fist

yumuk closed (eyes)
yumurcak a mischievous child
yumurta egg; **yumurta akı** the white of an egg; **yumurta sarısı** yolk
yumurtlamak lay eggs
yumuşak soft, mild
yumuşakçalar molluscs
yumuşaklık softness
yumuşamak become soft, calm down
yumuşatmak soften, appease
Yunan Greek
Yunanca Greek
Yunanistan Greece
yunusbalığı dolphin
yurt native country / home / student dormitory
yurtsever patriotic
yurttaş fellow countryman
yurttaşlık bilgisi civics
yusyuvarlak quite round
yutkunmak swallow one's spittle, gulp
yutmak swallow, gulp / win (at a game) / fall for
yutturmak cause to swallow / swindle
yuva nest
yuvalanmak settle down
yuvar globule, corpuscle
yuvarlak round
yuvarlaklık roundness
yuvarlamak roll / swallow
yuvarlanmak revolve, roll / become round
yuvarlatmak cause to rotate, make round
yüce high, exalted
Yüve Divan (Danıştay) Supreme Court
yük load, cargo, burden
yüklem predicate
yüklemek load / throw the blame on
yüklenme taking the blame, undertaking
yüklenmek be loaded / attack
yüklü loaded
yüklük closet for bedding
yüksek high, loud (voice) / **yüksek öğretim** higher education
yükseklik height, altitude
yükselmek rise; **yükseltmek** raise, promote

yüksük thimble
yüksünmek regard as burdensome, grumble
yükümlü compulsory, obligatory, responsible
yün wool / woollen
yürek heart / courage
yürekli brave, bold
yüreksiz faint-hearted
yürekten sincere, cordial
yürük nomad
yürümek walk, advance, march
yürürlük validity
yürütmek cause to walk / steal (argo)
yürüyüş walk
yüz face / surface; **yüz çevirmek** turn away; **yüz tutmak** begin; **yüz vermek** give encouragement, spoil
yüz hundred
yüzakı personal honour
yüzbaşı captain
yüzde per cent, percentage
yüzdürmek float
yüzer a hundred each
yüzey surface, face
yüzeysel superficial
yüzgeç fin
yüzgöz olmak be too intimate
yüzkarası disgrace
yüzlerce (in) hundreds
yüzleş(tir)mek meet face to face, confront
yüzmek swim, float
yüzölçümü area
yüzsüz shameless; **yüzsüzlük** effrontery
yüzük ring
yüzükoyun face downwards, prone
yüzüncü hundredth
yüzüstü bırakmak leave somebody in the lurch
yüzyıl century
yüzyüze face to face

Z

zaaf weakness
zabıt taking down in

writing, recording
zabıt tutmak put on official record
zabıta the police
zaçyağı sulphuric acid
zade noble, son
zafer victory
zafiyet weakness
zahir external, outward, outside / evidently
zahire cereal, provisions
zahiren outwardly
zâhiri outward, in appearance
zahmet trouble, difficulty; **zahmet etmek** give oneself trouble, take the trouble of; **zahmet vermek** cause trouble
zahmetli troublesome, difficult, wearing
zahmetsiz easy
zahmetsizce easily
zail olmak disappear
zait additional, superfluous / plus; **zait işareti** the puls sign
zakkum oleander
zalim unjust; **zalimlik** cruelty
zam rise / surcharge, additional charge
zaman time, period, era / when / tense (dilbilgisi)
zaman zaman every now and then, from time to time
zambak lily
zamir pronoun (dilbilgisi)
zamk gum; **zamklı** gummed, having gum
zamklamak gum, stick with gum
zampara womanizer, lecher
zan opinion, suspicion
zanaat handicraft
zangırdamak clank, rattle
zangır zangır trembling, with teeth chattering
zannetmek think
zapt etmek hold firmly, seize, grasp / take down in writing
zaptiye gendarme
zapturapt discipline
zar film, thin skin, membrane
zar dice
zarafet elegance, grace
zarar damage, loss, harm; **zarar etmek** suffer loss; **zarar görmek**

ziyaret visit; **ziyaret etmek** pay a visit
ziyaretçi visitor, caller
ziynet ornament
zoka artificial bait
zonklamak throb with pain
zooloji zoology
zor force, violence, dificulty / difficult, hard
zoraki forced, under compulsion, by force
zorba tyrant, bully
zorla with difficulty / by force
zorlamak force, use force, handle roughly
zorlanmak force oneself, be forced
zorlaşmak become harder
zorlu strong, powerful, brutal
zorluk difficulty
zorunlu necessary, compulsory
zorzoruna with difficulty
zuhur appearance, happening; **zuhur etmek** appear, come into existence
zuhurat sudden occurrences, unexpected events, hazards
zulmetmek treat unjustly, tyrannize
zulüm cruelty, oppression, tyranny
zurna shrill pipe
züccaciye glassware, china
züğürt penniless
züğürtleşmek become penniless
Zühal Saturn
Zühre Venüs
zührevi venereal
zül abasement, humility
zülüf side-lock of hair
zümre party, set of people, group
zümrüt emerald, emerald green
züppe affected, snobbish, dandy
zürafa giraffe
zürriyet descendants, offspring

be damaged
zararlı harmful; **zararlı çıkmak** come out the loser
zararsız harmless, not so bad
zarf envelope, cover
zarf adverb (dilbilgisi)
zarfında during, within
zargana garfish
zarif elegant, graceful
zariflik elegance, grace
zarp multiplication; **zarp işareti** multiplication sign
zaruret need, necessity / poverty
zaruri indispensable, necessary
zar zor with difficulty / by force
zat person
zaten essentially, in any case, and then
zati personal, private
zatülcenp pleurisy
zatürre pneumonia
zavallı miserable, unlucky, poor
zaviye angle, corner
zayıf weak, thin
zayıflamak become thin, lose weight
zayıflık weakness, thinness
zayi lost; **zayi etmek** lose; **zayiat vermek** suffer (cause) losses
zebani demon of hell
zebella huge, huge man, monstrous
zecri restrictive, violent
zede stricken by, sufferer
zedelemek damage, bruise
zehap belief, surmise
zehir poison, venom
zehirlemek poison
zehirli poisonous
zekâ intelligence
zekât canonical yearly alms, purification
zeki intelligent
zelil low, base
zelzele earthquake
zem blame, censure, backbiting
zemberek spring (of a watch)
zembil bush basket
zemheri extreme cold
zemin ground
zemin katı ground-floor, basement

zemmetmek censure, disparage
zencefil ginger
zenci negro
zengin rich, wealthy
zenginlik wealth
zerdali wild apricot
zerde sweetened rice with saffron
zerketmek inject
zerre atom, molecule
zerzevat vegetables; **zerzevatçı** greengrocer
zevahir appearance
zeval decay, fall
zevat persons
zevce wife
zevç mate, pair, husband
zevk taste, pleasure
zevk almak enjoy
zevkli amusing, enjoyable
zevksiz tasteless
zevzek talkative, giddy
zeyil appendix, post script, sequence
zeytin olive
zeytinlik olive grove
zeytinyağı olive-oil
zeytuni olive-green
zıbarmak lose consciousness / die (argo)
zıbın padded jacket (for a baby)
zıddiyet opposition, contrast
zıkkım any bitter food
zılgıt scolding; **zılgıt vermek** scold, reprimand; **zılgıt yemek** get a scolding
zımba punch, metal stamp
zımbalı perforated
zımbırdatmak twang, strum
zımbırtı twanging
zımpara kağıdı emery paper
zındık misbeliever, atheist
zıngırdamak tremble violently, rattle
zıngırtı rattling noise
zıpır hare-brained, madcap
zıpkın harpoon
zıplamak jump, hop
zıplatmak bounce
zıpzıp marble
zırdeli raving mad
zırh armour
zırhlı armoured, battleship
zırıldamak keep up an incessant chatter, nag
zırıltı continuous chatter, nagging
zırlak bawing
zırlamak weep (contemptously)
zırnık yellow arsenic
zırva silly chatter, nonsense
zırvalamak talk nonsense
zıt the opposite, the contrary, antonym
zıvana tenon; **zıvana testeresi** tenon-saw
zıvanadan çıkmak go mad
zibidi oddly dressed
zifaf nuptial; **zifaf odası** bridal chamber
zifiri pitch-dark
zifos splash of mud
zift pitch, tar
ziftlemek daub with pitch
zihin mind, intelligence
zihnen mentally, in mind
zihni mental
zihniyet mentality
zikir mention
zikretmek mention
zikzak zigzag
zil bell, cymbal
zillet abasement, shame
zimmet debt / charge / embezzlement
zina adultery
zincir chain, succession
zincirleme in a continuous series, in links
zincirlemek chain up
zincirli chained
zindan dungeon
zindancı jailer
zinde vigorous, alive, energetic
zinhar by no means
zira because, for
ziraat agriculture
zirai agricultural
zirve summit
ziya light
ziyadar luminous
ziyade more, excess, too much, excessive, more than
ziyadeleşmek increase
ziyadesiyle largely, amply
ziyafet feast, banquet
ziyan loss, damage; **ziyan görmek** suffer loss
ziyankâr wasteful
ziyanlı injured, losing harmful
ziyansız harmless, not so bad

ENGLISH · TURKISH

İNGİLİZCE OKUNUŞ BİLGİLERİ

Bir cep sözlüğü ihtiyacını tam anlamıyla karşılayacak olan bu sözlük telaffuz konusunda da İngilizce öğrenenler için güvenilir bir rehber olacaktır.

Sözlüğü kullananların ilkönce telaffuz konusunda aşağıdaki açıklamaları dikkatli bir şekilde okumaları yararlı olur.

İngilizce sözcüklerin nasıl okunacağını gösteren köşeli parantez içindeki telaffuzlarda bazı [ı, e, o, ö, t, d] harfleri siyah olarak yazılmıştır. Bu harfler Türkçedekinden biraz farklı olan sesleri belirtmek için kullanılmıştır.

ı İngilizcede, Türkçedeki [ı] sesine benzeyen bir ses vardır. Ağız normal [ı] sesini çıkarmak için yapıldığından biraz daha fazla açılmak suretiyle [ı] denirse siyah [**ı**] ile gösterilen ses elde edilmiş olur. Türkçedeki [ı] dan farkını belirtmek için telaffuzlarda bu sesi gösterirken normal [ı] yerine siyah [**ı**] kullanılmıştır. Köşeli parantez içindeki siyah [**ı**] lar Türk alfabesindeki [ı] dan farklı ve yukarıda söylendiği gibi okunmalıdır.

e Siyah [**e**] harfleri, Türk alfabesindeki [e] ile [a] arası bir sestir. Ağız [a] demek için açılmışken [e] denirse siyah [**e**] ile gösterilen ses elde edilmiş olur.

o Ağız [a] demek için açılmışken [o] denecek olursa siyah [**o**] ile gösterdiğimiz ses elde edilmiş olur.

ö Bu ses aslında siyah [**ı**] ile gösterdiğimiz sesin uzunudur. Fakat bu, Türkçedeki [ö] sesine pek yaklaşık olduğundan [ö] ile gösterilmiş, sadece farkını belirtmiş olmak için siyah [**ö**] kullanılmıştır.

t İngilizcedeki **th** harfleri yanyana oldukları vakit bazı sözcüklerde Türkçedeki [t] sesine benzer bir ses verirler. Bu sesi tam olarak çıkarmak için şöyle bir yol izlenir: Dilin ucu üst dişlerin uç kısmına hafifçe dokunur durumdan ayrılırken [t] denecek olursa siyah [**t**] ile gösterdiğimiz ses çıkmış olur.

d **th** bazı sözcüklerde siyah [**d**] ile gösterdiğimiz sesle okunur. Bu [**d**] sesi de dilin ucu üst dişlerin uç kısmına hafifçe dokunur durumdan ayrılırken [d] demekle elde edilir.

Okunuşlarda karşılaşılacak bu siyah [**ı, e, o, ö, t, d**] sesleri Türkçedeki [ı, e, o, ö, t, d] gibi değil, yukarıda tarif edildiği şekilde okunmalıdır.

İngilizce sözcük sonlarındaki ng harflerinin okunuşu bu harfleri ayrı ayrı belirtmek suretiyle değil, dilin gerisi arka damakta dayalı haldeyken [n] sesi çıkarmak suretiyle yapılır.

Okunuşlarda görülen [eı], [au], [ou], [iı] gibi yanyana iki sesli harfi okurken bir sesten diğerine kesiksiz şekilde, adeta aralarında pek belirsiz ve kısa bir [ğ] sesi varmış gibi geçmelidir.

Sesli harflerin yanında bulunan iki nokta (:) o sesin uzun okunacağını gösterir.

Sözcüklerin Türkçe karşılıkları verilirken birbirine az çok yakın anlamlı karşılıklar (,) ile, yakın olmayan karşılıklar ise (/) işareti ile ayrılmışlardır. Anlamları aynı olduğu halde dilbilgisinde yerleri ayrı olan sözcükler de (/) işareti ile ayrılmışlardır. Örnek:

answer [a:nsı] cevap / cevap vermek

Hacimce küçük olmasına rağmen, sadece en lüzumlu karşılıklar verildiği için, bu sözlüğün İngilizce-Türkçe bölümü on binden fazla İngilizce sözcüğü kapsamaktadır. Bu durumuyla gerek okullar, gerekse kendi kendine İngilizce öğrenenler için her türlü ihtiyacı karşılayacak niteliktedir.

Birinci bölümde bulunan Türkçe - İngilizce sözlükte de on bin sözcük bulunmaktadır. Türkçede halihazırda yerleşmiş yeni sözcükleri olduğu gibi nispeten eski, fakat halen kullanılanları da içeren bu bölüm küçük hacimli olmasına rağmen ihtiyacı geniş ölçüde karşılayacak kapsamdadır.

Önceki sayfalarda vermiş olduğumuz okunuş bilgileri arasında siyah harfle gösterdiğimiz sesler uluslararası fonetik birliği tarafından aşağıdaki sembollerle gösterilir. Başka sözlüklerde karşılaştığınızda kolayca anlayabilmeniz için bunları aşağıda veriyoruz.

Uluslararası sembol	FONO sözlüğünde karşılığı
δ	**d**
θ	**t**
ɔ	**o**
ə	**ı**
æ	**e**
ə:	**ö:**

A

a [ı, ey] (herhangi) bir
abandon [ıbendın] terketmek, bırakmak
abate [ıbeyt] azaltmak, hafifletmek
abbreviate [ıbri:vieyt] kısaltmak, **abbreviation** [ıbri:vieyşın] kısaltma
abdomen [ebdoumın] karın
ability [ıbiliti] yetenek, iktidar, kabiliyet
ablaze [ıbleyz] tutuşmuş
able [eybıl] güçlü, muktedir
abnormal [ebno:mıl] anormal
aboard [ıbo:d] gemide, gemiye
abolish [ıboliş] yürürlükten kaldırmak
abolition [ebılişın] yok etme, yürürlükten kaldırma
abominable [ıbominıbıl] iğrenç, berbat
abortion [ıbo:şın] çocuk düşürme / düşük
abound [ıbaund] bol olmak
about [ıbaut] hakkında / aşağı yukarı / civarında / üzere
above [ıbav] fevkinde, üstünde
abridge [ıbric] kısaltmak, özetlemek
abroad [ıbro:d] hariçte, yabancı ülkede
abrupt [ıbrapt] anî
abscess [ebses] apse
absence [ebsıns] yokluk, bulunmayış
absent [ebsınt] namevcut, yok
absolute [ebsılu:t] mutlak, tam
absolutaly [ebsılu:tli] tamamen, mutlaka
absorb [ıbso:b] emmek, (sünger gibi) çekmek

abstain [ıbsteyn] çekinmek, uzak durmak
abstention [ıbstenşın] çekinme
abstract [ebstrekt] soyut, anlaşılması zor / özet / [ıbstrekt] çıkarmak
absurd [ıbsö:d] saçma, abes
abundance [ıbandıns] bolluk
abuse [ıbyu:s] küfür / suistimal, kötüye kullanma
abuse [ıbyu:z] fena muamele etmek, küfretmek
abstinence [ebstinıns] perhiz / sakınma
acacia [ıkeysı] akasya
academic [ekıdemik] akademik
accelerate [ekselıreyt] hızlandırmak
accept [ıksept] kabul etmek
acceptable [ıkseptıbıl] kabul edilebilir, münasip
access [ekses] giriş,
accessible [ıksesibıl] girilebilir, erişilebilir
accessory [eksesıri] ilave parçalar, aksesuvar
accident [eksidınt] olay, kaza (trafik vs.) / tesadüf
accidental [eksidentıl] tesadüfî
accommodate [ıkomıdeyt] yerleştirmek, barındırmak
accommodation [ıkomıdeyşın] oturma yeri, yaşama yeri
accompany [ıkampıni] eşlik etmek
accompaniment [ıkampınimınt] refakat, eşlik
accomplice [ıkomplis] suç ortağı
accomplish [ıkompliş] yapmak, meydana getirmek
accord [ıko:d] anlaşma, uygunluk / akort / uymak
according to ....e göre
accordingly [ıko:dingli] uygun şekilde, gerektiği şekilde
accordion [ıko:diın] akordeon
account [ıkaunt] rapor, izahat, hesap
account addetmek, hesap vermek
accountancy [ıkauntınsi] muhasebecilik
accountant [ıkauntınt] muhasebeci

accumulate [ıkiu:miuleyt] toplamak, toplanmak, biriktirmek
accumulator [ıki:miuleytı] akümülatör
accuracy [ekiurisi] doğruluk / katilik
accurate [ekiurit] doğru, kat'î, kesin, tam
accusation [ekiu:zeyşın] suçlama
accuse [ıkiu:z] itham etmek, suçlamak
accustom [ıkastım] alıştırmak
accustomed [ıkastımd] alışık
ace [eys] kâğıt oyununda birli, as
ache [eyk] ağrımak / ağrı
achieve [ıçi:v] başarmak, elde etmek
achievement [ıçi:vmınt] başarı
acid [esid] asit / ekşi
acknowledge [eknolic] tasdik etmek, tanımak
acoustics [ıku:stiks] akustik, ses düzeni
acquaint [ıkweynt] bildirmek, tanıtmak
acquaintance [ıkweyntıns] bilgi, malûmat / tanıdık, aşina
acquire [ıkwayı] elde etmek, edinmek
acquit [ıkwit] suçlu bulmamak, beraat etmek
acre [eykı] İngiliz dönümü (4000 m²)
acrobat [ekrobet] cambaz, akrobat
across [ıkros] karşıdan karşıya, çapraz, öbür tarafa, bir taraftan öbür tarafa
act [ekt] iş, fiil / (piyes) perde / kanun / davranış
act harekette (davranışta) bulunmak
action [ekşın] hareket, iş
active [ektiv] faal, hareketli, etken (fiil), aktif
activity [ektiviti] faaliyet, meşgale, etkenlik
actor [ektı] aktör
actress [ektris] aktris
actual [ekçuıl] gerçek, hakiki
actually [ekçuıli] hakiki olarak, gerçekten
acute [ıkyu:t] keskin
A. D. [eydi:] Milattan sonra
adapt [ıdept] intibak ettir-

mek, uydurmak, tadil etmek
adaptation [edıpteyşın] adaptasyon, değiştirerek uydurma, uyarlama
add [ed] ilave etmek, toplamak
addict [edikt] müptela
addition [ıdişın] ilave, ek / toplama
additional [ıdişınıl] ilave, eklenen
address [ıdres] hitap / hitap etmek
address [ıdres] adres
adept [ıdept] mahir, usta
adequate [edikwit] uygun, münasip
adhere [ıdhiı] yapışmak
adhesion [ıdhi:jın] yapışma
adhesive [ıdhi:siv] yapıştırıcı, tutkal
adjacent [ıceysınt] bitişik
adjective [eciktiv] sıfat (dilbilgisinde)
adjoin [ıcoyn] bitişik olmak
adjourn [ıcö:n] tehir etmek, ertelemek
adjust [ıcast] doğrultmak / tadil etmek / ayarlamak
administer [ıdministı] idare etmek / (ilaç vs.) vermek
administration [ıdministreyşın] idare, hükümet
admirable [edmirıbıl] takdire değer
admiral [edmirıl] amiral
admire [ıdmayı] hayran olmak, çok beğenmek
admission [ıdmişın] giriş (bir yere) / itiraf
admissible [ıdmisıbıl] kabul olunabilen
admit [ıdmit] kabul etmek, içeri almak / itiraf etmek
admittance [ıdmitıns] giriş, kabul
adolescent [edılesınt] genç, yetişkin, delikanlı
adopt [ıdopt] benimsemek / evlat edinmek
adorable [ıdo:rıbıl] sevilecek, tapılacak, çok sevilecek
adore [ıdo:] taparcasına sevmek
adorn [ıdo:n] donatmak, süslemek
adult [ıdalt] [edalt] büyük, yetişkin
adultery [ıdaltıri] zina, evlilik dışı ilişki
advance [ıdva:ns] ilerleme,

terakki / avans
advance ilerlemek, ilerletmek
advantage [ıdva:ntic] avantaj, yarar
advantageous [ıdva:nticıs] yararlı, avantajlı
adventure [ıdvençı] macera, serüven
adverb [edvö:b] zarf (dilbilgisinde)
adversary [edvısıri] muhalif, düşman
adverse [edvö:s] karşı gelen, aksi
advertise [edvıtayz] ilan etmek
advertisement [ıdvö:tismınt] ilan, reklam
advice [ıdvays] öğüt
advise [ıdvayz] öğüt vermek / fikir vermek
adviser [ıdvayzı] müşavir, danışman
advocate [edvıkeyt] avukat, savunucul / savunmak
Aegean [i:ci:ın] Ege (Denizi)
aerial [eıriıl] havaî / anten
aeroplane [eıropleyn] uçak
aesthetics [i:stetiks] estetik
affair [ıfeı] iş, mesele, macera
affect [ıfekt] tesir etmek, etkilemek
affect gibi görünmek, yapmacık yapmak
affection [ıfekşın] sevgi
affirm [ıfö:m] doğrulamak
affirmative [ıfö:mıtiv] olumlu, müspet
afflict [ıflikt] acı vermek
afford [ıfo:d] bir şeyi yapmak veya almak için parası, zamanı vb. olmak
affront [ıfrant] (aleni) hakaret
afraid [ıfreyd] korkmuş, müteessir
afresh [ıfreş] yeniden
Africa [efrikı] Afrika
African Afrikalı
after [a:ftı] sonra, arkasından
afternoon [a:ftınu:n] öğleden sonra
afterwards [a:ftıwıdz] sonraları, sonra
again [ıgen, ıgeyn] tekrar, yine
against [ıgenst, ıgeynst] karşı, aleyhinde
age [eyc] yaş / çağ
ageless [eyclis] eskimez, değişmez, ölümsüz

agency [eycınsi] acente, vasıta
agenda [ıcendı] gündem
agent [eycınt] acente / fail, yapan
aggression [ıgreşın] saldırı
agile [ecayl] çevik
agitate [eciteyt] oynatmak, heyecan vermek
ago [ıgou] önce
agonizing [egınayzing] ıstırap veren
agony [egıni] şiddetli acı
agree [ıgri:] uyuşmak, razı olmak
agreeable [ıgriıbıl] hoş, uygun
agreement [ıgri:mınt] anlaşma, uyuşma
agriculture [egrikalçı] ziraat, tarım
ahead [ıhed] ileriye, ilerde
aid [eyd] yardım / yardım etmek
ail [eyl] rahatsız etmek / hastalanmak
ailment [eylmınt] hastalık
aim [eym] amaç, hedef / amaç edinmek / nişan almak
aimless [eymlis] amaçsız
air [eı] hava
air brake [eı breyk] hava freni
air conditioned [eıkındişınd] havalandırma tesisatlı
aircraft [eıkra:ft] uçak(lar)
airfield [eıfi:ld] havaalanı
air force [eıfo:s] hava kuvvetleri (askerî)
airline [eılayn] hava yolları
airmail [eımeyl] uçak postası
airplane [eıpleyn] uçak
airport [eıpo:t] havalimanı
air raid [eıreyd] hava hücumu
aisle [ayl] iki kısım koltuk arasında uzanan yol (sinema, otobüs, kilise)
alarm [ıla:m] tehlike işareti, alarm; **alarm clock** çalar saat
alas [ıla:s] maalesef, heyhat, yazık
Albania [elbeynyı] Arnavutluk
Albanian [elbeynyın] Arnavut
album [elbım] albüm
alcohol [elkıhol] alkol
ale [eyl] bira

alert [ılöt] dikkatli, tetik
algebra [elcebrı] cebir (matematik)
Algeria [elciıriı] Cezayir **-n** Cezayirli
alibi [elibay] suç işlendiği zaman başka yerde olduğunu ispat etme
alien [eylyın] yabancı
alight [ılayt] inmek, konmak / yanan, tutuşmuş
alike [ılayk] benzer, aynı şekilde
alimony [elimıni] nafaka
alive [ılayv] canlı, hayatta
all [o:l] bütün, sırf, hepsi, hep
allege [ılec] ileri sürmek, iddia etmek
allegory [eligıri] öğretici hikâye, kıssa
alley [eli] dar yol
alliance [ılayıns] ittifak, birleşme
allied [elayd] birleşik, müttefik
alligator [eligəytı] Amerikan timsahı
allocate [elokeyt] tahsis etmek, ödenek ayırmak
allot [ılot] pay dağıtmak, payını vermek
allow [ılau] müsaade etmek, izin vermek
allowance [ılauıns] tahsisat, istihkak
alloy [eloy] halita, alaşım
allude (to) [ılu:d] imâ etmek
allure [ıliu:ı] çekmek, cezbetmek, kandırmak
allusion [ılu:jın] imâ
ally [elay] müttefik
almanac [o:lmınek] almanak, yıllık, takvim
almighty [o:lmayti] Kadiri mutlak, Allah
almond [a:mınd] badem
almost [olmoust] hemen hemen
alms [a:mz] sadaka
alone [ıloun] yalnız, tek, sade
along [ılong] boyunca, uzunluğunca
aloud [ılaud] yüksek sesle, bağırarak
alphabet [elfıbet] alfabe
already [o:lredi] halihazırda, daha şimdiden
also [o:lsou] dahi, de, da, keza
alter [o:ltı] değiştirmek, değişmek
alteration [o:ltıreyşın] deği-

şiklik
alternate [o:ltö:nit] mütenavip, sırayla değişen
alternate [o:ltıneyt] sırayla değişmek
alternative [o:ltö:nıtiv] iki seçenek, alternatif
although [oldou] her ne kadar, ise de
altimeter [eltimi:tı] yükseklik ölçme aleti
altitude [eltityu:d] irtifa, yükseklik
altogether [oltıgedı] hep beraber, tamamen
aluminium [elyuminiyım] alüminyum
always [o:lweyz] daima, her zaman
am [em, ım] **"to be"** fiilinin **"I"** ile kullanılan şekli
a. m. [eyem] öğleden evvel
amateur [emıtö:] amatör
amaze [ımeyz] şaşırtmak
ambassador [ımbesıdı] büyük elçi
amber [embı] sarı, koyu sarı / amber, kehribar
ambiguity [embigiu:iti] müphemlik, belirsizlik
ambition [embişın] tutku, ihtiras
ambitious [embişıs] tutkulu, muhteris, hırslı
ambulance [embyulıns] hasta arabası
ambush [embuş] pusu / pusuya düşürmek
amen [a:men] amin (din)
amend [ımend] düzeltmek, ıslah etmek
America [ımerikı] Amerika
Amerikan [ımerikın] Amerikalı
amiable [eymiıbıl] cana yakın
amid [ımid] ortasında
ammonia [ımounyı] amonyak
ammunition [emiunişın] cephane
amnesty [emnisti] af
among [ımang] arasında
amongst [ımangst] arasında
amorous [emırıs] âşikane, sevdalı
amortize [emıtayz] amortise etmek
amount [ımaunt] miktar, tutar, toplam / baliğ olmak, o miktara varmak
ampere [empeı] amper
ample [empıl] bol, çok

amplifier [emplifayı] amplifikatör, kuvvetlendirici
amputate [empyuteyt] bir uzvu kesmek
amuse [ımiu:z] eğlendirmek
amusement [ımiuzmınt] eğlence
an [en, ın] (sesli harflerle başlayan isimler için) bir, herhangi bir
anaemia [ıni:miı] kansızlık, anemi
anaesthesia [eni:sti:ziı] anestezi, uyuşma
analogy [ınelıci] benzerlik, mukayese
analyse [enılayz] tahlil etmek, çözümlemek, analiz yapmak
analysis [ınelisis] analiz, çözümleme
anarchist [enıkist] anarşist
anarchy [enıki] anarşi
anatomy [ınetımi] anatomi, beden yapısı
ancestor [ensestı] ata
anchor [enkı] gemi demiri / demirlemek
anchovy [ençıvi] ançüez
ancient [eynşınt] (tarihte) çok eski
and [end, ınd] ve
anecdote [enikdout] fıkra, hikâye
angel [eyncıl] melek
anger [engı] öfke
anguish [engwiş] ıstırap
angle [engıl] açı
angry [engri] kızgın, öfkeli
angular [engyulı] köşeli
animal [enimıl] hayvan, hayvansal
animate [enimeyt] canlandırmak
annex [ıneks] eklemek
ankle [enkıl] ayak bileği
annihilate [ınayhileyt] imha etmek, yok etmek
anniversary [enivö:sıri] yıldönümü
announce [ınauns] haber vermek
announcer [ınaunsı] radyo spikeri
annoy [ınoy] kızdırmak
annual [enyuıl] yıllık
annul [ınal] iptal etmek
anonymous [ınonimıs] isimsiz, anonim
another [ınadı] diğer bir, başka, bir daha
answer [a:nsı] cevap / cevap vermek
ant [ent] karınca

antenna [entenı] anten
anthem [entım] milli marş
anthology [entoloci] antoloji
anti— [enti] e— karşı, düşman, muhalif, gayri anlamında önek
antibiotic [entibayotik] antibiyotik (tıp)
anticipate [entisipeyt] ummak, beklemek
antidote [entidout] zehire karşı ilaç (tıp)
antifreeze [entifri:z] antifriz
antipathy [entipıti] antipati
antiquarian [entikweırıın] antikacı / antikaya ait
antique [enti:k] antika
antiseptic [entiseptik] antiseptik (tıp)
antonym [entonim] zıt anlamda olan, karşıt
anvil [envil] örs
anxiety [engzayıti] endişe
anxious [enkşıs] endişeli, üzüntülü / hevesli
any [eni] herhangi bir
anybody [enibodi] biri, bir kimse
anyhow [enihau] nasıl olursa, ne olursa olsun
anyone [eniwan] biri, bir kimse
anything [eniting] herhangi bir şey
anyway [eniwey] ne olursa olsun
anywhere [eniweı] herhangi bir yer(de)
apart [ıpa:t] ayrı
apartment [ıpa:tmınt] daire (ev)
ape [eyp] maymun
apiece [ıpi:s] adam başına, birer birer
apologize [ıpolıcayz] özür dilemek
apology [ıpolıci] özür
apoplexy [epıpleksi] felç
apostrophe [ıpostrıfi] virgül, apostrof
appal [ıpo:l] korkutmak
apparatus [epıreytıs] alet, cihaz, aygıt
apparent [ıperınt] açık, belli, aşikâr
appeal [ıpi:l] cazibe / başvurmak / cezbetmek
appear [ıpiı] görünmek, meydana çıkmak
appendix [ıpendiks] ilave / kör barsak
appetite [epıtayt] iştah, istek, arzu

appetizer [epitayzı] iştah açıcı, meze
applaud [ıplo:d] alkışlamak, takdir etmek
applause [ıplo:z] alkış
apple [epıl] elma
appliance [ıplayıns] cihaz, aygıt
applicable [eplikıbıl] uygulanabilen, uygun olan
applicant [eplikınt] aday
application [eplikeyşın] kullanma, uygulama / dilekçe / müracaat
apply [ıplay] uygulamak / kullanmak / başvurmak
appoint [ıpoynt] tayin etmek / kararlaştırmak
appointment [ıpoyntmınt] tayin / iş / randevu
appreciate [ıpri:şieyt] takdir etmek, kıymetini bilmek
apprehend [eprihend] anlamak / tutuklamak
apprehension [eprihenşın] kuşku, kuruntu / anlayış / tutuklama
apprentice [ıprentis] çırak, stajyer
approach [ıprouç] yaklaşmak
appropriate [ıprouprieyt] uygun
approval [ıpru:vıl] onama, uygun bulma
approve [ıpru:v] onamak, uygun bulmak
approximate [ıproksimit] yaklaşık, aşağı yukarı
approximately [ıproksimitli] yaklaşık olarak, aşağı yukarı
apricot [eyprikot] kayısı
April [eypril] nisan
apron [eyprın] önlük
apt [ept] uygun / istidatlı, eğilimli
aptitude [eptityu:d] yetenek, eğilim
aquarium [ıkweıryım] akvaryum
Arab [erıb] Arap
Arabic [erıbik] Arapça
arc [a:k] kavis, yay
arcade [a:keyd] pasaj, üstü kapalı çarşı
arch [a:ç] kemer, tak
archaeology [a:kioloci] arkeoloji
archaic [a:keyik] modası geçmiş
architect [a:kitekt] mimar
architecture [a:kitekçı] mi-

marlık, mimarî
archives [a:ka:yvz] arşiv
arctic [a:ktik] kuzey kutbuna ait
ardent [a:dınt] ateşli, heyecanlı
are [a:] -dırlar, -sınız, -iz
area [eırii] alan, bölge
arena [ıri:nı] arena, boğa güreşi alanı
Argentina [a:cınti:nı] Arjantin
argue [a:giu:] tartışmak
argument [a:giu:mınt] tez, sav, fikir, tartışma
arise [ırayz] yükselmek / doğmak
aristocracy [eristokrısi] aristokrasi
arithmetic [eritmıtik] aritmetik
arm [a:m] kol / silah / silahlandırmak
armchair [a:mceı] koltuk
armistice [a:mistis] ateşkes
armour [a:mı] zırh
armpit [a:mpit] koltuk altı
army [a:mi] ordu
aroma [ıroumı] güzel koku
around [ıraund] etrafında
arouse [ırauz] uyandırmak, canlandırmak / teşvik etmek
arrange [ıreync] tertip etmek, düzenlemek
arrangement [ıreyncmınt] düzen, hazırlık / anlaşma
array [ırey] tanzim etmek, süslemek
arrest [ırest] tutuklama / tutuklamak
arrival [ırayvıl] varış
arrive [ırayv] vasıl olmak, varmak
arrogance [erıgıns] kibir, gurur
arrogant [erıgınt] kibirli
arrow [erou] ok
arsenic [a:sınik] arsenik
art [a:t] güzel sanat
artery [a:tıri] atardamar
artesian [a:tizyın] artezyen (kuyusu)
article [a:tikıl] makale / eşya, belirtici (dilbilgisinde)
artificial [a:tifişıl] sunî, yapma, yapay
artillery [a:tilıri] topçu, topçuluk
artist [a:tist] sanatkâr, ressam
artistic [a:tistik] sanatkârane
as [ez] gibi / kadar / olarak

/ iken
as a rule, genellikle
as if, sanki
as soon as, ...ince, ...ir ...mez (gelir gelmez)
ascend [ısend] yükselmek
ascertain [esıteyn] soruşturmak, sorup öğrenmek
ash [eş] kül
ashamed [ışeymd] mahçup, utanmış
ash-tray [eştrey] kül tablası
Asia [eyşı] Asya
aside [ısayd] kenara
ask [a:sk] sormak / istemek, rica etmek
asleep [ısli:p] uykuda
aspect [espekt] görünüş
asphalt [esfelt] asfalt
aspire [ıspayı] arzulamak
aspirin [espirin] aspirin
ass [es] eşek
assail [ıseyl] saldırmak
assassin [ısesin] suikastçı (resmî kişiye)
assault [ıso:lt] saldırı / saldırmak
assemble [ısembıl] toplamak / monte etmek
assent [ısent] onama / razı olmak
assert [ısö:t] iddia etmek
assess [ıses] kıymet biçmek, değerlendirmek
asset [eset] kâr, zimmet
assiduous [ısidyuıs] çalışkan, sebatkâr
assign [ısayn] tahsis etmek, ayırmak
assignment [ısaynmınt] tayin, atama / görev, ödev
assimilate [ısimileyt] hazmetmek, sindirmek
assist [ısist] yardım etmek
asistance [ısistıns] yardım
assistant [ısistınt] yardımcı
associate [ısouşieyt] birleştirmek / katılmak
associate [ısouşiit] ortak, ilişkili / tam hak sahibi olmayan üye
association [ısouşieyşın] birlik, dernek
assort [ıso:t] cinslerine göre ayırmak
assume [ısyu:m] (tavır) takınmak / farzetmek, var saymak
assumption [ısampşın] tavır takınma, / farzetme, var sayım
assurance [ışurıns] temin, teminat / sigorta
assure [ışuı] temin etmek,

garanti vermek
asterisk [estırisk] noktalamada (★) yıldız işareti
asthma [esmı] astım (tıp)
astonish [ıstoniş] şaşırtmak
astonishment [ıstonişmınt] hayret, şaşkınlık
astray [ıstrey] yoldan çıkmış
astrology [ıstroloci] müneccimlik
astronaut [estrınout] astronot
astronomer [ıstronomı] astronom
astronomy [ıstronımi] astronomi
astute [ıstyu:t] kurnaz
asylum [ısaylım] sığınak / tımarhane
at [et, ıt] ...de, ...da
ate [eyt] bak **eat**
atheism [eytiyizm] dinsizlik
athlete [etli:t] atlet, sporcu
Atlantic [ıtlentik] Atlas Okyanusu
atlas [etlıs] (coğrafya) atlas
atmosphere [etmısfiı] hava, atmosfer
atom [etım] atom
attach [ıteç] bağlamak
attaché [ıteşey] ateşe
attack [ıtek] saldırış, hücum / saldırmak
attain [ıteyn] erişmek, elde etmek
attempt [ıtempt] teşebbüs / teşebbüs etmek, kalkışmak
attend [ıtend] (derse, okula) devam etmek
attendance [ıtendıns] hazır bulunma
attention [ıtenşın] dikkat / ilgi gösterme
attentive [ıtentiv] dikkatli
attest [ıtest] tasdik etmek
attic [etik] çatı odası
attitude [etityu:d] vaziyet, tavır, tutum
attorney [ıtö:ni] vekil, avukat
attract [ıtrekt] çekmek, cezbetmek
attraction [ıtrekşın] ilgi çekici şey / çekicilik
attractive [ıtrektiv] çekici, cazip
attribute [etribyu:t] atfetmek, ona yormak
auburn [obın] kestane rengi (saç)
auction [o:kşın] açık arttırma ile satış, müzayede

audible [o:dibıl] duyulabilir
audience [o:dyıns] dinleyiciler, seyirciler (bir salonda)
auditorium [o:ditoriım] konferans salonu
August [o:gıst] ağustos
aunt [a:nt] teyze, hala
austere [o:styı] sert, haşin / süssüz
Australia [o:streylyı] Avustralya
Australian [ostreyliın] Avustralyalı
Austria [ostriı] Avusturya
Austrian [ostriın] Avusturyalı
author [o:tı] yazar
authority [o:toriti] selahiyet, otorite / makam / yetkili
authorize [o:tırayz] selahiyet vermek, yetki vermek
authentic [o:tentik] hakiki
autobiography [o:toubayogrıfi] otobiyografi
autocracy [o:tokrısi] istibdat
automatic [o:tımetik] otomatik
automobile [o:tımoubi:l] otomobil
autonomy [o:tonomi] özerklik
autopsy [o:topsi] otopsi
autumn [o:tım] sonbahar
auxiliary [o:gzilyıri] yardımcı (fiil)
available [ıveylıbıl] elde edilebilir, geçerli, var
avalanche [evıla:nş] çığ
avarice [evıris] para hırsı
avenge [ıvenc] öç almak
avenue [evınyu] geniş cadde, bulvar
average [evıric] vasat, vasati, ortalama / alelade
aversion [ıvö:şın] nefret
aviation [eyvieyşın] havacılık
avoid [ıvoyd] kaçınmak
await [ıweyt] beklemek
awake [ıweyk] uyanık / uyandırmak / uyanmak
award [ıwo:d] hüküm / ödül / ödül vermek
aware [ıweı] haberdar
away [ıwey] uzağa, uzakta / yok
awe [o:w] korku, saygı
awful [o:fıl] müthiş, korkunç
awhile [ıwayl] bir süre
awkward [o:kwıd] beceriksiz / kullanışsız / şaşkınlık yaratan

axe [eks] balta
axis [eksis] eksen
axle [eksıl] mil, aks
azure [ejur] gök mavisi

B

bable [bebıl] şırıldamak / şırıltı
baby [beybi] bebek
bachelor [beçılı] bekâr
bacillus [besilıs] basil
back geri, arka, sırt
back arka çıkmak, desteklemek
backbone [bekboun] belkemiği
backgammon [bekgemın] tavla oyunu
backward [bekwıd] geri / geriye doğru / gelişmemiş
background [bekgraund] arka plan / geçmiş
backwards [bekwıdz] geriye doğru
bacon [beykın] domuz pastarması
bacteria [bektiıriı] bakteriler
bad [bed] fena, kötü
badge [beç] rozet
badger [becı] porsuk
baffle [befıl] engel olmak, şaşırtmak
bag [beg] torba, çanta
baggage [begic] bagaj
baggy [begi] torba gibi
bail [beyl] kefalet / kefil
bait [beyt] olta yemi
bake [beyk] fırında pişirmek
baker [beykı] fırıncı
balance [belıns] denge / terazi
balcony [belkıni] balkon
bald [bo:ld] dazlak
bale [beyl] balya
ball [bo:l] top mermi / balo
ballerina [belıri:nı] balerin
ballet [beley] bale
balloon [bılu:n] balon
balm [ba:m] pelesenk / yatıştırıcı
balot [belıt] oy verme / oy pusulası
bamboo [bembu:] İngiliz kamışı
ban [ben] yasak / yasak etmek
banana [bına:nı] muz
band [bend] güruh, çete / bandaj / şerit, kuşak
bandage [bendic] sargı

bandit [bendit] haydut, eşkiya
bang [beng] patlama
banish [beniş] sürmek, kovmak
banister [benistı] tırabzan, merdiven kenarlığı
bank [benk] banka / nehir kıyısı / set / kanepe
banknote [benknout] kâğıt para
bankrupt [benkrapt] müflis, iflas etmiş
bankruptcy [benkrıptsi] iflas
banner [benı] bayrak
banquet [benkwit] ziyafet, şölen
bantam [bentım] ispenç
bar [ba:] çubuk / engel / baro / içki satılan yer / engel olmak
barbarian [ba:beyriın] barbar
barbarous [ba:bırıs] barbar, vahşi
barbed [ba:bıd] dikenli (tel)
barber [ba:bı] berber
bare [beı] çıplak / çorak
barely [beıli] sadece, ancak, zar zor
barefoot [beıfut] yalınayak
bareheaded [beıhedıd] açık başla, sapkasız
bargain [ba:gin] pazarlık etmek / pazarlık / kelepir
barge [ba:c] mavna
bark [ba:k] ağaç kabuğu / havlamak (köpek)
barley [ba:li] arpa
barn [ba:n] ambar
barometer [beromitı] barometre
baron [beron] baron
barrack(s) [berıks] kışla
barrage [bera:j] bend, baraj
barrel [berıl] varil
barren [berın] çorak, kısır
barricade [berikeyd] barikat
barrier [beriı] engel
barrister [beristı] avukat
barrow [berou] el arabası
barter [ba:tı] takas, takas yapmak
base [beys] esas, temel / üs / üzerine kurmak
baseball [beysbo:l] beyzbol oyunu
basement [beysmınt] bodrum katı
bashful [beşful] mahçup, utangaç
basic [beysik] esas, temel
basin [beysin] leğen, lavabo

basis [beysis] temel, prensip
bask [ba:sk] güneşlenmek
basket [ba:skit] sepet
basketball [ba:skibo:l] basketbol
bastard [ba:stıd] piç
bat [bet] yarasa / çomak / raket
bath [ba:t] yıkanmak / hamam, banyo
bathe [beyd] (nehir veya denizde) banyo yapmak / deniz banyosu
bathroom [ba:trum] banyo odası, banyo
battalion [bıtelyın] tabur
battery [betıri] batarya, pil
battle [betıl] muharebe / çarpışmak
battleship [betılşip] muharebe gemisi
bawl [bo:l] bağırmak
bay [bey] körfez / havlamak / defne
bayonet [beyınit] süngü
bazaar [bıza:] çarşı
B.C. (before Christ) [bi:si:] milattan önce
be [bi:] olmak
beach [bi:ç] kumsal, plaj
bead [bi:d] boncuk, tane, tespih tanesi
beak [bi:k] gaga
beam [bi:m] şua, ışın / kiriş, putrel / neşe saçmak
bean [bi:n] fasulye
bear (bore, borne) [beı, bo:, bo:n] taşımak / doğurmak / tahammül etmek / (meyva) vermek / ayı
beard [biıd] sakal
bearing [beıring] yatak (makinede) / tavır
beast [bi:st] (dört ayaklı, yabani) hayvan
beat (beat, beaten) [bi:t, bi:t, bi:tın] dövmek / çarpmak / vurmak / tempo
beautiful [biu:tifıl] güzel
beauty [biu:ti] güzellik / güzel kimse
beauty parlour [biu:ti pa:lı] güzellik salonu
because [bikoz] çünkü, yüzünden
beckon [bekın] (birine) işaret etmek
become (became, become) [bikam, bikeym, bikam] olmak / yakışmak
bed [bed] yatak, karyola
bedclothes [bedkloudz] yatak takımı

bedroom [bedrum] yatak odası
bee [bi:] arı
beef [bi:f] sığır eti
beefsteak [bi:fsteyk] biftek
beehive [bi:hayv] arı kovanı
been [bi:n] **be**'nin üçüncü şekli
beer [biı] bira
beet [bi:t] pancar
before [bifo:] önce, önünde, ...den önce
beforehand [bifo:hend] daha önce
before long [bifo: long] çok geçmeden
beg [beg] yalvarmak / dilenmek
began bak **begin**
beggar [begı] dilenci
begin (began, begun) [bigin, bigen, bigan] başlamak
beginner [biginı] acemi, yeni başlayan
begun bak **begin**
behalf [biha:f] namına, adına
behave [biheyv] davranmak
behaviour [biheyviı] tavır, davranış
behind [bihaynd] gerisinde, arkasında
behold [bihould] (fevkalade bir şey) görmek, bakmak
being [bi:ing] mevcudiyet, varlık, oluş
belch [belç] geğirmek
Belgian [belcın] Belçikalı
Belgium [belcım] Belçika
belief [bili:f] inanç
believe [bili:v] inanmak
bell [bel] çan, zil
bellow [belou] kükremek
bellows [belouz] körük
belly [beli] karın, göbek
belong [bilong] ait olmak
belongings [bilongingz] eşya, bir kimseye ait olan şeyler
beloved [bilavd] sevgili
below [bilou] aşağıda, altında
belt [belt] kayış, kemer
bench [benç] sıra, tezgâh
bend (bent, bent) [bend, bent, bent] eğilmek, eğmek / dönemeç
beneath [bini:t] altında
benefactor [benifektı] iyilik eden
benefit [benifit] yardım, yarar / yararlanmak
bent [bent] bak **bend**
beret [beret] bere

berry [beri] çekirdeksiz ve kabuksuz meyve
berth [bö:t] ranza
beseech [bisi:ç] yalvarmak
beside [bisayd] yanında / yanına
besides [bisaydz] buna ek olarak, de, da, yanısıra, buna ilaveten
besiege [bisi:c] kuşatmak
best [best] en iyi
bestow [bistou] vermek, hediye etmek
bet [bet] bahis / bahse girmek
betray [bitrey] ihanet etmek
betrayal [bitreyıl] ihanet etmek, ele vermek
better [betı] daha iyi
between [bitwi:n] (iki şey) arasında
beverage [bevıric] içilen şey
beware [biweı] sakınmak, uzak durmak
bewilder [biwildı] şaşırtmak
bewitch [biwiç] büyülemek
beyond [biyond] öteye, ötesinde
beyond doubt [biyond daut] şüphesiz
bias [bayıs] yanlamasına, verev / peşin hüküm, önyargı
biased [bayısd] ön yargı sahibi
Bible [baybıl] İncil
bibliography [bibliogrıfi] bibliyografya
bicycle [baysikıl] bisiklet
bib (bid, bidden) [bid, bid, bidın] emretmek / fiyat teklif etmek
bidding [biding] emir, kumanda / artırma
big [big] büyük
bigamy [bigımi] üstüne evlenme
bike [bayk] bisiklet
bile [bayl] safra
bilingual [baylingwıl] iki dilli
bill [bil] tasarı / hesap / afiş, ilan / kâğıt para / fatura
billiards [bilyıdz] bilardo
billion [bilyın] milyar
billow [bilou] büyük dalga
bin [bin] (çöp, kömür...) tenekesi
bind (bound, bound) [baynd, baund, baund] bağlamak / ciltlemek
binder [bayndı] mücellit
binoculars [binokyulız] dürbün

biography [bayogrıfi] biyografi
biology [bayolıci] biyoloji
bird [bö:d] kuş
birth [bö:t] doğum
birth control [bö:t kıntroul] doğum kontrolu
birthday [bö:tdey] doğum günü
birth-place [bö:tpleys] doğum yeri
birth rate [bö:t reyt] doğum oranı
biscuit [biskit] bisküvi
bishop [bişıp] piskopos
bit [bit] parça, kırıntı
bit bak **bite**
bitch [biç] dişi köpek
bite (bit, bitten) [bayt, bit, bitın] ısırmak / ısırış / lokma
biting [bayting] acı, yakıcı
bitter [bitı] şiddetli, keskin, acı
bitterness [bitınis] acılık, sertlik
black [blek] kara, siyah
blackboard [blekbo:d] yazı tahtası, karatahta
blacken [blekın] karartmak
blackmail [blekmeyl] şantaj / şantaj yapmak
black market, karaborsa
blacksmith [bleksmit] demirci, nalbant
bladder [bledı] sidik torbaśı
blade [bleyd] bıçak ağızı
blame [bleym] ayıplamak / kabahat, suç
blank [blenk] boş, yazısız / boşluk
blanket [blenkit] battaniye
blast [bla:st] patlama / patlamak
blaze [bleyz] alev, parlama / tutuşmak, parlamak
blazer [bleyzı] spor ceket, armalı ceket
bleach [bli:ç] beyazlatmak
bleak [bli:k] soğuk, çıplak
bleat [bli:t] melemek
bleed (bled, bled) [bli:d, bled, bled] kanamak
blemish [blemiş] kusur, leke / bozmak
blend [blend] (çay, vb.) harman / harmanlamak
bless (blessed, blest) [bles, blest, blest] Allahtan (birisi için) iyilik dilemek
blessed [blesid] mubarek
blessing [blesing] lütuf / dua

blest, bak **bless**
blew, bak **blow**
blind [blaynd] kör etmek / kör / stor, güneşlik
blind alley [blaynd eli] çıkmaz sokak
blink [blink] göz kırpıştırmak
bliss [blis] saadet
blister [blistı] kabarcık
blizzard [blizıd] tipi
block [blok] kütük, kaya vs. parçası / apartman bloku / arsa parçası / makara / tıkanma / tıkamak
blockade [blokeyd] abluka, kuşatma
blond(e) [blond] sarışın
blood [blad] kan
bloodshed [bladşed] kan dökme
bloodstone [bladstoun] kantaşı
bloody [bladi] kanlanmış / Allahın belası
bloom [blu:m] çiçek / çiçek açmak
blossom [blosım] (ağaç) çiçek açmak
blot [blot] leke / lekelemek
blouse [blauz] bulüz
blow (blew blown) [blou, blu: bloun] eşmek; üflemek / darbe, vuruş
blow up [blou ap] havaya uçurmak
blue [blu:] mavi
blues [blu:z] hüzünlü müzik
bluff [blaf] sarp / blöf
bluish [bluiş] mavimsi
blunder [blandı] hata, gaf
blunt [blant] kör (bıçak)
blur [blö:] bulaştırmak / net olmamak
blush [blaş] (yüzü) kızarmak
boa [bouı] boa yılanı
boar [bo:] erkek domuz
board [bo:d] tahta / yemek (pansiyonda) / yönetim / gemiye vs. binmek
board and lodging [bo:d ınd locing] yiyecek ve yatacak, pansiyon
boarder [bo:dı] pansiyoner
boarding school yatılı okul
boastful [boustful] öğütücü
boat [bout] sandal, kayık, gemi
bodice [bodis] korse
bodily [bodili] vücuda ilişkin, bedeni
body [bodi] vücut, beden, gövde

body guard [-ga:d] koruyucu
boil [boyl] çıban
boil kaynamak, kaynatmak
boiler [boylı] kazan
bold [bould] cesur / küstah / çarpıcı
boldly [bouldli] cesurca / küstahça / çarpıcı bir şekilde
bolt [boult] cıvata / kapı sürgüsü / kaçmak
bomb [bom] bomba
bombard [bomba:d] bombardıman etmek
bombastic [bombestik] tumturaklı
bond [bond] senet, bono / ilişki, bağ
bondage [bondic] kölelik
bone [boun] kemik
bonnet [bonit] çocuk veya kadın başlığı / araba kaputu
bonus [bounıs] ikramiye
bony [bouni] kemikli
boo [bu:] yuha / yuhalamak
book [buk] kitap / (yer, vs.) tutmak, bilet almak, yer ayırtmak
bookbinder [bukbayndı] mücellit
bookcase [bukkeys] kitap rafı
booking-clerk [buking kla:k] gişedeki biletçi
booking office [buking ofis] bilet gişesi
book-keeper [buk ki:pı] muhasebeci
booklet [buklit] kitapçık, broşür
bookseller [bukselı] kitapçı
bookshop [bukşop] kitapçı dükkanı
bookstall [buksto:l] kitap sergisi
boom [bu:m] gürleme, uğultu / büyük rağbet
boot [bu:t] ayakkabı, çizme
booth [bu:t] kulübe, baraka
bootlace [bu:tleys] ayakkabı bağı
booty [bu:ti] ganimet, yağma
border [bo:dı] sınır, kenar / bitişik olmak
bore bak **bear**
bore [bo:] delmek, sondaj yapmak / usandırmak, sıkmak / usandırıcı şey
boredom [bo:dım] can sıkıntısı
boring [bo:ring] can sıkıcı
born [bo:n] doğmuş

borne bak **bear**
borrow [borou] borç almak
borough [barı] kasaba
bosom [buzım] göğüs / kucak / yakın
Bosphorus [bosfırıs] Boğaziçi
boss [bos] patron
botany [botıni] botanik, bitki bilimi
both [bout] her ikisi de, her iki
bother [bodı] taciz etmek, canını sıkmak / zahmet etmek
bottle [botıl] şişe
bottom [botım] dip, kıç
bough [bau] dal
bought, bak **buy**
boulder [bouldı] kaya
bounce [bauns] zıplama / zıplamak
bound [baund] hudut, sınır / sınırlamak / sıçramak / gitmeğe hazır (gemi vs.) / ciltli
boundary [baundıri] hudut
bow [bou] yay, kavis / [bau] eğilme / eğilmek
bowels [bauılz] kalın bağırsak
bowl [boul] kâse, çanak
bowler [boulı] melon şapka
box [boks] kutu / loca / boks yapmak
boxer [boksı] boksör
box office [boks ofis] tiyatro (sinema) gişesi
boy [boy] (erkek) çocuk, oğlan
boycott [boykot] boykot
boyhood [boyhud] (erkek) çocukluk çağı
boyish [boyiş] çocukca, çocuk gibi
boy scout [boy skaut] izci
bra [bra:] sütyen
bracelet [breyslit] bilezik
braces [breysiz] pantalon askısı
bracket [brekit] parantez / parantez içine almak
brag [breg] övünmek
brain [breyn] beyin, dimağ, akıl
brainless [breynlis] ahmak, beyinsiz
brake [breyk] fren
branch [bra:nç] dal / şube
brand [brend] damga, marka / çeşit
brand new [brendniyu:] yepyeni
brandy [brendi] kanyak

brass [bra:s] pirinç (maden)
brassiere [breziı] sütyen
brat [bret] yumurcak
brave [breyv] cesur
brawl [bro:l] kavga
bray [brey] anırmak
brazier [breyziı] mangal
Brazil [brızil] Brezilya
Brazilian [brızilyın] Brezilyalı
breach [bri:ç] kırık, kırma / gedik açmak
bread [bred] ekmek
breadth [bredt] genişlik
break (broke, broken) [breyk, brouk, broukın] kırmak, kırılmak / bozmak / fasıla, ara
breakdown [breykdaun] bozulma, arıza
breakfast [brekfıst] sabah kahvaltısı
breakwater [breykwo:tı] mendirek, dalgakıran
breast [brest] göğüs, meme
breath [bret] nefes, nefes alma
breathe [bri:d] nefes almak, solumak
breeches [bri:çiz] kısa erkek pantalonu
bred bak **breed**
breed (bred, bred) [bri:d, bred, bred] yavrulamak / yetiştirmek, beslemek / cins
breeze [bri:z] meltem
brewery [bru:ıri] bira fabrikası
bribe [brayb] rüşvet
brick [brik] tuğla
bride [brayd] gelin
bridegroom [braydgrum] güvey, damat
bridge [bric] köprü / biriç (oyunu)
bridle [braydıl] yular
brief [bri:f] kısa
brigade [brigeyd] tugay
brigand [brigınd] eşkiya / haydut
bright [brayt] parlak / zeki
brighten [braytın] parlatmak
brilliance [brilyıns] parlaklık, şaşaa
brilliant [brilyınt] pırlanta
brim [brim] kenar, ağız
bring (brought, brought) [bring, bro:t, bro:t] getirmek
brink [brink] kenar
brisk [brisk] faal, canlı
Britain [britın] Britanya
British [britiş] İngiliz

brittle [britıl] gevrek
broad [bro:d] geniş
broadcast [bro:dka:st] radyo yayını / radyo ile yayınlamak
broaden [bro:dın] genişletmek
brochure [brouşuı] broşür
broil [broyl] kavga, gürültü
broke, broken bak **break**
broken [broukın] kırık
broker [broukı] simsar
bronchitis [bronkaytis] bronşit
bronze [bronz] tunç
brooch [brouç] broş
brood [bru:d] kuluçkaya yatmak / kara kara düşünmek
brook [bruk] dere, ırmak
broom [bru:m] süpürge
broth [brot] et suyu
brothel [brotıl] genelev
brother [bradı] erkek kardeş, birader
brought bak **bring**
brow [brau] alın
brown [braun] kahverengi
bruise [bru:z] bere, çürük
brush [braş] fırça / fırçalamak
brutal [bru:tıl] zalim, vahşi
brute [bru:t] hayvan / canavar / kaba
bubble [babıl] hava kabarcıkları yapmak / hava kabarcığı
bucket [bakit] kova
buckle [bakıl] toka, kopça / kopçalamak
bud [bad] konca / tomurcuklanmak
budget [bacit] bütçe
buffalo [bafılou] manda
buffer [bafı] tampon
buffet [bufey] büfe
bug [bag] tahtakurusu
bugle [biu:gıl] borazan
build (built, built) [bild, bilt, bilt] inşa etmek, kurmak
building [bilding] bina
bulb [balb] elektrik ampulü / çiçek soğanı
Bulgaria [balgeıriı] Bulgaristan
bulge [balc] dışarı fırlamak, şiş yapmak
bulk [balk] hacim, cüsse
bull [bul] boğa
bulldozer [buldouzı] buldozer
bullet [bulit] mermi
bulletin [bulıtin] bülten
bum [bam] tembel, işe yara-

maz, serseri / kıç
bump [bamp] çarpma, sarsıntı / şiş / çarpmak, sarsılmak
bumper [bampı] otomobil tamponu
bumpy [bampi] yamrı yumru, çıkıntılı
bun [ban] kuru üzümlü kek
bunch [banş] salkım, demet
bundle [bandıl] çıkın, deste
bungalow [bangılou] tek katlı kır evi
buoy [boy] şamandıra
burden [bö:dın] yük
bureau [biurou] yazıhane, büro
bureaucracy [biuırokrısi] kırtasiyecilik, bürokrasi
burglar [bö:glı] hırsız (ev, dükkân soyan)
burial [beriıl] defnetme, gömme
burly [bö:li] iriyarı
burn (burnt, burnt) [bö:n, bö:nt, bö:nt] yakmak, yanmak / yanık (yer)
burst [bö:st] patlamak / birden olmak / patlama
bury [beri] gömmek, defnetmek
bus [bas] otobüs
bush [buş] çalı, fidan
bushy [buşi] çalılık
business [biznis] iş, meşguliyet, görev / ticaret
bust [bast] büst
bustle [basıl] telaşlı faaliyet / telaş etmek
busy [bizi] meşgul / işlek
but [bat] fakat
butcher [buçı] kasap
butt [bat] dipçik / tos / tos vurmak / fıçı
butter [batı] tereyağı
butterfly [batıflay] kelebek
buttermilk [batımilk] yayık ayranı
button [batın] düğme / düğmelemek
buttonhole [batınhoul] ilik
buy (bought, bought) [bay, bo:t, bo:t] satın almak
buyer [bayı] satın alıcı
buzz [baz] vızıltı / vızıldamak
by [bay] tarafından / yanında / ile, vasıtasıyla / göre
bye-bye [baybay] Allahaısmarladık, güle güle
bystander [baystendı] seyirci, uzaktan bakan

C

cab [keb] taksi
cabaret [kebırey] kabare
cabbage [kebic] lahana
cabin [kebin] kamara / kulübe
cabinet [kebinit] dolap / kabine, bakanlar kurulu
cabinet maker [kebinit meykı] marangoz, mobilyacı
cable [keybıl] halat / kablo / telgraf
cadet [kıdet] harb okulu öğrencisi
café [kefey] çayhane, kahvehane, küçük lokanta
cafeteria [kefitiırıı] kafeterya
cage [keyc] kafes
cake [keyk] pasta, kek
clamity [kılemiti] felaket
calculate [kelkiuleyt] hesaplamak
calendar [kelindı] takvim
calf [ka:f] dana / baldır
calibre [kelibı] çap / değer
call [ko:l] isimlendirmek / seslenmek / ziyaret etmek / telefon etmek / çağırma, bağırma / ziyaret
calm [ka:m] sakin, durgun
calorie [kelıri] kalori
came bak **come**
camel [kemıl] deve
camera [kemırı] fotoğraf makinesi
camouflage [kemufla:j] örtmek, kamufle etmek / kamuflaj
camp [kemp] kamp / kamp kurmak
campaign [kempeyn] kampanya
can [ken, kın] muktedir olmak, ...bilmek / maşrapa / teneke kutu
Canada [kenıdı] Kanada
Canadian [kıneydyın] Kanadalı
canal [kınel] kanal
canary [kıneıri] kanarya
cancel [kensıl] feshetmek, iptal etmek
cancer [kensı] kanser / yengeç burcu
candid [kendid] samimi, açık konuşan
candidate [kendideyt] namzet, aday
candle [kendıl] mum
candlestick [kendılstik]

şamdan
candy [kendi] şekerleme
cane [keyn] değnek, kamış
cannibal [kenibıl] yamyam
cannon [kenın] top (askeri)
canoe [kınu:] tek kürekli kayık, kano
canteen [kenti:n] kantin
canvas [kenvıs] çadır bezi / kanaviçe
cap [kep] kep, kasket / kapak
capability [keypıbiliti] yetenek, kabiliyet
capable [keypıbıl] yetenekli, kabiliyetli
capacious [kıpeyşıs] geniş kapasiteli
capacity [kıpesiti] kapasite, yetenek
cape [keyp] (coğrafyada) burun / pelerin
capital [kepitıl] başkent / sermaye / büyük harf
capitalism [kepitılizm] kapitalizm
caprice [kıpri:s] kapris
capricious [kıprişıs] kaprisli
capricorn [kepriko:n] oğlak dönencesi, oğlak burcu
capsule [kepsiul] kapsül
captain [keptin] kaptan / yüzbaşı
captivate [keptiveyt] cezbetmek, büyülemek
captive [keptiv] esir
capture [kepçı] esir almak / zaptetmek
car [ka:] otomobil
caravan [kerıven] kervan
carbon [ka:bın] karbon
carbon paper kopya kâğıdı
carburettor [ka:biuretı] karbüratör
carcass [ka:kıs] ceset (hayvan)
card [ka:d] kart / iskambil
cardboard [ka:dbo:d] karton
cardigan [ka:digın] örgü ceket, hırka
cardinal [ka:dinıl] kardinal / esaslı
care [keı] kaygı, üzüntü / özen / bakım / aldırmak, umursamak / canı istemek
career [kıriı] meslek
carefree [keıfri:] kaygısız
careful [keıfıl] dikkatli
careless [keılis] dikkatsiz
caress [kıres] okşama / okşamak
caretaker [keıteykı] ev bekçisi

cargo [ka:gou] hamule, yük
caricature [kerikıtiuı] karikatür
carnation [ka:neyşın] karanfil
carnival [ka:nivıl] karnaval
carp [ka:p] sazan balığı
carpenter [ka:pintı] dülger, marangoz
carpet [ka:pit] halı
carriage [keric] araba / nakliye, taşıma
carrier [keriı] taşıyıcı
carrot [kerıt] havuç
carry [keri] taşımak, nakletmek
cart [ka:t] atlı yük arabası
carton [ka:tın] mukavva, karton kutu
cartoon [ka:tu:n] karikatür
cartridge [ka:tric] fişek / kaset
cart-wheel [ka:twi:l] araba tekerleği
carve [ka:v] oymak
cascade [keskeyd] çağlayan
case [keys] durum / vaka / kılıf
cash [keş] nakit para / peşin
cashier [keşiı] kasadar
casino [kısi:nou] gazino, kumarhane
cask [ka:sk] fıçı
cast [ka:st] atmak, saçmak / rol dağıtmak / atış / bir piyesin kişileri / demir dökme
castle [ka:sıl] hisar / şato
castor [ka:stı] tuzluk, biberlik
castor oil [ka:stı oyl] hintyağı
casual [kejiuıl] rastgele
casualty [kejuılti] kaza / zayiat
cat [ket] kedı
catalogue [ketılog] katalog
catapult [ketıpalt] sapan
cataract [ketırekt] katarakt / çağlayan
catastrophe [kıtestrıfi] felaket
catch, (caught, caught) [keç, ko:t, kot] yetişmek / yakalamak, tutmak
category [ketıgıri] kategori, sınıf
cater [keytı] beslemek / yemek vermek
caterpillar [ketıpilı] tırtıl
cathedral [kıti:drıl] büyük kilise
catholic [ketılik] katolik

cattle [ketıl] sığır
caught bak **catch**
cauldron [ko:ldrın] kazan
cauliflower [koliflauı] karnabahar
cause [ko:z] neden, sebep / dava / sebep olmak
caution [ko:şın] dikkat, tedbir / ikaz etmek
cautious [ko:şıs] ihtiyatlı
cavalry [kevılri] süvari
cave [keyv] mağara
caviar [kevia:] havyar
cavity [keviti] oyuk, boşluk
cease [si:s] durmak / bitmek / kesilmek
ceiling [si:ling] tavan
celebrate [selibreyt] kutlamak
celebrated [selibreytid] meşhur, ünlü
celebrity [silebriti] şöhretli kişi
celery [selıri] kereviz
celestial [silestiıl] ilahî / göğe ait
cell [sel] hücre / küçük oda
cellar [selı] mahzen
cement [siment] çimento / tutkal
cemetery [semitri] mezarlık
censor [sensı] sansür yapan / sansür etmek
censure [senşı] tenkit etmek, eleştirmek
census [sensıs] nüfus sayımı
cent [sent] yüzde / doların yüzde biri
centenary [sentınıri] yüz yıllık, yüzüncü yıl
centigrade [sentigreyd] santigrad
centimeter [sentimi:tı] santimetre
centipede [sentipi:d] kırkayak
central [sentrıl] merkez, merkezi
centre [sentı] merkez
centrifugal [sentrifiugıl] merkezkaç
century [sençıri] asır, yüzyıl
ceramics [seremiks] seramik
cereal [siıriıl] hububat
cerebral [serebrıl] beyine ait
ceremony [serimıni] tören
certain [sö:tin] belli / muhakkak / emin
certainly [sö:tinli] elbette
certainty [sö:tinti] kesinlik
certificate [sö:tifikit] belge, vesika, sertifika

certify [sö:tifay] doğrulamak, tasdik etmek, onaylamak
chagrin [şegrin] iç sıkıntısı
chain [çeyn] zincir
chair [çeı] sandalye
chairman [çeımın] başkan (toplantıda), kürsü başkanı
chalk [ço:k] tebeşir
challenge [çelinc] meydan okumak
chamber [çeymbı] oda / meclis
Chamber of Commerce [çeymbı ıv komö:s] Ticaret Odası
champagne [şempeyn] şampanya
champion [çempiın] şampiyon
chance [ça:ns] fırsat, ihtimal, şans
chandelier [şendıliı] avize
change [çeync] değişiklik / değiştirmek / değişmek / bozuk para
channel [çenıl] kanal, geçit
chaos [keyos] karmakarışık hal, kaos
chap [çep] arkadaş / adam
chapel [çepıl] küçük kilise
chapter [çeptı] bölüm, kısım
character [keriktı] vasıf, karakter
characteristic [keriktıristik] özellik, hususiyet, karakteristik
charcoal [ça:koul] mangal kömürü
charge [ça:c] itham, suçlama / sorumluluk / görev / şarj / harcama / suçlamak / fiyat koymak / hücüm etmek / şarj etmek, doldurmak
charitable [çeritıbıl] hayırsever
charity [çeriti] iyilik, merhamet / bağış
charm [ça:m] cazibe / tılsım / cezbetmek
charming [ça:ming] çekici, güzel, hoş
charter [ça:tı] imtiyaz, patent / (gemi, uçak) kiralama
charwoman [ça:wumın] temizlikçi kadın
chase [çeys] kovalamak
chassis [şesi] şasi
chaste [çeyst] iffetli
chat [çet] sohbet / sohbet etmek

chatter [çetı] çene çalmak
cheap [çi:p] ucuz / âdi
cheat [çi:t] dolandırmak / kopya çekmek (sınavda) / hilekâr / hile
check [çek] kontrol etmek / durdurmak / kontrol
check in [çek in] (otele, havaalanına) gelişini kaydettirmek
check out [çek aut] (otelden) ayrılma zamanı
checkers [çekız] dama
cheek [çi:k] yanak / küstahlık
cheer [çiı] neşe / alkışlamak
cheerful [çiıfıl] neşeli
cheese [çi:z] peynir
chemical [kemikıl] kimyevi, kimyasal
chemist [kemist] eczacı, kimyager
chemistry kimya
cheque [çek] çek (banka)
cherry [çeri] kiraz
chess [çes] satranç
chest [çest] göğüs / sandık
chestnut [çesnat] kestane
chew [çu:] çiğnemek
chewing gum [çuing gam] çiklet
chick [çik] civciv
chicken [çikin] piliç / tavuk eti
chickenpox [çikinpoks] su çiçeği hastalığı
chief [çi:f] başlıca, esas / şef
chiefly [çi:fli] başlıca, bilhassa, özellikle
child [çayld] çocuk
childhood [çayldhud] çocukluk
childish [çayldiş] çocukça
children [çildrın] çocuklar
chill [çil] soğuk algınlığı
chimney [çimni] baca
chin [çin] çene
China [çaynı] Çin / çini
Chinese [çayni:z] Çinli, Çince
chip [çip] küçük parça, kırıntı / kızarmış patates / çentmek
chocolate [çoklit] çikolata
chirp [çö:p] cıvıldamak
choice [çoys] seçme, tercih / çeşit / seçkin
choir [kwayı] koro
choke [çouk] tıkanma, boğulma / tıkanmak / boğmak
cholera [kolırı] kolera
choose (chose, chosen)

[çu:z, çouz, çouzın] seçmek
chop [çop] pirzola / doğramak
chord [ko:d] tel / akord
chorus [korıs] koro
chose, chosen bak **choose**
Christ [krayst] İsa
Christian [kristyın] Hıristiyan
Christmas [krismıs] Noel
chrome (chromium) [kroum] [kroumyım] krom
chronic [kronik] müzmin, devamlı
chronology [kronoloci] hadiseleri tarih sırasına göre veren cetvel
chuckle [çakıl] kendi kendine gülmek
chum [çam] ahbap
church [çö:ç] kilise
churn [çö:n] yayık
cigar [siga:] sigar, puro
cigarette [sigıret] sigara
cinema [sinımı] sinema
cipher [sayfı] sıfır / şifre
circle [sö:kıl] daire / çevre / etrafını dönmek
circuit [sö:kit] dolaşım / (elektrik) devre
circular [sö:kyulı] dairevî / tâmim, genelge, sirküler
circulate [sö:kyuleyt] dolaştırmak / dolaşmak
circumcise [sö:kımsayz] sünnet etmek
circumstance [sö:kımstıns] hal, durum, koşul
circus [sö:kıs] sirk
cistern [sistö:n] sarnıç
citizen [sitizın] yurttaş / hemşehri
city [siti] şehir, kent
civic [sivik] şehre ait
civil [sivil] medeni, uygar / sivil / terbiyeli
civilian [siviliın] sivil
civilize [sivilayz] medenileştirmek
civilized [sivilayzd] uygar
civilization [sivilizeyşın] medeniyet, uygarlık
claim [kleym] hakkını isteme / hak iddia etmek
clamp [klemp] mengene, kenet
clan [klen] kabile, klan
clang [kleng] çınlamak / çınlatmak
clap [klep] el çırpma / el çırpmak, alkışlamak
clarify [klerifay] tasfiye etmek / izah etmek
clash [kleş] çarpma / çar-

pışmak

clasp [kla:sp] toka / kavramak / bağlamak

class [kla:s] sınıf, sosyal sınıf, / çeşit, tür

classic [klesik] değerli eser, klasik

classification [klesifikeyşın] tasnif, sınıflama

classify [klesifay] sınıflamak

classmate [kla:smeyt] sınıf arkadaşı

classroom [kla:srum] sınıf

clatter [kletı] takırtı / takırdamak

clause [klo:z] ibare, yan cümle (dilbilgisi) / fıkra, madde

claw [klo:] pençe

clay [kley] kil

clean [kli:n] temiz / temizlemek

clear [kliı] açık / berraklaşmak, temizlemek

clearly [kliıli] açık bir şekilde

cleft bak **cleave**

clench [klenç] sıkmak, sıkıca tutmak

clerk [kla:k] kâtip

clever [klevı] zeki

click [klik] çatırtı / takırdamak

client [klayınt] müvekkil, müşteri

cliff [klif] uçurum, kayalık

climate [klaymit] iklim

climax [klaymeks] en yüksek derece, doruk

climb [klaym] tırmanmak

cling (clung, clung) [kling, klang, klang] sarılmak, tutunmak

clinic [klinik] klinik

clink [klink] tıklama

clip [klip] kırkma / kırpmak / kesmek / raptiye

clippers [klipız] saç tıraş makinası / tırnak makası

cloak [klouk] pelerin

cloakroom, vestiyer

clock [klok] saat (duvar, masa saati v.s.) / saati söylerken kullanılan "saat" sözcüğü

clog [klog] takunya / tıkamak

close [klous] kapalı / yakın, bitişik / candan / dar

close [klouz] kapatmak / sona ermek

closet [klozit] hela / gardrop

cloth [klot] kumaş, bez

clothe [kloud] giydirmek
clothes [kloudz] elbise
clothing [klouding] giyim
cloud [klaud] bulut
cloudy [klaudi] bulutlu
clover [klouvı] yonca
clown [klaun] palyaço
club [klab] kulüp / sopa
clue [klu:] ipucu
clump [klamp] küme
clumsy [klamzi] hantal, sakar
cluster [klastı] salkım, küme
clutch [klaç] kavrama / kavramak, tutmak / debreyaj
Co. (company) [kampıni] şirket
c/o (care of...) eli ile (mektup v.s.)
coach [kouç] yolcu arabası, vagon / antrenör
coal [koul] maden kömürü
coalition [kouılişın] birleşme, koalisyon
coarse [ko:s] kaba
coast [koust] sahil, kıyı
coat [kout] ceket / kaplamak
cobra [kobrı] kobra yılanı
cobwed [kobweb] örümcek ağı
cocaine [koukeyn] kokain
cock [kok] horoz / tetik (tüfekte)
cockpit [kokpit] pilot yeri
cocktail [kokteyl] kokteyl
coconut [koukonat] Hindistan çevizi
cocoon [koku:n] koza
code [koud] şifre / kanunlar
co-education [kouediukeyşın] kız erkek karışık öğretim
coffee [kofi] kahve
coffin [kofin] tabut
cohere [kouhiı] yapışmak, birbirini tutmak
coherent [kouhiırınt] birbirini tutan
coil [koyl] kangal, bobin, spiral
coin [koyn] sikke, madeni para
coincide [koinsayd] tesadüf etmek / uymak
Col (colonel) [kö:nıl] albay
cold [kould] soğuk / soğuk algınlığı, nezle
collaborate [kılebıreyt] işbirliği yapmak
collaboration [kılebıreyşın] işbirliği
collapse [kıleps] çökmek, yıkılmak

collar [kolı] yaka, tasma
colleague [koli:g] meslekdaş
collect [kılekt] toplamak, biriktirmek
collection [kılekşın] koleksiyon
college [kolic] yüksek okul
collide [kılayd] çarpmak, çarpışmak
collision [kılijın] çarpma
colloquial [kıloukwiıl] konuşma diline ait (deyim, tabir v.s.)
colon [koulın] iki nokta üstüste
colonel [kö:nıl] albay
colony [kolıni] sömürge / yerleşenler
colour [kalı] renk / boyamak
coloured [kalıd] renkli / zenci
colourful [kalıfıl] renkli
colourless [kalılis] renksiz, soluk
colt [koult] tay
column [kolım] sütun, direk, kolon
comb [koum] tarak / taramak
combat [kombet] muharebe / mücadele etmek
combination [kombineyşın] birlik, birleşme
combine [kımbayn] birleşmek / birleştirmek
combustion [kımbasçın] yanma, tutuşma
come (came, come) [kam, keym, kam] gelmek
comedian [kımi:diın] komedi aktörü
comedy [komıdi] komedi
comet [komit] kuyruklu yıldız
comfort [kamfıt] ferahlık / konfor / teselli etmek
comfortable [kamfıtıbıl] rahat, konforlu
comic [komik] komik
coming [kaming] gelecek / varış / gelen
comma [komı] virgül
command [kıma:nd] emir / idare / emretmek, kumanda etmek
commander [kıma:ndı] kumandan
commemorate [kımemıreyt] kutlamak, anmak
commence [kımens] başlamak
commend [kımend] övmek, tavsiye etmek

comment [koment] yorum / açıklama, mütalâa / fikrini söylemek
commentary [komınteri] yorum
commerce [komö:s] ticaret
commercial [kımö:şıl] ticari
commission [kımişın] görev / hizmet / kurul, komisyon / yüzdelik
commit [kımit] yapmak, işlemek / teslim etmek, emanet etmek
committee [kımiti] heyet, komite
commodity [kımoditi] mal, alıp satılan şey
common [komın] herkese ait, genel, alelade
commonly [komınli] genellikle
common sense [komınsens] sağduyu, aklıselim
Commonwealth [komınwelt] İngiliz İmparatorluğu
commotion [kımouşın] karışıklık, heyecan
communal [komyu:nıl] ortak
communicate [kımyu:nikeyt] nakletmek / tebliğ etmek
communism [komyunizm] komünizm
community [komyu:niti] cemiyet, toplum
compact [kımpekt] pudralık / sıkı, toplu
companion [kımpeniın] arkadaş, yoldaş
company [kampıni] şirket / bölük / refakat, eşlik
compare [kımpeı] karşılaştırmak
comparison [kımperisın] karşılaştırma
compartment [kımpa:tmınt] bölme / kompartıman
compass [kampıs] pusula
compasses [kampısiz] pergel
compassion [kımpeşın] merhamet
compassionate [kımpeşınit] merhametli
compatriot [kımpetriıt] vatandaş
compel [kımpel] mecbur etmek, zorlamak
compensate [kompınseyt] tazmin etmek, telafi etmek
competence [kompitıns]

maharet, yeterlik
competition [kompitişın] rekabet, yarışma
competitor [kımpetitı] müsabık, yarışmacı
compile [kımpayl] (yazı) derlemek
complain [kımpleyn] şikayet etmek
complaint [kımpleynt] şikâyet
complement [komplimınt] tamamlayıcı, tümleç
complete [kımpli:t] tam / tamamlamak
complex [kompleks] birçok kısımlardan oluşan, karışık
complexion [kımplekşın] ten (rengi)
complicate [komplikeyt] karıştırmak
complicated [komplikeytid] karışık, komplike
compliment [komplimınt] iltifat
comply [kımplay] razı olmak, uymak
component [kımpounınt] parça (bir bütünün)
compose [kımpouz] meydana getirmek / yazmak / bestelemek
composer [kımpouzı] besteci
composition [kompızişın] yazma, kompozisyon / terkip, bileşim
compositor [kımpozitı] mürettip / kompozitör
compound [kımpaund] tertip etmek / [kompaund] bileşim
comprehend [komprihend] anlamak / içine almak
comprehensible [komprihensibıl] anlaşılabilir
compress [kompres] kompres / sıkmak, teksif etmek, yoğunlaştırmak
compromise [komprımayz] uzlaşma / uzlaşmaya varmak / tehlikeye atmak
compulsion [kımpalşın] zorlama
compulsory [kımpalsıri] zorunlu
compute [kımpyu:t] hesap yapmak, hesaplamak
computer [kımpyu:tı] elektronik hesap makinesi, bilgisayar
comrade [komrid] arkadaş, yoldaş

concave [konkeyv] çukur, içbükey
conceal [kınsi:l] gizlemek
conceit [kınsi:t] kibir
conceivable [kınsi:vıbıl] akla uygun, makul
conceive [kınsi:v] düşünmek, tasavvur etmek / gebe kalmak
concentrate [konsıntreyt] bir noktada toplamak
concentration [konsıntreyşın] bir yere toplama / aklı bir noktada toplama
concept [konsept] kavram / fikir
concern [kınsö:n] ilgili olmak, ilgilendirmek / ilişkin / kuşku
concert [konsıt] konser
concession [kınseşın] imtiyaz, ayrıcalık
concise [kınsays] kısa, özlü
conclude [kınklu:d] sonuca varmak
conclusion [kınklu:jın] netice, sonuç
concord [konko:d] uygunluk, barış
concrete [konkri:t] müşahhas, somut / beton
concur [kınkö:] uyuşmak, razı olmak
condemn [kındem] mahkûm etmek
condense [kındens] yoğunlaştırmak
condition [kındişın] şart, koşul / durum
conditional [kındişınıl] şarta bağlı
condole [kındoul] teselli etmek, avutmak
conduct [kondıkt] davranış
conduct [kındakt] rehberlik etmek / yapmak / icra etmek / yönetmek
cone [koun] koni
confectionery [kınfekşınıri] şekerlemeler
confederate [kınfedırit] müttefik, birleşmiş
confer [kınfö:] müzakere etmek, görüşmek
conference [konfırıns] konferans
confess [kınfes] itiraf etmek, kabul etmek
confession [kınfeşın] itiraf
confidant [konfident] sırdaş
confide [kınfayd] (sır vs.) tevdi etmek, sır vermek, güvenmek

confidence [konfidıns] güven, itimat, emniyet / mahremiyet, gizlilik
confident [konfidınt] emin, güvenilir
confidential [konfidenşıl] mahrem, gizli
confine [kınfayn] hapsetmek, kapatmak
confirm [kınfö:m] onaylamak, tasdik etmek
confiscate [konfiskeyt] el koymak
conflict [konflikt] mücadele
conform [kınfo:m] uymak
confront [kınfrant] karşı gelmek, yüzleştirmek
confuse [kınfiu:z] şaşırtmak, karıştırmak
confusion [kınfiu:jın] karışıklık / şaşkınlık
congratulate [kıngretiu:leyt] tebrik etmek
congregate [kongrigeyt] toplanmak
congregation [kongrigeyşın] toplantı / cemaat
congress [kongres] kongre
conic [konik] konik
conjecture [kıncekçı] tahmin / tahmin etmek
conjugate [koncyugeyt] fiilin çekimini yapmak
conjunction [kıncankşın] birleşme / bağlaç
connect [kınekt] birleştirmek, bağlamak
connection [kınekşın] bağ, ilişki, bağlantı
conquer [konkı] fethetmek, altetmek
conqueror [konkırı] fatih
conquest [konkwest] fethetme, fetih
conscience [konşıns] vicdan
conscientious [konşienşıs] vicdanlı, dürüst
conscious [konşıs] haberdar, şuurlu, bilinçli
consecutive [kınsekyutiv] art arda gelen
consent [kınsent] razı olmak / müsaade
consequence [konsikwıns] sonuç / önem
consequently [konsikwıntli] sonuç olarak, onun için
conservation [konsıveyşın] muhafaza, koruma, saklama
conservative [kınsö:vıtiv] muhafazakâr, tutucu
conserve [kınsö:v] korumak,

saklamak / konserve

consider [kınsidı] diye düşünmek, fikrinde olmak, etraflıca düşünmek, göz önünde tutmak

considerable [kınsidırıbıl] hatırı sayılır, epeyi

considerate [kınsidırit] saygılı, hatırşinas

consideration [kınsidıreyşın] düşünme, düşünce

considering [kınsidıring] düşünülürse, göz önüne alınırsa

consign [kınsayn] sevketmek, göndermek

consignment [kınsaynmınt] sevk, teslim

consist [kınsist] ibaret olmak, oluşmak

consistent [kınsistınt] tutarlı, değişmeyen

console [kınsoul] teselli etmek

consolidate [kınsolideyt] sağlamlaştırmak

consonant [konsınınt] sessiz harf

conspiracy [kınspirısi] suikast, ihanet (vatan)

conspirator [kınspirıtı] suikastçı

constable [kanstıbıl] polis

constant [konstınt] daimi, sabit

constellation [konstıleyşın] burç, takım yıldız

constipation [konstipeyşın] kabızlık

constitute [konstitiu:t] tayin etmek / kurmak, meydana getirmek

constitution [konstitiuşın] anayasa / yaratılış, karakter

construct [kınstrakt] inşa etmek

construction [kınstrakşın] yapı

consul [konsıl] konsolos

consulate [konsyulit] konsolosluk

consult [kınsalt] danışmak

consultation [konsılteyşın] danışma, konsültasyon

consume [kınsiu:m] istihlak etmek, tüketmek

consumption [kınsampşın] istihlak, tüketim

contact [kontekt] temas, münasebet / (elek.) kontak

contagious [kınteycıs] sari, bulaşıcı

contain [kınteyn] ihtiva etmek, içine almak
contemplate [kontımpleyt] seyretmek / enine boyuna düşünmek
contemplation [kontımpleyşın] düşünme, tefekkür
contemporary [kıntempırıri] çağdaş
contempt [kıntempt] küçümseme, hakir görme
contemptible [kıntemptıbıl] rezil, alçak
contend [kıntend] yarışmak, yarışmaya girmek
content [kıntent] memnun [kontent] muhteva, içerik
contents [kontents] içindekiler (kitapta)
contest [kontest] müsabaka, yarışma
continent [kontinınt] kıta (coğrafya) / Avrupa
continental [kontinentıl] kıtaya ilişkin
continual [kıntinyuıl] devamlı, sık sık olan
continuance [kıntinyuıns] devamlılık
continue [kıntinyu:] devam etmek
continuous [kıntinyuıs] devamlı, sürekli
continuously [kıntinyuısli] devamlı, durmadan
contra— [kontra] karşıt, zıt anlamında önek
contract [kıntrekt] büzülmek / kısaltmak / kontrat yapmak
contract [kontrekt] kontrat
contradict [kontrıdikt] yalanlamak
contradiction [kontrıdikşın] çelişki, anlaşmazlık
contrary [kontrıri] aksi, muhalif, zıt
contrast [kontra:st] tezat, karşıt
contribute [kıntribyu:t] vermek / iştirak etmek / bağışlamak
contribution [kontribi:uşın] bağış, yardım
control [kıntroul] idare, hakimiyet / hakim olmak
controversy [kontrıvö:si] ihtilaf, anlaşmazlık
convalescence [konvılesıns] nekahat
convenience [kınvi:nyıns] uygunluk, müsaitlik, kolaylık / yararlı şey

convenient [kınvi:nyınt] elverişli, uygun
convention [kınvenşın] anlaşma / topluluk
conventional [kınvenşınıl] göreneğe göre / basmakalıp
conversation [konvıseyşın] konuşma
converse [kınvö:s] konuşmak / [konvö:s] zıt
convert [kınvö:t] tahvil etmek, değiştirmek
convertible [kınvö:tibıl] değiştirilebilir
convex [konveks] dışbükey
convey [kınvey] nakletmek, ifade etmek
convict [kınvikt] suçunu isbat etmek / [konvikt] mahkûm
conviction [kınvikşın] kanı, inanma / mahkûmiyet
convince [kınvins] ikna etmek, inandırmak
convoy [konvoy] konvoy
cook [kuk] aşçı / pişmek, pişirmek
cool [ku:l] serin / serinletmek / sakin
co-operate [kouopıreyt] işbirliği yapmak
co-operation [kouopıreyşın] işbirliği
co-ordinate [kouodineyt] düzenlemek
cop (argo) [kop] polis
copious [koupiıs] bol, çok
copper [kopı] bakır
copy [kopi] kopya, nüsha / kopya çıkarmak
copyright [kopirayt] telif hakkı
coral [korıl] mercan
cord [ko:d] ip, şerit
cordial [ko:diıl] samimi / kalbe kuvvet veren
corduroy [ko:dıroy] çizgili kadife kumaş
core [ko:] öz, nüve
cork [ko:k] mantar (şişe)
corkscrew [ko:kskru:] tirbuşon, burgu
corn [ko:n] hububat / mısır / nasır
corner [ko:nı] köşe
coronation [korıneyşın] taç giyme
coroner [korını] sorgu yargıcı
corporal [ko:pıril] onbaşı / bedeni
corporation [ko:pıreyşın] dernek, kurum

corps [ko:] heyet / kolordu
corpse [ko:ps] ceset
correct [kırekt] düzeltmek / doğru
correction [kırekşın] düzeltme, tashih
correspond [korispond] uymak / karşılamak, tekabül etmek / yazışmak
correspondence [korispondıns] muhabere, yazışma
corridor [korido:] koridor
corrosion [kıroujın] aşındırma
corrupt [kırapt] bozuk / bozmak / çürümek
corruption [kırapşın] rüşvet yeme, yolsuzluk
corset [ko:sit] korse
cosmetic [kozmetik] kozmetik, makyaja ait
cosmonaut [kozmınot] kozmonot, astronot
cosmopolitan [kozmopolitın] bütün dünyaya ait, ulus inancı olmayan, geniş fikirli
cosmos [kozmos] kâinat, evren
cost [kost] bedel / fiyatı ...olmak, mal olmak
costume [kostiu:m] kostüm
cosy [kouzi] rahat, sıcak, kuytu
cot [kot] çocuk karyolası / kulübe
cottage [kotic] kır evi, küçük ev
cotton [kotın] pamuk
couch [kauç] kanepe
cough [kof] öksürük / öksürmek
could, bak **can**
council [kaunsil] meclis
counsel [kaunsıl] fikir / danışmak / avukat
count [kaunt] (sayı) saymak
counter [kauntı] marka, fiş / gişe / tezgâh
counter [kauntı] karşı, aksi anlamında önek
counterfeit [kauntıfi:t] sahte, sahte şey
country [kantri] ülke / kır / köy
countryman [kantrimın] yurttaş
countryside [kantrisayd] kır
county [kaunti] vilayet, ilçe
couple [kapıl] çift
coupon [ku:pon] kupon
courage [karic] cesaret
courageous [kıreycıs] cesur

courier [kurıı] kurye
course [ko:s] seyir, cereyan / rota / kurs
court [ko:t] mahkeme / saray / kur yapmak
courteous [kö:tiıs] nazik
courtesy [kö:tısi] nezaket
courtyard [ko:tya:d] bahçe, avlu
cousin [kazın] kuzen
cover [kavı] örtmek / (masrafı) karşılamak / (mesafe) katetmek / örtü, kapak / örterek saklamak
covering [kavıring] örtü
covet [kavit] şiddetli arzu etmek, imrenmek
cow [kau] inek
coward [kauwıd] korkak
cowboy [kauboy] kovboy
crab [kreb] yengeç
crack [krek] çatlak / çatlamak, çatlatmak / çatırtı
cradle [kreydıl] beşik
craft [kra:ft] sanat, marifet / gemiler / uçaklar
cram [krem] izdiham / yığılmak / sınav için alelacele çalışmak
cramp [kremp] kramp / mengene
crane [kreyn] turna kuşu / kren, vinç
crank [krenk] krank
crash [kreş] patırtıyla düşmek, çarpmak / çatırtı, gürültü / iflas etmek
crater [kreytı] krater
crave [kreyv] arzu etmek
crawl [kro:l] yerde sürünmek / kravl yüzmek
crayon [kreyın] renkli kalem, tebeşir
crazy [kreyzi] çılgın
creak [kri:k] gıcırtı / gıcırdamak
cream [kri:m] kaymak / krem
crease [kri:s] kat / buruşturmak
create [krieyt] yaratmak
creation [krieyşın] yaratma
creative [krieytiv] yaratıcı
creator [krieytı] yaratan
creature [kri:çı] yaratık
credible [kredibıl] inanılabilir
credit [kredit] kredi / itimat, güven
creditor [kreditı] alacaklı
creed [kri:d] iman, inanç
creek [kri:k] koy (coğrafya)
creep (crept, crept) [kri:p, krept krept] sürünmek, sürünerek ilerlemek

crept, bak **creep**
crescent [kresınt] hilâl
crest [krest] tepe (dağ, dalga vs.)
crew [kru:] tayfa, ekip
crime [kraym] cürüm, suç
criminal [kriminıl] cürüm sayılan / cani
crimson [krimzın] kızıl
crinkle [krinkıl] kıvrım / kıvırmak
cripple [kripıl] malul, sakat / sakat etmek
crisis [kraysis] kriz
crisp [krisp] gevrek
critic [kritik] eleştirici
critical [kritikıl] kritik, tehlikeli / kusur bulan, tenkitci
crocodile [krokıdayl] timsah
crook [kruk] kanca / dolandırıcı
crop [krop] mahsul, ekin
cross [kros] karşıdan karşıya geçmek / haç / kesişmek / çarpı / dargın
crossword [kroswö:d] bulmaca
crouch [krauç] çömelmek
crow [krou] ötmek (horoz) / karga
crowd [kraud] kalabalık, güruh / kalabalık yapmak / doldurmak
crown [kraun] taç / taç giydirmek
crude [kru:d] ham, kaba
cruel [kruıl] zalim
cruelty [kruılti] gaddarlık
cruise [kru:z] deniz gezintisi
crumb [kram] ekmek kırıntısı
crumple [krampıl] buruşturmak
crunch [kranç] gıcırdatmak / kıtırdatarak yemek
crusade [kru:seyd] Haçlı seferi
crush [kraş] ezmek, yok etmek
crust [krast] kabuk (ekmek vs.)
crutch [kraç] koltuk değneği
cry (cried, cried) [kray, krayd, krayd] bağırmak / ağlamak / haykırış
crystal [kristıl] kristal
cub [kab] aslan, köpek vs. yavrusu
cube [kiu:b] mikâp, küp
cucumber [kiu:kambı] salatalık, hıyar
cuddle [kadıl] sarmak, ku-

caklamak, sarılmak
cue [kiu:] işaret, ipucu
cuff [kaf] kol ağzı, yen
cultivate [kaltiveyt] toprağı işlemek / terbiye etmek
cultural [kalçırıl] kültürle ilgili, kültürel
culture [kalçı] kültür
cultured [kalçıd] kültürlü
cunning [kaning] kurnaz
cup [kap] fincan, bardak / kupa (sporda)
cupboard [kabıd] dolap
cupola [kiu:pılı] kubbe
cure [kiuı] tedavi etmek / çare / ilaç
curfew [kö:fyu] sokakta dolaşma yasağı
curiosity [kiuriositi] tecessüs, merak / antika
curious [kiuriıs] acayip / meraklı
curl [kö:l] kıvrım, bukle / kıvrılmak, kıvırmak
currant [karınt] frenk üzümü
currency [karınsi] revaç, geçerlilik / nakit para
curriculum [kırikyulım] okul müfredat programı
current [karınt] akım / akıntı / bugünkü / geçerli
curse [kö:s] küfür etmek, lanetlemek / lanet, beddua
curtain [kö:tın] perde
curtsey [kö:tsi] diz bükerek reverans yapmak
curve [kö:v] eğri, yay / dönemeç
cushion [kuşın] yastık
custody [kastıdi] himaye / tutuklama
custom [kastım] âdet
customary [kastımıri] âdet olan
customs [kastımz] gümrük
cut [kat] kesik / ara / biçki
cut (cut, cut) [kat] kesmek
cutlery [katlıri] sofrada bıçaklar
cutlet [katlit] pirzola
cycle [saykıl] devir / daire / bisiklet
cyclone [saykloun] kasırga
cylinder [silindı] silindir
cymbal [simbıl] büyük zil
cynic [sinik] insanları küçümseyen
cypress [saypris] selvi
Cypriot [sipriyıt] Kıbrıslı
Cyprus [saypris] Kıbrıs
Czech [çek] Çek
Czechoslovakia [çekouslouvekyı] Çekoslovakya

D

dad, daddy [ded, dedi] baba, babacığım
daffodil [defıdil] sarı nergis
dagger [degı] hançer
daily [deyli] günlük
dairy [deıri] süthane, mandıra
daisy [deyzi] papatya
dam [dem] bend, baraj
damage [demic] hasar, zarar / hasar vermek
damn [dem] küfür / lanetlemek / kahrolsun!
damp [demp] nem / nemli, rutubetli / nemlendirmek
dance [da:ns] dans etmek / dans
Dane [deyn] Danimarkalı
danger [deyncı] tehlike
dangerous [deyncırıs] tehlikeli
dangle [dengıl] asılıp sallanmak
Danish [deniş] Danimarkaca
dare [deı] cüret etmek
daring [deıring] cesur, atılgan, cüretkâr
dark [da:k] karanlık, koyu
darken [da:kın] karartmak
darkness [da:knis] karanlık, koyuluk
darling [da:ling] sevgili
darn [da:n] (örerek) tamir etmek
dash [deş] atılma, hamle / imlada tire (-) işareti / fırlamak
dashing [deşing] atılgan
data [deytı] veriler, bilgi
date [deyt] tarih / randevu / tarihini atmak
daughter [do:tı] kız evlat
dawn [do:n] şafak / şafak sökmek
day [dey] gün, gündüz
daylight [deylayt] gün ışığı
day off [dey of] izin günü
daze [deyz] şaşkınlık / sersemletmek
dazzle [dezıl] (gözleri) kamaştırmak
dead [ded] ölü, ölmüş
deaden [dedın] körletmek, azaltmak
deadline [dedlayn] son tarih
deadly [dedli] amansız, müthiş, öldürücü
deaf [def] sağır
deafen [defın] sağır etmek

deal [di:l] muamele etmek / uğraşmak / oyun kâğıdını dağıtmak / ticari anlaşma
dealer [di:lı] tüccar
dean [di:n] dekan
dear [diı] aziz / sevgili / değerli, pahalı
death [det] ölüm
debate [dibeyt] müzakere, münakaşa / tartışmak
debit [debit] borç, zimmet (defterde)
debris [debri:] enkaz
debt [det] borç
decade [dekeyd] on yıl
decay [dikey] bozulmak, (sağlık, güç) kaybetmek, çürümek
deceased [disi:sd] merhum
deceit [disi:t] aldatma, hile
deceive [disi:v] aldatmak
December [disembı] aralık (ayı)
decent [di:sınt] nezih, münasip
deception [disepşın] aldatma, hile
decide [disayd] karar vermek
decidedly [disaydidli] kesin olarak, şüphesiz
decimal [desimıl] ondalık (matematik)
decision [disijın] karar
decisive [disaysiv] kesin
deck [dek] güverte / donatmak
declaration [deklıreyşın] bildiri, beyan, ilan
declare [dikleı] beyan etmek, ifade etmek / ilan etmek
decline [diklayn] inme / zayıflama / azalma / kabul etmemek / azaltmak / çekmek (dilbilgisi)
decorate [dekıreyt] donatmak, süslemek
decoration [dekıreyşın] süsleme, dekorasyon
decrease [dikri:s] azalmak, azaltmak / azalma
decree [dikri:] yargı, hüküm / hüküm vermek
dedicate [dedikeyt] ithaf etmek, adamak
deduct [didakt] çıkarmak, azaltmak
deduction [didakşın] tenzilat, indirim / tümden gelim
deed [di:d] fiil, hareket
deep [di:p] derin

deeply [di:pli] şiddetle
deer [dii] geyik(ler)
defaat [difi:t] mağlûp etmek, yenmek / yenilgi
defect [difekt] kusur, sakatlık
defective [difektiv] kusurlu, sakat
defence [difens] savunma, müdafaa, koruma
defend [difend] savunmak
defendant [difendınt] sanık
defensive [difensiv] savunan, müdafaa eden
defer [difö:] ertelemek, geciktirmek
defiance [difayıns] meydan okuma
deficiency [difişınsi] eksiklik
deficit [defisit] açık, eksiklik, yokluk
define [difayn] tarif etmek, açıklamak
definite [definit] belli, muayyen
definitely [definitli] muhakkak, kat'i olarak
deform [di:fo:m] deforme etmek
deft [deft] becerikli, eli çabuk
defy [difay] karşı koymak, meydan okumak
degenerate [di:cenıreyt] soysuzlaşmak / [dicenırit] soysuz
degrade [digreyd] alçaltmak, azaltmak
degree [digri:] derece / kademe / üniversite diploması
dejected [dicektid] üzgün
delay [diley] erteleme / vakit kaybetmek / geciktirmek
delegate [deligit] delege
delegation [deligeyşın] delegasyon, temsilci heyet
deliberate [dilibırit] kasdi / [dilibıreyt] görüşmek, tartışmak
delicate [delikıt] nazik (mesele, durum), zarif, nefis, hassas, duygun
delicious [dilişıs] hoş, leziz, lezzetli
delight [dilayt] zevk / zevklendirmek
delightful [dilaytfıl] zevk verici, hoş
delirium [dilirıım] sayıklama / çılgınlık
deliver [dilivı] teslim etmek / tevzi etmek, dağıtmak /

ulaştırmak / konuşma yapmak / kurtarmak

delivery [diliviri] dağıtım / kurtarma / teslim

demand [dima:nd] istek / istekte bulunmak

demi— [demi] yarı... anlamında önek

demobilize [di:moubilayz] terhis etmek

democracy [dimokrısi] demokrasi

demolish [dimoliş] yıkmak

demon [di:mın] iblis

demonstrate [demınstreyt] izah etmek / göstermek / gösteri yapmak

demonstration [demınstreyşın] gösterme / nümayiş / gösteri

demoralize [dimorılayz] maneviyatını bozmak

den [den] in / küçük oda

denial [dinayıl] inkâr

Denmark [denma:k] Danimarka

denote [dinout] göstermek, işaret etmek

denounce [dinauns] aleyhinde bulunmak, itham etmek / ihbar etmek

dense [dens] kesif, yoğun

dental [dentıl] dişlere ait

dentist [dentist] dişçi

deny [dinay] inkâr etmek

depart [dipa:t] ayrılmak

department [dipa:tmınt] şube, kısım

departure [dipa:çı] ayrılma, kalkış

depend [dipend] tâbi olmak, ...e bağlı olmak

dependence [dipendıns] bağımlılık

dependent [dipendınt] bağlı

deplore [diplo:] üzüntü duymak, uygun bulmamak

deposit [dipozit] tortu / emanet / depozito / emanete bırakmak / pey vermek

depot [depout] ambar

depress [dipres] bastırmak / alçaltmak / kasvet vermek

depression [dipreşın] kasvet, durgunluk / çöküntü

deprive [diprayv] mahrum etmek

depth [dept] derinlik

deputy [depiuti] vekil, mebus, milletvekili / yardımcı, muavin

derive [dirayv] çıkarmak, tü-

retmek / elde etmek / ... kökünden gelmek (dilbilgisi)
descend [disend] inmek, alçalmak
descent [disent] iniş / nesil
describe [diskrayb] tasvir etmek, anlatmak
description [diskripşın] tarif / tasvir, niteleme
desert [dezıt] çöl
desert [dizö:t] terketmek, kaçmak
deserve [dizö:v] hak etmek, layık olmak
design [dizayn] desen, model / çizmek / tasarlamak
desirable [dizayrıbıl] makbul, arzu edilen
desire [dizayı] arzu / arzu etmek
desk [desk] okul sırası / yazı masası / kürsü
desolate [desıleyt] çöl haline sokmak, harap etmek / üzmek / çorak / viran / yalnız, kimsesiz
despair [dispeı] yeis, umutsuzluk / umudunu kesmek
desperate [despırit] çılgın / umutsuz
despise [dispayz] küçük görmek, hakir görmek
despite [dispayt] rağmen
dessert [dizö:t] meyve veya tatlı (yemek sonunda)
destination [destineyşın] gidilecek yer, hedef
destiny [destini] kader, nasip, alınyazısı
destroy [distroy] tahrip etmek, yok etmek
destruction [distrakşın] tahribat
destructive [distraktiv] tahrip edici
detach [diteç] ayırmak
detail [diteyl] tafsilat, ayrıntı
detain [diteyn] tutmak, geciktirmek
detect [ditekt] meydana çıkarmak, sezmek
detection [ditekşın] meydana çıkarma
detective [ditektiv] dedektif
detention [ditenşın] alıkoyma, tutma
determine [ditö:min] tespit etmek, saptamak / karar vermek / azmetmek
determination [ditö:mineyşın] azim, karar
detest [ditest] hoşlanma-

mak, nefret etmek
deuce [diu:s] şeytan
devaluation [divelìueyşın] devalüasyon
develop [divelıp] gelişmek, geliştirmek
development [divelıpmınt] gelişme
deviate [di:vieyt] sapmak
deviation [di:vieyşın] sapma, sapıklık
device [divays] cihaz, alet
devil [devıl] şeytan
devoid [divoyd] mahrum, yoksun, olmayan
devote [divout] adamak, vakfetmek, hasretmek
devour [divauı] yutmak, yiyip bitirmek
devout [divaut] dindar
dew [diu:] çiğ
diabetes [dayıbi:tiz] şeker hastalığı
diabolical [dayıbolikıl] şeytani
diagnose [dayıgnouz] teşhis etmek
diagnosis [dayıgnousis] teşhis (hastalık)
dial [dayıl] kadran / (telefon numaralarını) çevirmek
dialect [dayılekt] lehçe
dialogue [dayılog] diyalog, konuşma
diameter [dayemitı] çap
diamond [dayımınd] elmas / karo (iskambil)
diaper [dayıpı] çocuk bezi
diarrhoea [dayırii] diyare, ishal
diary [dayıri] hatıra defteri
dice [days] (oyun için) zarlar
dictate [dikteyt] yazdırmak / zorla kabul ettirmek
dictator [dikteytı] diktatör
diction [dikşın] diksiyon, konuşma şekli
dictionary [dikşınıri] sözlük
didactic [didektik] öğretici, didaktik
die [day] ölmek / oyun zarı
did, bak **do**
diet [dayıt] perhiz, rejim
differ [difı] farklı olmak, fark etmek
difference [difrıns] fark
different [difrınt] farklı, ayrı
difficult [difikılt] zor, güç / müşkülpesent
difficulty [difikılti] zorluk, güçlük
dig (dug, dug) [dig, dag, dag] kazmak

digest [daycest] hazmetmek, sindirmek / özet
digestion [daycesçın, dicesçın] sindirim
digit [dicit] parmak / rakam (0 - 9)
dignified [dignifayd] ağır başlı
dignity [digniti] vakar
dilemma [daylemı] güç durum, çıkmaz, açmaz
diligent [dilicınt] çalışkan
dim [dim] bulanık, belirsiz, silik
dimension [daymenşın] ebat, boyut
diminish [diminiş] azalmak, azaltmak
dimple [dimpıl] gamze
dine [dayn] akşam yemeği yemek
diner [daynı] trende restoran vagonu
dinner [dinı] akşam yemeği
dip [dip] daldırmak, batırmak
diphtheria [diftiıriı] difteri
diphthong [diftong] iki seslinin bir hecede kaynaşması
diploma [diploumı] diploma
diplomacy [diploumısi] diplomasi, siyaset
diplomat [diplımet] diplomat
direct [dayrekt, direkt] direkt, doğrudan doğruya / idare etmek, yönetmek / yöneltmek
direction [direkşın] yön / talimat / yönetim
directly [direktli] doğrudan doğruya
director [direktı] müdür
dirt [dö:t] kir
dirty [dö:ti] kirli
disable [diseybıl] sakat etmek
disadvantage [disıdva:ntic] mahzur, sakınca
disagree [disıgri:] uyuşmamak
disagreement [disıgri:mınt] anlaşmazlık, uyuşmazlık
disappear [disıpiı] gözden kaybolmak
disappoint [disıpoynt] hayat kırıklığına uğratmak
disappointment [disıpoyntmınt] hayal kırıklığı
disapprove [disıpru:v] uygun bulmamak
disarmament [disa:mımınt] silahsızlanma

disaster [diza:stı] felaket
disc [disk] disk
discern [disö:n] ayırdetmek, sezmek
discharge [disça:c] boşaltmak / salıvermek / işten çıkarmak / boşalma / atış / serbest bırakma
discipline [disiplin] disiplin
disclaim [diskleym] kabul etmemek
disclose [disklouz] açığa vurmak
discomfort [diskamfıt] rahatsızlık
disconnect [diskınekt] bağlantısını kesmek
discontent [diskontent] hoşnutsuzluk
discord [disko:d] ihtilaf, anlaşmazlık
discotheque [diskıtek] diskotek
discount [diskaunt] iskonto / iskonto etmek
discourage [diskaric] ümidini kırmak, cesaretini kırmak
discourse [disko:s] nutuk, söylev
discover [diskavı] keşfetmek
discoverer [diskavırı] kâşif
discovery [diskavıri] keşif
discredit [diskredit] itibarsızlık
discreet [diskri:t] ihtiyatlı, ketum
discretion [diskreşın] ihtiyat
discriminate [diskrimineyt] ayırt etmek
discuss [diskas] tartışmak, müzakere etmek
disdain [disdeyn] hakir görmek
disease [dizi:z] hastalık
disembark [disimba:k] karaya çıkmak, çıkarmak
disengage [disingeyc] serbest bırakmak / çözmek
disgrace [disgreys] ayıp, rezalet
disguise [disgayz] kıyafet değiştirme
disgust [disgast] tiksinti
dish [diş] yemek / yemek tabağı
dishwasher [dişwoşı] bulaşık makinası
disillusion [disilu:jın] hayalini yıkmak
disinclined [disinklaynd] is-

teksiz
disinfect [disinfekt] dezenfekte etmek
disinfectant [disinfektınt] antiseptik, mikrop öldürücü
dislike [dislayk] hoşlanmamak
dislocate [dislıkeyt] yerinden çıkarmak
dismal [dizmıl] kederli, neşesiz
dismay [dismey] cesaretini kırmak / korku
dismiss [dismis] kovmak, işinden çıkarmak, serbest bırakmak
dismount [dismaunt] (attan vs.) inmek
disobey [disoubey] itaat etmemek
disorder [diso:dı] karışıklık
dispatch [dispeç] göndermek / çabucak bitirmek / gönderme / rapor
dispel [dispel] dağıtmak / gidermek
dispensary [dispensıri] dispanser
disperse [dispö:s] dağıtmak, dağılmak
displace [displeys] yerinden oynatmak, başka yere koymak
display [displey] gösteri / sergilemek
displease [displi:z] gücendirmek, memmun etmemek
dispose [dispouz] başından atmak, savmak
disposition [dispızişın] mizaç / düzen
disprove [dispru:v] yalanlamak
dispute [dispyu:t] münakaşa, tartışma / tartışmak
disqualify [diskwolifay] diskalifiye etmek
disregard [disriga:d] ihmal etmek, saymamak
disrespect [disrispekt] hürmetsizlik
dissolution [disılu:şın] çözülme / sona erme / parçalanma
dissolve [dizolv] suda erimek / çözmek / son vermek
dissuade [disweyd] caydırmak
distance [distıns] mesafe, uzaklık
distant [distınt] uzak

distil [distil] damıtmak
distinct [distinkt] vazıh, açık, ayrı
distinction [distinkşın] ayırma, fark, alâmet
distinguish [distingwiş] ayırdetmek / kendini göstermek, sivrilmek
distinguished, ünlü
distort [disto:t] şeklini bozmak
distract [distrekt] (zihni) başka tarafa çekmek
distress [distres] elem, sıkıntı / ızdırap vermek
distribute [distribiu:t] dağıtmak, tevzi etmek, taksim etmek
distribution [distribiu:şın] tevzi, dağıtım
district [distrikt] bölge, semt
distrust [distrast] itimat etmemek
disturb [distö:b] rahatsız etmek, tedirgin etmek
disturbance [distö:bıns] karışıklık, rahatsızlık
ditch [diç] hendek, çukur
dive [dayv] (suya) dalmak
diver [dayvı] dalgıç
diverse [dayvö:s] çeşitli
diversion [dayvö:şın] oyalama / eğlence
divert [dayvö:t] başka tarafa çevirmek / oyalamak / eğlendirmek
divide [divayd] bölmek, ayırmak, taksim etmek
divine [divayn] ilâhî, ulu
division [divijın] tümen / kısım, bölme, bölüm
divorce [divo:s] boşanma/ boşanmak
divulge [divalc] ifşa etmek, meydana vurmak
dizzy [dizi] başı dönen
do (did, done) [du:, did, dan] yapmak, etmek
docile [dousayl] uysal
dock [dok] rıhtım
dockyard [dokya:d] tersane
doctor [doktı] doktor
doctrine [doktrin] öğreti, doktrin
document [dokiumınt] vesika, belge
dog [dog] köpek
doleful [doulfıl] kederli
doll [dol] bebek (oyuncak)
dollar [dolı] dolar
dolphin [dolfin] yunus balığı
dome [doum] kubbe
domestic [dımestik] eve ait,

aile içi / kendi ülkesine ait / evcil
dominate [domineyt] hâkim olmak
donation [douneyşın] bağış
done, bak **do**
donkey [donki] eşek
donor [dounı] bağışta bulunan
doom [du:m] kader / mahkûm etmek
doomsday [du:mzdey] kıyamet günü
door [do:] kapı
doorkeeper [do:ki:pı] kapıcı
doorstep [do:step] kapı eşiği
dope [doup] çiriş / sersemletici ilaç
dormitory [domitıri] yatakhane
dose [dous] doz
dot [dot] nokta, benek / noktalamak
double [dabıl] çift, duble / iki misli olmak
double bed [dabıl bed] iki kişilik yatak
double room [dabıl rum] iki yataklı oda
doubt [daut] şüphe, kuşku / şüphe etmek, kuşkulanmak
doubtful [dautfıl] kuşkulu
doubtless [dautlis] kuşkusuz
dough [dou] hamur
dove [dav] kumru
dowdy [daudi] kılıksız
down [daun] aşağı, aşağıya
downcast [daunka:st] kederli
downright [daunrayt] kati, tamamen
downstairs [daunsteız] evin alt katı / aşağıda, aşağıya
dowry [dauri] çeyiz
doze [douz] uyuklamak
dozen [dazın] düzüne
draft [dra:ft] müsvedde / tasarı / poliçe / taslağını yapmak / askere almak (Amerika)
drag [dreg] sürüklemek
dragon [dregın] ejderha
drain [dreyn] lağım / (suyunu) boşaltmak
drainage [dreynic] drenaj, süzülme / süzülen su
drainer [dreynı] süzgeç
drama [dra:mı] dram
drank bak **drink**
draught [dra:ft] çekme / ha-

va cereyanı / ilaç
draughts [dra:fts] dama oyunu
draw (drew, drawn) [dro:, dru:, dro:n] çekmek / resim yapmak / çizmek
drawer [dro:ı] çekmece
drawn bak **draw**
dread [dred] korku / korkmak
dream [dri:m] rüya / rüya görmek
dreary [driıri] kasvetli
dregs [dregs] tortu
drench [drenç] sırılsıklam ıslatmak
dress [dres] elbise / giydirmek, giyinmek
dressing [dresin] giyinme / sos, salça
dressmaker [dresmeykı] kadın terzisi
drew, bak **draw**
dribble [dribıl] damlama / damlatmak, damlamak
dried [drayd] kurutulmuş
drift [drift] sürüklenmek
drill [dril] matkap / delmek / talim, alıştırma
drink (drank, drunk) [drink, drenk, drank] (su v.s.) içmek / içki
drip [drip] damlamak, damlatmak
drive (drove, driven) [drayv, drouv, drivın] sürmek / yürütmek / (araba v.s.) kullanmak
driver [drayvı] şoför
driving license [drayving laysıns] ehliyet
drizzle [drizıl] çiselemek / çisenti
droop [dru:p] sarkmak
drop [drop] damla / düşürmek / damlatmak
dropper [dropı] damlalık
drought [draut] kuraklık
drove, bak **drive**
drown [draun] suda boğmak, boğulmak
drowsy [drawzi] uykulu
drug [drag] ilaç / uyuşturucu madde
druggist [dragist] eczacı
drum [dram] davul / davul çalmak / varil
drunk [drank] bak, **drink** / sarhoş
dry [dray] kuru / kurutmak / yavan (kitap, espri vs.)
dual [diuıl] çift, ikili
dubious [diu:byıs] şüpheli
duchess [daçis] düşes

duck [dak] ördek
duckling [dakling] ördek yavrusu
due [diu:] uygun, münasip / hak / ödeme zamanı gelmiş / varış saati gelmiş (tren v.s.)
duel [diuıl] düello
duke [diu:k] duka, dük
dull [dal] sıkıntılı, sıkıcı, donuk / aptal, durgun
duly [diuli] uygun bir şekilde (zamanında)
dumb [dam] dilsiz
dummy [dami] manken (cansız)
dump [damp] atmak / damping yapmak
dung [dang] gübre
dungeon [dancın] zindan
duplex [diu:pleks] çift
duplicate [diu:plikeyt] suret / suretini çıkarmak
duplicator [diu:plikeytı] teksir makinesi
durable [diu:rıbıl] dayanıklı
duration [diureyşın] süre
during [diu:ring] esnasında, süresince
dusk [dask] akşam karanlığı
dust [dast] toz / tozunu almak
dustbin [dastbin] çöp tenekesi
duster [dastı] toz bezi, silgi
dustman [dastmın] çöpçü
dustpan [dastpen] faraş
dusty [dasti] tozlu
Dutch [daç] Hollandalı
dutiful [diu:tifıl] hürmetkâr / vazifeşinas
duty [diu:ti] görev / gümrük vergisi
dwarf [dwo:f] cüce
dwell [dwel] ikamet etmek
dwindle [dwindıl] azalmak
dye [day] boya / (kumaş, saç, deri v.s.) boyamak
dynamic [daynemik] dinamik
dynamite [daynımayt] dinamit
dynamo [daynımou] dinamo
dynasty [dinısti] hanedan
dysentery [disıntri] dizanteri

E

each [i:ç] her bir
eager [i:gı] istekli, gayretli
eagerly [i:gıli] istekle, gayretle

eagle [i:gıl] kartal
ear [iı] kulak
ear-ring [iırring] küpe
earl [ö:l] kont
early [ö:li] erken, erkenden
earn [ö:n] (çalışarak) kazanmak, hak etmek
earnest [ö:nist] ciddi, istekli
earnings [ö:ningz] kazanç
earth [ö:t] toprak, yeryüzü
earthly [ö:tli] dünyevi
earthquake [ö:tkweyk] yer sarsıntısı, deprem
earthworm [ö:twö:m] solucan
ease [i:z] rahatlık, kolaylık / rahatlamak
easily [i:zili] kolayca
east [i:st] doğu
Easter [i:stı] Paskalya
eastern [i:stın] doğuya ait
easy [i:zi] kolay, rahat
easychair [i:ziçeı] koltuk
eat (ate, eaten) [i:t, et, (eyt) i:tın] yemek
eatable [i:tıbıl] yenir
eavesdrop [i:vzdrop] kulak misafiri olmak
ebb [eb] cezir, denizin çekilmesi
eccentric [iksentrik] eksantrik
echo [ekou] yankı / yankılamak
eclipse [iklips] güneş tutulması
economic [i:kınomik] iktisadî, ekonomik
economize [i:konımayz] idareli kullanmak
economy [i:konımi] ekonomi, iktisat
ecstasy [ekstısi] kendinden geçme, vecd
eddy [edi] anafor, girdap
edge [ec] kenar
edged [ecd] ağızlı, kenarlı
edible [edibıl] yenebilir
edition [idişın] baskı, basım, nüsha
editor [editı] gazete müdürü, editör
educate [edyukeyt] eğitmek, tahsil ettirmek
education [edyukeyşın] eğitim, tahsil
eel [i:l] yılan balığı
effect [ifekt] sonuç / etki / sonuç vermek
effective [ifektiv] etkili
effervescent [efıvesınt] köpüren
efficiency [ifişınsi] yeterlilik, ehliyet

efficient [ifişınt] yeterli, ehil, randımanlı
effort [efıt] gayret, çabalama
effrontery [ifrantıri] küstahlık
effusive [ifyu:siv] bol bol, canı gönülden
e.g. [i:ci:] örnek olarak, örneğin
egg [eg] yumurta
eggplant [egpla:nt] patlıcan
egoist [egouist] bencil
Egypt [i:cipt] Mısır
Egyptian [i:cipşın] Mısırlı
eiderdown [aydıdaun] kuştüyü yorgan
eight [eyt] sekiz
eighteen [eyti:n] on sekiz
eighty [eyti] seksen
either [aydı] ikisinden biri, her biri
elaborate [ilebırit] özenle hazırlanmış
elapse [ileps] (vakit) geçmek
elastic [ilestik] esnek
elasticity [ilestisiti] esneklik
elbow [elbou] dirsek
elder [eldı] daha yaşlı olan (ailede)
elect [ilekt] seçmek, seçkin
election [ilekşın] seçim
electric [ilektrik] elektriki
electricity [ilektrisiti] elektrik
electrician [ilektrişın] elektrikçi
elegance [eligıns] zerafet, şıklık
elegant [eligınt] zarif
elegy [elici] ağıt
element [elimınt] unsur, eleman, öğe
elementary [elimentıri] başlangıç, yeni başlayanlar için
elephant [elifınt] fil
elevate [eliveyt] yükseltmek
elevator [eliveytı] asansör
eleven [ilevın] on bir
eligible [elicibıl] uygun, seçilebilir
eliminate [ilimineyt] çıkarmak, kaldırmak
ellipse [ilips] elips
elm [elm] karaağaç
eloquence [elıkwıns] etkili konuşma
eloquent [elıkwınt] belagatli, iyi konuşan
else [els] başka, diğer
elsewhere [elsweı] başka

yerde
elude [ilyu:d] ...den sıyrılmak
elusive [ilyu:siv] tutulmaz, hatırda kalmaz
emanate [emıneyt] meydana gelmek, doğmak
embargo [emba:gou] ambargo
embark [emba:k] gemiye bindirmek, yüklemek
embarrass [imberıs] şaşırtıp utandırmak / rahatsız etmek
embassy [embısi] sefaret, elçilik
embellish [imbeliş] süslemek
ember [embı] kor
embezzle [imbezıl] zimmetine geçirmek
emblem [emblım] remiz, amblem
embody [imbıdi] göz önünde canlandırmak
embrace [imbreys] kucaklamak
embroidery [imbroydıri] nakış
embryo [embrio] rahimdeki yavru, embriyo
emend [imend] düzeltmek, tashih etmek
emerald [emırıld] zümrüt
emerge [imö:c] ortaya çıkmak, zuhur etmek
emergency [imö:cınsi] fevkalade hal / buhran / ani tehlike
emery [emıri] zımpara
emigrant [emigrınt] muhacir, göçmen
emigrate [emigreyt] göç etmek
eminence [eminıns] paye, yükseklik
emotion [imouşın] heyecan, his
emperor [empırı] imparator
emphasis [emfısis] belirtme, vurgu
emphasize [emfısayz] belirtmek, vurgulamak
empire [empayı] imparatorluk
empirical [empirikıl] ampirik, deneysel
employ [imploy] kullanmak / iş vermek, işe almak
employee [imployi:] işçi, memur
employer [imployı] patron işveren
employment [imploymınt]

iş, görev
empress [empris] imparatoriçe
empty [empti] boş / boşaltmak
enable [ineybıl] güçlendirmek, imkân vermek
enamel [inemıl] mine
enchant [inça:nt] büyülemek
encircle [insö:kıl] çevrelemek, kuşatmak
enclose [inklouz] içine almak, çevrelemek
enclosure [inkloujı] kuşatma, içine alma / mektup içine konan ek / çevrilmiş arsa
encounter [inkauntı] karşılaşmak, rastlamak
encourage [inkaric] teşvik etmek, cesaret vermek
encouragement [inkaricmınt] teşvik, cesaret verme
encyclopedia [insayklıpi:dyı] ansiklopedi
end [end] son, uç, bitim / sona ermek, son vermek
endeavour [indevı] gayret etmek, çaba sarfetmek
endless [endlis] sonsuz
endorse [indo:s] ciro etmek / desteklemek
endure [indyuı] tahammül etmek, dayanmak
enemy [enimi] düşman
energetic [enıcetik] enerjik
energy [enıci] kuvvet, güç
enfold [infould] sarmak
engage [ingeyc] hizmetine almak / tutmak
engaged [ingeycd] nişanlanmış / meşgul
engagement [ingeycmınt] nişanlanma / angajman
engaging [ingeycing] hoş, dikkati çeken
engine [encin] makine, motor
engineer [enciniı] mühendis
England [inglınd] İngiltere
English [ingliş] İngiliz, İngilizce
Englishman [inglişmın] İngiliz
engrave [ingreyv] hakketmek, oymak
enigma [enigmı] muamma
enjoy [incoy] zevk almak, hoşlanmak
enjoyment [incoymınt] zevk, eğlence
enlarge [inla:c] büyütmek

enlighten [inlaytın] aydınlatmak
enlist [inlist] asker olmak / kaydetmek
enliven [inlayvın] canlandırmak
enmity [enmiti] düşmanlık
enormous [ino:mıs] pek büyük
enough [inaf] yeterli
enrage [inreyc] kızdırmak
enrich [inriç] zenginleştirmek
enrol [inroul] asker olmak / üye olmak, kaydolmak
ensure [inşuı] temin etmek, garanti vermek
entangle [intengıl] karmakarışık etmek
entente [a:nta:nt] anlaşma
enter [entı] girmek
enterprise [entıprayz] teşebbüs girişim
entertain [entıteyn] ağırlamak, eğlendirmek
entertainment [entıteynmınt] eğlence, ağırlama, ziyafet
enthusiasm [intiuziezm] şevk, heves
enthusiastic [intiuziestik] coşkun, hevesli
entice [intays] ayartmak
entire [intayı] bütün, tekmil tüm
entirely [intayıli] tamamen
entitle [intaytıl] yetki vermek
entrance [entrıns] giriş
entreat [intri:t] yalvarmak
entrust [intrast] tevdi etmek, emanet etmek
entry [entri] antre, giriş
envelop [invelıp] sarmak kuşatmak
envelope [enviloup] zarf
envious [enviıs] kıskanç
environment [invayrınmınt muhit, çevre
envoy [envoy] elçi
envy [envi] haset / haset etmek, kıskanmak
epic [epik] destan
epidemic [epidemik] salgın (hastalık)
episode [episoud] olay
epitaph [epita:f] mezar kitabesi
epoch [i:pok] devir, çağ
equal [i:kwıl] eşit
equality [i:kwoliti] eşitlik
equally [i:kwıli] eşit olarak, ayni derecede
equator [ikweytı] ekvator

equip [ikwip] donatmak, teçhiz etmek
equipment [ikwipmınt] teçhizat, donatım
equity [ekwiti] adalet
era [iırı] çağ, devir
erase [ireyz] silmek
eraser [ireyzı] silgi
erect [irekt] dikmek, inşa etmek / dimdik
errand [erınd] iş, sipariş
erotic [erotik] aşka ait, şehvani
err [ö:] yanılmak
error [erı] yanlışlık, hata
erupt [irapt] fışkırmak
escape [iskeyp] kaçmak, firar etmek / firar
escort [esko:t] muhafız / refakat etmek
especial [ispeşıl] özel
especially [ispeşıli] bilhassa, özellikle
espionage [espiına:j] casusluk
essay [esey] deneme, makale
essence [esıns] öz, esas / esans
essential [isenşıl] gerekli, lüzumlu
essentially [isenşıli] mutlaka, esas olarak
establish [istebliş] ihdas etmek, kurmak
establishment [istebli şmınt] kurum, müessese
estate [isteyt] arazi / mülk
esteem [isti:m] itibar / hürmet etmek
estimate [estimeyt] tahmin etmek
etc. (et cetera) [etsetırı] vesaire (v.s.)
eternal [itö:nıl] sonsuz
eternity [itö:niti] ebediyet
ether [i:tı] eter
ethics [etiks] ahlak ve terbiye kuralları
Ethiopia [i:tiopiı] Habeşistan
etiquette [etiket] adabı muaşeret, görgü
Europe [yuırıp] Avrupa
European [yuırıpiın] Avrupalı
evacuation [ivekyueyşın] tahliye, boşaltma
evade [iveyd] sakınmak
evaluate [ivelyueyt] değerlendirmek
evaporate [ivepıreyt] buharlaşmak / ortadan kaybolmak

evasion [iveyjın] kaçınma, yan çizme
eve [i:v] arife
even [i:vın] hatta, bile / düz / çift (sayı)
evening [i:vning] akşam
event [ivent] olay
eventual [ivençuıl] sonuç olarak
eventually [iventyuıli] sonuçta
ever [evı] herhangi bir vakitte, daima / hiç
everlasting [evıla:sting] dayanıklı / sonsuz
every [evri] her, her bir
everbody [evribodi] herkes
everyday [evridey] her günkü
everything [evriting] her şey
everyhwhere [evriweı] her yere, her yerde
evidence [evidıns] delil
evident [evidınt] aşikâr
evil [i:vıl] kötü, şer, günah
evoke [ivouk] uyandırmak, hasıl etmek
evolution [i:vılu:şın] evrim, gelişim
ex— [eks] sabık, eski anlamında önek
exact [igzekt] tam, aynen, kati
exactly [igzektli] aynen, tamamen
exaggerate [igzecıreyt] abartmak
exaggeration [igzecıreyşın] abartma
examination [igzemineyşın muayene, sınav
examine [igzemin] muayene etmek / tetkik etmek / sınav yapmak
example [igza:mpıl] örnek
exasperate [igza:spıreyt] sabrını tüketmek
excavate [ekskıveyt] kazmak, oymak
exceed [iksi:d] tecavüz etmek, aşmak
excel [iksel] üstün olmak, geçmek
excellence [eksılıns] mükemmellik
excellent [eksılınt] mükemmel
except [iksept] istisna etmek, ayrı tutmak
except müstesna, hariç
exception [iksepşın] istisna, ayrılık
excess [ikses] ifrat, aşırı, fazla (bagaj v.b.)

exchange [iksçeync] para değiştirme (yabancı parayı), değiş tokuş, değiştirme / değiştirmek
excite [iksayt] heyecanlandırmak, uyandırmak, kışkırtmak
excitement [iksaytmınt] heyecan
exclaim [ekskleym] bağırmak (sevinç veya hayretle)
exclamation [eksklımeyşın] nida, ünlem
exclude[iksklu:d] çıkarmak, hariç tutmak
exclusion [iksklu:jın] içeri almama, ayırma
exclusive [iksklu:siv] müstesna, özel
excursion [ikskö:şın] tenezzüh, gezinti
excuse [ikskiu:z] affetmek / bahane, mazeret
execute [eksikyu:t] yapmak, yerine getirmek / idam etmek
execution [eksikyuşın] icra, yapma / idam
executive [igzekiutiv] icra eden
exempt [igzempt] muaf
exemption [igzempşın] muafiyet, bağışıklık
exercise [eksısayz] kullanmak / harekete getirmek / kullanma / çalıştırma, idman
exert [igzö:t] çaba harcamak / ortaya koymak, kullanmak
exertion [igzö:şın] çaba
exhale [eksheyl] nefesi dışarı vermek
exhaust [igzo:st] tüketmek / egzoz
exhibition [eksibişın] sergi
exile [egzayl] sürgün
exist [igzist] var olmak / yaşamak
existence [igzistıns] var oluş / yaşayış
exit [eksit] çıkış
exotic [igzotik] yabancı ülkeden gelen
expand [ikspend] genleşmek, genişlemek
expect [ikspekt] ummak, beklemek
expectation [ekspekteyşın] ümit, umma
expedition [ekspidişın] sefer, gezi heyeti
expel [ikspel] kovmak, çı-

karmak
expend [ikspend] harcamak
expenditure [ikspendiçı] harcama, sarf
expense [ikspens] sarfiyat, harcama, gider
expensive [ikspensiv] pahalı
experience [ikspiıriıns] tecrübe, deneyim / yaşantı / tecrübe etmek / görüp geçirmek
experiment [iksperimınt] deneme, deney, tecrübe
experimental [iksperimentıl] deneysel
expert [ekspö:t] uzman
expire [ikspayı] sona ermek, ölmek
explain [ikspleyn] izah etmek, açıklamak
explanation [eksplıneyşın] izahat, açıklama
explicit [iksplisit] sarih, açık
explode [iksploud] patlamak, patlatmak
exploit [iksployt] istismar etmek, çıkarına kullanmak, sömürmek
exploration [eksplo:reyşın] keşif, araştırma
explore [iksplo:] araştırmak, keşfetmek
explorer [iksplo:rı] kâşif
explosion [iksploujın] infilâk, patlama
explosive [iksplo:siv] patlayıcı (madde)
export [ekspo:t] ihrac etmek / ihracat / ihrac maddesi
expose [ikspouz] maruz bırakmak / teşhir etmek
exposure [ikspoujı] poz (fotoğraf) / ifşa etme
express [ikspres] ifade etmek, söylemek / ekspres (tren)
expression [ikspreşın] ifade, yüz ifadesi / anlatış / deyim
expulsion [ikspalşın] çıkarma, defetme
exquisite [ekskwizit] latif, şahane
extend [ikstend] uzatmak, uzamak
extension [ikstenşın] yayılma, ilâve, uzatma
extensive [ikstensiv] geniş, büyük çapta
extent [ikstent] derece / ölçü / miktar
exterior [ekstiıriı] harici, dış

taraf
exterminate [ikstö:mineyt] imha etmek
external [ikstö:nıl] harici
extinct [ikstinkt] sönmüş, tükenmiş
extinguish [ikstingwiş] söndürmek
extra [ekstrı] fazladan, ekstra, ilave olarak
extract [ekstrekt] parça, iktibas / çıkarmak
extraordinary [ikstro:dinri] olağanüstü
extravagance [ikstrevıgıns] müsriflik, ifrat
extreme [ikstri:m] son derece, son had, aşırı
extremely [ikstri:mli] aşırı derecede
exuberant [igziu:bırınt] coşkun, taşkın, bol
eye [ay] göz / iğne deliği
eyebrow [aybrau] kaş
eyelash [ayleş] kirpik
eyelid [aylid] gözkapağı
eye-witness [aywitnis] görgü tanığı

F

fable [feybıl] masal
fabric [febrik] yapı / kumaş
fabricate [febrikeyt] imal etmek
fabulous [febyulıs] efsanevi
face [feys] çehre, yüz / karşılaşmak / nazır olmak
facility [fısiliti] kolaylık
facilities [fısiliti:z] olanak ve araçlar
facing [feysing] bakan, dönük, karşısında
fact [fekt] gerçek, olan
factor [fektı] etken, sebep, faktör
factory [fektıri] fabrika
faculty [fekılti] fakülte
fade [feyd] solmak, eriyip gitmek, kaybolmak
fail [feyl] başarısızlığa uğramak / yetmemek, tükenmek / zayıflamak
failure [feylıı] başarısızlık
faint [feynt] zayıf, hafif / bayılmak / baygınlık
fair [feı] adalete uygun, hakkaniyetli, doğru, dürüst / orta karar / sarışın / pa-

nayır, fuar
fairly [feıli] az çok, orta karar, şöyle böyle / hakkıyle
fairy [feıri] peri
faith [feyt] itikat, sadakat, güven, inanç
faithful [feytfıl] sadık
faithfully [feytfıli] sadakatle, bağlı kalarak
fake [feyk] kalp, sahte
falcon [folkın] şahin
fall (fell, fallen) [fo:l, fel fo:lın] düşmek, çökmek / azalmak, hafiflemek
fall [fo:l] düşüş, çöküş / çağlayan / sonbahar
fallen bak **fall;** dökülmüş, düşük
false [fo:ls] yanlış, uygunsuz / sahte, takma
falsify [fo:lsifay] tahrif etmek
falter [fo:ltı] bocalamak
fame [feym] şöhret, ün
familiar [fımilyı] bildik / alışkın, teklifsiz, samimi
family [femili] aile
family name [femili neym] soyadı
famine [femin] kıtlık, açlık
famous [feymıs] ünlü
fan [fen] yelpaze / vantilatör / yelpazelenmek
fanatic [fınetik] mutaassıp, yobaz, sabit fikirli
fancy [fensi] hayal / tasavvur etmek / heves
fantastic [fentestik] hayali, acayip / fevkalade
fantasy [fentısi] hayal
far [fa:] uzak, uzakta, uzağa
fare [feı] seyahat ücreti
farewell [feıwel] elveda, allahısmarladık
farm [fa:m] çiftlik
farmer [fa:mı] çiftçi
farther [fa:dı] daha öte
fascinate [fesineyt] teshir etmek, büyülemek
fashion [feşın] moda, tarz, biçim
fashionable [feşınıbıl] modaya uygun
fast [fa:st] hızlı / sıkı / oruç / oruç tutmak
fasten [fa:sın] bağlamak, raptetmek, iliklemek
fastener [fa:sını] kopça, raptiye, fermuar
fastidious [festidiıs] müşkülpesent
fat [fet] şişman, yağlı / kalın, dolu / yağ

fatal [feytıl] öldürücü / kaderde olan
fate [feyt] kader, yazgı
father [fa:dı] baba
fathom [fedım] kulaç
fatigue [fıti:g] yorgunluk
fatten [fetın] semirtmek
fault [fo:lt] kusur, noksan
faulty [fo:lti] kusurlu
favour [feyvı] lehinde / taraftar olmak, yardımcı olmak, iltimas etmek / lütuf
favourable [feyvırıbıl] uygun, muvafık
favourite [feyvırit] favori, en beğenilen, gözde
fear [fiı] korku / korkmak / endişe etmek
fearful [fiıfıl] korkunç
fearless [fiılis] korkusuz
feasible [fi:zıbıl] yapılabilen, mümkün
feast [fi:st] ziyafet, festival
feather [fedı] kuş tüyü
feature [fi:çı] özellik / çehre
February [februıri] şubat
fed, bak **feed**
federal [fedırıl] federal
federation [fedıreyşın] birlik, federasyon
fee [fi:] ücret
feeble [fi:bıl] zayıf
feed (fed, fed) [fi:d, fed, fed] beslemek, beslenmek, yemek
feel (felt, felt) [fi:l, felt, felt] hissetmek, duymak / ellemek
feeling [fi:ling] his, duygu
feet, bak **foot**
fell bak **fall**
fellow [felou] adam, yoldaş
felt [felt] bak **feel,** keçe
female [fi:meyl] dişi
feminine [feminin] dişi
fence [fens] çit, parmaklık / çitle çevirmek
ferment [fö:ment] maya / mayalandırmak / heyecanlandırmak
fermentation [fö:menteyşın] mayalanma
ferry [feri] feribot, araba vapuru
ferryboat [feribout] feribot
fertile [fö:tayl] verimli
fertilizer [fö:tilayzı] (suni) gübre
fervour [fö:vı] hararet, istek, hırs
festival [festivıl] festival, bayram
fetch [feç] gidip getirmek

feud [fiu:d] kan davası
feudal [fiu:dıl] derebeyliğe ait
fever [fi:vı] vücut harareti, ateş
few [fiu:] az, az şey veya kişi
financé(e) [fiansey] nişanlı
fiasco [fieskou] fiyasko
fibre [faybı] lif, tel
fickle [fikıl] kararsız
fiction [fikşın] hikâye, roman nevi
fictitious [fiktişıs] hayali, uydurma
fidelity [fideliti] sadakat
fidget [ficit] huzursuzlanmak, kıpırdamak
field [fi:ld] tarla / alan
fierce [fiıs] azgın, şiddetli
fiery [fayıri] ateşli, atılgan
fifteen [fifti:n] on beş
fifth [fift] beşinci
fifty [fifti] elli
fig [fig] incir
fight (fought, fought) [fayt, fo:t, fo:t] dövüşmek / harp etmek
fight [fayt] kavga, savaş
fighter [faytı] dövüşen, savaşçı
fighting [fayting] dövüş
figure [figı] rakam / hesap / şekil / vücut
filament [filımınt] ince tel
file [fayl] eğe / eğelemek / dosya / dosyaya koymak
fill [fil] dolmak, doldurmak
fillet [filit] fileto
filling [filing] doldurma / dolgu
filling station [filing steyşın] benzin istasyonu
film [film] film / ince tabaka
filter [filtı] filtre, süzgeç / süzmek
filth [filt] pislik
filthy [filti] pis
fin [fin] (balıkta) yüzgeç
final [faynıl] nihai, kati
finance [faynens] maliye
financial [faynenşıl] mali
find (found, found) [faynd, faund, faund] bulmak, keşfetmek
fine [fayn] güzel / iyi / ince / para cezası
finger [fingı] parmak
finish [finiş] bitirmek, bitmek / son, bitirme
finite [faynayt] hudutlu, sınırlı
Finland [finlınd] Finlandiya
fir [fö:] köknar
fire [fayı] ateş / yangın /

ateşlemek / ateş etmek / (işten) atmak
fireman [fayımın] ateşçi, itfaiyeci
fireplace [fayıpleys] ocak, şömine
fireproof [fayıpru:f] yanmaz
firewood [fayıwu:d] odun
firm [fö:m] sağlam, sıkı / değişmez / katı / ticarethane, firma
first [fö:st] birinci, ilk önce
fiscal [fiskıl] devlet gelirine ait, mali
fish [fiş] balık avlamak / balık
fishbone [fişboun] kılçık
fisherman [fişımın] balıkçı
fishing [fişing] balık avı
fishing-line [fişing layn] olta
fishmonger [fişmangı] balık satıcısı
fishy [fişi] şüpheli
fist [fist] yumruk
fit [fit] uygun / uymak / uydurmak
five [fayv] beş
fix [fiks] tespit etmek, saptamak / takmak, tamir etmek
flabby [flebi] sarkık, gevşek
flag [fleg] bayrak
flagship [flegşip] amiral gemisi
flake [fleyk] tane **snowflake** kar tanesi
flame [fleym] alev / alevlenmek
flank [flenk] böğür / ordu cenahı / yan
flannel [flenıl] fanila
flap [flep] çarpma sesi, çarpış / örtü
flare [fleı] alevlenmek
flash [fleş] şimşek, alev / ışıldamak, şimşek gibi çakmak
flask [fla:sk] küçük şişe / termos
flat [flet] düz, yassı / apartman dairesi
flatten [fletın] yassıltmak
flatter [fletı] pohpohlamak, iltifat etmek
flattery [fletıri] dalkavukluk
flavour [fleyvı] lezzet
flaw [flo:] kusur / çatlak, yarık
flax [fleks] keten
flea [fli:] pire
fled, bak **flee**
flee (fled, fled) [fli: fled, fled] kaçmak
fleet [fli:t] filo, donanma

flesh [fleş] et / vücut
fleshy [fleşi] şişman, etli
flew bak **fly**
flexible [fleksibıl] bükülebilir
flick [flik] hafif vuruş
flicker [flikı] yanıp sönmek / titrek ışık
flight [flayt] uçuş, uçma / merdiven (iki kat arasındaki) / kaçış
flimsy [flimzi] ince
fling (flung, flung) [fling, flang, flang] fırlatmak
flint [flint] çakmaktaşı
flip [flip] fiske
flirt [flö:t] flört etmek
float [flout] yüzmek, batmamak / yüzdürmek / havada gitmek
flock [flok] sürü
flood [flad] sel, seylap
floor [flo:] oda zemini / kat / döşeme
flop [flop] çırpınmak, devrilmek, düşürmek
florist [flo:rist] çiçekçi
flour [flauı] un
flourish [flariş] gelişmek, ilerlemek
flourishing [flarişing] müreffeh, mamur, bayındır
flow [flou] akmak
flower [flawı] çiçek
flu [flu:] grip
fluctuate [flakçueyt] değişmek, inip çıkmak
fluency [flu:ınsi] belâgat, akıcılık (dil)
fluent [flu:ınt] akıcı
fluid [flu:id] mayi, sıvı
flung bak **fling**
fluorescent [flu:oresınt] floresan
flurry [flari] birden bastıran yağmur, kar, rüzgâr / telaş
flush [flaş] (yüz) kızarmak / su fışkırtarak temizlemek / fışkırma
flutter [flatı] çırpınmak
fly [flay] sinek
fly [flew, flown] [flay, flu:, floun] uçmak / uçak ile gitmek / hızla gitmek / uçuş
flying [flaying] uçma
foam [foum] köpük
focus [foukıs] odak
foe [fou] düşman
fog [fog] sis
foggy [fogi] sisli
foil [foyl] ince madeni tabaka, levha

fold [fould] katlanmak / kıvrım, kat / ağıl
folk [fouk] halk
folklore [fouklo:] folklor
follow [folou] izlemek, takip etmek
follower [folouwı] taraftar / halef
following [folouwing] aşağıdaki, takip eden
folly [foli] budalalık
fond [fond] seven, hoşlanan
fondle [fondıl] okşamak
food [fu:d] besin, yiyecek
fool [fu:l] aptal / aldatmak
foolish [fuliş] akılsız
foot (çoğulu **feet**) [fut, fi:t] ayak
football [futbo:l] futbol
footnote [futnout] sayfa dibindeki not, dip not
footpath [futpa:t] patika
footprint [futprint] ayak izi
footstep [futstep] ayak izi / ayak sesi
for [fo:, fı] için / müddetle / çünkü
forbade, bak **forbid**
forbear (forbore, forborne) [fo:beı, fo:bo:, fo:bo:n] sakınmak, çekinmek
forbid (forbade, forbidden) [fıbid, fıbeyd, fıbidın] yasaklamak
forebode [fo:boud] işareti olmak / önceden sezmek
forbore, forborne, bak **forbear**
force [fo:s] kuvvet / mecbur etmek
forced [fo:sd] mecburi
forceps [fo:seps] pens
fore [fo:] ön taraf
forecast [fo:ka:st] tahmin (hava)
forefinger [fo:fingı] şehadet parmağı
foreground [fo:graund] ön plan
forehead [forid] alın
foreign [forin] ecnebi, harici, yabancı
foreign currency [forin karinsi] döviz
foreigner [forinı] yabancı, ecnebi
foreman [fo:mın] işçibaşı
foresee (foresaw, foreseen) [fo:si, fo:so:, fo:si:n] önceden sezmek
foresight [fo:sayt] önsezi, basiret, ihtiyat
forest [forist] orman
forestry [foristri] ormancılık

foretell [fo:tel] önceden haber vermek
forever [fırevı] ebediyen
for example [fo: igza:mpıl] örneğin, mesela
forgave, bak **forgive**
forge [fo:c] demir dökmek / uydurmak
forget (forgot, forgotten) [fıget, fıgot, fıgotın] unutmak
forgetful [fıgetfıl] unutkan
forgive (forgave, forgiven) [fıgiv, fıgeyv, fıgivın] affetmek
forgot, forgotten bak **forget**
fork [fo:k] çatal
forlorn [fılo:n] kimsesiz, metruk, kederli
form [fo:m] biçim, şekil / teşkil etmek / meydana gelmek, oluşmak
formal [fo:mıl] resmî
formality [fo:meliti] formalite
formation [fo:meyşın] meydana geliş, oluşum
former [fo:mı] önceki, evvelki
formerly [fo:mıli] eskiden, evvelce
formidable [fo:midıbıl] heybetli, korkunç
formula [fo:myulı] formül
formulate [fo:myuleyt] formül haline koymak
forsake (forsook, forsaken) [fıseyk, fısuk, fıseykın] terketmek
fort [fo:t] kale
forth [fo:t] ileri
forthcoming [fo:tkaming] gelecek
forthright [fo:trayt] açıkça
fortieth [fo:tiıt] kırkıncı
fortification [fo:tifikeyşın] tahkim etme, sağlamlaştırma / hisar
fortify [fo:tifay] tahkim etmek, sağlamlaştırmak
fortnight [fo:tnayt] iki hafta
fortress [fo:tris] kale
fortunate [fo:çınıt] talihli
fortune [fo:çın] talih / servet
forty [fo:ti] kırk
forward [fo:wıd] ileri / ilerletmek
fossil [fosil] fosil
foster [fostı] büyütmek, bakmak
fought, bak **fight**
foul [faul] kirli, adi, fena / faul / kirletmek
found [faund] tesis etmek

found, bak **find**
foundation [faundeyşın] kuruluş / vakıf / temel
founder [faundı] kurucu
foundry [faundri] dökümhane
fountain [fauntin] fıskiye, çeşme
fountain pen [fauntin pen] dolmakalem
four [fo:] dört
fourteen [fo:ti:n] on dört
fourth [fo:t] dördüncü
fowl [faul] tavuk / kuş
fox [foks] tilki
foyer [fwayei] (tiyatrolarda) giriş, fuaye
fracture [frekçı] kırıklık (kemikte)
fragile [frecayl] kolay kırılır
fragment [fregmınt] parça, kesir
fragrance [freygrıns] güzel koku
frame [freym] çerçeve, çatı, iskelet / çerçevelemek / taslağını yapmak / kurmak
framework [freymwö:k] çatı, iskelet
France [fra:ns] Fransa
frank [frenk] samimi
frankly [frenkli] açıkça
frantic [frentik] çılgın
fraternity [frıtö:niti] kardeşlik (erkek)
freak [fri:k] kapris / acayip şey veya insan
freckle [frekıl] çil
free [fri:] hür, özgür, serbest / bedava / serbest bırakmak
freedom [fri:dım] hürriyet, özgürlük
freeze (froze, frozen) [fri:z, frouz, frouzın] donmak, dondurmak
freight [freyt] navlun, yük
French [frenç] Fransız / Fransızca
frenzy [frenzi] çılgınlık
frequency [fri:kwınsi] tekerrür, frekans, sıklık
frequent [frikwınt] sık sık olan
frequently [frikwıntli] sık sık
fresco [freskou] duvar resmi, fresko
fresh [freş] taze, yeni / diğer bir / temiz (hava)
fret [fret] kemirmek / rahatsız etmek
friction [frikşın] sürtünme,
Friday [fraydi] cuma

fried [frayd] kızarmış (yağda)
friend [frend] arkadaş
friendly [frendli] arkadaşça, sokulgan
friendship [frendşip] dostluk, arkadaşlık
fright [frayt] büyük korku
frighten [fraytın] korkutmak
frightful [fraytfıl] korkunç
frigid [fricid] soğuk
fringe [frinc] saçak, kenar
frivolous [frivılıs] havai
frizzy [frizi] kıvırcık
fro [frou] **to and fro** ileri geri / bir yerden bir yere
frog [frog] kurbağa
from [from] ...den, ...dan
front [frant] ön, cephe
frontage [frantic] ön, cephe
frontier [frantiı] cephe, sınır
frost [frost] ayaz, don
froth [frot] köpük
frown [fraun] kaş çatmak
frozen [frouzın] bak **freeze,** donuk, donmuş
frugal [fru:gıl] tutumlu
fruit [fru:t] meyva
fruitful [fru:tfıl] verimli
fruitless [fru:tlis] sonuçsuz, verimsiz
frustrate [frastreyt] engellemek, bozmak
fry [fray] tavada kızartmak
frying-pan [frayingpen] tava
fuel [fiuıl] akaryakıt
fugitive [fiu:citiv] kaçak, firari
fulfil [fulfil] yerine getirmek, ifa etmek
full [ful] dolu
fully [fuli] tamamen
fumble [fambıl] beceriksizce yapmak, tutamamak
fume [fiu:m] buhar, duman
fun [fan] eğlence, neşe
function [fankşın] görev / amaç / fonksiyon / iş görmek, çalışmak
fund [fand] sermaye, fon, para
fundamental [fandımentıl] asli, bellibaşlı
funeral [fiu:nırıl] cenaze töreni
funnel [fanıl] huni, vapur bacası
funny [fani] tuhaf, komik
fur [fö:] kürk
furious [fiuıriıs] kızgın, azgın
furnace [fö:nis] fırın
furnish [fö:niş] döşemek, donatmak

furniture [fö:niçı] mobilya
further [fö:dı] daha ileri, daha uzak / ayrıca / daha
furtive [fö:tiv] sinsi
fury [fiuıri] kızgınlık, hiddet, öfke
fuse [fiu:z] tapa / sigorta (elektrik) / erimek / birleşmek
fusion [fiujın] erime
fuss [fas] sebepsiz telaş
futile [fiu:tayl] boş yere
future [fiu:çı] istikbal, gelecek

G

gag [geg] ağız tıkacı, şaka
gage [geyc] teminat
gaiety [geyıti] neşe
gain [geyn] kazanç / kazanmak
galaxy [gelıksi] gökyüzünde samanyolu
gale [geyl] fırtına
gall [go:l] safra / kin
gallant [gelınt] yiğit
gallery [gelıri] galeri
gallon [gelın] galon
gallop [gelıp] dörtnal / dörtnala koşmak
gallows [gelouz] darağacı
gamble [gembıl] kumar / kumar oynamak
game [geym] oyun
gang [geng] güruh, çete
gangster [gengstı] gangster
gangway [gengwey] geçit, dehliz
gap [gep] gedik, aralık, boşluk
gape [geyp] ağzı açık kalmak
garage [gera:j] garaj
garbage [ga:bic] süprüntü
garden [ga:dın] bahçe
gardener [ga:dnı] bahçıvan
garlic [ga:lik] sarımsak
gargle [ga:gıl] gargara
garland [ga:lınd] çiçekten yapılmış taç
garment [ga:mınt] giyim eşyası
garnish [ga:niş] (yemek) süslemek
garniture [ga:niçı] süs
garrison [gerisın] garnizon
garter [ga:tı] çorap bağı
gas [ges] gaz
gasoline [gesıli:n] benzin
gasp [ga:sp] zorlukla solumak

gastric [gestrik] midevi
gate [geyt] (bahçe v.s.) kapı
gather [gedı] toplanmak, toplamak
gathering [gedıring] toplantı
gauge [geyç] ölçü / ölçü aleti
gaunt [go:nt] zayıf, sıska
gave, bak **give**
gay [gey] şen
gaze [geyz] gözünü dikerek bakmak
gazelle [gızel] ceylan
gear [giı] takım, levazımat / çark tertibatı / vites
gelatine [celıti:n] jelatin
gem [cem] kıymetli taş, mücevher
gendarme [janda:m] jandarma
gender [cendı] ismin cinsi (dilbilgisi)
general [cenırıl] genel / general
in general genellikle
generally [cenrıli] genellikle, çoğu kez
generate [cenıreyt] meydana getirmek / doğurmak
generation [cenıreyşın] nesil, meydana getirme
generosity [cenırositi] cömertlik
generous [cenırıs] cömert, eli açık
genial [ci:nyıl] hoş, güler yüzlü
genius [ci:nyıs] deha, dahi
gentle [centıl] nazik, kibar, hafif
gentleman [centılmın] kibar erkek, bey
gentleness [centılnis] nezaket
gently [centli] nazik şekilde
genuine [cenyuin] hakiki / samimi
geography [ciogrıfi] coğrafya
geology [ciolıci] jeoloji
geometry [ciomıtri] geometri
germ [cö:m] mikrop
German [cö:mın] Alman / Almanca
Germany [cö:mıni] Almanya
gerund [cerınd] fiilden yapılma isim (dilbilgisi)
gesture [cesçı] el, kol, yüz hareketi / jest
get (got, got veya **gotten)** [get, got, gotın] elde et-

mek / almak / kazanmak / erişmek
ghastly [ga:stli] korkunç, ölü gibi
ghost [goust] hortlak
giant [cayınt] dev
giddy [gidi] başı dönmüş / başdöndürücü
giddiness [gidinis] başdönmesi
gift [gift] hediye, armağan / yetenek
gigantic [caygentik] kocaman
giggle [gigıl] kıkır kıkır gülmek
gild [gild] yaldızlamak
gill [gil] solungaç
gilt [gilt] yaldızlı
gimlet [gimlit] matkap
gin [cin] cin (içki)
ginger [cincı] zencefil
gipsy [cipsi] çingene
giraffe [cira:f] zürafa
girdle [gö:dıl] kuşak, korse
girl [gö:l] kız / sevgili
give (gave, given) [giv, geyv, givın] vermek
glacier [glesiı] buzul
glad [gled] memnun
glamour [glemı] çekicilik, cazibe, sihir
glamorous [glemırıs] cazibeli, çekici
glance [gla:ns] bakış / bakıvermek
gland [glend] (vücutta) bez, gudde
glare [gleı] parıldamak
glass [gla:s] cam / bardak
glasses [gla:siz] gözlük
glassy [gla:si] cam gibi
glaze [gleyz] sır / cam geçirmek / sırlamak
glazier [gleyziı] camcı
gleam [gli:m] pırıltı / parıldamak
glee [gli:] sevinç / şarkı
glide [glayd] kaymak, kanat çırpmadan uçmak
glider [glaydı] planör
glimmer [glimı] donuk ışık
glimpse [glimps] bir anlık bakış
glint [glint] parıltı
glisten [glisın] parlamak
glitter [glitı] parıltı / parıldamak
globe [gloub] küre, dünya
gloom [glu:m] karanlık, hüzün
gloomy [glu:mi] hüzünlü / ışıksız
glorify [glorifay] tapmak /

yüceltmek
glorious [glo:riıs] şanlı, şerefli / günlük güneşlik (gün)
glory [glo:ri] şan, debdebe, ihtişam
gloss [glos] cila / cilalamak
glossary [glosıri] küçük sözlük
glossy [glosi] perdahlı
glove [glav] eldiven
glow [glou] kızıllık / hararet / parıldamak
glue [glu:] tutkal, zamk / yapıştırmak
glutton [glatın] obur
gnash [neş] (dişleri) gıcırdatmak
gnaw [no:] kemirmek
go (went, gone) [gou, went, gon] gitmek
goad [goud] dürtmek
goal [goul] hedef, amaç / kale / gol
goalkeeper [goulki:pı] kaleci
goat [gout] keçi
goblet [goblit] kadeh
God [god] Tanrı
goddess [godis] tanrıça
gold [gould] altın
golden [gouldın] altın renginde, altından
goldsmith [gouldsmit] kuyumcu
gone, bak **go** gitmiş
good [gud] iyi
good-bye [gudbay] allahaısmarladık, gülegüle
goodness [gudnis] iyilik, hayır
goods [gudz] eşya, emtia
goose (çoğulu **geese**) [gu:s, gi:s] kaz
gorge [go:c] gırtlak / geçit (coğrafya)
gorgeous [go:cıs] debdebeli, şahane
gossip [gosip] dedikodu / dedikoducu / dedikodu yapmak
got [got] bak **get**
gourd [guıd] su kabağı
govern [gavın] yönetmek, hüküm sürmek
governess [gavınis] mürebbiye, dadı
government [gavınmınt] hükümet, yönetim
governor [gavını] vali
gown [gaun] cüppe
grab [greb] kapmak, ele geçirmek
grace [greys] zerafet

graceful [greysfıl] zarif, nazik

gracious [greyşıs] mültefit **Good gracious! Gracious me!** Aman yarabbi! Allah Allah!

grade [greyd] mertebe, basamak / sınıf / derecelere ayırmak

gradual [grecyuıl] tedrici, azar azar

gradually [grecuıli] tedrici olarak, yavaş yavaş

graduate [grecuit] üniversite mezunu / [grecueyt] (üniversiteden) mezun olmak

grain [greyn] tahıl

grammar [gremı] dilbilgisi

gram(me) [grem] gram

gramophone [gremıfoun] gramofon

grand [grend] muhteşem, büyük

grandchild [grençayld] torun

granddaughter [grendo:tı] kız torun

grandfather [grenfa:dı] büyükbaba

grandmother [grenma:dı] büyükanne

grandpa [grenpa] dede, büyükbaba

grandson [grensan] erkek torun

granite [grenit] granit

grant [gra:nt] bağışlamak, ihsan etmek, vermek / burs

granule [greniul] tanecik

grape [greyp] üzüm

graphic [grefik] yazı, çizilen, grafik

grass [gra:s] çimen, ot

grasshopper [gra:shopı] çekirge

grassy [gra:si] çimenli

grate [greyt] rendelemek / gıcırdamak

grateful [greytfıl] minnettar, müteşekkir

grater [greytı] rende

gratification [gretifikeyşın] memnuniyet

grating [greyting] parmaklık / gıcırtı

gratis [greytis] bedava

gratitude [gretityu:d] minnettarlık, şükran

grave [greyv] mezar / ciddi / düşünceli / önemli

gravel [grevıl] çakıl taşı

gravestone [greyvstoun]

mezar taşı
graveyard [greyvya:d] mezarlık
gravitate [greviteyt] çekilmek / çökmek
gravity [greviti] çekici kuvvet / ciddiyet / yer çekimi
graze [greyz] otlamak
grease [gri:s] yağlamak / makina yağı
great [greyt] büyük, ulu
Greece [gri:s] Yunanistan
greed [gri:d] hırs, tamah
greedy [gri:di] haris, tamahkâr, açgözlü
Greek [gri:k] Yunanlı / Rumca
green [gri:n] yeşil
greengrocer [gri:ngrousı] manav
green house [gri:n haus] limonluk
greet [gri:t] selamlamak
grew, bak **grow**
grey [grey] gri
greyhound [greyhaund] tazı
grid [grid] ızgara
grief [gri:f] keder, hüzün
grievance [gri:vıns] dert, şikayet, keder
grieve [gri:v] kederlenmek
grievous [gri:vıs] elim, keder veren
grill [gril] ızgara
grim [grim] haşin, merhametsiz / korkunç
grimy [graymi] kirli
grin [grin] sırıtmak / sırıtma
grind (ground, ground) [graynd, graund, graund] öğütmek / (dişleri) gıcırdatmak
grip [grip] kavramak / sıkı tutma / pençe
groan [groun] inilti / sızlanmak
grocer [grousı] bakkal
groom [gru:m] seyis / damat
groove [gru:v] yiv
grope [group] el yordamıyla aramak
gross [grous] grosa (12 düzine) / hantal / gayrısafi / toptan / brüt
grotesque [groutesk] gülünç, garip
ground [graund] yer, zemin / arazi / sebep
groundless [graundlis] sebepsiz, asılsız
group [gru:p] grup
grove [grouv] koru (ağaç)
grow (grew, grown) [grou gru:, groun] büyümek,

yetişmek, yetiştirmek
growl [graul] homurdanmak
grown bak **grow** yetişkin
growth [grout] büyüme, gelişme
grudge [grac] garaz, hınç / çok görme
gruesome [gru:sım] korkunç, korku veren
grumble [grambıl] dırdır etmek / şikayet etmek, homurdanmak
guarantee [gerınti:] garanti, kefalet / kefil / kefil olmak, garanti etmek
guard [ga:d] korumak / muhafız, bekçi
guardian [ga:dyın] bekçi, gardiyan
guerilla [gırilı] çete / çete muharebesi
guess [ges] tahmin etmek / tahmin
guest [gest] misafir
guidance [gaydıns] rehberlik
guide [gayd] rehber, kılavuz / yol göstermek / rehberlik etmek
guidebook [gaydbuk] rehber kitap, seyahat rehberi
guideline [gaydlayn] prensip
guilt [gilt] suçluluk
guilty [gilti] suçlu
guitar [gita:] gitar
gulf [galf] körfez
gull [gal] martı
gullet [galit] gırtlak
gulp [galp] yudum / yutmak
gum [gam] diş eti / zamk / yapıştırmak
gun [gan] silah, top, tüfek
gunpowder [ganpaudı] barut
gurgle [gö:gıl] lık lık su sesi
gush [gaş] fışkırmak
gust [gast] bora
gusto [gastou] zevk
guts [gats] bağırsaklar / cesaret
gutter [gatı] oluk
guttural [gatırıl] gırtlaktan çıkan ses
guy [gay] adam, herif
gymnasium [cimneyziım] jimnastik salonu
gymnastics [cimnestiks] jimnastik
gynaecologist [gaynıkolıcist] kadın hastalıkları doktoru
gypsy [cipsi] çingene

H

haberdasher [hebıdeşı] tuhafiyeci

habit [hebit] adet, huy, alışkanlık

habitual [hebiçuıl] mutat, her zamanki

had, bak **have**

haemorrhage [hemıric] kanama (iç)

haemorrhoids [hemıroydz] basur

haggard [hegıd] yüzü yorgun, bitkin

hail [heyl] dolu / dolu yağmak / çağırmak, seslenmek / selamlamak, alkışlamak

hair [heı] saç

haircut [heıkat] saç kesme

hairdo [heıdu] mizampli

hairdresser [heıdresı] kuaför

hairpin [heıpin] firkete, toka (saç)

hairy [heıri] tüylü, kıllı

half [ha:f] yarım, yarı

halftime [haftaym] haftaym, oyunun yarısı

hall [ho:l] salon, hol

hallo [halou] alo

hallucination [hılu:sineyşın] hayal görme

halo [heylou] hale

halt [ho:lt] duruş, mola / duraklamak, durdurmak

halter [ho:ltı] yular

ham [hem] jambon

hamburger [hembö:gı] köfteli sandöviç

hammer [hemı] çekiç / çekiçle çakmak

hammock [hemık] hamak

hamper [hempı] hareketine engel olmak

hand [hend] el

handbag [hendbeg] el çantası

handbook [hendbuk] el kitabı, rehber

handcuff [hendkaf] kelepçe

handful [hendfıl] avuç dolusu

handicap [hendikep] hendikap, engel

handicraft [hendikra:ft] el sanatı

handiwork [hendiwö:k] el işi

handkerchief [henkıçif] mendil

handle [hendıl] ele almak,

yönetmek, kullanmak / sap, kulp
handsome [hensım] yakışıklı
handwriting [hendrayting] el yazısı
handy [hendi] el altında, kullanışlı / becerikli
hang (hung, hung) [heng, hang, hang] asılı durmak, sarkmak
hang [heng] asmak, idam etmek
hanger [hengı] çengel, askı
haphazard [hephezıd] gelişigüzel
happen [hepın] olmak, vuku bulmak
happiness [hepinis] mutluluk
harass [herıs] rahat vermemek
harbour [ha:bı] liman, barınak / barındırmak
hard [ha:d] zor, güç / katı, sert / kuvvetle, gayretle
harden [ha:dın] katılaştırmak
hardly [ha:dli] hemen hemen hiç
hardness [ha:dnis] katılık, güçlük
hardship [ha:dşip] zorluk
hardware [ha:dweı] madeni eşya, nalburiye
hardy [ha:di] dayanıklı
hare [heı] tavşan
harm [ha:m] zarar, ziyan / zarar vermek, zedelemek
harmful [ha:mfıl] zararlı
harmless [ha:mlis] zararsız
harmony [ha:mıni] ahenk, uyum, bağlılık
harness [ha:nis] koşum takımı / (atı) koşumlamak / nehiri sulama veya elektrik için kullanmak
harp [ha:p] harp (çalgı)
harpoon [ha:pu:n] zıpkın
harsh [ha:ş] hırçın, sert
harvest [ha:vist] hasat, ürün / hasat yapmak
has, bak **have**
haste [heyst] acele
hasten [heysın] acele etmek, acele ettirmek
hastily [heystili] aceleyle
hasty [heysti] acele, çabuk, aceleci
hat [het] şapka
hatchet [heçit] küçük balta
hate [heyt] nefret / nefret etmek
hatred [heytrid] nefret

haunted [ho:ntid] perili
have (had, had) [hev, hed, hed] sahip olmak
haven [hevın] sığınacak yer
hawk [ho:k] atmaca
hay [hey] saman
hazard [hezıd] tehlike / şansa bırakmak
haze [heyz] pus, sis
hazelnut [heyzılnat] fındık
hazy [heyzi] puslu
he [hi:, hi] o (erkek)
head [hed] baş / tepe / reis
headache [hedeyk] başağrısı
headlight [hedlayt] far, ön ışık
headline [hedlayn] manşet, başlık
headmaster [hedma:stı] başöğretmen, müdür
headquarters [hedkwo:tız] karargâh
headstrong [hedstrong] inatçı
heal [hi:l] iyileştirmek, iyileşmek
health [helt] sıhhat, sağlık
healthy [helti] sıhhatli
heap [hi:p] küme / yığmak
hear (heard, heard) [hiı, hö:d, hö:d] işitmek, duymak
hearsay [hiısey] şayia, dedikodu, söylenti
heart [ha:t] kalp, yürek
hearten [ha:tın] teşvik etmek
hearty [ha:ti] samimi / sağlam
heat [hi:t] sıcaklık / ısıtmak
heathen [hidın] kâfir
heating [hi:ting] ısıtma
central heating, kalorifer
heave [hi:v] zorlukla kaldırmak / kaldırıp atmak / (deniz gibi) yükselip alçalmak
heaven [hevın] gök, sema / cennet / Tanrı
heavenly [hevınli] semavi, ilahi / fevkalade
heavily [hevili] ağır bir şekilde, şiddetle
heavy [hevi] ağır, güç / şiddetli, yoğun
Hebrew [hi:bru:] Musevi / İbranice
hedge [hec] çit
heed [hi:d] aldırmak, dikkat etmek
heel [hi:l] topuk, ökçe
height [hayt] yükseklik
heir [eı] vâris

heiress [eıris] kadın vâris
held, bak **hold**
helic [helikoptı] helikopter
hell [hel] cehennem
hello [helou] merhaba / alo
helmet [helmit] miğfer
help [help] yardım etmek / yardım / **(can't help)** elinde olmamak, yapmadan edememek
helpful [helpfıl] yardımcı
helpless [helplis] çaresiz
hemisphere [hemisfiı] yarım küre
hen [hen] tavuk
hence [hens] buradan, bu sebepten
her [hö:] onu, onun, ona (kadın)
herald [herıld] haberci / ilan etmek, duyurmak
herd [hö:d] sürü
here [hiı] burada, buraya
hereabout(s) [hiırıbaut] bu civarda
hereditary [hireditıri] irsi
heredity [hirediti] irsiyet, kalıtım
heritage [heritic] miras
hero [hiırou] kahraman
heroic [hirouik] kahramanca
heroin [herouin] eroin
heroine [herouin] kadın kahraman (roman vs.)
herring [hering] ringa balığı
hers [hö:z] onunki (kadın için)
herself [hö:self] kendisi (kadın için)
hesitate [heziteyt] tereddüt etmek, duraksamak
hew (hewed, hewn) [hiu: hiu:d, hiu:n] yontmak / yarmak
heyday [heydey] en iyi günler, gençlik çağı
hi [hay] merhaba
hiccough, hiccup [hikap] hıçkırık / hıçkırmak
hid, bak **hide**
hidden [hidın] (bak, **hide**) saklı, gizli
hide (hid, hidden) [hayd, hid, hidın] saklamak, saklanmak / hayvan derisi
hideous [hidyıs] çirkin
high [hay] yüksek
high fidelity [hay fideliti] sesi çok tabii veren
highly [hayli] son derece / hayli
highway [haywey] anayol,

karayolu

hijack [haycek] (uçak v.s.) kaçırmak

hill [hil] tepe

him [him] onu, ona (erkek)

himself [himself] kendisi

hind [haynd] arka

hinder [hindı] engel olmak

hint [hint] ima etmek

hip [hip] kalça

hire [hayı] kira / kiralamak

his [hiz] onun, onunki (erkek)

hiss [his] tıslama

historian [histo:riın] tarihçi

historical [histo:rikıl] tarihi

history [histıri] tarih

hit [hit] vurmak

hitchhike [hiçhayk] otostop yapmak

hive [hayv] arı kovanı

hoard [ho:d] biriktirmek

hoarse [ho:s] boğuk

hobble [hobıl] köstek / kösteklemek

hobby [hobi] zevk için meşguliyet, merak

hockey [hoki] hokey

hoe [hou] çapa / çapalamak

hoist [hoyst] yükseltme / kaldırma

hold [hould] tutunacak yer / gemi ambarı

hold (held, held) [hould, held, held] içine almak, tutmak / sahip olmak / korumak / düzenlemek

holding [houlding] şirketler topluluğu

hole [houl] çukur, delik

holiday [holıdi] tatil günü, tatil, bayram

Holland [holınd] Hollanda

hollow [holou] içi boş, çukur, oyuk

holy [houli] kutsal

home [houm] aile ocağı, ev / yurt

homemade [hoummeyd] evde yapılmış

homesick [houmsik] yurt özlemi çeken

homicide [homisayd] cinayet

homosexual [houmısekşuıl] eşcinsel

honest [onist] dürüst, namuslu

honesty [onisti] dürüstlük

honey [hani] bal

honeymoon [hanimu:n] balayı

honorary [onırıri] fahri, onursal

honour [onı] namus, şeref / hürmet göstermek
honourable [onırıbıl] muhterem, şerefli
honoured [onıd] şerefli
hood [hud] başlık / (otomobil v.s.) kaput
hook [huk] kanca / kanca ile tutmak
hoop [hu:p] halka, çember
hoot [hu:t] ötmek, boru çalmak, düdük çalmak
hop [hop] sekmek, sıçramak
hope [houp] umut / ummak
hopeful [houpfıl] umutlu, umut verici
hopeless [houplis] umutsuz
horizon [hırayzın] ufuk
horizontal [horizontıl] yatay
horn [ho:n] boynuz / klakson
horoscope [horıskoup] yıldız falı, burç
horrible [horibıl] müthiş, berbat
horrid [horid] müthiş, iğrenç
horrify [horifay] dehşet vermek
horror [horı] dehşet
horse [ho:s] at, beygir
horseman [ho:smın] atlı
horse race [ho:s reys] at yarışı
horseshoe [ho:s şu:] nal
hose [houz] hortum
hospital [hospitıl] hastane
hospitality [hospiteliti] konukseverlik
host [houst] ev sahibi, otel sahibi / çokluk, kalabalık
hostage [hostic] rehine
hostel [hostıl] öğrenci (işçi) yurdu
hostess [houstis] ev sahibesi / hostes
hostile [hostayl] düşman
hostility [hostiliti] düşmanlık
hot [hot] sıcak, kızgın
hotel [houtel] otel
hound [haund] av köpeği
hour [auı] saat (zaman)
hourly [auıli] saatte bir
house [haus] ev, mesken / iskan etmek, barındırmak
household [haushould] ev halkı
housewife [hauswayf] ev kadını
hovercraft [hovıkreft] tazyikli hava üzerinde giden ta-

şıt

how [hau] nasıl

however [hauevı] her ne şekilde, her ne kadar

howl [haul] ulumak

hubbub [habıb] gürültü

huddle [hadıl] toplanmak, yumaklanmak

hue [hiu:] renk

hug [hag] kucaklamak

huge [hiu:c] çok iri

hull [hal] gemi teknesi

hullo [halou] alo, merhaba

hum [ham] vızıldamak / vızıltı, uğultu, mırıltı

human [hiu:mın] insan / beşeri, insani

humane [hiumeyn] şefkatli, insancıl

humanism [hiu:mınizm] hümanizm

humanity [hiumeniti] beşeriyet, insanlık

humble [hambıl] mütevazi, alçak gönüllü

humbug [hambag] şarlatan / saçma

humid [hiu:mid] rutubetli

humidity [hiu:miditi] rutubet

humiliate [hiu:milieyt] küçük düşürmek

humorous [hiu:mırıs] nükteli, güldürücü

humour [hiu:mı] mizah / mizaç, huy

hump [hamp] kambur, hörgüç / tümsek

hunch [hanş] kambur / içine doğma

hundred [handrıd] yüz (sayı)

hung, bak **hang**

Hungary [hangıri] Macaristan

hunger [hangı] açlık / şiddetli istek

hungry [hangri] aç

hunt [hant] avlamak, aramak

hunter [hantı] avcı

hunting [hanting] avcılık

huntsman [hantsmın] avcı

hurdle [hö:dıl] mania, enge

hurl [hö:l] fırlatmak

hurray [hurey], **hurrah** [hura:] yaşasın, yaşa

hurricane [harikın] kasırga

hurry [hari] acele etmek, acele ettirmek / acele

hurt (hurt, hurt) [hö:t] incitmek, yaralamak

husband [hazbınd] koca

hush [haş] sükut / susturmak / sus!

husky [haski] kısık (ses)
hustle [hasıl] itip kakma
hut [hat] kulübe
hybrid [haybrid] melez
hydraulic [haydro:lik] hidrolik
hydro- [haydrou] suya ait anlamında ek
hydrogen [haydrıcin] hidrojen
hydrophobia [haydrofobiı] kuduz
hygiene [hayci:n] sağlık bilgisi
hymn [him] ilahi (müzik)
hyphen [hayfın] tire
hypnotism [hipnıtizm] ipnotizma
hypocrisy [hipokrisi] mürailik, yalancılık
hypothesis [haypotisis] iki yüzlülük
hysteria [histiıriı] sinir bozukluğu, isteri

I

I [ay] ben (şahıs)
ice [ays] buz
iceberg [aysbö:g] aysberg buzdağı
ice-cream [ayskri:m] dondurma
iceland [ayslınd] izlanda
icy [aysi] buzlu
idea [aydiı] fikir
ideal [aydiıl] ideal, mükemmel / ideal, ülkü
idealist [aydiılist] idealist, ülkücü
identical [aydentikıl] aynı, farksız, özdeş
identification [aydentifikeyşın] hüviyet, kimlik
identify [aydentifay] teşhis etmek, kimliğini tanımak
identity [aydentiti] hüviyet / benzerlik
ideology [aydiolıci] ideoloji
idiocy [idiısi] ahmaklık
idiom [idyım] deyim
idiot [idyıt] çok aptal, bön
idle [aydıl] aylak, boş, tembel / işsiz, çalışmayan / boş gezmek
idol [aydıl] tapılan kimse / put
i.e. [ay i:] yani, demek ki
if [if] eğer, ise
ignite [ignayt] tutuşturmak

ignition [ıgnişın] tutuşturma / kontak (oto)
ignorance [ignırıns] cehalet, bilgisizlik
ignorant [ignırınt] cahil, bihaber
ignore [igno:] aldırmamak, görmemezlikten gelmek
il— [il] zıddı, gayri, olmayan anlamında önek
ill [il] hasta, fena
illegal [ili:gıl] kanunsuz
illegible [ilecibıl] okunaksız
illegitimate [ilicitimit] gayrimeşru, piç
illicit [ilisit] kanuna aykırı
illiterate [ilitırit] ümmi, cahil
illness [ilnis] hastalık
illogical [ilocikıl] mantıksız
illuminate [ilyu:mineyt] aydınlatmak
illumination [ilyu:mineyşın] aydınlatma
illusion [ilu:jın] hayal, aldatıcı görünüş
illusionist [ılu:jınist] hokkabaz, illüzyonist
illustrate [ilıstreyt] resimlemek / açıklamak
illustrated [ilıstreytid] resimli
illustration [ilıstreyşın] resim
im— [im] olmayan, değil anlamında önek
image [imic] görüntü
imagine [imecin] tahayyül etmek, göz önünde canlandırmak, düşünmek
imaginary [imecinıri] hayali
imagination [imecineyşın] muhayyele, tahayyül, imge
imbecile [imbisi:l] ahmak
imitate [imiteyt] taklit etmek
imitation [imiteyşın] taklit, imitasyon
immature [imıtyuı] ham, olmamış
immediate [imi:dyıt] acele, pek yakın / doğrudan
immediately [imi:dyıtli] derhal, hemen
immense [imens] uçsuz bucaksız
immigrant [imigrınt] muhacir, göçmen
immigrate [imigreyt] hicret etmek, göçmek
immigration [imigreyşın] muhaceret, göç
immortal [imo:tıl] ölümsüz
immune [imyu:n] muaf, ba-

ğışık

impact [impekt] çarpma

impartial [impa:şıl] tarafsız, taraf tutmayan

impatience [impeyşıns] sabırsızlık

impatient [impeyşınt]sabırsız

impending [impending] yakında olacak, beklenen

impenetrable [impenitrıbıl] nüfuz edilmez, içine işlenmez

imperative [imperıtiv] zorunlu / emir (kipi)

imperceptible [impıseptibıl] hissedilmez

imperfect [impö:fikt] kusurlu / (dilbilgisinde) geçmişte devamlı hal

imperial [impiıriıl] şahane / imparatora ait

imperil [imperil] tehlikeye atmak

impermeable [impö:miıbıl] (su) geçirmez

impersonal [impö:sınıl] şahsi olmayan

impersonate [impö:sıneyt] rolüne girmek, canlandırmak

impertinent [impö:tinınt] küstah, saygısız

imperturbable [impıtö:bıbıl] soğukkanlı

impetous [impeçyuıs] coşkun, atılgan

implement [implımınt] alet, vasıta, araç

implicate [implikeyt] sokmak, karıştırmak

implicit [implisit] kati, kesin / ima edilen

implied [implayd] kapalı bir şekilde söylenmiş, değinilen, ima edilen

implore [implo:] istirham etmek, yalvararak istemek

imply [implay] delalet etmek, demek istemek

impolite [impılayt] nezaketsiz, terbiyesiz

import [impo:t] ithal / İthal etmek

importance [impo:tıns] önem

important [impo:tınt] önemli

importer [impo:tı] ithalatçı

impose [impouz] yüklemek / zorlamak / empoze etmek

imposing [impouzing] heybetli

impossibility [imposibiliti] imkânsızlık
impossible [imposibıl] imkânsız, olanaksız
impotence [impıtıns] iktidarsızlık, güçsüzlük
impoverish [impovıriş] fakirleşmek
impracticable [imprektikıbıl] yapılamaz / idaresi güç
impregnate [impregneyt] aşılamak, döllemek
impress [impres] (damga v.s.) basmak / iz bırakmak, etkilemek
impression [impreşın] izlenim, intiba, etki / nüsha, baskı
impressive [impresiv] etkileyici, tesir edici
imprint [imprint] basmak, tab etmek
imprison [imprizın] hapsetmek
improbable [improbıbıl] muhtemel olmayan
improper [impropı] münasebetsiz, yersiz
improve [impru:v] iyileştirmek, ıslah etmek, düzeltmek
improvement [impru:vmınt] ilerleme, gelişim
imprudence [impru:dıns] ihtiyatsızlık
imprudent [impru:dınt] düşüncesiz, tedbirsiz
impudence [impiu:dıns] arsızlık, yüzsüzlük
impudent [impyudınt] arsız, yüzsüz
impulse [impals] itme, ani arzu
impulsive [impalsiv] atılgan
impure [impyuı] pis, iffetsiz
in [in] ...de, içinde, içine
in— [in] olmayan, değil anlamında önek
inability [inıbiliti] iktidarsızlık, güçsüzlük
inaccessible [ineksesıbıl] sokulunmaz, yanaşılmaz
inaudible [ino:dibıl] işitilemez
inaugurate [ino:gyureyt] resmi açılış veya başlangıç yapmak
inborn [inbo:n] doğuştan
incapable [inkeypıbıl] yeteneksiz, kabiliyetsiz
incessant [insesınt] fasılasız, hiç durmayan

inch [inç] pus: 25,4 mm
incident [insidınt] küçük olay
incite [insayt] harekete geçirmek, kışkırtmak
inclination [inklineyşın] meyil / eğilim
incline [inklayn] yokuş / eğmek
inclined [inklaynd] eğilimli / eğik, yatkın
include [inklu:d] içine almak, kapsamak
inclusion [inklu:jın] kapsam
inclusive [inklu:siv] içine alan, her şey dahil
incognito [inkognitou] takma adla
income [inkam] irat, gelir
income tax [inkam teks] gelir vergisi
incomparable [inkompırıbıl] emsalsiz
incompetent [inkompitınt] kabiliyetsiz, yeteneksiz
inconsistent [inkınsistınt] kararsız, uymaz
inconvenient [inkınvi:nyınt] sakıncalı, uygun olmayan
incorporation [inko:pıreyşın] birleşme, kooperatif, şirket
incorrect [inkırekt] doğru olmayan, yanlış
increase [inkri:s] çoğaltmak, artmak / artma
incredible [inkredibıl] inanılmaz
incurable [inkyu:rıbıl] tedavi edilemez
indebted [indetid] medyun, borçlu, minnettar
indecent [indi:sınt] hayasız, müstehcen
indecision [indisijın] tereddüt, kararsızlık
indeed [indi:d] gerçekten
indefinite [indefinit] belirsiz
indelible [indelibıl] silinmez
independence [indipendıns] bağımsızlık
independant [indipendınt] bağımsız
index [indeks] fihrist, endeks
India [indiı] Hindistan
Indian [indiın] Hintli, **Red Indian** [red indiın] Kızılderili
indicate [indikeyt] göstermek
indict [indikt] suçlamak
indifference [indifırıns] ala-

kasızlık, ilgisizlik
indifferent [indifırınt] ilgisiz, aldırış etmeyen, kayıtsız
indigestion [indicesçın] hazımsızlık
indignant [indignınt] kızgın
indirect [indirekt] dolaşık, dolaylı
indiscreet [indiskri:t] tedbirsiz, boşboğaz
indispensable [indispensıbıl] zaruri, kaçınılmaz
indisputable [indispyutıbıl] muhakkak, tartışılmaz
indistinct [indistinkt] belli belirsiz
individual [individyuıl] birey / bireysel, kişisel / tek
individually [individyuıli] ferden, teker teker
indolence [indılıns] haylazlık
indoor [indo:] ev içinde olan veya yapılan
indoors [indo:z] ev içinde
induce [indyu:s] müsebbip olmak, ikna etmek, yol açmak
indulge [indalc] müsamaha etmek, göz yummak, düşkün olmak
industrial [indastriıl] endüstriye ait, sınai
industrious [indastriıs] çalışkan
industry [indıstri] sanayi, endüstri
inefficient [inifişınt] etkisiz, yetersiz, az
inequality [inikwoliti] eşitsizlik
inert [inö:t] atıl, yumuşak, hareketsiz
inertia [inö:şyı] atalet, uyuşukluk
inevitable [inevitıbıl] kaçınılmaz, çaresiz
inexhaustible [inigzo:stıbıl] tükenmez, yorulmaz
inexperience [inikspiıriıns] tecrübesizlik
infallible [infelıbıl] kat'i, hatasız, şaşmaz
infamous [infımıs] kötü şöhretli, rezil
infamy [infımi] fena şöhret, rezalet
infant [infınt] küçük çocuk
infantry [infıntri] piyade
infect [infekt] bulaştırmak, aşılamak
infection [infekşın] bulaşma, sirayet
infectious [infekşıs] sari,

bulaşıcı
infer [inf**ö**:] sonuç çıkarmak
inferior [infıırıı] aşağısında, ikinci derecede
infernal [inf**ö**:nıl] cehennemi
infidel [infidıl] kâfir
infidelity [infideliti] sadakatsizlik, ihanet
infiltrate [infiltreyt] sızmak, girmek
infinite [infinit] sonsuz
infinitive [infinitiv] mastar (dilbilgisi)
infinity [infiniti] sonsuzluk
infirm [inf**ö**:m] hastalıklı, metanetsiz
infirmity [inf**ö**:miti] sakatlık, zayıflık
inflame [infleym] alevlendirmek, tutuşturmak
inflammable [inflemıbıl] çabuk ve kolay yanar, tutuşur
inflate [infleyt] şişirmek / enflasyon yapmak
inflation [infleyşın] enflasyon, şişme
inflexible [infleksıbıl] bükülmez
inflict [inflikt] duçar etmek, (ağrı, acı, ceza) vermek
influence [influıns] etki, kuvvet / etkilemek
influential [influenşıl] etkili
influenza [influenzı] grip
inform [inf**o**:m] haber vermek
informal [inf**o**:mıl] teklifsiz, resmi olmayan
information [infımeyşın] haber, enformasyon
informer [inf**o**:mı] gammaz
infringe [infrinc] ihlal etmek, düzeni bozmak
infuriate [infyuırieyt] kızdırmak, öfkelendirmek
ingenuity [incinyuiti] hüner, marifet
ingenious [inci:nyıs] marifetli, akıllı
inhabit [inhebit] ikamet etmek, barınmak
inhabitant [inhebitınt] oturan, sakin, nüfus
inhale [inheyl] nefes çekmek
inherit [inherit] miras olarak almak
inheritor [inheritı] varis
inhibit [inhibit] engel olmak
inhuman [inhiu:mın] gaddar
inimitable [inimitıbıl] eşsiz, taklit edilemez

initial [inişıl] ilk, ilk harf
initiation [inişleyşın] başlama, ilk adımını atma
initiative [inişıtiv] kişisel girişim, inisiyatif
inject [incekt] enjeksiyon yapmak, içeri sokmak
injure [incı] zarar vermek, zedelemek
injured [incıd] yaralı
injury [incıri] yara, zarar
injustice [incastis] haksızlık
ink [ink] mürekkep
inkling [inkling] ima, seziş
inland [inlınd] etrafı kara (arazi) olan, iç bölge
in-law [inlo:] kayın (peder v.s.); **mother-in-law** kayınvalide
inlet [inlet] giriş yolu / koy
inn [in] han / meyhane
inner [inı] dahili, iç
innocence [inısıns] masumiyet, suçsuzluk
innocent [inisınt] masum
innovation [inıveyşın] yenilik
innumerable [inyu:mırıbıl] sayısız
inoculate [inokyuleyt] (hastalık için) aşılamak
input [input] girdi, veri
inquest [inkwest] bir ölüm üzerinde yapılan adli soruşturma
inquire [inkwayı] sormak, soruşturmak
inquiry [inkwayıri] sorgu, soruşturma
inquisitive [inkwizitiv] mütecessis, meraklı
insane [inseyn] mecnun, deli
insatiable [inseyşıbıl] açgözlü, doymaz
inscription [inskripşın] yazı, kitabe
insect [insekt] haşere, böcek
insecure [insikyuı] emniyetsiz, tehlikede
insensitive [insensitiv] hassas olmayan, hissiz
inseparable [insepırıbıl] ayrılmaz
insert [insö:t] sokmak, eklemek, ilave etmek
inside [insayd] iç, içeride, içinde, içine
insight [insayt] anlayış, seziş
insignificant [insignifikınt] önemsiz
insincere [insinsiı] mürai,

yüze gülen
insipid [insipid] yavan
insist [insist] ısrar etmek
insolent [insılınt] küstah
insoluble [insolyubıl] halledilemez, çözümlenemez / erimez
insomnia [insomniı] uykusuzluk
inspect [inspekt] denetlemek, teftiş etmek
inspection [inspekşın] teftiş, denetim
inspector [inspektı] müfettiş
inspiration [inspireyşın] ilham
inspire [inspayı] ilham etmek
instability [instıbiliti] sebatsızlık, kararsızlık
install [insto:l] kurmak, yerleştirmek
instalment [insto:lmınt] taksit / tefrika
instance [instıns] örnek, misal
instant [instınt] an, ani
instantaneous [instınteyniıs] enstantane, ani
instantly [instıntli] aniden, derhal
instead [insted] yerine
instigate [instigeyt] tahrik etmek, kışkırtmak
instinct [instinkt] içgüdü
institute [instityu:t] tesis etmek, kurmak / enstitü
institution [instityu:şın] tesis, müessese
instruct [instrakt] öğretmek, talimat vermek
instruction [instrakşın] talimat
instrument [instrumınt] alet
instrumental [instrumentıl] aletle yapılan
insufficient [insıfişınt] kifayetsiz, yetersiz
insulate [insyuleyt] izole etmek, tecrit etmek
insulator [insyuleytı] izolatör, yalıtkan
insult [insalt] hakaret / hakaret etmek
insurance [inşuırıns] sigorta
insure [inşuı] sigorta etmek, garantilemek
intact [intekt] bozulmamış, zedelenmemiş
intake [inteyk] giriş noktası
integral [integrıl] tamamlayıcı / tam, bütün / integ-

ral (matematik)
integrity [integriti] bütünlük, tamlık / dürüstlük
intelect [intilekt] akıl, zeka
intellectual [intilekçuıl] kültürlü, entellektüel
intelligence [intelicıns] zekâ / istihbarat
intelligent [intelicınt] zeki
intend [intend] niyet etmek
intense [intens] şiddetli
intensify [intensifay] şiddetlendirmek
intensive [intensiv] şiddetli, yoğun
intent [intent] kasıt / kararlı, niyetli
intention [intenşın] niyet
intentional [intenşınıl] kasti
inter [intı] arasında anlamına gelen önek
intercept [intısept] yolunu kesmek
interchange [intıçeync] karşılıklı değiştirmek / değiş tokuş yapmak
intercommunication [intıkomyunikeyşın] haberleşme
intercourse [intıko:s] ilişki / cinsel birleşme
interest [intrist, intırest] ilgilendirmek, ilgi çekmek / ilgi, merak, heves / pay / kazanç / faiz
interested [intristid] ilgili, ilgi duyan
interesting [intıresting] enteresan, ilginç
interfere [intıfiı] karışmak, burnunu sokmak, müdahale etmek
interference [intıfiırıns] müdahale, karışma
interior [intiıriı] iç, dahil
interlock [intılok] kenetlenmek
interlude [intılu:d] ara, aralık
intermediate [intımi:dyıt] orta, ortadaki
intern [intö:n] enterne etmek, tecrit etmek
internal [intö:nıl] dahili
international [intıneşınıl] uluslararası
interpret [intö:prit] tercümanlık etmek, yorumlamak
interrogate [interıgeyt] sorguya çekmek
interrogation [interıgeyşın] sorgu

interrupt [intırapt] sözünü kesmek / kesmek
interruption [intırapşın] kesilme, inkıta
intersect [intısekt] kesişmek
interval [intıvıl] fasıla, ara
intervene [intıvi:n] araya girmek, karışmak
intervention [intıvenşın] müdahale
interview [intıvyu:] mülakat, görüşme
intestine [intestin] bağırsak
intimacy [intimısi] gizlilik / yakın dostluk, samimiyet
intimate [intimıt] içten, yakın
intimidate [intimideyt] korkutmak
into [intu] içine, içeriye
intolerable [intolırıbıl] çekilmez, tahammül edilmez
intonation [intouneyşın] sesin ahengi
intoxicate [intoksikeyt] sarhoş etmek
intransitive [intra:nsitiv] geçişsiz (fiil)
intrigue [intri:g] entrika
introduce [intrıdyu:s] sokmak / tanıştırmak, takdim etmek / başlatmak
introduction [intrıdakşın] takdim, tanıtma / başlangıç
intrude [intru:d] zorla girmek
intuition [intyuişın] sezme, içgüdü
invade [inveyd] istila etmek
invalid [invelid] hükümsüz, geçersiz
invalid [invıli:d] malul, sakat, hasta
invaluable [invelyuıbıl] çok değerli, paha biçilmez
invariable [inveıriıbıl] değişmez
invasion [inveyjın] istila
invent [invent] icat etmek
invention [invenşın] icat, buluş
inventor [inventı] mucit
inverse [invö:s] ters
invert [invö:t] ters çevirmek
invest [invest] kuşatmak / yatırım yapmak
investigate [investigeyt] soruşturmak
investigation [investigeyşın] soruşturma, tahkikat

investment [investmınt] (bir işe) para yatırma, yatırım
invisible [invizibıl] gözle görülmez
invitation [inviteyşın] davet, çağrı
invite [invayt] davet etmek, çağırmak
inviting [invayting] cazibeli, çekici
invoice [invoys] fatura
involve [involv] sarmak, karıştırmak, gerektirmek
inward [inwıd] içe doğru
iodine [ayıdi:n] iyod
ir- [ir] değil, zıddı anlamında önek
Ireland [ayılınd] İrlanda
Irish [ayriş] İrlandalı
iron [ayın] demir / ütü / ütülemek
ironic [ayronik] istihzalı, alaylı
irony [ayrıni] istihza, alay
irrational [ireşınıl] mantıksız
irregular [iregyulı] düzensiz
irrelevant [irelıvınt] konu dışı, sadet harici
irresistible [irezistibıl] karşı konulmaz, dayanılmaz
irresponsible [irisponsibıl] sorumsuz
irrigate [irigeyt] su vermek, su sevketmek
irrigation [irigeyşın] sulama, irigasyon
irritate [iriteyt] kızdırmak, öfkelendirmek
Islam [izla:m] İslam
island [aylınd] ada
isolate [aysıleyt] ayırmak, tecrit etmek
Israel [izreyl] İsrail
issue [işyu] çıkış, neşir / mesele / çıkmak / yayımlamak
it [it] (cansız ve hayvanlar için) o, onu, ona
Italy [itıli] İtalya
Italian [itelyın] İtalyan, İtalyanca
itch [iç] kaşınmak / uyuz
item(s) [aytims] müfredat, madde
itinerary [aytinırıri] yolculukta izlenecek yol
its [its] onun (hayvan, cansız)
itself [itself] (cansız ve hayvanlar için) kendisi
ivory [ayvıri] fildişi
ivy [ayvi] sarmaşık

J

jack [cek] kriko / bacak, vale (iskambilde)
jackal [ceko:l] çakal
jacket [cekit] ceket
jail [ceyl] hapishane / hapsetmek
jam [cem] sıkıştırmak, sıkışmak / sıkışıklık / reçel
janitor [cenitı] kapıcı
January [ceniuıri] Ocak ayı
Japan [cıpen] Japonya
Japanese [cepıni:z] Japonyalı, Japonca
jar [ca:] kavanoz, çömlek / gıcırtı / sarsmak
jaundice [co:ndis] sarılık hastalığı
javelin [cevlin] mızrak, sırık, cirit
jaw [co:] çene
jawbone [co:boun] çene kemiği
jazz [cez] caz
jealous [celıs] kıskanç
jealousy [celısi] kıskançlık
jeep [ci:p] cip
jeer [ciı] alay etmek
jelly [celi] pelte
jeopardize [cepıdayz] tehlikeye koymak
jerk [cö:k] sarsıntı / sarsmak
jersey [cö:zi] kazak / jarse kumaş
jest [cest] şaka / şaka etmek
Jesus [ci:zıs] İsa peygamber
jet [cet] kehribar / fışkırma / fışkırmak / jet
Jew [cu:] Yahudi, Musevi
jewel [cu:ıl] mücevher
jewelry [cu:ılri] mücevherat
jingle [cingıl] çıngırtı / çıngırdamak
job [cob] görev, hizmet, meslek, iş
jobless [coblis] işsiz
jockey [coki] cokey
jog [cog] sarsmak / yavaş yavaş yol almak, koşmak
join [coyn] birleşmek, katılmak
joiner [coynı] doğramacı
joint [coynt] müşterek / eklem, mafsal / parça et (pişirmek için)
jointly [coyntli] ortaklaşa
joist [coyst] kiriş
joke [couk] şaka / şaka yap-

mak
jolly [coli] neşeli
jolt [coult] sarsıntı
Jordan [co:dın] Ürdün
jostle [cosıl] itip kakmak
journal [cö:nıl] gazete / gündem
journalist [cö:nılist] gazeteci
journey [cö:ni] seyahat
jovial [couviıl] keyifli
joy [coy] sevinç, büyük kıvanç
jubilee [cu:bili:] (ellinci v.s.) yıldönümü, jübile
judge [cac] yargıç, hakem / hüküm vermek
judgement [cacmınt] hüküm, yargı / fikir / muhakeme
judicial [cu:dişıl] adli, kanuni
jug [cag] su kabı
juggler [caglı] jonklör, hokkabaz
juice [cu:s] meyva suyu
July [culay] temmuz
jumble [cambıl] karmakarışık / karıştırmak
jump [camp] sıçrayış / atlamak, zıplamak
junction [cankşın] kavşak
juncture [cankçı] birleşme yeri / durum, zaman
June [cu:n] haziran
jungle [cangıl] vahşi ve sık orman
junior [cu:nyı] genç, kıdemsiz
junk [cank] pılı pırtı
just [cast] tam, henüz, ancak / adil, doğru
justice [castis] adalet, hak
justify [castifay] haklı çıkarmak
justly [castli] hakkıyla
juvenile [cu:vınayl] gençliğe ait, gençlikle ilgili

K

kangaroo [kengıru:] kanguru
karat [kerıt] ayar
keel [ki:l] gemi omurgası
keen [ki:n] keskin / hassas / şiddetli / gayretli
keep (kept, kept) [ki:p, kept, kept] tutmak, saklamak, muhafaza etmek
keeper [ki:pı] bekçi

keepsake [ki:pseyk] yadigâr, hatıra
kennel [kenıl] köpek kulübesi
kept, bak **keep**
kerb [kö:b] kaldırım kenarı
kernel [kö:nıl] çekirdek içi, öz
kettle [ketıl] çaydanlık
key [ki:] anahtar
khan [ka:n] han (kral)
kick [kik] tekmelemek / tekme
kid [kid] oğlak / çocuk / (argo) muziplik etmek
kidnap [kidnep] bir insan kaçırmak
kidney [kidni] böbrek
kill [kil] öldürmek
killer [kilı] katil
kilogram [kilougrem] kilo
kin [kin] akraba
kind [kaynd] cins, tür / müşfik, nazik
kindergarten [kindıga:tın] ana okulu, yuva
kindness [kayndnis] nezaket
king [king] kral
kingdom [kingdım] kraliyet
king size [king sayz] büyük boy
kiss [kis] öpmek / öpücük
kit [kit] eşya, avadanlık
kitchen [kiçin] mutfak
kite [kayt] uçurtma
kitten [kitın] yavru kedi
knack [nek] maharet
knead [ni:d] yoğurmak
knee [ni:] diz
kneel (knelt, knelt) [ni:l, nelt, nelt] diz çökmek
knelt, bak **kneel**
knife (çoğulu **knives)** [nayf, nayvz] bıçak, çakı
knight [nayt] şövalye
knit [nit] örgü örmek
knob [nob] topak, kelle / kapı tokmağı
knock [nok] vurmak, (kapıyı) çalmak / çakmak / vuruş, darbe
knot [not] düğüm / düğümlemek / ağaç budağı / deniz mili
know (knew, known) [nou, niu, noun] bilmek / tanımak
knowledge [nolic] bilgi, malumat
known [noun] bak **know** tanınmış, bilinen
knuckle [nakıl] parmak mafsalı, eklem

L

label [leybıl] etiket
laboratory [lıborıtri] laboratuvar
laborious [lıbo:rııs] zahmetli
labour [leybı] iş, çalışma, emek
labyrinth [lebırint] labirent, dehliz
lace [leys] (ayakkabı) bağ / tül, dantel
lack [lek] eksiklik / eksik olmak
lacking [leking] eksik
lacquer [lekı] vernik
lad [led] delikanlı
ladder [ledı] merdiven
ladle [leydıl] kepçe
lady [leydi] hanımefendi
lager [la:gı] bir cins bira
laggard [legıd] geri kalan, ağır hareket eden
laid, bak **lay**
lain, bak **lie**
lake [leyk] göl
lamb [lem] kuzu
lame [leym] topal / yetersiz, ikna etmeyen
lament [lıment] yas tutmak / yas
lamp [lemp] lamba
lamp-shade [lempşeyd] abajur
lance [la:ns] mızrak
land [lend] ülke / toprak, kara, arazi / karaya çıkmak / (uçak) inmek
landing [lending] karaya çıkma / sahanlık, antre
landlady [lendleydi] ev sahibesi
landlord [lendlo:d] ev sahibi / otelci / pansiyoncu
landscape [lendskeyp] manzara
landslide [lendslayd] heyelan (coğrafya)
lane [leyn] dar yol
language [lengwic] dil, lisan
languid [lengwid] baygın, yorgun, hareketsiz
languish [lengwiş] mecalsiz
lantern [lentö:n] el feneri
lap [lep] dizin üstü, kucak / kedi gibi içmek, şıpırdatmak
lapse [leps] (zaman) geçmek / hata
large [la:c] iri, büyük
largely [la:cli] büyük ölçüde

lark [la:k] tarlakuşu
lascivious [lısivyıs] şehvete düşkün
lash [leş] kamçı darbesi / kamçılamak
lass [les] genç kız
lassitude [lesityu:d] yorgunluk
last [la:st] son / geçen / dayanmak / sürmek
lasting [la:sting] dayanıklı
latch [leç] mandal
late [leyt] geç / merhum
lately [leytli] son zamanlarda, geçenlerde
lather [la:dı] sabun köpüğü / sabunlanmak / köpürtmek
Latin [letin] Latince
latitude [letityu:d] enlem, arz derecesi (coğrafya)
latter [letı] sonraki
lattice [letis] kafes
laugh [la:f] gülüş / gülmek
laughable [la:fıbıl] gülünç
laughter [la:ftı] kahkaha
launch [lo:nç] gemiyi suya indirmek / fırlatmak
laundry [lo:ndri] çamaşırhane / çamaşır
lavatory [levıtri] tuvalet, hela
lavender [levindı] lavanta
lavish [leviş] müsrif / bol bol vermek
law [lo:] kanun, yasa, kural
lawful [lo:fıl] kanuna uygun
lawn [lo:n] çimenlik
lawyer [lo:yı] avukat
lax [leks] dikkatsiz, dalgacı
lay, bak **lie**
lay (laid, laid) [ley, leyd, leyd] koymak / yatırmak / sermek / (sofrayı) hazırlamak / yumurtlamak
layer [leyı] kat, tabaka
lay-out [leyaut] plan
lazy [leyzi] tembel
lead [led] kurşun
lead (led, led) [li:d, led, led] götürmek / liderlik etmek
leader [li:dı] reis, lider, elebaşı, önder
leadership [li:dışip] liderlik, önderlik
leading [li:ding] en önemli, belli başlı
leaf [li:f] yaprak
leaflet [li:flet] broşür

league [li:g] cemiyet, dernek / lig / fersah
leak [li:k] sızıntı, akıntı / sızmak (sıvı)
lean (leant, leant) [li:n, lent, lent] meyletmek / sarkmak / dayamak / dayanmak / zayıf, yağsız
leant, bak **lean**
leap (leaped veya **leapt)** [li:p, li:pt, lept] sıçramak
learn (learned veya **learnt)** [lö:n, lö:nd, lö:nt] öğrenmek
lease [li:s] kiralama
least [li:st] en az, asgari
at least hiç olmazsa
leather [ledı] deri (işlenmiş)
leave (left, left) [li:v, left, left] terketmek, ayrılmak / bırakmak / müsaade, izin
Lebanon [lebının] Lübnan
lecture [lekçı] konferans / konferans vermek
led bak **lead**
leek [li:k] pırasa
left, bak **leave** sol
leg [leg] bacak
legacy [legısi] miras, kalıntı
legal [li:gıl] meşru, kanuni, yasal
legalize [li:gılayz] meşru kılmak
legend [lecınd] menkibe, efsane
legible [lecibıl] okunaklı
legislative [lecisleytiv] kanun yapan
legitimate [licitimıt] meşru, yasal
leisure [lejı] boş vakit
leisurely [lejıli] acele etmeden, ağır ağır
lemon [lemın] limon
lemonade [lemıneyd] limonata
lend (lent, lent) [lend, lent, lent] ödünç vermek
length [lengt] uzunluk
lengthen [lengtın] uzatmak
lengthy [lengti] mufassal, etraflıca, ayrıntılı
lenient [li:nyınt] müşfik, yumuşak
lens [lenz] mercek
lent bak **lend**
lentil [lentil] mercimek
leopard [lepıd] pars
leprosy [leprısi] cüzzam
leprous [leprıs] cüzzamlı

less [les] daha az
lessen [lesın] azaltmak
lesson [lesın] ders
lest [lest] olmasın diye
let [let] müsaade etmek, izin vermek / **let's** şeklinde teklif anlamı verir / kiraya vermek
lethal [li:dıl] öldürücü
lethargy [letıci] rehavet, uyuşukluk
letter [letı] mektup / harf
lettuce [letis] salata, marul
level [levıl] seviye, düzey / düz, yatay / tesviye etmek
lever [li:vı] kaldıraç
levy [levi] toplamak / vergi
lewd [liu:d] müstehcen
liability [layıbiliti] sorumluluk / borç
liable [layıbıl] mükellef, tâbi, sorumlu
liar [layı] yalancı
libel [laybıl] iftira / iftirada bulunmak
liberal [libırıl] cömert, liberal, serbest fikirli
liberate [libıreyt] serbest bırakmak, koyuvermek
liberty [libıti] özgürlük, serbestlik, serbesti
librarian [laybreırıın] kütüphaneci
library [laybrıri] kütüphane
licence [laysıns] ruhsat, izin, lisans
license [laysıns] ruhsat vermek
lick [lik] yalamak / dövmek
lid [lid] kapak
lie (lied, lied) [lay, layd, layd] yalan / yalan söylemek
lie (lay, lain) [lay, ley, leyn] yatmak, uzanmak
lieutenant [leftenınt] teğmen
life çoğulu **lives** [layf, layvz] hayat, yaşam / can
lifebelt [layfbelt] cankurtaran kemeri
lifebuoy [layfboy] şamandıra
lifeless [layflis] cansız
lifelong [layflong] ömür boyunca
lift [lift] kaldırmak, yükseltmek, yükselmek / asansör
light [layt] ışık, aydınlık,

far / hafif (yük) / açık (renk)
light (lighted veya **lit)** [layt, laytid, lit] tutuşturmak / aydınlatmak
lighten [laytın] ışıldamak / şimşek çakmak / hafifletmek (yükü)
lighter [laytı] şat / çakmak
lighthouse [laythaus] fener kulesi
lightly [laytli] hafifçe
lightning [laytning] şimşek
like [layk] gibi, benzer / sevmek, beğenmek
likelihood [layklihud] ihtimal
likely [laykli] muhtemel, olasılı
likeness [layknis] benzerlik
liking [layking] sevme, ilgi, düşkünlük
lilac [laylık] leylak
lily [lili] zambak
limb [lim] uzuv, organ
lime [laym] kireç
limestone [laymstoun] kireç taşı
limit [limit] tahdit etmek, sınırlandırmak / sınır, hudut / had
limp [limp] topallamak / yumuşak, pörsük
line [layn] satır / hat, çizgi / mısra / nevi
lined [laynd] çizgili / astarlı
linen [linın] keten / çamaşır
liner [laynı] bir organizasyona ait yolcu vapuru veya uçağı
linesman [laynzmın] yan hakem
linger [lingı] (acele etmeyip) gecikmek
linguist [lingwist] dilci
lining [layning] astar (kumaş)
link [link] rabıta / bağlamak
lion [layın] aslan
lip [lip] dudak
lipstick [lipstik] dudak boyası, ruj
liqueur [likyuı] likör
liquid [likwid] sıvı
liquidate [likwideyt] ortadan kaldırmak, tasfiye etmek
liquor [likı] içki (alkollü)

list [list] liste
listen [lisın] dinlemek
listener [lisnı] dinleyici
listless [listlis] ilgisiz, ruhsuz
lit, bak **light**
literal [litırıl] hakiki / sözcük sözcük
literary [litırıri] edebi
literature [litrıçı] edebiyat / mesleki rehber
litre [li:tı] litre
litter [litı] tahterevan, teskere / çerçöp
little [litıl] küçük, az
a little biraz
live [layv] canlı
live [liv] yaşamak / ikamet etmek, oturmak
livelihood [layvlihud] maişet, geçim
liveliness [layvlinis] canlılık
lively [layvli] canlı, neşeli
liver [livı] karaciğer
livestock [layvstok] çiftlik hayvanları
living [living] canlı / yaşama, geçim
livingroom [living rum] oturma odası
lizard [lizıd] kertenkele
load [loud] yük / yüklemek
loaf çoğulu **loaves** [louf, louvz] ekmek (somunu)
loan [loun] ödünç verme
loathe [loud] iğrenmek
lobby [lobi] dehliz, salon / kulis yapanlar
lobe [loub] kulak memesi
lobster [lobstı] istakoz
local [loukıl] mahalli, yerel
locate [loukeyt] yerini tayin etmek / yerleştirmek
lock [lok] kilit / kilitlemek
locker [lokı] kilitli dolap
locket [lokit] madalyon
lockjaw [lokco:] tetanos, sara
locksmith [loksmit] çilingir
locomotive [loukımoutiv] lokomotif
locust [loukıst] çekirge
lodge [loc] kirada oturmak, barındırmak
lodging [locing] pansiyon, kiralık oda
lofty [lofti] yüksek, ulvi
log [log] kütük

logic [locik] mantık
logical [locikıl] mantıki
loiter [loytı] boş gezmek, sallanmak
lone [loun] kimsesiz
lonely [lounli] yalnız, kimsesiz, tenha
lonesome [lounsım] yapayalnız
long [long] uzun / çok arzu etmek
longitude [loncityu:d] tül, boylam (coğrafya)
look [luk] bakmak / görünmek / bakış, görünüş
looking-glass [luking gla:s] ayna
loom [lu:m] dokuma tezgahı / hayal meyal görünmek
loop [lu:p] ilmik / ilmiklemek
loose [lu:s] serbest, başıboş / gevşek, bol / çözmek
loosen [lu:sın] gevşetmek
loot [lu:t] yağma
lord [lo:d] efendi, lord
  the Lord Allah
lorry [lori] kamyon
lose (lost, lost) [lu:z, lost, lost] kaybetmek
loser [lu:zı] kaybeden
loss [los] kayıp, ziyan
lot [lot] miktar, adet / kur'a / kısmet, pay / arsa
lotion [louşın] losyon
lottery [lotırı] piyango
loud [laud] gürültülü
loudspeaker [laudspi:kı] hoparlör
lounge [launc] hol, salon
louse (çoğulu **lice)** [laus, lays] bit
lousy [lauzi] bitli / çok fena, berbat
love [lav] sevmek / aşk, sevgi / sevgili
lovely [lavli] sevimli, hoş
lover [lavı] aşık
loving [laving] seven
low [lou] alçak, düşük
lower [louı] daha aşağı / indirmek, azaltmak
loyal [loyıl] sadık
loyalty [loyılti] sadakat
lozenge [lo:zinc] eşkenar dörtgen / pastil
lubricate [lu:brikeyt] yağlamak (makine)
lucid [lu:sid] berrak
luck [lak] talih, şans
lucky [laki] talihli

ludicrous [lu:dikrıs] gülünç
luggage [lagic] bagaj, eşya
lukewarm [lu:kwo:m] ılık
lull [lal] teskin etmek
lullaby [lalıbay] ninni
lumber [lambı] kereste
luminous [lu:minıs] ışıklı, parlak
lump [lamp] parça, tane, topak
lump sugar kesme şeker
lunacy [lu:nısi] delilik
lunar [lu:nı] ayla ilgili olan, aya ait
lunatic [lu:nıtik] deli
lunch [lanç] öğle yemeği
lung [lang] akciğer
lunge [lanc] saldırış
lurch [lö:ç] sendelemek
lure [liuı] ayartmak / tuzak
lust [last] şehvet, hırs
lustre [lastı] parlaklık
lusty [lasti] dinç, kuvvetli
lute [liu:t] ut
luxurious [laksyuırıs] tantanalı, süslü, lüks
luxury [laksıri] lüks
lynch [linç] linç etmek

M

macaroni [mekırouni] makarna
machine [mışi:n] makine
machine gun makineli tüfek
machinery [mışi:nıri] makineler, mekanizma
mackerel [mekrıl] uskumru
mackintosh [mekintoş] yağmurluk
mad [med] deli, çılgın
madam [medım] bayan
madden [medın] delirtmek
made, bak **make**
magazine [megızi:n] mecmua, dergi
magic [mecik] sihirli, sihir
magician [mıcişın] sihirbaz
magistrate [mecistrit] sulh yargıcı
magnanimous [megnenimıs] alicenap
magnet [megnit] mıknatıs

magnificence [megnifisıns] ihtişam, görkem
magnificent [megnifisınt] muhteşem, görkemli
magnifier [megnifayı] pertavsız, büyüteç
magnify [megnifay] büyütmek
magpie [megpay] saksağan
mahogany [mıhogıni] maun
Mahomet [mıhomit] Muhammet
maid [meyd] kız / hizmetçi
maiden [meydın] kız, bakire
mailbox [meylboks] posta kutusu
mail [meyl] posta / posta ile göndermek
main [meyn] ana, esas
mainly [meynli] başlıca
maintain [meynteyn] muhafaza etmek / bakmak / savunmak
maintenance [meyntınıns] bakım
maize [meyz] mısır, darı
majestic [mıcestik] muhteşem, görkemli
majesty [mecisti] majeste / ihtişam
major [meycı] binbaşı / esas, başlıca
majority [mıcoriti] ekseriyet, çoğunluk
make (made, made) [meyk, meyd, meyd] yapmak, imal etmek / marka / yapım
maker [meykı] yapıcı, yapan
malady [melıdi] hastalık
malaria [mıleırii] sıtma
male [meyl] erkek
malevolent [mılevılınt] kötü niyetli
malice [melis] kötü niyet
malignant [mılignınt] kötü yürekli, uğursuz, habis
malnutrition [melniutrişın] gıdasızlık, kötü beslenme
maltreat [meltri:t] fena muamele etmek
mammal [memıl] memeli hayvan
mammy [memi] anneciğim / siyahi dadı
man çoğulu **men** [men, men] erkek, adam / insan / adam vermek, personel koymak

manage [menic] idare etmek / becermek
management [menicmınt] idare, yönetim
manager [menicı] müdür, yönetici
mane [meyn] yele
mangle [mengıl] parçalamak / çamaşırı merdane ile sıkmak
manhood [menhud] erkeklik (çağı)
maniac [meynyek] manyak
manicure [menikyuı] manikür
manifest [menifest] aşikar / göstermek, açıklamak / manifesto
manifesto [menifestou] beyanname, bildiri
manipulate [mınipyuleyt] işletmek, çalıştırmak
mankind [menkaynd] insanoğlu, insanlık
manly [menli] yiğitçe
mannequin [menikin] manken
manner [menı] davranış, terbiye / tarz, usul
manners [menı:s] terbiye, görgü
manoeuvre [mınu:vı] manevra
mantelpiece [mentılpi:s] şömine rafı
mantle [mentıl] manto, pelerin
manual [menyuıl] elle yapılan / elkitabı
manufacture [menyufekçı] imal etmek, imalat
manure [mınyuı] gübre
manuscript [menyuskript] (el) yazma / müsvedde
many [meni] çok, birçok
map [mep] harita
marble [ma:bıl] mermer
March [ma:ç] mart
march [ma:ç] yürümek (asker gibi) / yürüyüş / marş (müzik)
mare [meı] kısrak
margarine [ma:cıri:n] margarin
margin [ma:cin] pay, tolerans
marine [mıri:n] denize veya denizciliğe ilişkin
mariner [merinı] gemici
marionette [meryınet] kukla
maritime [meritaym] denize ilişkin

mark [ma:k] işaret koymak, işaretlemek / işaret, iz / not (okulda)
marked [ma:kd] işaretli
market [ma:kit] çarşı / piyasa
marketing [ma:kiting] pazarlama
marksman [ma:ksmın] nişancı
marmalade [ma:mıleyd] (portakallı) marmelat
marriage [meric] evlenme, evlilik, izdivaç
married [merid] evli
marrow [merou] ilik, öz
marry [meri] evlenmek, evlendirmek
marsh [ma:ş] bataklık
marshal [ma:şıl] mareşal
martial [ma:şıl]savaşla ilgili
martial law, örfi idare, sıkı yönetim
martyr [ma:tı] şehit
marvel [ma:vıl] mucize
mascot [meskıt] tılsım / maskot
masculine [meskyulin] müzekker, erkek cinsi
mash [meş] ezme, lapa
mask [ma:sk] maske / maskelemek
mason [meysın] duvarcı / mason
mass [mes] küme / yığmak
massacre [mesıkı] katliam, kırım
massage [mesa:j] masaj
masseur [mesö:] masör
masseuse [mesö:z] masöz
massive [mesiv] kocaman, kütle halinde
mast [ma:st] gemi direği, direk
master [ma:stı] sahip / usta / öğretmen / hakim olmak
masterpiece [ma:stıpi:s] şaheser, sanat eseri
mat [met] paspas / mat
match [meç] kibrit / maç / eş / uymak
matchless [meçlis] emsalsiz
mate [meyt] eş, ortak / çiftleştirmek
material [mıtiırıl] madde / malzeme
maternal [mıtö:nıl] analığa ait
mathematics [metımetiks]

matematik
matrimony [metrimıni] evlilik
matron [meytrın] kadın (evli veya dul) / okul veya hastanede idareci kadın
matter [metı] madde / mesele, iş / önemli olmak
mattress [metris] minder, somye
mature [mıçuı] olgun / olgunlaştırmak
maturity [mıçu:riti] olgunluk
mausoleum [mo:sıli:ım] türbe
maxim [meksim] düstur, vecize, özdeyiş
maximum [meksimım] maksimum, azami
May [mey] mayıs
may (might) [mey, mayt] (izin ve olanak gösterir) mümkün olmak / muhtemel olmak
maybe [meybi] belki
mayor [meyı] belediye reisi
maze [meyz] karmakarışık (yol, hat...) şebekesi / karışıklık
me [mi:] beni, bana
meadow [medou] çayır, otlak
meagre [mi:gı] zayıf, kıt
meal [mi:l] yemek, öğün
mean (meant, meant) [mi:n, ment] anlamında olmak, demek istemek / vasıta
meaning [mi:ning] anlam
means [mi:nz] vasıta
meant, bak **mean**
meantime [mi:ntaym] bu arada, bu sırada
meanwhile [mi:nwayl] bu arada, bu sırada
measles [mi:zılz] kızamık
measure [mejı] ölçü / tedbir, önlem / ölçmek
measurement [mejımınt] ölçü, ölçme
meat [mi:t] et
mechanic [mikenik] teknisyen, makineci
mechanical [mikenikıl] makineyle olan, makineyle işleyen, makine gibi
mechanism [mekınizm] mekanizma
medal [medıl] madalya
meddle [medıl] karışmak, müdahale etmek

mediate [mi:dieyt] aracılık yapmak / uzlaştırmak
medical [medikıl] tıbbi
medicine [medsin] ilaç, tıp
medi(a)eval [medii:vıl] orta çağlara ait
meditate [mediteyt] düşünmek
meditation [mediteyşın] derin düşünme
Mediterranean [meditıreyniın] Akdeniz
medium [mi:dyım] orta / çevre / vasıta
meet (met, met) [mi:t, met, met] rastlamak, karşılaşmak / buluşmak, toplanmak
meeting [mi:ting] toplantı, miting
melancholy [melınkıli] melankoli
mellow [melou] olgun, tatlı
melodrama [melıdra:mı] melodram
melody [melıdi] melodi
melon [melın] kavun
water melon karpuz
melt [melt] erimek, eritmek / yumuşamak
member [membı] üye
membership [membışip] üyelik
memo [memou] not, muhtıra
memoir [memwa:] anı
memorandum [memırendım] not, muhtıra
memorial [mimoriıl] anıt
memorize [memırayz] ezberlemek
memory [memıri] hafıza, bellek / hatıra
men [men] erkekler, adamlar
menace [menıs] tehlike, tehdit
mend [mend] tamir etmek
mental [mentıl] zihni
mentality [menteliti] zihniyet
mention [menşın] lafını etmek, anmak, zikretmek / anma
menu [menyu] yemek listesi
mercenary [mö:sınıri] para veya mükafat için çalışan
merchandise [mö:çındayz] mal (satılan)
merchant [mö:çınt] tüc-

car
merciful [mö:sifıl] merhametli
merciless [mö:silis] merhametsiz
mercury [mö:kyuri] cıva
mercy [mö:si] merhamet
mere [miı] sadece, sırf
merely [miıli] sadece
merge [mö:c] birleştirmek, birleşmek
meridian [mıridyın] boylam
merit [merit] meziyet
mermaid [mö:meyd] deniz kızı
merriment [merimınt] neşe
merry [meri] neşeli
merry-go-round [merigouraund] atlıkarınca
mess [mes] karışıklık, pislik
message [mesic] haber
messenger [mesincı] haberci
met, bak **meet**
metal [metıl] madeni / metal
meteor [mi:tiı] meteor
meteorology [mi:tiırolıci] meteoroloji
meter [mi:tı] sayaç
method [metıd] metot, yöntem
meticulous [mıtikyulıs] titiz
metre [mi:tı] metre
metropolis [mitropılis] büyük şehir, başşehir
metropolitan [metropolitın] başkentle ilgili
mew [miu:] miyavlamak
mice [mays] fareler
microbe [maykroub] mikrop
microphone [maykrıfoun] mikrofon
microscope [maykroskoup] mikroskop
mid— [mid] orta anlamında önek
midday [middey] öğle üzeri, gün ortası, öğle
middle [midıl] orta
midget [micit] cüce
midnight [midnayt] gece yarısı
midway [midwey] ortada, orta yolda
midwife [midwayf] ebe
might [mayt] (**may**'in geçmiş şekli) ihtimal / kudret

migrant [maygrınt] göçebe
migrate [maygreyt] göçmek
mild [mayld] mutedil, hafif
mildew [mildyu:] küf
mile [mayl] mil
military [militıri] askeri
milk [milk] süt / sağmak
milkman [milkmın] sütçü
milky [milki] sütlü, süt gibi
mill [mil] fabrika / değirmen / öğütmek
miller [milı] değirmenci
millet [milit] darı
million [milyın] milyon
mimic [mimik] taklit / taklit etmek
minaret [minıret] minare
mince [mins] kıyma / kıymak (et)
minced meat [minst mi:t] kıyma et
mind [maynd] akıl, fikir / aldırış etmek
mine [mayn] benimki / maden ocağı / mayın
miner [maynı] madenci
mineral [minırıl] madeni
mingle [mingıl] karıştırmak, karışmak
miniature [minyıçı] minyatür
minimize [minimayz] azaltmak, küçümsemek
minimum [minimım] asgari, minimum, en az
mining [mayning] madencilik
minister [ministı] bakan / papaz
ministry [ministri] bakanlık
mink [mink] vizon
minor [maynı] küçük, önemsiz
minority [maynoriti, minoriti] azınlık
mint [mint] nane / darphane
minus [maynıs] eksik / eksi işareti
minute [minit] dakika / kısa süre, an
minute [maynyu:t] ufak
miracle [mirıkıl] mucize
mirage [mira:j] serap
mire [mayı] bataklık
mirror [mirı] ayna
mis— [mis] yanlış anlamına gelen önek

niscarriage [miskeric] başarısızlık / çocuk düşürme

niscellaneous [misıleynyıs] çeşitli

nischief [misçif] şeytanlık, zarar, felaket

nischievous [misçivıs] yaramaz, zararlı

nisconduct [miskondıkt] yanlış hareket

nisdeed [misdi:d] yanlış iş, kötü iş

niser [mayzı] cimri

niserable [mizrıbıl] sefil, mutsuz, berbat

nisery [mizıri] sefalet / dert, bedbahtlık

nisfortune [misfo:tyun] talihsizlik

nisgiving [misgiving] kuşku

nishap [mishep] aksilik

nislead (misled, misled) [misli:d, misled] yanlış yola yöneltmek

nisprint [misprint] dizgi hatası, baskı hatası

Miss [mis] bayan (kız)

niss [mis] boşa gitmek / ıska / kaçırmak / özlemini çekmek

missile [misayl] mermi / füze

missing [mising] eksik, kayıp

mission [mişın] görev, elçilik

missionary [mişınıri] misyoner

mist [mist] sis

mistake [misteyk] hata / hata etmek / yanlış anlamak

Mister [mistı] (kısaltılmışı: **Mr**) bey, bay

mistress [mistris] (kısaltılmışı: **Mrs**) bayan / sahibe / öğretmen / metres

mistrust [mistrast] güvenmemek / güvensizlik

misty [misti] sisli

misunderstand [misandıstend] yanlış anlamak

misuse [misyu:z] suiistimal etmek, kötüye kullanmak

mitigate [mitigeyt] hafifletmek, azaltmak

mix [miks] karıştırmak / birleştirmek / birleşmek / karışık

mixture [miksçı] karışım, terkip

moan [moun] inilti, inlemek
mob [mob] ayaktakımı
mobile [moubayl] müteharrik, gezici, hareketli
mock [mok] alay etmek
mode [moud] moda, usul, tarz / kip
model [modıl] model, örnek, tip
moderate [modırit] makul, orta karar, ılımlı
modern [modın] modern
modernize [modınayz] modernize etmek
modest [modist] mütevazi, alçak gönüllü
modesty [modisti] tevazu
modify [modifay] değişiklik yapmak
Mohammedan [mouhemidın] Müslüman
moist [moyst] nemli
moisten [moysın] nemlendirmek
moisture [moysçı] nem
mole [moul] ben / leke / köstebek
molecule [molikyu:l] molekül
molest [mılest] taciz etmek
mollify [molifay] sakinleştirmek, yatıştırmak
moment [moumınt] an
momentary [moumıntır ani, bir anlık, geçici
monarch [monık] kral
monastery [monıstri] manastır
Monday [mandi] pazartesi
monetary [manitıri] para il ilgili
money [mani] para
monitor [monitı] sınıf mümessili / kontrol ekranı (televizyon)
monk [mank] keşiş
monkey [manki] maymun
monopoly [mınopıli] tekel
monotonous [mınotınıs] sıkıcı, monoton
monster [monstı] canava azman
monstrous [monstrıs] müthiş, korkunç
month [mant] ay (30 gün)
monthly [mantli] ayda bi aylık
monument [monyumın anıt
mood [mu:d] ruh hali. ruhsa durum / kip
moon [mu:n] ay / uydu

moonlight [mu:nlayt] ay ışığı
moor [muı] kır, çalılık
mop [mop] tahta bezi / bezle kurulamak
moral [mo:rıl] ahlaki / ahlak
morale [mora:l] maneviyat
morbid [mo:bid] hastalık derecesinde, marazi
more [mo:] daha, daha fazla
morello [mırelou] vişne
moreover [mo:rouvı] bundan başka
morgue [mo:g] morg
morning [mo:ning] sabah
Morocco [mırokou] Fas
morose [mırous] huysuz
morphia [mo:fiı] morfin
morsel [mo:sıl] lokma, parça
mortal [mo:tıl] fani, ölümlü
mortality [mo:teliti] ölüm oranı
mortar [mo:tı] harç (beton) / havan topu / havaneli
mortgage [mo:gic] rehin / ipotek etmek
mortify [mo:tifay] kırmak (bir kimseyi) / nefse hakim olmak / kangren olmak
Moslem [mozlım] Müslüman
mosque [mosk] cami
mosquito [moski:tou] sivrisinek
moss [mos] yosun
mossy [mosi] yosunlu
most [moust] en, son derece, çoğu
mostly [moustli] çoğunlukla
motel [moutel] motel
moth [mot] güve
mother [madı] anne
mother-in-law [madı in lo:] kaynana
motion [mouşın] hareket
motive [moutiv] sebep / harekete geçiren
motor [moutı] motor
motorbike [moutıbayk] motosiklet
motorcycle [moutısaykıl] motosiklet
motto [motou] düstur, prensibi gösteren söz
mould [mould] küf / kalıp

mound [maund] tümsek
mount [maunt] (at v.s.) binmek / tırmanmak
mountain [mauntin] dağ
mountaineer [mauntinii] dağcı
mountainous [mauntinyıs] dağlık
mourn [mo:n] yas tutmak
mourning [mo:ning] yas
mouse (çoğulu **mice**) [maus, mays] fare
moustache [mısta:ş] bıyık
mouth [maut] ağız
mouthful [mautfıl] ağız dolusu
movable [mu:vıbıl] hareket edebilen, sabit olmayan, menkul
move [mu:v] hareket etmek, hareket ettirmek, kımıldatmak / ev nakletmek / tahrik etmek / hareket
movement [mu:vmınt] hareket
movies [mu:viz] sinema
moving [mu:ving] hareket eden, hareketli / acıklı
mow [mou] (ot) biçmek
Mr (Mister) [mistı] bay
Mrs [misiz] bayan
much [maç] çok
mucus [miukıs] sümük
mud [mad] çamur
muddle [madıl] karıştırmak
muddy [madi] çamurlu
mudguard [madga:d] çamurluk (otomobil vs.)
muffle [mafıl] sarmak / sesi azaltmak
muffler [maflı] atkı / susturucu
mug [mag] maşrapa
mulberry [malberi] dut
mule [miu:l] katır
multi [malti] birçok anlamında önek
multiple [maltipıl] müteaddit, çeşitli
multiply [maltiplay] çoğaltmak / çarpmak (matematik)
multiplication [maltiplikeyşın] çarpım
multitude [maltityu:d] kalabalık
mumble [mambıl] mırıldanmak
mummy [mami] anneciğim

/ mumya

mumps [mamps] kabakulak

munch [manç] çiğnemek

municipality [miunisipeliti] belediye

munition [miunişın] mühimmat, cephane

murder [mö:dı] cinayet / öldürmek

murderer [mö:dırı] katil

murmer [mö:mı] mırıltı / mırıldanmak

muscle [masıl] kas

muse [miu:z] düşünmek

museum [miu:ziım] müze

mushroom [maşrum] mantar (bitki)

music [miu:zik] müzik

musical [miu:zikıl] müzikli, müziğe ait

musician [miu:zişın] müzisyen

Muslim [mazlim] Müslüman

mussel [masıl] midye

must [mast] ...meli, ...malı

mustard [mastıd] hardal

musty [masti] küflü

mute [miu:t] sessiz, dilsiz

mutilate [myutileyt] kırarak, koparararak, keserek zarar vermek

mutineer [miu:tinii] asi

mutiny [miu:tini] isyan

mutter [matı] mırıldanmak

mutton [matın] koyun eti

mutual [miu:çuıl] karşılıklı, ortak

my [may] benim

myself [mayself] kendim

mysterious [mistiıriıs] esrarengiz

mystery [mistıri] esrarlı şey

mystic [mistik] mistik

mysticism [mistisizm] mistisizm, tasavvuf

mystify [mistifay] esrarengizleştirmek, şaşırtmak

mythology [maytolıci] mitoloji

N

nag [neg] vırvır etmek

nail [neyl] çivi / tırnak / çivilemek

naive [na:i:v] saf, çocuğumsu

naked [neykid] çıplak

name [neym] isim, ad / isimlendirmek

namely [neymli] yani

namesake [neymseyk] adaş

nap [nep] kısa uyku

nape [neyp] ense

napkin [nepkin] peçete

narcotic [na:kotik] uyuşturucu madde

narrate [nıreyt] anlatmak, hikaye etmek

narrow [nerou] dar

nasty [na:sti] nahoş, fena, iğrenç

nation [neyşın] ulus, millet

national [neşınıl] ulusal

nationality [neşıneliti] milliyet, uyruk

nationalize [neşınılayz] millileştirmek

native [neytiv] yerli, o yerde doğmuş, o yere özgü

natural [neçırıl] doğal, tabii

naturally [neçırıli] tabii, kuşkusuz, doğal olarak

nature [neyçı] tabiat, doğa / mizaç

naughty [no:ti] yaramaz, haylaz

naval [neyvıl] bahriyeye ilişkin

navel [neyvıl] göbek

navigation [nevigeyşın] denizcilik

navy [neyvi] bahriye

near [nii] yakın, yanında

nearly [niıli] aşağı yukarı, hemen hemen

neat [ni:t] temiz, tertipli, zarif

necessary [nesisıri] gerekli, lüzumlu

necessitate [nisesiteyt] icabetmek, gerektirmek

necessity [nisesiti] gereklilik, zorunluluk

neck [nek] boyun

necklace [neklis] gerdanlık, kolye

need [ni:d] ihtiyacında olmak / zorunda olmak / ihtiyaç, zorunluluk

needle [ni:dıl] iğne (dikiş), ibre

needless [ni:dlis] gereksiz

negative [negıtiv] negatif, olumsuz

neglect [niglekt] ihmal etmek, savsaklamak / ih-

mal, savsaklama
negligence [neglicıns] ihmal
negotiate [nigouşieyt] müzakere etmek
negotiation [nigouşieyşın] müzakere
negro [ni:grou] zenci
neigh [ney] kişnemek
neighbour [neybı] komşu
neighbourhood [neybıhud] civar, dolay
neither [naydı] (iki şeyden) hiçbirisi
neither ...nor ne... ne de
nephew [nefyu] yeğen (erkek)
nerve [nö:v] sinir / cesaret
nervous [nö:vıs] sinire ait, sinirli
nest [nest] yuva
nestle [nesıl] yerleşmek, sığınmak
net [net] ağ / net / safi
network [netwö:k] şebeke, teşkilat
neurotic [niurotik] sinir hastası
neuter [niu:tı] tarafsız
never [nevı] asla, hiç
nevertheless [nevıdıles] mamafih, bununla birlikte
new [niu:] yeni
newly [niu:li] yakında, yeni bir şekilde
news [niu:z] haber
newspaper [niu:zpeypı] gazete
next [nekst] gelecek / ertesi / bitişik
nibble [nibıl] çimlenmek
nice [nays] hoş, nefis
nicely [naysli] hoş bir şekilde
nick [nik] çentmek / çentik
nickname [nikneym] takma ad
niece [ni:s] yeğen (kız)
niggardly [nigıdli] pinti
night [nayt] gece
nightingale [naytingeyl] bülbül
nil [nil] sıfır
nimble [nimbıl] çevik
nine [nayn] dokuz
ninety [nayntl] doksan
nineteen [naynti:n] on dokuz
ninth [naynt] dokuzuncu
nipple [nipıl] meme ucu
no [nou] hayır / hiç

nobility [noubiliti] soyluluk
noble [noubıl] soylu kişi
nobody [noubıdi] hiç kimse
nod [nod] başla işaret / başını sallamak
noise [noyz] gürültü
noisy [noyzi] gürültülü, gürültücü
nomad [noumed] göçebe
nominal [nominıl] itibari, sözde
nominate [nomineyt] aday göstermek, atamak
non— [non] hiçbir anlamında önek, gayri
none [nan] hiç, hiçbir
nonsense [nonsıns] saçma, anlamsız
nonstop [nonstop] doğrudan, durmadan
noodle [nu:dıl] şehriye
noon [nu:n] öğle vakti
noose [nu:s] ilmik
nor [no:] ne de
norm [no:m] standart, norm
normal [no:mıl] normal
north [no:t] kuzey
northern [no:dın] kuzeye ait
Norway [no:wey] Norveç
Norwegian [no:wi:cyın] Norveçli, Norveçce
nose [nouz] burun
nostril [nostril] burun deliği
not [not] değil
notable [noutıbıl] tanınmış, geçerli
notary [noutıri] noter
notch [noç] kertik / çentmek
note [nout] not / tezkere / nota / not etmek
note-book [nout buk] defter
noted [noutid] maruf, seçkin, meşhur, ünlü
nothing [nating] hiçbir şey
notice [noutis] farkında olmak / dikkat / ilan / ihbar
notify [noutifay] bildirmek
notification [noutifikeyşın] bildirme, bildiri
notion [nouşın] kavram
notorious [nouto:riıs] fena şöhretli
notwithstanding [notwidstending] rağmen
nought [no:t] sıfır

noun [naun] isim (dilbilgisi)
nourish [nariş] beslemek
nourishing [narişing] besleyici, gıdalı
novel [novıl] roman / yeni
novelty [novılti] yenilik
November [nouvembı] kasım (ay)
novice [novis] acemi
now [nau] şimdi
nowadays [nauıdeyz] bu günlerde
nowhere [nouweı] hiçbir yerde
nuclear [niu:klii] çekirdeğe ait , öz, nükleer
nude [niu:d] çıplak
nudge [nac] dürtmek
nugget [nagit] altın külçesi
nuisance [niu:sıns] sıkıntı, bela
null [nal] hükümsüz
numb [nam] uyuşuk / uyuşturmak
number [nambı] adet / numara / sayı / numaralamak
numeral [niu:mırıl] sayısal, rakam, sayı
numerous [niu:mırıs] bir çok, çok sayıda
nun [nan] rahibe
nurse [nö:s] hemşire, hastabakıcı / bakmak
nursery [nö:sıri] çocuk odası / fidanlık
nut [nat] fındık / cıvata somunu
nutriment [niu:trimınt] besin
nutrition [niu:trişın] beslenme
nutritious [niu:trişıs] besleyici
nylon [naylon] naylon
nymph [nimf] peri

O

oak [ouk] meşe
oar [o:] kürek (kayık)
oath [out] yemin
oats [outs] yulaf
obedience [obi:dyıns] itaat
obedient [obi:dyınt] itaatkâr
obey [obey] itaat etmek
object [obcikt] madde, nesne / hedef, amaç

object [obcekt] itiraz etmek
objection [obcekşın] itiraz
objektive [obcektiv] hislerine kapılmadan, objektif
obligation [obligeyşın] mecburiyet, zorunluluk
obligatory [obligıtıri] zorunlu
oblige [oblayc] zorunlu kılmak / lütuf göster mek
obliging [oblaycing] lütufkâr
oblique [obli:k] meyilli, yatık
oblivion [oblivyın] unutulma
oblong [oblong] dikdörtgen
obscene [obsi:n] müstehcen, açık saçık
obscure [obskiuı] karartmak / çapraşık, belirsiz
obscurity [obskiu:riti] karışıklık, belirsizlik
observation [obzö:veyşın] gözlem, tetkik, inceleme
observatory [ıbzö:vıtıri] rasathane
observe [ıbzö:v] gözetlemek, dikkat etmek, gözlem yapmak
obsess [ıbses] zihnini tamamen kaplamak
obstacle [obstıkıl] engel
obstinacy [obstinısi] inatçılık
obstinate [obstinit] inatçı
obstruct [obstrakt] engel olmak
obtain [obteyn] elde etmek, ele geçirmek
obvious [obviıs] besbelli, aşikar, apaçık
occasion [ıkeyjın] olay, fırsat, münasebet
occasional [ıkeyjınıl] arada sırada olan
occasionally [ıkeyjınıli] arada sırada
occupant [okyupınt] işgal eden, oturan
occupation [okyupeyşın] meşgale, iş / işgal
occupy [okyupay] işgal etmek
occur [ıkö:] vuku bulmak, olmak
ocean [ouşın] okyanus
o'clock [ıklok] saat (vakit

bildirme)
octagon [oktıgın] sekiz köşeli şekil, sekizgen
October [oktoubı] ekim (ay)
octopus [oktıpıs] ahtapot
oculist [okyulist] göz hekimi
odd [od] tek (sayı) / tuhaf
odour [oudı] koku
of [ov, ıv] ...in, ...nın, ...den
off [o:f] uzakta / dışarıya, ...den
offence [ofens] kabahat / hücum
offend [ıfend] gücendirmek, kızdırmak
offensive [ıfensiv] saldırıcı
offer [ofı] teklif, öneri / teklif etmek, önermek
office [ofis] yazıhane, büro / (hükümette) iktidar / bakanlık
officer [ofisı] subay / memur
official [ofişıl] memur / resmi
officious [ofişıs] işgüzar
offside [ofsayd] ofsayd, kenardan dışarda
offspring [ofspring] döl, evlat
often [ofın] sık sık, ekseriya
oil [oyl] yağ / gaz / yağlamak, petrol
ointment [oyntmınt] merhem
O.K. [oukey] peki, tamam
okey [oukey] pekala, olur
old [ould] yaşlı / eski
olive [oliv] zeytin
omelet [omlit] omlet
ominous [ominıs] meşum, uğursuz
omission [omişın] bırakma, atlama, çıkarılma
omit [oumit] atlamak / bırakmak
omnibus [omnibıs] otobüs
on [on] üzerinde, üstünde. üstüne
once [wans] bir defa, eskiden, vaktiyle
one [wan] bir (tane)
oneself [wanself] kendisi
onion [anyın] soğan
onlooker [onlukı] (bir olaya)

seyirci

only [ounli] sadece, yalnız, yegane

ooze [u:z] sızıntı / sızmak

opaque [oupeyk] saydam olmayan

open [oupın] açmak / açılmak / açık

opening [oupınıng] açma / başlangıç / delik, açıklık

openly [oupınli] açıkça, saklamadan

opera [opırı] opera

operate [opıreyt] işlemek, işletmek / ameliyat yapmak

operation [opıreyşın] işleme, faaliyet / harekat / ameliyat

opinion [ıpinyın] fikir, düşünce, mütalaa

opium [oupyım] afyon

opportunity [opıtyu:niti] fırsat

oppose [ıpouz] muhalefet etmek, aleyhte olmak, karşı gelmek

opposite [opızit] aksi, karşı, zıt

opposition [opızişın] muhalefet, itiraz

oppress [ıpres] bastırmak, baskı yapmak / eziyet vermek

oppression [ıpreşın] zulüm, baskı, sıkıntı

optician [optişın] gözlükçü

optics [optiks] optik

optimism [optimizm] iyimserlik

optimist [optimist] iyimser

option [opşın] tercih hakkı, seçme

optional [opşınıl] ihtiyari, isteğe göre

or [o:] yahut, veya / yoksa

oral [o:rıl] şifahi, sözlü / ağızdan

orange [orinc] portakal

orator [orıtı] hatip

orbit [o:bit] yörünge

orchard [o:çıd] meyve bahçesi

orchestra [o:kistrı] orkestra

orchid [o:kid] orkide

ordeal [o:diıl] çetin tecrübe

order [o:dı] düzen, tertip, sıra / emir / sipariş

order [**o**:dı] emretmek / sipariş etmek, ısmarlamak
orderly [**o**:dıli] düzenli / emir eri
ordinal [**o**:dinıl] sıra sayısı (birinci, ikinci...)
ordinary [**o**:dinıri] mutat, her zamanki, alelade
ore [**o**:] maden filizi
organ [**o**:gın] uzuv
organic [o:genik] uzvi
organize [**o**:gınayz] tertip etmek, düzenlemek, kurmak
organization [**o**:gınayzeyşın] teşekkül, örgüt / düzenleme
organizer [**o**:gınayzı] tertip eden, organizatör
orient [oriınt] doğu
oriental [**o**:riyentıl] doğuya ait, oryantal
origin [**o**ricin] menşe, asıl
original [o:ricinal] asli, ilk şekli, orijinal / yeni / asli nüsha
originality [**o**ricineliti] orijinallik, yenilik
originate [**o**ricineyt] meydana gelmek
ornament [**o**:nımınt] süs, süslemek
ornamental [**o**:nımentıl] süs için, süse ilişkin
orphan [**o**:fın] öksüz, yetim
orthodox [**o**:tıd**o**ks] ortodoks
orthography [**o**:t**o**grıfi] imla
oscillate [**o**sileyt] sallanmak
oscillation [**o**sileyşın] salınma
ostrich [**o**striç] deve kuşu
other [adı] diğer, öteki
otherwise [adıwayz] aksi takdirde / başka türlü / başka bakımdan
Ottoman [**o**tımın] Osmanlı
ought [**o**:t] -meli, -malı anlamında yardımcı fiil
ounce [auns] ağırlık ölçüsü (28.35 gr.)
our [auı] bizim
ours [auız] bizimki
ourselves [auıselvz] kendimiz
out [aut] dışarı, dışarda
outbreak [autbreyk] vuku bulma, olma
outburst [autb**ö**:st] infilak,

patlama
outcast [autka:st] serseri, kimsesiz
outcome [autkam] sonuç
outdoor [autdo:] ev dışında olan, açık havada yapılan
outdoors [autdo:z] ev dışında, dışarda
outfit [autfit] donatım, takım
outlaw [autlo:] kanun kaçağı / toplum dışına sürmek / yasaklamak
outlet [autlet] menfez, çıkış yeri
outline [autlayn] taslak / taslağını çizmek / özet
outlook [autluk] dış görünüş, manzara
output [autput] verim, randıman
outrage [autreyc] tecavüz, zorbalık / tecavüz etmek
outright [autrayt] büsbütün / derhal / kesin
outside [autsayd] dış, dış taraf, dışında, dışarı
outsider [autsaydı] mensup olmayan kimse, yabancı
outskirts [autskö:ts] civar, kenar, banliyö
outstanding [autstending] göze çarpan
outwit [autwit] zekaca bastırmak
oval [ouvıl] oval
oven [avın] fırın
over [ouvı] üzerinden, üzerinde, fevkinde / bitmiş
over— [ouvı] aşırı, lüzumundan fazla anlamında önek
overall [ouvıro:l] göğüslük, iş önlüğü / her şey dahil
overcast [ouvıka:st] bulutlu / hüzünlü
overcharge [ouvıçac] fazla hesap çıkarmak
overcoat [ouvıkout] palto
overcome (overcame, overcome) [ouvıkam, ouvıkeym, ouvıkam] hakkından gelmek, yenmek
overdo [ouvıdu:] ifrata vardırmak
overflow [ouvıflou] taşmak, su basmak

overhear [ouvıhiı] tesadüfen işitmek
overlook [ouvıluk] nazır olmak / gözden kaçırmak / hoş görmek
oversea [ouvısi:] deniz aşırı
overthrow (—threw, —thrown) [ouvıtrou, —tru: —troun] yıkmak, altetmek
overtime [ouvıtaym] fazla mesai
overture [ouvıtyuı] uvertür / (dostluk kurmak için) başlangıç
overturn [ouvıtö:n] devirmek, tepe taklak etmek
overwhelm [ouvıwelm] batırmak, garketmek
overwork [ouvıwö:k] fazla çalışma (mesai)
owe [ou] borçlu olmak
owing to [ouing tu] dolayısıyla
owl [aul] baykuş
own [oun] kendi / sahip olmak
owner [ounı] sahip
ox [oks] öküz, sığır
oxen [oksın] öküzler
oxygen [oksicın] oksijen
oyster [oystı] istiridye

P

pace [peys] adım / sürat / adımlamak
pacific [pısifik] barışçı
Pacific Ocean [pısifik ouşın] Büyük Okyanus
pacify [pesifay] yatıştırmak, barışı sağlamak
pack [pek] istif etmek, paket yapmak, ambalaj yapmak / paket, deste
package [pekic] paket yapmak / paket, deste
packet [pekit] paket
packing [peking] ambalaj
pact [pekt] mukavele, pakt, sözleşme
pad [ped] pamuk v.s. tampon / tıkaç / not defteri / istampa
paddle [pedıl] kısa kürek
padlock [pedlok] asma kilit
page [peyc] sayfa

paid, bak **pay**
pail [peyl] kova
pain [peyn] acı, ağrı, elem
painful [peynfıl] acı veren
painstaking [peynsteyking] itinalı, özenli
paint [peynt] yağlı boya resim yapmak / boyamak / boya
painter [peyntı] ressam, boyacı
painting [peynting] resim, tablo / ressamlık
pair [peı] çift / eş / eş olmak
pal [pel] arkadaş, ahbap
palace [pelıs] saray
palate [pelıt] damak
pale [peyl] soluk, uçuk
Palestine [pelistayn] Filistin
palette [pelit] palet
pallid [pelid] solgun
palm [pa:m] palmiye / avuç (içi)
palpitate [pelpiteyt] çarpıntı yapmak, (kalp) atmak
palpitation [pelpiteyşın] çarpıntı
pamphlet [pemflit] broşür, kitapçık
pan [pen] çanak, tava
pan— [pen] hepsi, bütün anlamında önek
pancake [penkeyk] bir çeşit kek
pane [peyn] pencere camı
panel [penıl] levha / tabla / heyet
pang [peng] sancı
panic [penik] ürkme, panik
panorama [penıra:mı] manzara, panaroma
pant [pent] sık solumak
panther [pentı] pars, panter
pantomime [pentımaym] pantomim
pantry [pentri] kiler
pants [pents] pantalon / don
papa [pıpa:] baba, babacığım
paper [peypı] kağıt / gazete
paprika [peprikı] kırmızı biber
parachute [perışu:t] paraşüt

parachutist [perışu:tist] paraşütçü
parade [pıreyd] gösteriş / tören / gezinti yeri / teşhir etmek, sergilemek
paradise [perıdays] cennet
paragraph [perıgra:f] paragraf
parallel [perılel] paralel / benzemek
paralyse [perılayz] felce uğratmak
paralysis [pırelisis] felç
paramount [perımaunt] üstün
parasite [perısayt] tufeyli, parazit, asalak
parcel [pa:sıl] paket
parch [pa:ç] kurumak / kavurmak
parchment [pa:çmınt] parşömen
pardon [pa:dın] af, bağışlama / affetmek
pare [peı] meyve kabuğunu soymak
parent [peırınt] ebeveyn, ana-baba
parenthesis [pırentisis] parantez
park [pa:k] park / (bir vasıtayı) park etmek
parliament [pa:lımınt] parlamento
parlour [pa:lı] salon, oturma odası
parody [perıdi] bir eserin taklidi / taklit etmek (gülünç hale koyarak)
parquet [pa:key] parke
parrot [perıt] papağan
parsley [pa:sli] maydanoz
part [pa:t] kısım, parça / pay / rol / ayırmak, ayrılmak
partake (—took, —taken) [pa:teyk, —tuk, —teykın] katılmak, iştirak etmek
partial [pa:şıl] kısmi / taraf tutan
participate [pa:tisipeyt] iştirak etmek, katılmak
participle [pa:tisipıl] fiilden yapılma sıfat veya zarf, ortaç
particle [pa:tikıl] zerre, parçacık / küçük önemsiz sözcükler (dilbilgisi)
particular [pıtikyulı] özel / belirli / müşkülpesent, titiz
particularly [pıtikyulıli] özel-

likle
parting [pa:ting] ayrılma, veda
partisan [pa:tizen] partili, partizan
partition [pa:tişın] bölme duvarı, bölüm
partly [pa:tli] kısmen
partner [pa:tnı] ortak, eş
part time [pa:t taym] günün bir kısmında
party [pa:ti] parti / takım (askeri) / toplantı
pass [pa:s] geçit / paso / geçmek / uzatmak
passage [pesic] geçit, pasaj / (kitapta) bölüm
passenger [pesincı] yolcu
passerby [pesıbay] yoldan geçen
passion [peşın] ihtiras, şehvet
passionate [peşınit] ihtiraslı
passive [pesiv] mukavemet etmeyen, pasif / edilgen (dilbilgisi)
passport [pa:spo:t] pasaport
password [pa:swö:d] parola
past [pa:st] geçmiş / geçe / mazi / önünden
paste [peyst] macun, pasta, tutkal
pasteboard [peystbo:d] mukavva
pasteurize [pestırayz] pastörize etmek
pastime [pa:staym] eğlence
pastoral [pa:stırıl] kır ve köylere ilişkin
pastry [peystri] hamur işi, pasta
pasture [pa:sçı] otlak, çayır
pat [pet] (el ile) hafifçe vurmak / parça
patch [peç] yama / arazi parçası
patent [peytınt] patent
paternity [pıtö:niti] babalık
path [pa:t] patika, yol
pathetic [pıtetik] acıklı
pathway [pa:twey] patika
patience [peyşıns] sabır
patient [peyşınt] sabırlı / hasta
patriot [petriıt] yurtsever
patriotic [petriotik] yurtsever

patriotism [petriyıtizm] yurtseverlik
patrol [pıtroul] devriye / devriye gezmek (askeri)
patron [peytrın] koruyucu, himaye eden
patter [petı] pıtırtı, yağmur damlalarının sesi
pattern [petın] nümune, örnek / resim
pauper [po:pı] yoksul
pause [po:z] duraklamak / durma, duraklama
pave [peyv] kaldırım döşemek
pavement [peyvmınt] kaldırım
pavilion [pıvilyın] pavyon, kulübe
paw [po:] pençe
pawn [po:n] rehin / rehine koymak, tehlikeye koymak / piyon
pay [pey] maaş, ücret
pay (paid, paid) [pey, peyd, peyd] ödemek, (para) vermek
payment [peymınt] ödeme
payroll [peyroul] ücret bordrosu
pea [pi:] bezelye
peace [pi:s] barış, sulh, sükûnet
peach [pi:ç] şeftali
peacock [pi:kok] tavus
peak [pi:k] zirve, en yüksek nokta
peanut [pi:nat] fıstık
pear [peı] armut
pearl [pö:l] inci
peasant [pezınt] köylü
pebble [pebıl] çakıl taşı
peck [pek] gagalamak
peculiar [pikyu:liı] kendine has, acayip
peculiarity [pikyu:lieriti] özellik
pedal [pedıl] pedal
peddle [pedıl] seyyar satıcılık yapmak
pedestrian [pıdestriın] yaya
pedigree [pedigri:] soy
pedlar [pedlı] seyyar satıcı
peel [pi:l] kabuğunu soymak
peep [pi:p] gözetlemek
peer [piı] eş, emsal
peerless [piılis] eşsiz
peevish [pi:viş] hırçın
peg [peg] ağaç çivi / mandal, çengel
pen [pen] dolmakalem, mü-

rekkepli kalem
penalize [pi:nılayz] cezalandırmak
penalty [penılti] ceza / penaltı
penance [penıns] kefaret, kendi kendine ceza
pencil [pensıl] kurşun kalem
pending [pending] sallantıda, kararlaştırılmamış
penetrate [penitreyt] nüfuz etmek, içine girmek
penetration [penitreyşın] nüfuz etme, içine işleme
penguin [pengwin] penguen
peninsula [peninsyulı] yarımada
penitent [penitınt] nadim, pişman
penknife [pennayf] çakı
penniless [penilis] meteliksiz
penny [peni] 1 Pound'ın yüzde biri
pension [penşın] emekli maaşı / [pansiyon] pansiyon
pensioner [penşını] emekli
pensive [pensiv] düşünceli, dalgın
pentagon [pentıgın] beş köşeli
penthouse [penthaus] sarkıtma / saçak / çatı katı
people [pi:pıl] halk / ulus / kişiler
pepper [pepı] biber
peppermint [pepımint] nane
per [pö:] vasıtasiyle / tarafından / her biri için
per cent [pö:sent] yüzde (matematik)
perambulator [pırembiyuleytı] çocuk arabası
perceive [pısi:v] hissetmek, farkına varmak, sezmek
percentage [pısentic] yüzdelik
perceptible [pıseptibıl] hissedilir
peremptory [pıremptıri] kesin / itirazsız
perennial [pırenyıl] mütemadi, seneden seneye
perfect [pö:fikt] mükemmel, tam / tamamlamak

perfection [pö:fekşın] mükemmellik
perfectly [pö:fiktli] tamamen, adamakıllı
perforate [pö:fıreyt] delik açmak / pul kenarı
perform [pıfo:m] yapmak, yerine getirmek / rol yapmak (tiyatro)
performance [pıfo:mıns] yapım, icra, temsil
perfume [pö:fyum] parfüm, güzel koku
pergola [pö:golı] çardak
perhaps [pıheps] belki
peril [peril] tehlike
perilous [perilıs] tehlikeli
period [piıriıd] devir, devre
periodical [piıriyodikıl] zaman zaman yapılan / dergi
perish [periş] mahvolmak, bozulmak
perjury [pö:cıri] yalan yere yemin
permanent [pö:mınınt] daimi, sürekli, kalıcı
permanently [pö:mınıntli] sürekli olarak
permission [pımişın] müsaade
permit [pımit] müsaade etmek
permit [pö:mit] permi, lisans
perpendicular [pö:pındikyulı] dikey, dik (açı)
perplex [pıpleks] şaşırtmak
persecute [pö:sikyu:t] zulmetmek
persecution [pö:sikyu:şın] zulüm
persevere [pö:siviı] sebat etmek
perseverance [pö:siviırıns] sebat
Persia [pö:şı] İran
Persian [pö:şın] İranlı, İranca
persist [pısist] ısrar etmek, sebat etmek
persistence [pı:sistıns] ısrar, sebat
person [pö:sın] şahıs, kişi
personage [pö:sınic] önemli kişi
personal [pö:sınıl] kişisel
personality [pö:sıneliti] karakter, kişilik
personally [pö:sınıli] şah-

sen / bizzat
personnel [pö:sınel] personel
perspective [pıspektiv] perspektif, görüş açısı
perspire [pıspayı] terlemek
perspiration [pö:spıreyşın] terleme, ter
persuade [pısweyd] ikna etmek, razı etmek
persuasion [pısweyjın] ikna, razı etme / inanç
persuasive [pısweysiv] ikna edici, inandırıcı
pertain [pıteyn] ilişkin olmak
perturb [pıtö:b] rahatsız etmek / korkutmak
pervade [pıveyd] istila etmek, yayılmak
perverse [pıvö:s] ters, bozuk
pervert [pıvö:t] bozmak, saptırmak / sapık
pessimism [pesimizm] kötümserlik
pessimist [pesimist] kötümser
pest [pest] baş belası
pester [pestı] usandırmak, canını sıkmak
pestle [pesıl] havaneli
pet [pet] ev hayvanı / sevilen
petal [petıl] çiçek yaprağı
petition [petişın] dilekçe
petrify [petrifay] taşlaşmak
petrol [petrıl] benzin
petroleum [pıtroulyım] petrol
petticoat [petikout] eteklik, kombinezon
petty [peti] önemsiz / küçük / adi
pew [piu:] (kilisede) peyke, sıra
phantom [fentım] hayal, hayalet
pharmacy [fa:mısi] eczane / eczacılık
phase [feyz] safha
pheasant [fezınt] sülün
philanthropy [filentrıpi] hayırseverlik
philately [filetıli] pulculuk
philology [filolıci] filoloji, lisaniyat, dilbilim
philosopher [filosıfı] filozof, düşünür
philosophy [filosıfi] felse-

fe
phobia [foubyı] fobi
phone [foun] telefon etmek
phonetic [fınetik] fonetik, ses bilimine ilişkin
photo [foutou] fotoğraf
photocopy [foutoukopi] fotokopi
photograph [foutıgra:f] fotoğraf / fotoğraf çekmek
photographer [fıtogrıfı] fotoğrafçı
photography [fıtogrıfi] fotoğrafçılık sanatı
phrase [freyz] deyim, ibare
physical [fizikıl] maddi, bedene ait
physics [fiziks] fizik
physician [fizişın] doktor
physicist [fizisist] fizikçi
physique [fizi:k] bünye
piano [piyenou] piyano
pianist [pi:ınist] piyanist
pick [pik] toplamak / almak / seçmek / delmek
picket [pikit] kazık
pickle [pikıl] turşu
pickpocket [pikpokit] yankesici
pickup [pikap] kamyonet / pikap
picnic [piknik] piknik
pictorial [piktoıryıl] resimli
picture [pikçı] resim
the pictures sinema
picturesque [pikçıresk] resim gibi güzel
pie [pay] börek
piece [pi:s] parça
piecemeal [pi:smi:l] parça parça
pier [piı] iskele
pierce [piıs] delmek
piety [payıti] dindarlık
pig [pig] domuz
pigeon [picın] güvercin
pile [payl] yığmak, kümelemek / yığın, küme
pilfer [pilfı] yürütmek, tırtıklamak, aşırmak
pilgrim [pilgrim] hacı
pill [pil] hap
pillage [pilic] çapul / yağma etmek
pillar [pilı] direk, sütun
pillow [pilou] yastık
pilot [paylıt] kılavuz, pilot / yol göstermek
pimp [pimp] pezevenk

pimple [pimpıl] sivilce
pin [pin] (toplu, kancalı) iğne / iğnelemek
pincers [pinsız] kerpeten
pinch [pinç] çimdik / çimdiklemek / sıkmak
pine [payn] çam / hasretini çekmek
pineapple [paynepıl] ananas
pink [pink] pembe / karanfil
pint [paynt] bir galonun sekizde biri
pioneer [payınii] öncü
pious [payıs] sofu
pip [pip] çekirdek
pipe [payp] pipo / boru
pipeline [payplayn] petrol borusu
piracy [payrısi] korsanlık
pirate [payrıt] korsan
piss [pis] işemek
pistachio [pista:şyou] Antep fıstığı
pistol [pistıl] tabanca
piston [pistın] piston
pit [pit] çukur, kuyu
pitch [piç] zift / ziftlemek / mertebe, yükseklik / ses perdesi / atmak / kurmak / konmak
pitcher [piçı] testi
piteous [pityıs] acıklı, acındıran
pitfall [pitfo:l] tuzak
pith [pit] öz, kudret
pitiable [pitiıbıl] acınacak durumda
pitiful [pitifıl] acıklı
pitiless [pitilis] merhametsiz, acımasız
pity [piti] merhamet / yazık **what a pity,** ne yazık
pivot [pivıt] eksen, mil / dönmek
placard [pleka:d] üzerine ilan yazısı yazılıp asılmış kağıt
place [pleys] yer, mahal / yerleştirmek
placid [plesid] sakin, durgun
plague [pleyg] veba / musibet / taciz etmek
plaice [pleys] pisi balığı
plain [pleyn] ova / açık, sarih / sade
plainly [pleynli] açık ve sarih şekilde, açıkça
plaintiff [pleyntif] davacı
plan [plen] plan / planını çizmek / planlamak, tasarla-

mak
plane [pleyn] rende / uçak
planet [plenit] gezegen
plank [plenk] kalas
plant [pla:nt] bitki / fabrika / (fidan v.s.) dikmek
plantation [pla:nteyşın] fidanlık, tarla
plaster [pla:stı] sıva / yakı / sıvamak / yakı yapıştırmak / plaster
plastic [plestik] plastik
plate [pleyt] tabak / levha / plaka / tabaka
platform [pletfo:m] platform / peron / taraça
plating [pleyting] kaplama
platinum [pletinım] platin
platoon [plıtu:n] (askeri) takım
plausible [plo:zibıl] sözde haklı, görünüşte doğru
play [pley] oynamak / piyes / çalmak (çalgı) / oyun / şaka
player [pleyı] oyuncu / müzisyen / aktör
playground [pleygraund] oyun alanı
plaything [pleyting] oyuncak
playwright [pleyrayt] oyun yazarı
plea [pli:] savunma / rica
plead [pli:d] dava etmek / savunmak (mahkeme) / yalvarmak
pleasant [plezınt] hoş
please [pli:z] hoşuna gitmek, memnun etmek / lütfen
pleasing [pli:zing] hoş
pleasure [plejı] zevk, memnuniyet, kıvanç
pleat [pli:t] plise
plebiscite [plebisayt] plebisit, halk oylaması
pledge [plec] rehin / rehin vermek / vaat
plentiful [plentifıl] bol
plenty [plenti] bol, çok
pleurisy [pluırisi] zatülcenp
pliers [playız] kıskaç, pens, kerpeten
plight [playt] fena durum
plot [plot] arsa / entrika / pi-

yes veya hikayenin planı / dolap çevirmek
plough [plau] pulluk / çift sürmek / saban
pluck [plak] yolmak, koparmak / cesaret
plug [plag] tıkaç / fiş / buji / tıkamak
plum [plam] erik
plumb [plam] çekül
plumber [plamı] sıhhi tesisatçı, muslukçu
plump [plamp] tombul
plunder [plandı] yağma / yağma etmek
plunge [planc] daldırmak, sokmak, dalmak
plural [plu:rıl] çoğul
plus [plas] artı
ply [play] (gemi vs.) sefer yapmak
plywood [playwud] kontrplak
p.m. (post meridiem'in kısaltılmışı) [piem] öğleden sonra
pneumonia [niumounyı] zatürre
pocket [pokit] cep / cebe koymak
pocket-book [pokit buk] cep kitabı
poem [pouim] şiir
poet [pouit] şair, ozan
poetry [pouitri] şiir, şiir sanatı
poignant [poynınt] yakıcı keskin
point [poynt] işaret etmek / göstermek / nokta uç / husus / amaç / derece
pointed [poyntid] sivri uçlu
pointless [poyntlis] anlamsız, beyhude, boş
poise [poyz] denge / duruş / temkin
poison [poyzın] zehir / zehirlemek
poisonous [poyzınıs] zehirli
poke [pouk] dürtmek
poker [poukı] ocak demiri / poker
Poland [poulınd] Polonya
polar [poulı] kutba ait
pole [poul] kutup / sırık, direk
Pole [poul] Polonyalı
police [pıli:s] emniyet, zabıta, polis
police-station [pıli:s steyşın] karakol
policeman [pıli:smın] polis

memuru
policy [polisi] siyaset / poliçe
polish [poliş] parlatmak, cilalatmak / cila
Polish [pouliş] Polonyalı
polite [pılayt] terbiyeli, nazik
political [pılitikıl] siyasi
politician [politişın] politikacı, siyaset adamı
poll [poul] oy verme / oy vermek
pollution [pılu:şın] kirlenme
polygamy [poligımi] birden fazla kadın alma
pomegranate [pomgrenit] nar
pomp [pomp] tantana
pompous [pompıs] debdebeli, şatafatlı
pond [pond] su birikintisi
ponder [pondı] düşünmek
ponderous [pondırıs] ağır, yavaş, hantal
pony [pouni] midilli (at)
pool [pu:l] su birikintisi, havuz
poor [puı] yoksul / zavallı
pop [pop] patlama sesi / patlamak / popüler müzik
pope [poup] papa
poplar [poplı] kavak
poppy [popi] haşhaş, gelincik
popular [popyulı] halk için, halkın hoşuna giden, popüler
popularity [popyuleriti] popülerlik, rağbet
population [popyuleyşın] bir yerin nüfusu, halk
porcelain [po:slin] porselen
porch [po:ç] kapı önünde sundurma
pore [po:] kendini vermek / uzun uzun düşünmek / gözenek
pork [po:k] domuz eti
porous [po:rıs] suyu geçiren, sızdıran, delikli
porridge [poric] yulaf unu çorbası
port [po:t] liman
portable [po:tıbıl] portatif, taşınabilir
porter [po:tı] kapıcı / hamal
portion [po:şın] parça, por-

siyon

portly [po:tli] heybetli

portrait [po:trit] portre

Portugal [poçugıl] Portekiz

Portuguese [po:çıgi:z] portekizli / Portekizce

pose [pouz] vaziyet, poz

position [pızişın] durum / mevki, yer / görev

positive [pozitiv] müspet, olumlu / gerçek / emin

possess [pızes] sahibi olmak

possession [pızeşın] sahiplik / tasarruf / sahip olunan şeyler

possessive [pızeşiv] mülkiyet, aitlik, iyelik

possessor [pızesı] mal sahibi

possibility [posibiliti] imkân, olanak, olasılık

possible [posibıl] mümkün, olabilir

possibly [posibli] muhtemelen

post [poust] posta / postalamak / görev / direk, kazık / (ilan v.s.) yapıştırmak

postage [poustic] posta ücreti

postcard [poustka:d] kartpostal

poster [poustı] afiş

posterity [posteriti] zürriyet, gelecek nesiller

postman [poustmın] postacı

post-office [poustofis] postane

postpone [pouspoun] ertelemek, tehir etmek

postponement [pouspounmınt] tehir, erteleme

postscript [pousskript] (P.S.) mektup sonu notu, hamiş

posture [posçı] tavır

post-war [poustwo:] savaş sonrası

pot [pot] çömlek, kavanoz

potato [pıteytou] patates

potent [poutınt] kuvvetli

potential [pountenşıl] mevcut güç, gizli güç / potansiyel (fizik) / olasılık derecesi

potter [potı] çömlekçi

pottery [potıri] çömlekçilik / çanak çömlek

pouch [pauç] kese (para v.s.)
poultry [poultri] kümes hayvanları
pounce [pauns] atılmak
pound [paund] İngiliz lirası / libre / havanda dövmek / çarpmak
pour [po:] dökmek / üşüşmek / boşalmak
pout [paut] somurtmak
poverty [povıti] yoksulluk
powder [paudı] pudra / toz / barut
power [pauı] kuvvet, güç, yetki
powerful [pauıfıl] kuvvetli, güçlü
powerplant [pauıpla:nt] elektrik santralı
practicable [prektikıbıl] tatbiki mümkün, uygulanabilir
practical [prektikıl] pratik / becerikli
practically [prektikıli] hemen hemen
practice [prektis] uygulama, tatbikat / idman
practise [prektis] yapmak / uygulamak / pratik yapmak
prairie [preıri] ağaçsız ova
praise [preyz] övgü / methetmek
pram [prem] çocuk arabası
prance [pra:ns] sıçramak / şaha kalkmak
prattle [pretıl] çocuk gibi konuşmak
pray [prey] dua etmek / yalvarmak
prayer [preı] dua
pre— [pri:] önceden anlamında önek
preach [pri:ç] öğüt vermek, vaiz vermek
preacher [pri:çı] vaiz
precarious [prikeırııs] şüpheli / tehlikeli
precaution [priko:şın] ihtiyat, tedbir
precede [prisi:d] önünde gelmek
precept [pri:sept] düstur
precious [preşıs] değerli
precipice [presipis] uçurum
precis [preysi:] özet
precise [prisays] tam
precision [prisijın] kesinlik

preconception [pri:kınsepşın] peşin hüküm, önyargı
predecessor [pri:disesı] selef, kendinden önceki
predestination [pridestineyşın] kader, nasip
predicament [pridikımınt] fena ve müşkül durum
predicate [pri:dikit] bildirmek / onaylamak / [predikit] yüklem
predict [pridikt] kehanette bulunmak
prediction [pridikşın] kehanet, önceden haber
predominant [pri:dominınt] üstün
preface [prefis] önsöz
prefer [prifö:] tercih etmek
preferable [prefırıbıl] tercihe şayan
preference [prefırıns] tercih
prefix [pri:fiks] önek
pregnant [pregnınt] hamile, gebe
prejudice [precudis] peşin hüküm, önyargı
preliminary [priliminıri] başlangıca ait, ön
prelude [prelyud] başlangıç, giriş
premature [premıçı] mevsimsiz, erken
premeditate [pri:mediteyt] önceden tasarlayarak yapmak
premeditated [pri:mediteytid] kasdi, bilerek yapılan
premier [premyı] başbakan
premiere [premieı] gala
premises [premisiz] ev ve ona ait (bahçe, müştemilat gibi) her şey
premium [pri:myım] mükâfat, prim
premonition [pri:mınişın] önsezi
preoccupy [pri:okyupay] zihnini işgal etmek
preparation [prepıreyşın] hazırlama, hazırlık / müstahzar
prepare [pripeı] hazırlamak, hazırlanmak
preposition [prepızişın] edat, ilgeç
prescribe [priskrayb] reçete vermek
prescription [priskripşın] re

çete

presence [prezıns] mevcut oluş, bulunuş

present [prezınt] şimdiki, mevcut / halihazır / armağan, hediye

present [prizent] takdim etmek, sunmak

presentable [prizentıbıl] takdim edilebilir

presentiment [prizentimınt] önceden hissetme, önsezi

presently [prezıntli] biraz sonra

preservation [prizö:veyşın] koruma, muhafaza

preserve [prizö:v] muhafaza etmek, korumak / konservesini yapmak

preserved [prizö:vd] muhafaza edilmiş / konserve

preside [prizayd] başkanlık etmek

president [prezidınt] başkan

press [pres] basın / basımevi / ütülemek / basmak, sıkmak / zorlamak / pres

pressing [presing] acele / önemli

pressure [preşı] basınç, baskı, zorlama

prestige [presti:j] şöhret, prestij, saygınlık

presumably [prizyu:mıbli] galiba

presume [prizyu:m] tahmin etmek, farzetmek, varsaymak

presumption [prizamşın] ihtimal, faraziye, varsayım

pretence [pritens] yapmacık

pretend [pritend] ...gibi görünmek, yapmacık yapmak

pretext [pri:tekst] bahane

pretty [priti] güzel, hoş / epey, hayli

prevail [priveyl] hüküm sürmek, geçerli olmak

prevailing [priveyling] geçerli

prevalent [prevılınt] geçerli, her yerde olan

prevent [privent] engel olmak

prevention [privenşın] önleme, engel olma

preventive [priventiv] önleyici

previous [pri:vyıs] önceki, sabık

prey [prey] av, kurban

price [prays] fiyat

prick [prik] batmak / sokmak / iğnelemek

prickle [prikıl] iğne, diken / iğnelemek / kaşındırmak

prickly [prikli] dikenli

pride [prayd] gurur

priest [pri:st] papaz

primary [praymıri] as'l, en önemli / ilk

prime [praym] birinci, esas / âlâ, en iyi

primer [praymı] ilk okuma kitabı

primitive [primitiv] ilkel, iptidai, eski usul

prince [prins] prens

princess [prinses] prenses

principal [prinsipıl] başlıca / baş, reis, müdür

principle [prinsipıl] prensip, ilke, kural

print [print] (kitap v.s.) basmak, matbaada basmak / baskı

printer [printı] matbaacı / baskı yapan

printing [printing] matbaacılık, baskı

prior [prayı] sâbık, evvel

priority [prayoriti] öncelik

prison [prizın] hapishane

prisoner [priznı] tutuklu mahpus, esir

privacy [prayvısi] mahremlik, gizlilik

private [prayvit] özel, kişisel / mahrem / er

privilege [privilic] imtiyaz ayrıcalık / ayrıcalık tanımak

prize [prayz] ödül / değer vermek

probable [probıbıl] muhtemel

probability [probıbiliti] ihtimal, olasılık

probably [probıbli] muhtemelen

probation [probeyşın] deneme

problem [problım] sorun problem

procedure [prousi:cı] işlem, usul, gelişim

proceed [prousi:d] ilerlemek, devam etmek

proceeding [prousi:ding] hareket tarzı, gidiş / işlem
process [prouses] işlem, metod / eylem / süreç
procession [prıseşın] geçit resmi, alay
proclaim [prokleym] ilan etmek
procure [prokyuı] elde etmek, tedarik etmek
prod [prod] dürtme / dürtmek
prodigious [prodicıs] harikulade, muazzam
produce [prıdyu:s] üretmek / çıkarmak
producer [prıdyu:sı] yapımcı, prodüktör
product [prodıkt] ürün
production [prıdakşın] üretim / ürün
productive [prıdaktiv] mümbit, verimli
profess [prıfes] itiraf etmek, bildirmek
profession [prıfeşın] meslek
professional [prıfeşınıl] profesyonel / mesleki
professor [prıfesı] profesör
proficiency [profişınsi] yeterlilik, ehliyet
profile [proufayl] profil
profit [profit] kâr, kazanç / kâr etmek
profitable [profitıbıl] kârlı, yararlı
profiteer [profitiı] vurguncu
profound [prıfaund] derin, içten
profuse [prıfyu:s] mebzul, bol bol
programme [prougrem] program
progress [prougres] ilerleme, yürüme / gelişim
progression [prougreşın] gelişme, ilerleme
prohibit [prıhibit] yasak etmek
prohibition [prouhibişın] yasak, yasaklama
project [proucekt] plan, proje / tasarlamak / fırlatmak / çıkıntı teşkil etmek
projecting [proucekting] çıkıntılı
projection [proucekşın] projeksiyon
proletarian [prolıteıriın] üc-

retle çalışan işçi sınıfından, emekci
prolific [prolifik] verimli
prolong [prılong] uzatmak, geciktirmek
promenade [promına:d] gezinti / gezinmek
prominence [prominıns] çıkıntı / belirlilik
prominent [prominınt] çıkıntılı / şöhretli
promise [promis] vaat etmek, söz vermek / vaat
promising [promising] umut verici
promote [prımout] terfi ettirmek / teşvik etmek
prompt [prompt] tez davranan / harekete geçirmek
promptly [promptli] derhal
prone [proun] eğilimli / yüzükoyun
pronoun [prounaun] zamir
pronounce [prınauns] telaffuz etmek
pronunciation [prınansieyşın] telaffuz, okunuş
proof [pru:f] kanıt, delil / matbaa provası
prop [prop] destek, dayak / yaslamak
propaganda [propıgendı] propaganda
propel [prıpel] ileriye sürmek, itmek
propeller [propelı] pervane
proper [propı] uygun
properly [propıli] uygun bir şekilde
property [propıti] emlak, mal
prophesy [profisay] kehanette bulunmak
prophet [profit] peygamber
proportion [prıpo:şın] nispet, oran
proposal [prıpouzıl] teklif, evlenme teklifi
propose [prıpouz] teklif etmek / evlenme teklifi yapmak
proposition [propızişın] teklif, iş
proprietor [proprayıtı] mal sahibi, sahip
prose [prouz] nesir, düz yazı
prosecute [prosikyu:t] takip etmek / dava etmek, kovuşturmak

prosecution [prosikyu:şın] adli takibat / dava etme
prosecutor [prosikyu:tı] davacı / savcı
prospect [prospekt] görünüş / ihtimal
prospective [prospektiv] muhtemel, olasılı
prospectus [prospektıs] tarifname, prospektüs
prosper [prospı] başarıya ulaşmak, refaha ermek
prosperity [prosperiti] refah
prosperous [prospırıs] refah içinde
prostitute [prostityu:t] fahişe, orospu
prostrate [prostreyt] yere kapanmış, bitkin
protect [prıtekt] korumak
protection [prıtekşın] koruma, muhafaza
protector [prıtektı] hami, koruyucu
protest [prıtest] itiraz etmek
protest [proutest] itiraz
Protestant [protistınt] protestan
protocol [proutıkol] protokol
protractor [proutrektı] minkale, iletki
protrude [proutru:d] dışarı fırlamak
protruding [proutru:ding] fırlak, çıkıntılı
proud [praud] gururlu, mağrur
prove [pru:v] kanıtlamak, ispat etmek
proverb [provö:b] atasözü
provide [prıvayd] tedarik etmek, teçhiz etmek, donatmak
providence [providıns] ihtiyat / Cenab-ı Hak
province [provins] vilayet, il, eyalet / saha
provincial [provinşıl] taşralı
provision [provijın] tedarik, provizyon
provisions [provijınz] erzak
provisional [provijınıl] muvakkat, geçici
provocative [prıvokıtiv] tahrik edici, kışkırtıcı
provoke [prıvouk] tahrik etmek
prowl [praul] av peşinde dolaşmak

proximity [proksimiti] yakınlık

proxy [proksi] vekalet, başkasının yerine hareket etme yetkisi / vekil

prudence [pru:dıns] ihtiyat, basiret

prudent [pru:dınt] ihtiyatlı

prune [pru:n] budamak / kurutulmuş erik

pry [pray] tecessüs etmek, burnunu sokmak

P.S. [pi: es] mektup sonu notu, hamiş

psychiatry [saykayıtri] psikiatri

psycho-analysis [saykouınelisis] psikanaliz

psychology [saykolıci] psikoloji

pub [pab] birahane

puberty [piu:bö:ti] ergenlik çağı

public [pablik] umumi, aleni, herkese açık / halk

publication [pablikeyşın] neşretme, yayın

publicity [pablisiti] alenilik / reklam

publish [pabliş] (kitap vs.) neşretmek, yayımlamak

publisher [pablişı] yayıncı

pudding [puding] puding muhallebi

puddle [padıl] kirli su biri kintisi

puff [paf] üfleme, püf pudra pomponu / üfle mek

pull [pul] çekmek / çek me

pulley [puli] makara (yük) kasnak

pulp [palp] öz, özsu

pulse [pals] nabız / atmak (nabız)

pulverize [palvırayz] to: yapmak / toz gibi serp mek / toz haline ez mek

pump [pamp] tulumba pompa / pompalamak

pumpkin [pam(p)kin] bal ka bağı

punch [panç] muşta / nokt / zımbalamak / yumrukla mak / punç

punctual [pankçuıl] dakik zamanında

punctuality [pankçueliti] da kiklik

punctuate [panktiueyt] nok

talamak
punctuation [pankçueyşın] noktalama
puncture [pankçı] delmek, deşmek / patlak
pungent [pancınt] keskin, sert, acı
punish [paniş] cezalandırmak
punishment [panişmınt] ceza
pupil [piu:pıl] öğrenci / gözbebeği
puppet [papit] kukla
puppy [papi] köpek yavrusu
purchase [pö:çis] satın almak / mübayaa
pure [piu:ı] saf, halis, arı
puree [piurey] püre
purely [piuıli] sırf, tamamen
purgative [pö:gıtiv] müshil
purge [pö:c] temizlemek / müshil
purify [piuırifay] tasfiye etmek, temizlemek
purity [piuıriti] saflık, temizlik
purple [pö:pıl] mor
purpose [pö:pıs] maksat, niyet
purr [pö:] (kedi için) mırıldamak
purse [pö:s] para kesesi
pursue [pö:syu:] takip etmek, devam etmek
pursuit [pısyu:t] takip / meşgale
pus [pas] cerahat, irin
push [puş] itmek / itme
puss pussy [pus-pusi] pisi pisi
put (put, put) [put, put, put] koymak / ifade etmek
putrefy [piutrifay] çürümek
puzzle [pazıl] şaşırmak, şaşırtmak / bilmece / muamma
pyjamas [pica:mız] pijama
pylon [paylon] elektrik direği / kule
pyramid [pirımid]ehram, piramit

Q

quack [kwek] ördek sesi
quadrangle [kwodrengıl]

dörtgen / bahçe
quadrilateral [kwodriletırıl] dörtgen
quail [kweyl] bıldırcın / ürkmek
quaint [kweynt] tuhaf, antika
quake [kweyk] titremek
qualification [kwolifikeyşın] vasıf, şart, ehliyet
qualify [kwolifay] vasıflandırmak / ehliyet vermek
qualified [kwolifayd] ehliyetli, nitelikli
quality [kwoliti] kalite, vasıf
qualm [kwa:m] kuşku / mide bulantısı
quantity [kwontiti] miktar
quarantine [kworınti:n] karantina
quarrel [kwo:rıl] kavga / kavga etmek
quarrelsome [kworılsım] kavgacı
quarry [kwo:ri] taş ocağı
quart [kwo:t] galon'un dörtte biri
quarter [kwo:tı] çeyrek / yön / mahalle / ikametgâh
quarterly [kwo:tıli] üç aylık
quartz [kwo:ts] kuvarts
quay [ki:] rıhtım
queen [kwi:n] kraliçe
queer [kwiı] acayip / sapık
quell [kwel] teskin etmek, yatıştırmak / basmak, bastırmak
quench [kwenç] söndürmek, gidermek
query [kwiıri] soru / soru işareti / soruşturmak
quest [kwest] arama, araştırma
question [kwesçın] soru / söz konusu / mesele / soru sormak
question-mark soru işareti
questionnaire [kwesşıneı] soru kağıdı, anket soruları
queue [kiu:] bekleyen insanlar, sıra kuyruğu
quick [kwik] çabuk, süratli
quickly [kwikli] çabuk, hızlı
quiet [kwayıt] sakin, sessiz
quietly [kwayıtli] sakin bir şekilde, sessizce

quilt [kwilt] yatak örtüsü, yorgan
quince [kwins] ayva
quit [kwit] terketmek, vazgeçmek
quite [kwayt] tamamen, epey, oldukça
quiver [kwivı] titreme / titremek
quiz [kwiz] sınav / şaka yapmak / sınav yapmak
quota [kwoutı] hisse, pay, kota
quotation [kwouteyşın] iktibas, yazıdan parça alma / (ticarette) fiyat teklifi
quote [kwout] iktibas etmek, sözden veya yazıdan parça almak

R

rabbi [rebay] haham
rabbit [rebit] tavşan
rabies [reybi:z] kuduz
race [reys] yarış, yarışmak / ırk, cins
racial [reyşıl] ırka ilişkin
rack [rek] raf
racket [rekit] raket / velvele / çete
racketeer [rekitıı] zorba, gangster
radar [reyda:] radar
radiance [reydyıns] parlaklık
radiant [reydiınt] parlak, parıldayan
radiate [reydieyt] ısı veya ışık saçmak, ışın göndermek
radiation [reydieyşın] ışın gönderme, radyasyon
radiator [reydieytı] radyatör
radical [redikıl] köke ait, köklü, radikal
radio [reydiou] radyo
radish [rediş] turp
radium [reydiım] radyum
radius [reydiıs] yarıçap
raft [ra:ft] sal
rag [reg] paçavra
rage [reyc] hiddet, öfke / şiddetli arzu / öfkelenmek / kudurmak
ragged [regid] pejmürde, düzensiz, pürüzlü
raging [reycing] şiddetli,

hiddetli, gözü dönmüş
raid [reyd] akın, baskın / baskın yapmak
raider [reydı] akıncı, baskın yapan
rail [reyl] demiryolu rayı / tırabzan üstü / küpeşte
railroad [reylroud] demiryolu (Amerikan)
railway [reylwey] demiryolu
rain [reyn] yağmur / yağmur yağmak
rainbow [reynbou] gökkuşağı
raincoat [reynkout] yağmurluk
rainy [reyni] yağmurlu
raise [reyz] kaldırmak, yükseltmek / meydana getirmek, yetiştirmek / artırmak
raisin [reyzin] kuru üzüm
rake [reyk] tırmık / tırmıklamak
rally [reli] yeniden kuvvetlenmek, toparlanmak / otomobil ralisi
ram [rem] koç / şahmerdan
Ramadan [remıden] ramazan ayı
ramble [rembıl] keyfi dolaşmak, gezinmek
ramp [remp] meyil, rampa
rampart [rempa:t] savunma için kazılan çukur
ramshackle [remşekıl] kôhne
ran, bak **run**
ranch [ra:nç] hayvan yetiştiren çiftlik
rancour [renkı] hınç
random [rendım] rasgele
rang, bak **ring**
range [reync] düzene koymak, sıralamak / dolaşmak, gezmek / sıra, dizi / menzil
ranger [reyncı] korucu
rank [renk] rütbe, sıra
ransom [rensım] fidye
rap [rep] darbe / kapı çalmak, hafifçe vurmak
rape [reyp] zorla iğfal etmek
rapid [repid] hızlı
rapture [repçı] büyük sevinç, kendinden geçme
rare [reı] nadir, ender, müstesna / az pişmiş
rarely [reıli] nadiren
rascal [ra:skıl] çapkın, yara-

maz, serseri
ash [reş] ihtiyatsız, hesapsız, korkusuz
asp [ra:sp] raspa, törpü
aspberry [ra:zbıri] ahududu
at [ret] büyük fare
ate [reyt] oran / derece / rayiç / tasnif etmek
ather [ra:dı] oldukça / tercihan
atio [reyşiou] oran
ation [reşın] istihkak, tayın
ational [reşınıl] makul, uygun, rasyonal
attle [retıl] zırıltı, takırtı / takırdamak
attlesnake [retılsneyk] çıngıraklı yılan
attling [retling] takırtı
avage [revic] harap etmek, talan etmek
ave [reyv] çıldırmak
aven [reyvın] kuzgun
avenous [revınıs] haris
avishing [revişing] büyüleyici
aw [ro:] çiğ, ham
ay [rey] ışın,
ayon [reyon] suni ipek
azor [reyzı] ustura, tıraş makinesi
re— [ri:] yeniden, tekrar anlamında önek
reach [ri:ç] erişmek, yetişmek / uzanmak / varmak
react [ri:ekt] aksi tesir etmek, tepki göstermek
reaction [ri:ekşın] tepki
read (read, read) [ri:d, red, red] okumak
reader [ri:dı] okuyucu
reading [ri:ding] okuma
ready [redi] hazır
ready-made hazır (elbise v.b.)
real [riıl] gerçek, hakikat
real estate [riıl isteyt] mülk, gayrimenkul, mal
real estate agent emlakçı
realist [riılist] realist, gerçekçi
realistic [riılistik] gerçeğe uygun
reality [rieliti] gerçek, hakikat, realite
realize [riılayz] anlamak, idrak etmek, farkında olmak / gerçekleştirmek, uygulamak
really [riıli] hakikaten, ger-

çekten

realm [relm] memleket, ülke / kraliyet

reap [ri:p] ürün toplamak, orakla kesmek

rear [rıı] arka, geri / yetiştirmek, büyütmek

rearmament [ria:mımınt] yeniden silahlanma

reason [ri:zın] sebep, gerekçe / akıl / sonuç çıkarmak / muhakeme etmek

reasonable [ri:zınıbıl] makul

reassure [riışuı] tatmin etmek, güven vermek

rebel [rebıl] asi, [ribel] isyan etmek

rebellion [ribelyın] isyan

rebellious [ribelyıs] başkaldıran, asi

rebound [ribaund] geri sıçramak

rebuff [ribaf] red / reddetmek

rebuke [ribyu:k] azar / azarlamak

recall [riko:l] geri çağırmak / hatırlamak

recede [risi:d] geri çekilmek

receipt [risi:t] makbuz

receive [risi:v] (verilen veya gönderileni) almak / maruz kalmak / (bir kimseyi) kabul etmek

receiver [risi:vı] alıcı (radyo v.s.) / alan (kimse)

recent [ri:sınt] bu yakında, geçenlerde

recently [ri:sıntli] geçenlerde, yakında

reception [risepşın] kabul, alma / resepsiyon

recess [rises] istirahat, teneffüs / bucak, köşe

recession [riseşın] çekilme / istirahate çekilme / girinti / piyasada durgunluk

recipe [resipi] reçete, yemek yapma tarifesi

recite [risayt] ezbere (şiir) söylemek

recital [risaytıl] resital

reckless [reklis] pervasız, korkusuz

reckon [rekın] hesap etmek, tahmin etmek

reclaim [rikleym] ıslah etmek, düzeltmek

recline [riklayn] dayanmak.

uzanmak
recognition [rekıgnişın] tanıma, onaylama
recognize [rekıgnayz] tanımak / tasdik etmek
recognized [rekıgnayzd] tanınmış, muteber
recoil [rikoyl] geri tepmek / çekilmek
recollect [rekılekt] hatırlamak
recollection [rekılekşın] hatırlama / hatıra, anı
recommend [rekımend] tavsiye etmek, önermek
recommendation [rekımendeyşın] tavsiye, öneri
recompense [rekımpens] telafi etmek, tazmin etmek
reconcile [rekınsayl] barıştırmak, uzlaştırmak, telif etmek
reconstruct [ri:kınstrakt] yeniden kurmak
record [reko:d] kayıt / rekor / plak
record [riko:d] kaydetmek
recorder [riko:dı] kaydeden kimse / kaydeden alet
recover [rikavı] tekrar ele geçirmek / iyileşmek / ayılmak
recovery [rikavıri] geri alma / iyileşme, kalkınma
recreation [rekrieyşın] eğlence / dinlenme
recruit [rikru:t] yeni asker / yeni üye / yeni işçi / (işçi, üye, asker) kaydetmek
rectangle [rektengıl] dikdörtgen
rectify [rektitay] düzeltmek, tashih etmek
recur [rikö:] tekrar olmak
recurrence [rikarıns] tekrar olma, (tıp) nüks
red [red] kırmızı
Red Crescent [red kresınt] Kızılay
Red Cross [red kros] Kızılhaç
redden [redın] kızarmak, kırmızılaştırmak
redeem [ridi:m] kurtarmak, telafi etmek / ifa etmek
redemption [ridemşın] ödeme, kurtarma
reduce [ridyu:s] azaltmak
reduction [ridakşın] azalma,

indirim
reek [ri:k] fena koku / fena koku yaymak
reel [ri:l] makara, bobin / halk oyunu / sendelemek
refer [rifö:] havale etmek / ilgili olmak
referee [refıri:] hakem
reference [refırıns] müracaat / ima / referans
refill [ri:fil] tekrar doldurmak
refine [rifayn] arılaştırmak, tasfiye etmek
refinement [rifaynmınt] kibarlık, incelik
refinery [rifaynıri] tasfiyehane, rafineri
reflect [riflekt] yansıtmak / düşünmek
reflection [riflekşın] yansıma, düşünme
reflex [ri:fleks] aksetme, yansıma
reform [ri:fʌ:m] ıslah / ıslah etmek / reform
reformer [rifo:mı] ıslahatçı
refrain [rifreyn] nakarat, ara nağme / kendini tutmak, kaçınmak
refresh [rifreş] tazelemek, canlandırmak
refreshment [rifreşmınt] serinletici şey (içki v.b.)
refrigerator [rifricıreytı] buzdolabı, soğutucu
refuge [refyu:c] sığınak
refugee [refyuci:] mülteci
refund [ri:fand] (parayı) geri vermek
refusal [rifyu:zıl] red
refuse [rifyu:z] reddetmek, kabul etmemek
refuse [refyu:s] süprüntü, çerçöp
refute [rifyu:t] yalanlamak
regain [ri:geyn] tekrar elde etmek
regard [riga:d] bakmak / telakki etmek / ilişki / itibar, saygı
regarding [riga:ding] hakkında, hususunda
regardless [riga:dlis] bakmaksızın
regime [reyji:m] rejim, hükümet sistemi
regiment [recimınt] (askeri) alay
region [ri:cın] mıntıka, nahiye, bölge
register [recistı] sicil, kayıt /

kaydetmek
registered [recistıd] taahhütlü / kayıtlı
registration [recistreyşın] tescil, kayıt
regret [rigret] esef, teessüf / esef etmek
regular [regyulı] muntazam, düzenli
regularity [regyuleriti] intizam, düzen
regularly [regyulıli] düzenli olarak
regulate [regyuleyt] düzenlemek, bir seviyede tutmak
regulation [regyuleyşın] nizam, yönetmelik, talimat
regulator [regyuleytı] regülatör, ayar edici
rehearsal [rihö:sıl] prova (tiyatroda)
rehearse [rihö:s] prova etmek
reign [reyn] saltanat sürmek
rein [reyn] dizgin
reinforce [ri:nfo:s] takviye etmek, kuvvetlendirmek
reject [ricekt] reddetmek
rejection [ricekşın] red, iade
rejoice [ricoys] sevinmek, sevindirmek
rejoin [ricoyn] iltihak etmek, yeniden katılmak
relapse [rileps] nüks / nüksetmek, eski haline dönmek
relate [rileyt] bağlantısı olmak / nakletmek
relation [rileyşın] ilgi, ilişki / akraba / anlatış
relationship [rileyşınşip] akrabalık
relative [relıtiv] nisbi, oranlı / akraba
relatively [relıtivli] nispeten
relativity [relıtivıti] ilişkinlik, izafiyet, görelik
relax [rıleks] gevşetmek, gevşemek / dinlenmek
relaxation [rilekseyşın] dinlenme, rahatlama
relay [ri:ley] yeniden döşemek / naklen yaymak
release [rili:s] serbest bırakmak / piyasaya çıkarmak / salıvermek
relent [rilent] merhamete gelmek, gevşemek
relentless [rilentlis] aman-

sız

relevant [relivınt] ilgili

reliable [rilayıbıl] güvenilebilir, emniyetli

reliance [rilayıns] güvenç

relic [relik] kutsal emanet / kalıntı

relief [rili:f] kurtarma / rahatlama / kabartma resim

relieve [rili:v] hafifletmek, dindirmek, yatıştırmak / kurtarmak / nöbetini almak

religion [rilicın] din

religious[rilicıs] dindar, dine ait

relinquish [rilinkwiş] vazgeçmek, bırakmak

relish [reliş] zevk, istek / lezzet / zevk almak

reluctance [rilaktıns] isteksizlik

reluctant [rilaktınt] isteksiz

rely [rilay] güvenmek

remain [rimeyn] kalmak, geride kalmak

remark [rima:k] söz, mülahaza / söylemek, beyan etmek

remarkable [rima:kıbıl] dikkate değer

remedy [remidi] çare, ilaç / iyi etmek

remember [rimembı] hatırlamak

remind [rimaynd] hatırlatmak

remit [rimit] affetmek, vazgeçmek / havale göndermek

remittance [rimitıns] posta havalesi

remnant [remnınt] artan, geri kalan

remonstrate [rimonstreyt] protesto etmek

remorse [rimo:s] pişmanlık

remorseless [rimo:slis] vicdansız, zalim

remote [rimout] uzak, hücra

remove [rimu:v] kaldırmak / çıkarmak / silmek

removal [rimu:vıl] nakil / kaldırma

Renaissance [rineysıns] Rönesans

rend (rent, rent) [rend, rent rent] yırtmak, yarmak

render [rendı] vermek, yap-

mak. etmek
renew [rinyu:] yenilemek
renounce [rinauns] vazgeçmek. feragat etmek
renovate [renıveyt] yenilemek
renown [rinaun] şöhret
renowned [rinaund] ünlü
rent [rent] kira / kiralamak / yırtık, yarık
reorganize [ri:ogınayz] yeniden tertiplemek
repair [ripeı] tamir / tamir etmek, onarmak
reparation [repıreyşın] tazminat
repay (repaid, repaid) [ri:pey, ri:peyd, ri:peyd] borç ödemek / telafi etmek
repeat [ripi:t] tekrarlamak
repel [ripel] defetmek, reddetmek
repelling [ripeling] iğrenç
repent [ripent] pişman olmak
repentance [ripentıns] pişmanlık, nedamet
repetition [repitişın] tekrar
replace [ripleys] yerine başkasını koymak / tekrar yerine koymak
reply [riplay] cevap / cevap vermek
report [ripo:t] rapor / haber vermek / rapor etmek
reporter [ripo:tı] muhabir (gazetede)
repose [ripouz] dinlenmek, yaslanmak
represent [reprizent] temsil etmek / göstermek / vekili olmak
representation [reprizenteyşın] temsil, mümessillik
representative [reprizentıtiv] temsilci, mümessil, delege
repress [ripres] bastırmak
reprimand [reprima:nd] azarlamak / ayıplamak / azarlama
reprint [riprint] yeni baskı / yeniden tabetmek, tekrar basmak
reprisal [riprayzıl] karşılık, misilleme
reproach [riprouç] tekdir / ayıplamak

reproduce [ri:prıdyu:s] aynen kopya etmek / doğurmak
reproduction [ri:prıdakşın] kopya, yeniden basma, röprodüksiyon / üretme
reproof [ripru:f] serzeniş, ayıplama, azarlama
reprove [ripru:v] tekdir etmek, azarlamak
reptile [reptayl] sürüngen, yılan
republic [ripablik] cumhuriyet
repugnance [ripagnıns] nefret, tiksinme
repulse [ripals] red / defetmek / püskürtmek
repulsive [ripalsiv] iğrenç, soğuk, itici
reputable [repyutıbıl] iyi namı olan, saygıdeğer
reputation [repyuteyşın] şöhret
repute [ripyu:t] şöhret
request [rikwest] talep, istek / rica / talep etmek, rica etmek
require [rikwayı] istemek / icabetmek, gerektirmek
requirement [rikwayımınt] ihtiyaç, icap, şart
requisite [rikwizit] zorunlu
rescue [reskiu:] kurtarma / kurtarmak
research [risö:ç] tetkik, araştırma
resemblance [rizemblıns] benzeyiş
resemble [rizembıl] benzemek
resent [rizent] gücüne gitmek, alınmak
resentful [rizentfıl] küskün, gücenik
resentment [rizentmınt] küskünlük
reservation [rezıveyşın] saklama / yer ayırtma
reserve [rizö:v] ihtiyat / ayırmak, kenara koymak
reserved [rizö:vd] ketum / çekingen / tutulmuş
reservoir [rezıwa:] sarnıç, su deposu
residence [rezidıns] ikametgâh, konut
resident [rezidınt] (bir yerde) devamlı yaşayan, ikamet eden

residue [rezidyu:] tortu
resign [rizayn] istifa etmek / teslim etmek
resignation [rezigneyşın] istifa / tevekkül / kabullenme
resigned [rizaynd] mütevekkil, kabullenmiş
resin [rezin] reçine
resist [rizist] direnmek, mukavemet etmek
resistance [rizistıns] mukavemet, direnç
resistant [rizistınt] mukavim, dayanıklı
resolute [rezılu:t] sebatkâr, azimli, kararlı
resolution [rezılu:şın] azim / teklif, önerge
resolve [rizo:lv] karar vermek / halletmek
resort [rizo:t] başvurmak / (yazlığa) gitmek / başvurma / çare / sayfiye
resound [rizaund] tınlamak
resource [riso:s] çare / kaynak
respect [rispekt] bakım, münasebet / saygı / saygı göstermek
respectable [rispektıbıl] saygıdeğer / bir hayli
respected [rispektid] saygıdeğer, muhterem
respectful [rispektfıl] saygılı
respiration [respireyşın] nefes alma
respond [rispond] cevap vermek, yanıtlamak
response [rispons] cevap
responsible [risponsibıl] sorumlu
responsibility [risponsibiliti] sorumluluk
rest [rest] kalan, ötesi, diğerleri / dinlenme, istirahat / dinlenmek / dayanmak
restaurant [restırınt] lokanta
restful [restfıl] dinlendirici
restless [restlis] huzursuz, tezcanlı
restoration [restıreyşın] eski haline getirme / tamir, onarma
restore [risto:] iade etmek, eski haline getirmek / tamir etmek, onarmak
restrain [ristreyn] tutmak, frenlemek

restrict [ristrikt] sınırlamak, kısıtlamak
restricted [ristriktid] mahdut, tahditli, sınırlı
result [rizalt] sonuç / sonuçlanmak
resume [rizyu:m] yeniden almak, (söze) tekrar devam etmek
retail [riteyl] perakende satış
retailer [riteylı] perakende satıcı
retain [riteyn] alıkoymak
retire [ritayı] çekilmek, emekli olmak / yatmağa gitmek
retirement [ritayımınt] çekilme / emekli olma
retort [rito:t] sert cevap vermek
retrace [ritreys] (izini) takip etmek
retreat [ritri:t] ricat / ricat etmek, çekilmek
retrieve [ritri:v] ele geçirmek / düzeltmek / kurtarmak
return [ritö:n] dönmek / dönüş / iade / karşılık / kazanç / geri vermek
reveal [rivi:l] ifşa etmek, açığa vurmak
revelation [revıleyşın] ifşa, açığa vurma
revenge [rivenc] intikam / intikam almak
revenue [revınyu:] varidat, gelir
revere [riviı] hürmet etmek
reverence [revırıns] muhterem (papaz için)
reverse [rivö:s] ters, zıt / tersine çevirmek, geri götürmek
review [rivyu:] kitap tenkidi / gözden geçirmek
revise [rivayz] gözden geçirmek, düzeltmek
revision [rivijın] tashih, düzeltme, revizyon
revival [rivayvıl] canlanma
revive [rivayv] canlandırmak
revoke [rivouk] iptal
revolt [rivoult] isyan etmek, ayaklanmak
revolution [revılu:şın] inkilap, devrim, ihtilal
revolve [rivolv] dönmek
revolver [rivolvı] tabanca

reward [riwo:d] mükâfat / mükâfatını vermek
rheumatism [ru:mıtizm] romatizma
rhyme [raym] kafiye
rhythm [ridım] ahenk
rib [rib] kaburga kemiği
ribbon [ribın] kurdela, şerit
rice [rays] pirinç (yiyecek)
rich [riç] zengin / verimli / bol
riches [riçiz] servet
rid [rid] kurtarmak
get rid of, başından atmak, kurtulmak
ridden, bak **ride**
riddle [ridıl] bilmece / kalbur
ride (rode, ridden) [rayd, roud, ridın] (at, bisiklet v.b. ile) gitmek / binmek
rider [raydı] binici
ridge [ric] sırt, tepe
ridicule [ridikyu:l] gülünçleştirme / gülünçleştirmek / alay etmek
ridiculous [ridikyulıs] gülünç
riding [rayding] binicilik
rifle [rayfıl] tüfek
right [rayt] hak / doğru / sağ / uygun / sağ tarafa / tam
righteous [rayçıs] dürüst
rightful [raytfıl] haklı, hak sahibi
rightly [raytli] doğru olarak, haklı bir şekilde
rigid [ricid] sert, eğilmez, müsamahasız
rigorous [rigırıs] sert, şiddetli, eğilmez
rim [rim] kenar, çerçeve, ağız (fincan v.s.)
ring [ring] (çan, zil) çalmak, tınlamak / halka, yüzük / ring / zil sesi
rinse [rins] durulamak, çalkalamak
riot [rayıt] kargaşalık, isyan, ayaklanma
riotous [rayıtıs] gürültülü
rip [rip] yırtık / yırtmak
ripe [rayp] olgun
ripen [raypın] olgunlaşmak
ripple [ripıl] dalgacık
rise (rose, risen) [rayz, rouz, rizın] kalkmak, yükselmek / (güneş) doğmak / yükselme / doğuş

risk [risk] tehlike, rizi-ko / tehlikeyi göze almak
risky [riski] tehlikeli
rival [rayvıl] rakip / rekabet etmek
rivalry [rayvılri] rekabet
river [rivı] nehir, ırmak
rivet [rivit] perçin / perçinlemek
road [roud] yol
roam [roum] dalaşmak, gezmek
roar [ro:] gürleme / gürlemek, kükremek
roast [roust] kızartmak
rob [rob] soymak (hırsızlık)
robber [robı] soyguncu
robbery [robıri] hırsızlık
robot [roubot] makine adam, robot
robust [roubast] dinç
rock [rok] kaya / sallamak, sallanmak
rocket [rokit] roket
rocking-chair [roking çeı] salıncaklı koltuk
rocky [roki] kayalık
rod [rod] çubuk, sırık
rode, bak **ride**
role [roul] rol
roll [roul] yuvarlanmak, dönmek / yuvarlamak / tomar yapmak / tomar, rulo
roller [roulı] silindir / paten
romance [roumens] hikaye, aşk macerası
romantic [roumentik] şairane, romantik
roof [ru:f] çatı, dam
room [ru:m] oda / yer
rooster [ru:stı] horoz
root [ru:t] kök, esas / kökleşmek
rope [roup] ip, halat
rose [rouz] gül
rose, bak **rise**
rosy [rouzi] pembe
rot [rot] çürümek
rotary [routıri] dönen
rotten [rotın] çürük, berbat
rough [raf] taslak, müsvedde / kaba, pürüzlü, kaba saba / dalgalı (deniz)
roughly [rafli] yaklaşık olarak, kabaca
roulette [ru:let] rulet
round [raund] etrafında / yuvarlak / dairevi
roundabout [raundıbaut] dolambaçlı

rouse [rauz] uyandırmak, kışkırtmak
route [ru:t] rota, yol
routine [ru:tin] usul, adet, alışıldığı gibi
row [rou] dizi / sıra / kürek çekmek
row [rau] kavga, gürültü
rowdy [raudi] külhanbeyi / gürültülü
royal [royıl] krala ait, şahane
royalty [royılti] telif hakkı (yazar ücreti) / hükümdarlık
rub [rab] ovmak, ovalamak
rubber [rabı] kauçuk / lastik / silgi
rubbish [rabiş] süprüntü, çöp / boş laf
ruby [ru:bi] yakut
rudder [radı] dümen
rude [ru:d] nezaketsiz, haşin, kaba
ruffle [rafıl] buruşturmak, kırıştırmak / canını sıkmak
rug [rag] kilim
rugged [ragid] pürüzlü / kayalık
ruin [ru:in] harabe, enkaz / harap etmek
rule [ru:l] kural / idare / hüküm sürmek, yönetmek
ruler [ru:lı] hükümdar / cetvel
Rumania [rumeynyı] Romanya
rumble [rambıl] gümbürtü / gümbürdemek
rummage [ramic] araştırmak (altüst ederek)
rumour [ru:mı] şayia, söylenti
run, (ran, run) [ran, ren, ran] koşmak / akmak / işlemek, işletmek
rung, bak **ring**
runner [ranı] koşucu
running [raning] akan, akar / işleyen / koşma / idare
runway [ranwey] pist
rupture [rapçı] ani kırılma / inkita / fıtık
rural [ruırıl] taşraya ait
rush [raş] aceleyle gitmek / acele ettirmek / itip kakma / acele / hamle, saldırış
Russia [raşı] Rusya
Russian [raşın] Rusça / Rus

rust [rast] paslanmak
rustic [rastik] köye ait
rustle [rasıl] hışırtı / hışırdamak
rusty [rasti] paslı
ruthless [ru:tlis] merhametsiz
rye [ray] çavdar

S

sabotage [sebota:j] sabotaj
sack [sek] çuval / yağma, talan / işten çıkarmak
sacred [seykrid] kutsal
sacrifice [sekrifays] kurban etmek, feda etmek
sad [sed] üzgün / acıklı
saddle [sedıl] eyer / eyerlemek
safe [seyf] emniyette, salim / tehlikesiz
safely [seyfli] salimen
safety [seyfti] emniyet
safety pin [seyfti pin] çengelli iğne
safety razor [seyfti reyzı] jiletli tıraş makinesi
sag [seg] sarkmak / çökmek
sagacious [sıgeyşıs] dirayetli, anlayışlı
sail [seyl] yelken, gemi ile gitmek
sailor [seylı] gemici, denizci, bahriyeli
saint [seynt] aziz
sake [seyk] hatır
salad [selıd] salata
salary [selıri] maaş
sale [seyl] satış
salesman [seylzmın] satıcı
saliva [sılayvı] salya
salmon [semın] som balığı
saloon [sılu:n] bar / büfe / içki salonu
salt [so:lt] tuz / tuzlamak
salty [so:lti] tuzlu
salute [sılu:t] selamlaşmak / selam
salvage [selvic] (gemiyi) kurtarmak
salvation [selveyşın] kurtuluş, selamet
same [seym] aynı
sample [sa:mpıl] örnek, numüne
sanction [senkşın] onayla-

ma / onaylamak, uygun görmek
sanctuary [senktyuıri] sığınak / kutsal yer
sand [send] kum
sandal [sendıl] sandal (ayakkabı)
sandpaper [sendpeypı] zımpara
sands [sendz] plaj, kumsal
sandwich [sendwiç] sandviç
sandy [sendi] kumlu
sane [seyn] aklı başında, makul
sang, bak **sing**
sanitary [senitıri] sıhhi
sanity [seniti] aklı başında olma
sank, bak **sink**
sap [sep] bitkisel özsu
sarcasm [sa:kezm] alay, küçümseme
sarcastic [sa:kestik] küçümseyen, alaya alan
sardine [sa:di:n] sardalya
sardonic [sa:donik] küçümseyen, alaycı
sat, bak **sit**
Satan [seytın] şeytan
satchel [seçıl] okul çantası
satellite [setılayt] peyk, uydu
satiate [seyşieyt] doyurmak, haddinden fazla vermek
satire [setayı] hiciv, taşlama, yergi
satirical [setirikıl] hicivli
satisfaction [setisfekşın] memnuniyet, tatmin
satisfactory [setisfektıri] tatminkâr, ikna edici
satisfied [setisfayd] ikna olmuş / doymuş
satisfy [setisfay] tatmin etmek, ikna etmek
Saturday [setıdi] cumartesi
sauce [so:s] salça
saucepan [so:spın] uzun saplı tencere
saucer [so:sı] fincan tabağı
saunter [so:ntı] gezinmek
sausage [sosic] sucuk, salam, sosis
savage [sevic] vahşi
save [seyv] korumak / tasarruf etmek, artırmak / kurtarmak / ...den başka

savings [seyvingz] biriktirilmiş para, tasarruf
saviour [seyvıı] kurtarıcı
saw, bak, **see,** testere
sawdust [so:dast] talaş
say (said, said) [sey, sed, sed] demek, söylemek
saying [seying] söz, atasözü, özdeyiş
scabbard [skebıd] kın, kılıf
scaffold [skefıld] yapı iskelesi / darağacı
scald [sko:ld] (su ile) haşlamak
scale [skeyl] ölçü, ölçek / terazi kefesi / (balık v.s.) pul
scalp [skelp] başın derisi / derisini yüzmek
scan [sken] göz gezdirmek
scandal [skendıl] rezalet, skandal
scanty [skenti] az, kıt
scapegoat [skeypgout] başkasının günahı yükletilen kimse
scar [ska:] yara izi
scarce [skeıs] nadir, kıt
scarcely [skeısli] nadiren, zorla, ancak
scare [skeı] korku / korkutmak
scarecrow [skeıkrou] bostan korkuluğu
scarf [ska:f] eşarp
scarlet [ska:lit] kırmızı, kızıl
scatter [sketı] serpmek, dağıtmak
scenario [sina:riou] senaryo
scene [si:n] sahne / olay yeri / (piyeste) tablo
scenery [si:nıri] manzara
scent [sent] koku / koklamak / parfüm
sceptic [skeptic] şüpheci
schedule [şedyu:l] liste, program / program yapmak
scheme [ski:m] proje
scholar [skolı] burslu / bilgin / okumuş kişi
scholarship [skolışip] burs
school [sku:l] okul
science [sayıns] bilim
scientific [sayıntifik] bilimsel
scientist [sayıntist] bilim adamı, bilgin
scissors [sizız] makas
scold [skould] azarlamak

scoop [sku:p] kepçe (bakkal)
scooter [sku:tı] küçük tekerlekli motosiklet
scope [skoup] saha, alan / faaliyet alanı
scorch [sko:ç] kavurmak, dağlamak
score [sko:] kertik / oyunda kazanılan puan / çizmek / puan kazanmak / yirmi
scorn [sko:n] küçümseme, hor görme / hor görmek / tenezzül etmemek
scornful [sko:nfıl] hor gören
scorpion [sko:piın] akrep
Scotch [skoç] İskoçyalı
Scotland [skotlınd] İskoçya
scoundrel [skaundrıl] kötü adam, hain
scout [skaut] izci
scowl [skaul] kaş çatmak, kızgın bakmak
scramble [skrembıl] güçlükle çabalama / çabalamak, tırmanmak
scrap [skrep] kırıntı, artık / kavga
scrape [skreyp] kazıma / kazımak, tırmalamak
scratch [skreç] tırmalamak, kaşımak
scrawl [skro:l] çızıktırmak, kargacık burgacık yazmak
scream [skri:m] haykırış / haykırmak
screen [skri:n] perde / kalbur / korumak / kalburdan geçirmek / beyaz perde (sinema) / paravana
screw [skru:] vidalamak, (vida) çevirmek / vida / uskur
screwdriver [skru:drayvı] tornavida
scribble [skribıl] dikkatsiz yazı yazmak
script [skript] el yazısı / senaryo
scrub [skrab] çalılık / fırçalayarak yıkamak
scruple [skru:pıl] endişe
scrupulous [skru:pyu:lıs] dikkatli, titiz
scrutiny [skru:tini] dikkatli muayene
scuffle [skafıl] itişme, itip kakma / ayaklarını yere

sürmek
sculptor [skalptı] heykeltıraş
sculpture [skalpçı] heykeltıraşlık, heykel
scum [skam] köpük
scuttle [skatıl] kömür kovası / lumbuz / sıvışmak, kaçmak
scythe [sayd] tırpan, orak
sea [si:] deniz
seagull [si:gal] martı
seal [si:l] mühür / mühürlemek / tıkamak / fok
seam [si:m] dikiş yeri / maden damarı
seaman [si:mın] denizci
seaport [si:po:t] liman
search [sö:ç] araştırmak
searchlight [sö:çlayt] ışıldak, reflektör
seashore [si:şo:] sahil
seasick [si:sik] deniz tutmuş
seaside [si:sayd] deniz kenarı, sahil
season [si:zın] mevsim
seasonable [si:zınıbıl] mevsime uygun / tam vaktinde olan
seat [si:t] oturulacak şey, iskemle
seaweed [si:wi:d] yosun
seclusion [siklu:jın] inziva
second [sekınd] ikinci / saniye / desteklemek
secondary [sekındri] ikinci derecede, tali
secondary school, ortaokul, lise
second-hand [sekındhend] kullanılmış, müstamel
secrecy [si:krisi] gizlilik
secret [si:krit] sır, gizli
secretary [sekrıtıri] sekreter, kâtibe, kâtip
secrete [sikri:t] gizlemek
sect [sekt] tarikat
section [sekşın] kısım, bölüm / bölge / manga
sector [sektı] bölge, mıntıka / sektör
secular [sekyulı] dünyevi, laik / maddiyatçı
secure [sikyuı] sağlamak
security [sikyu:riti] emniyet / emniyet veren / rehin / garanti
sedan [sedın] kapalı otomobil

sedate [sideyt] sakin
sedative [sedıtiv] müsekkin, yatıştırıcı (ilaç)
sediment [sedimınt] tortu
seduce [sidyu:s] ayartmak / iğfal etmek / baştan çıkarmak
see, (saw, seen) [si:, so:, si:n] görmek / anlamak
seed [si:d] tohum
seek (sought, sought) [si:k, so:t, so:t] aramak
seem [si:m] görünmek, o şekilde gözükmek
seemly [si:mli] münasip, uygun
seen, bak **see**
see-saw [si:so:] tahterevalli
segment [segmınt] parça, bölüm, bölge
segregate [segrıgeyt] ayırmak, ayrı tutmak
seize [si:z] yakalamak, kavramak / el koymak
seizure [si:jı] yakalama, el koyma / felç
seldom [seldım] nadiren
select [silekt] seçmek / seçkin
selection [sileksın] seçme / seçilmiş parçalar
self (çoğulu **selves)** [self, selvz] kendi
selfish [selfiş] bencil
sell (sold, sold) [sel, sould, sould] satmak, satılmak
seller [selı] satıcı
semblance [semblıns] benzeyiş, benzerlik
semen [si:men] tohum, meni
semester [simestı] sömestire, dönem
semi— [semi] yarı anlamında önek
semicircle [semisö:kıl] yarım daire
semicolon [semikoulın] noktalı virgül
senate [senit] senato
senator [senıtı] senatör
send (sent, sent) [send, sent, sent] göndermek
sender [sendı] gönderen
senior [si:nyı] kıdemli
sensation [senseyşın] his, heyecan
sense [sens] anlam / beş duyunun her biri / duygu / akıl
senseless [senslis] kendin-

den geçmiş / abes, anlamsız
sensibility [sensibiliti] hassasiyet, duyarlık
sensible [sensibıl] makul
sensitive [sensitiv] hisli, hassas, duygulu
sensual [sensyuıl] şehvani, şehvetli
sensuality [sensyueliti] şehvet
sent, bak **send**
sentence [sentıns] cümle / hüküm / mahkûm etmek
sentiment [sentimınt] his, hassaslık
sentimental [sentimentıl] içli, duygusal
sentry [sentri] nöbetçi
separable [sepırıbıl] ayrılabilen
separate [sepırit] ayrı, müstakil / [sepıreyt] ayırmak, ayrılmak
separately [sepıritli] ayrı olarak
separation [sepıreyşın] ayrılma, ayırma, ayrılık
September [septembı] eylül
septic [septik] mikrop kapmış
sequel [si:kwıl] devam, arkası / sonuç
sequence [si:kwıns] silsile, zincirleme
serenade [serıneyd] serenad
serene [siri:n] durgun
serf [sö:f] köle
sergeant [sa:cınt] çavuş
serial [siırıl] sıra halinde, dizi, tefrika
series [siıriz] seri, dizi
serious [siıriıs] ciddi
sermon [sö:mın] vaiz
serpent [sö:pınt] yılan
serum [siırım] serum
servant [sö:vınt] uşak, hizmetçi
serve [sö:v] hizmet etmek / işe yaramak
serviceable [sö:visıbıl] işe yarar
sesame [sesımi] susam
session [seşın] celse, oturum
set [set] tanzim etmek / kurmak / tespit etmek / koymak / takım / (güneş) batmak
settee [seti:] kanepe
setter [setı] av köpeği

settle [setıl] yerleşmek, iskân etmek / halletmek / durulmak / (bir şeyin üstüne) yerleşmek / ödemek

settled [setıld] sabit / meskûn / yerleşmiş

settlement [setılmınt] yerleşme, iskan / anlaşma / ödeme

settler [setlı] yerleşen kimse

seven [sevın] yedi

seventeen [sevınti:n] on yedi

seventy [sevınti] yetmiş

sever [sevı] ayırmak / kesmek

several [sevrıl] bir miktar, birkaç

severe [sivii] şiddetli

sew [sou] dikiş dikmek

sewer [siu:ı] ana lağım

sex [seks] cins / seks

shabby [şebi] pejmürde

shack [şek] kulübe

shackle [şekıl] köstek

shade [şeyd] gölgelik, gölge / küçük fark

shadow [şedou] gölge / gölgelemek / gizlice takip etmek

shady [şeydi] gölgeli / şüpheli

shaft [şa:ft] ok / şua / sütun / şaft

shake (shook, shaken) [şeyk, şuk, şeykın] sallamak, sarsmak, sarsılmak / (el) sıkmak

shaky [şeyki] sarsak, kuvvetsiz

shall [şel] gelecek zaman kipini oluşturan yardımcı fiil

shallow [şelou] sığ

sham [şem] yapmacık, yalan / yalandan yapmak / sahte

shame [şeym] utanç, ayıp / yazık / utandırmak

shameful [şeymfıl] utandırıcı, ayıp

shameless [şeymlis] utanmaz

shampoo [şempu:] şampuan

shape [şeyp] şekil / şekil vermek

share [şeı] pay, hisse / paylaşmak

share holder [şeı houldı] hissedar

shark [şa:k] köpek balığı
sharp [şa:p] keskin / zeki
sharpen [şa:pın] bilemek
shatter [şetı] çatırdatarak kırmak / yok etmek
shave [şeyv] (sakal) tıraş / tıraş olmak
shawl [şo:l] şal
she [şi:] o (dişi)
sheaf [şi:f] demet
shear (shore, shorn) [şiı, şo:, şo:n] kırkmak
shed [şed] baraka, sundurma / dökmek
sheep [şi:p] koyun
sheer [şi:ı] saf, sırf / dik
sheet [şi:t] yatak çarşafı / kağıt yaprağı / maden v.b. yaprağı
sheik [şeyk] şeyh
shelf [şelf] raf
shell [şel] kabuk / mermi
shelter [şeltı] sığınak, barınacak yer / barındırmak
shepherd [şepıd] çoban
sheriff [şerif] (köyde) polis müdürü, şerif
sherry [şeri] İspanyol şarabı
shield [şi:ld] kalkan
shift [şift] değiştirme, iş nöbeti / yerini değiştirmek
shifty [şifti] hilekâr
shin [şin] incik kemiği
shine (shone, shone) [şayn, şon, şon] parlamak / parıltı
shining [şayning] parlak, parlayan
shiny [şayni] parlak
ship [şip] gemi / (gemi ile) mal göndermek
shipment [şipmınt] gemiye yükleme / gemi yükü / sevk
shipping [şiping] denizciliğe ait / nakliyat
shipyard [şipya:d] tersane, gemi yapım yeri
shire [şayı] eyalet, vilayet, kontluk
shirk [şö:k] (işten) kaçmak
shirt [şö:t] gömlek
shiver [şivı] titremek, üşümek, ürpermek
shock [şok] sarsıntı, darbe, şok / sarsmak
shoe [şu:] ayakkabı
shone, bak **shine**
shook, bak **shake**
shoot (shot, shot) [şu:t, şot, şot] vurmak / top veya tüfek atmak / ateş etmek

/ atmak / şut çekmek / atmak / filiz
shop [şop] dükkan
shop-assistant, tezgâhtar
shopkeeper [şopki:pı] dükkancı
shopping [şoping] alışveriş
shore [şo:] sahil, kıyı
short [şo:t] kısa
shortage [şo:tic] kıtlık
shortcoming [şo:tkaming] noksanlık
shorten [şo:tın] kısaltmak
shorthand [şo:thend] stenografi
shortly [şo:tli] hemen, yakında / kısaca
shorts [şo:ts] kısa pantalon, şort
shot, bak **shoot**
shot [şot] (tüfek v.b.nin) bir atış / şut
should [şud] -meli, -malı anlamında yardımcı fiil
shoulder [şouldı] omuz / omuzlamak
shout [şaut] bağırmak / bağırma
shove [şav] itmek, dürtmek
shovel [şavıl] kürek
show (showed, shown) [şou, şoud, şoun] göstermek
show [şou] gösteri / teşhir
shower [şauı] sağanak / duş
shrank, bak **shrink**
shred [şred] lime lime etmek / dilim
shrewd [şru:d] kurnaz
shriek [şri:k] feryat etmek / çığlık
shrill [şril] tiz sesli
shrimp [şrimp] karides
shrink (shrank, shrunk) [şrink, şrenk, şrank] büzülmek, çekmek
shrivel [şrivıl] büzülmek
shroud [şraud] kefen
shrub [şrab] çalı
shrug [şrag] omuz silkmek
shudder [şadı] ürpermek
shuffle [şafıl] ayak sürümek / iskambil kağıtlarını karıştırmak
shun [şan] sakınmak
shut (shut, shut) [şat] kapatmak, kapanmak / kapalı

shutter [şatı] kepenk, pancur
shuttle [şatıl] mekik
shy [şay] sıkılgan
sick [sik] hasta
sickle [sikıl] orak
sickness [siknis] hastalık
side [sayd] yan, taraf
sideboard [saydbo:d] büfe (mobilya)
sideways [saydweyz] yandan
siege [si:c] muhasara
sieve [siv] elek / elemek
sift [sift] elemek
sigh [say] iç çekmek
sight [sayt] görme / manzara
sight-seeing [saytsi:ing] turistik gezinti
sign [sayn] imzalamak / işaret, belirti
signal [signıl] işaret / işaret etmek
signature [signıçı] imza
signboard [saynbo:d] tabela
significant [signifikınt] anlamlı / önemli
signify [signifay] o anlama gelme, belirtmek
signpost [saynpoust] işaret tabelası
silence [saylıns] sükut / susturmak
silent [saylınt] sessiz
silk [silk] ipek
sill [sil] denizlik, eşik
silly [sili] aptal
silver [silvı] gümüş
silversmith [silvısmit] gümüşçü
similar [similı] benzeyen, gibi
simmer [simı] yavaş yavaş kaynamak
simple [simpıl] basit, yalın
simplicity [simplisiti] basitlik
simplify [simplifay] basitleştirmek
simply [simpli] sadece, sade bir şekilde
simulate [simyuleyt] taklidini yapmak
simultaneous [simılteynyıs] aynı zamanda olan
sin [sin] günah / günah işlemek
since [sins] ...den beri / mademki
sincere [sinsiı] candan, samimi, içten

sincerely [sinsıılı] samimi olarak, içtenlikle
sinew [sinyu] adele, kas
sing (sang, sung) [sing, seng, sang] şarkı söylemek / ötmek
singer [singı] şarkıcı
single [singıl] tek, yegane / (tren, vapur v.b. biletinde) sadece gidiş / bekâr
singular [singyulı] tekil
sinister [sinistı] meş'um
sink (sank, sunk) [sink, senk, sank] batmak, batırmak / lavabo
sinner [sinı] günahkâr
sip [sip] yudumlamak
siphon [sayfın] sifon
sir [sö:] efendi, efendim
siren [sayrın] fettan / canavar düdüğü
sirloin [sö:loyn] sığır filatosu
sister [sistı] kız kardeş
sister-in-law [sistı in lo:] görümce, baldız
sit (sat, sat) [sit, set, set] oturmak, oturtmak
site [sayt] yer, mahal / arsa
sitting [siting] oturum
sitting-room, oturma odası
situation [sityueyşın] yer, konum / durum
six [siks] altı
sixteen [siksti:n] on altı
sixty [siksti] altmış
size [sayz] büyüklük, hacim / ölçü
sizzle [sizıl] cızırdamak
skate [skeyt] paten / patenle kaymak
skeleton [skelitın] çatı, iskelet
sketch [skeç] kroki / küçük piyes / taslağını yapmak
skewer [skiuı] şiş (et pişirmek için)
ski [ski:] kayak / kaymak
skid [skid] takoz
skill [skil] maharet, hüner, yetenek
skilful [skillfıl] hünerli
skilled [skild] tecrübeli
skim [skim] köpüğünü sıyırmak / göz gezdirmek
skin [skin] deri / kabuğunu (derisini) soymak
skip [skip] sekmek, atlamak

skipper [skipı] kaptan
skirmish [skö:miş] kavga, çatışma
skirt [skö:t] eteklik, etek
skull [skal] kafatası
sky (çoğulu) **skies** [skay, skayz] gökyüzü
skylark [skayla:k] tarla kuşu
sky-scraper [skayskreypı] gökdelen bina
slack [slek] gevşek / tembel
slacks [sleks] pantalon
slain, bak **slay**
slake [sleyk] (susuzluğunu) gidermek
slam [slem] gürültü ile kapatmak
slander [sla:ndı] iftira / iftira etmek
slang [sleng] argo
slant [sla:nt] meyil / meyillenmek
slap [slep] tokatlamak
slattern [sletö:n] kılıksız (kadın)
slaughter [slo:tı] kesmek / katliam
slaughter-house, mezbaha
slave [sleyv] köle, esir
slavery [sleyvıri] kölelik
slay (slew, slain) [sley, slu:, sleyn] öldürmek
sledge [slec] kızak
sleek [sli:k] düz ve perdahlı
sleep (slept, slept) [sli:p, slept, slept] uyumak / uyku
sleepy, uykusu gelmiş
sleeve [sli:v] (gömlek, ceket) kolu, yen
slender [slendı] narin
slept, bak **sleep**
slew, bak **slay**
slice [slays] dilim
slick [slik] düz / kaygan / kurnaz
slid, bak **slide**
slide (slid, slid) [slayd, slid] kaymak, kaydırmak / kayma / slayt
slight [slayt] hafif, az, önemsiz
slightly [slaytli] biraz, hafifçe
slim [slim] narin, ince
sling (slung, slung) [sling, slang] sapanla atmak / fırlatmak / asmak
slip [slip] kayar gibi gitmek, kaymak, kaydır-

mak / yanlış yapmak / yanlış, sürçme / külot
slipper [slipı] terlik
slippery [slipıri] kaygan
slit [slit] yarık, aralık / yarmak
slogan [slougın] düstur
slope [sloup] yamaç, meyil, yokuş
sloppy [slopi] pis ve ıslak / dağınık
slot [slot] yarık (para veya jeton atmak için)
slot machine [slot mışi:n] içine para atılarak sigara vb. alınan makina
sloth [slout] tembellik
slouch [slauç] kamburu çıkmış, yorgun
slouching, hımbıl, kamburu çıkmış
sloven [slavın] şapşal
slow [slou] ağır, yavaş / geçikmiş / geri / yavaşlamak
slowly [slouli] yavaş yavaş
sluggish [slagiş] uyuşuk
slum [slam] teneke mahallesi, kenar mahalle
slung, bak **sling**
slur [slö:] zor anlaşılır şekilde konuşmak
slut [slat] pis kadın
sly [slay] sinsi, kurnaz
smack [smek] şaplamak / şamar
small [smo:l] küçük, ufak
smallpox [smo:lpoks] çiçek hastalığı
smart [sma:t] şık, zarif / kurnaz / çabuk / sızı / sızlamak
smash [smeş] çarpma / parçalamak
smear [smiı] lekelemek / sıvamak
smell (smelt, smelt) [smel, smelt, smelt] koku / koklamak, kokmak
smelly [smeli] pis kokan
smelt, bak **smell**
smile [smayl] tebessüm etmek / gülümseme
smith [smit] demirci, nalbant
smoke [smouk] duman / sigara içmek / tütmek
smoking [smouking] sigara içme
smooth [smu:d] düz, pürüzsüz / muntazam /

tesviye etmek, duzlemek
smother [smadı] boğmak
smudge [smac] leke / bulaştırmak
smug [smag] kendinden memnun
smuggle [smagıl] kaçakçılık yapmak
smuggler [smaglı] kaçakçı
snack [snek] hafif yemek
snail [sneyl] salyangoz
snake [sneyk] yılan
snap [snep] ısırmak için saldırmak / kopmak, koparmak / ısırış
snapshot [snepşot] acele fotoğraf, enstantane
snare [sneı] tuzak
snarl [sna:l] hırlamak
snatch [sneç] kapmak
sneak [sni:k] sinsi sinsi yapmak
sneer [sniı] istihza, alay / alayla gülmek
sneeze [sni:z] aksırmak
sniff [snif] burnunu çekmek / kokusunu almak
snob [snob] züppe / kibirli
snooze [snu:z] (uyku) kestirmek
snore [sno:] horlamak
snort [sno:t] burnundan sesli nefes çıkarmak
snow [snou] kar / kar yağmak
snowy [snouvi] karlı
snug [snag] kuytu ve sıcak / mahfuz
snuggle [snagıl] (yanına) sokulmak
so [sou] böyle, böylece / o kadar / bu nedenle
soak [souk] sırsıklam etmek, sırsıklam olmak, suya daldırmak
soap [soup] sabun / sabunlamak
soar [so:] uçmak, yükselmek
sob [sob] hıçkırık / hıçkırmak
sober [soubı] ayık, aklı başında
so-called [souko:ld] sözde, sözüm ona
soccer [sokı] futbol
sociable [souşıbıl] sokulgan, girgin
social [souşıl] sosyal
socialism [souşılizm] sosyalizm
socialist [souşılist] sosyalist

society [sısayıti] topluluk, toplum
sociology [sousiolıci] sosyoloji, toplumbilim
sock [sok] kısa çorap
socket [sokit] yuva / fiş
soda [soudı] soda
sofa [soufı] kanepe
soft [soft] yumuşak
soften [sofın] yumuşatmak, yumuşamak
soil [soyl] toprak / kirletmek
solace [solis] teselli
solar [soulı] güneşe ait
sold, bak **sell**
soldier [soulcı] asker
sole [soul] ayak tabanı / yegane / dil balığı
solemn [solım] vakarlı, ciddi
solicitor [solisitı] müşavir avukat
solid [solid] katı / sağlam
solidarity [solideriti] dayanışma
solitary [solitıri] ıssız / tek
solitude [solityu:d] ıssızlık, inziva
solo [soulou] solo
soluble [soliubıl] eriyebilir
solution [sılu:şın] çözüm / erime / solüsyon
solve [solv] halletmek
sombre [sombı] loş
some [sam] biraz / bazı / birkaç
somebody [sambıdi] birisi, bir kimse
somehow [samhau] her nasılsa
someone [samwan] birisi
somersault [samıso:lt] takla
something [samting] bir şey
sometimes [samtaymz] bazan
somewhat [samwot] biraz, oldukça
somewhere [samweı] bir yere, bir yerde
son [san] oğul
son-in-law [saninlo:] damat
song [song] şarkı
soon [su:n] yakında, çok geçmeden
soothe [su:d] teskin etmek, yatıştırmak
sophisticated [sofistikeytid] adabı bilen, incelikli

/ karmaşık
soporific [sopırifik] uyutucu (ilaç)
sordid [so:did] alçak, çıkarcı, menfaatçi
sore [so:] ağrılı, yaralı / küskün / yara
sorrow [sorou] keder
sorry [sori] müteessir, üzgün
sort [so:t] çeşit, tür
sought, bak **seek**
soul [soul] ruh / kişi
sound [saund] ses / ses çıkarmak / sağlam, sıhhatte
soup [su:p] çorba
sour [sauı] ekşi / hırçın, abus
source [so:s] kaynak, menba / menşe
south [saut] güney
southern [sadın] güneyde
souvenir [su:vınyı] hatıra
sovereign [sovrin] hükümdar
Soviet Union [souvyıt yu:nyın] Sovyetler Birliği
sow [sou] (ekin v.s.) ekmek
space [speys] uzay / alan / mesafe
spaceship [speysşip] uzay gemisi
speciality [speşieliti] özellik
spade [speyd] bahçıvan beli / (oyunda) maça
Spain [speyn] İspanya
span [spen] karış
Spaniard [spenyıd] İspanyol
spanner [spenı] somun anahtarı
spare [speı] ayırmak / kayırmak / boş (vakit) / yedek
sparing [speıring] idareli
spark [spa:k] kıvılcım / kıvılcım saçmak
sparkle [spa:kıl] parıldamak / parıltı
sparrow [sperou] serçe
sparse [spa:s] seyrek
spasm [spezm] ıspazmoz
spat, bak **spit**
spatter [spetı] sıçratmak
speak (spoke, spoken) [spi:k, spouk, spoukın] konuşmak
speaker [spi:kı] konuşmacı, sözcü
spear [spiı] mızrak
special [speşıl] özel

specialist [speşılist] uzman
specialize [speşılayz] uzmanlaşmak
specially [speşıli] özel olarak, özellikle
species [spi:şiz] cins
specific [spesifik] has, belli, muayyen / sarih
specify [spesifay] kesin olarak belirtmek
specimen [spesimin] örnek
speck [spek] benek
spectacle [spektıkıl] manzara
spectacles [spektıkılz] gözlük
spectacular [spektekyulı] hoş görünüşlü
spectator [spekteytı] (maç v.b.) seyirci
spectre [spektı] hayalet
speculate [spekyuleyt] düşünmek / tahmin etmek / istif yapmak
speculation [spekyuleyşın] nazariye, tahmin etme / istifçilik
sped, bak **speed**
speech [spi:ç] konuşma, nutuk
speed (sped, sped) [spi:d, sped, sped] hızlandırmak
speed [spi:d] hız
speedy [spidi] seri, hızlı
spell (spelt, spelt) [spel, spelt, spelt] sözcüğün harflerini söylemek veya yazmak / büyü
spellbound [spelbaund] büyülenmiş
spelling [speling] yazım
spelt, bak **spell**
spend (spent, spent) [spend, spent, spent] sarfetmek, harcamak
sperm [spö:m] meni
sphere [sfiı] küre / saha
spice [spays] baharat / bahar katmak
spicy [spaysi] baharlı
spider [spaydı] örümcek
spill [spil] (kazara) dökmek, dökülmek
spin (spun, spun) [spin, span, span] eğmek, bükmek / dönmek
spinach [spinıç] ıspanak
spindle [spindıl] mil, eksen
spine [spayn] belkemiği
spinster [spinstı] evlenme-

miş kız
spiral [spayrıl] helezoni
spirit [spirit] ruh, şevk, maneviyat / cin / ispirto
spirited [spiritid] cesur, ateşli
spiritual [spiriçuıl] ruhani
spiritualism [spriçuılizm] ispirtizma
spit (spat, spat) [spit, spet, spet] tükürük / tükürmek
spite [spayt] kin
spittle [spitıl] tükürük
splash [spleş] zifos / (su v.b.) sıçratmak
spleen [spli:n] dalak
splendid [splendid] mükemmel / görkemli
splendour [splendı] debdebe, ihtişam
splinter [splintı] kıymık
split (split, split) [split] yarmak, bölmek, yarılmak / yarık
spoil (spoiled, spoilt) [spoyl, spoyld, spoylt] bozmak / şımartmak
spoilt [spoylt] şımarık
spoke, bak **speak**
spokesman [spouksmın] sözcü
sponge [spanc] sünger / sünger ile silmek
sponsor [sponsı] kefil / kefil olmak / para vermek
spontaneous [sponteynyıs] kendiliğinden olan
spool [spu:l] makara
spoon [spu:n] kaşık
spoonful [spu:nfıl] kaşık dolusu
sport [spo:t] spor
sportsman [spo:tsmın] sporcu
spot [spot] yer, nokta / benek / lekelemek / farketmek / tanımak
spotless [spotlis] lekesiz
spotlight [spotlayt] projektör ışığı
spotted [spotid] benekli
spouse [spauz] koca veya karı
spout [spaut] fışkırmak / su (yağmur) borusu
sprain [spreyn] burkulma / burkmak
sprang, bak **spring**
spray [sprey] serpinti / püskürtmek
spread (spread, spread) [spred] yaymak, sermek

/ yayılmak / dağılma
spring [spring] ilkbahar / pınar / yay
spring (sprang, sprung) [spring, spreng, sprang] sıçramak
sprinkle [sprinkıl] serpmek
sprint [sprint] son sürat (kısa mesafe) koşmak
sprout [spraut] filizlenmek / tomurcuk
sprung, bak **spring**
spun, bak **spin**
spur [spö:] mahmuz / teşvik / mahmuzlamak / teşvik etmek
spy [spay] casus / casusluk etmek
squad [skwod] (askeri) takım, ekip
squadron [skwodrın] suvari taburu / uçak filosu
squander [skwondı] çarçur etmek
square [skweı] kare / alan, meydan
square-root, karekök (mat.)
squash [skwoş] ezmek / kabak (sebze)
squat [skwot] güdük / çömelmek
squeak [skwi:k] gıcırdamak, ciyaklamak
squeeze [skwi:z] sıkmak, sıkıştırmak / sıkma
squint [skwint] şaşılık
squirrel [skwirıl] sincap
squirt [skwö:t] fışkırmak
stab [steb] bıçaklamak, saplamak
stability [stebiliti] istikrar, denge
stabilize [steybilayz, stebilayz] denkleştirmek / sağlamlaştırmak
stable [steybıl] sabit, muhkem, sağlam / ahır
stack [stek] saman balyası, demet, yığın
stadium [steydyım] stadyum
staff [sta:f] kadro, elemah / kurmay
stage [steyc] merhale, derece / tiyatro (sahnesi)
stagger [stegı] sendelemek
stagnant [stegnınt] durgun (su v.b.)
stain [steyn] leke / leke yapmak

stainless [steinlıs] paslanmaz

staircase [steıkeyz] merdiven (tırabzanı ile birlikte

stairs [steız] merdiven

stake [steyk] kazık / desteklemek / bahse koymak / tehlike

stale [steyl] bayat

stall [sto:l] satış sergisi / ahırın bölmesi / (tiyatroda) koltuk

stallion [stelyın] aygır

stammer [stemı] kekelemek

stamp [stemp] pul / damga / damgaıamak / ayağını yere vurmak

stand (stood, stood) [stend, stud, stud] ayakta durmak / dayanmak / duruş / sehpa / tezgah

standard [stendıd] standart / seviye / bayrak

standardize [stendıdayz] standartlaştırmak

standpoint [stendpoynt] noktai nazar, görüş

standstill [stendstil] duraklama

star [sta:] yıldız

starboard [sta:bıd] sancak (geminin sağı)

starch [sta:ç] kola / kolalamak

stare [steı] dik dik bakmak

start [sta:t] başlamak, hareket etmek / çıkış, hareket, start

starter [sta:tı] otomobilde marş / bir işe veya yarışa başlama noktasında olan

starters [sta:tız] ana yemek öncesi yenilen şey (çorba, meyva suyu vb.)

startle [sta:tıl] ürkütmek, şaşırtmak

starvation [sta:veyşın] açlık

starve [sta:v] açlıktan ölmek

state [steyt] devlet / durum, vaziyet / ifade etmek / bildirmek

stately [steytli] muhteşem, heybetli

statement [steytmınt] ifade / söz

statesman [steytsmın] devlet adamı

static [stetik] statik

station [steyşın] durak yeri, istasyon / mahal / yerleştirmek
stationary [steyşınıri] sabit, duran
stationery [steyşınıri] kırtasiye
statistics [stıtistiks] istatistik
statue [steçu:] heykel
status [steytıs] durum
statute [steçu:t] kanun
stay [stey] kalmak / durmak / kalış
steadfast [stedfıst] metin, sabit
steady [stedi] değişmeyen, devamlı / sarsılmaz, metin / mazbut / teskin etmek, yatıştırmak
steak [steyk] biftek
steal (stole, stolen) [sti:l, stoul, stoulın] çalmak (hırsızlık)
stealthy [stelti] gizli
steam [sti:m] buhar
steamer [sti:mı] vapur
steel [sti:l] çelik
steep [sti:p] dik, yalçın
steeplechase [sti:pılçeys] engelli koşu
steer [stiı] (dümenle) idare etmek, yönetmek
steering-wheel, direksiyon
stem [stem] bitki gövdesi / sözcüğün kökü
stench [stenç] pis koku
stencil [stensıl] mumlu kağıt
stenography [stenogrıfi] stenografi
step [step] adım / basamak / adım atmak / kapı eşiği / ayak sesi
step—, üvey
step father [step fa:dı] üvey baba
step mother [step madı] üvey anne
steppe [step] bozkır
sterile [sterayl] kısır, semeresiz / mikropsuz
sterilize [sterilayz] sterilize etmek, kısırlaştırmak
sterling [stö:ling] İngiliz parası
stern [stö:n] sert, ciddi / geminin kıç tarafı
stew [stiu:] yavaş yavaş kaynamak
steward [stiu:ıd] kamarot /

vekilharç / iaşe idare memuru (otel, okul v.s.)
stick (stuck, stuck) [stik, stak, stak] çubuk, değnek / yapışmak, yapışık kalmak
sticky [stiki] yapışkan
stiff [stif] bükülmez, katı / nezaketsiz / zor
stiffen [stifın] sertleştirmek
stifle [stayfıl] boğmak
still [stil] hâlâ, elan / yine / hareketsiz
stimulant [stimyulınt] münebbih, uyarıcı
stimulate [stimyuleyt] canlandırmak, uyarmak
sting (stung, stung) [sting, stang] (arı, akrep v.b.) sokmak / acı, ıstırap / sokma, ısırma / iğne (hayvan veya bitki)
stingy [stinci] cimri
stink (stank veya stunk, stunk) [stink, stenk, stank] pis kokmak
stipulate [stipyuleyt] şart koşmak
stir [stö:] karıştırmak / tahrik etmek / kımıldatmak
stirrup [stirıp] üzengi
stitch [stiç] dikiş
stock [stok] stok / stok yapmak
stocks [stoks] hisse senedi ve tahvilat
Stock Exchange [stokeksçeync] borsa
stocking [stoking] uzun çorap
stocky [stoki] tıknaz
stole, bak **steal**
stolen, bak **steal**
stolid [stolid] duygusuz
stomach [stamık] mide / karın
stone [stoun] taş / çekirdek / kıymetli taş
stony [stouni] taşlı / taş gibi
stood, bak **stand**
stool [stu:l] tabure
stoop [stu:p] eğilmek / tenezzül etmek
stop [stop] durdurmak, engel olmak / durmak / kalmak / durma / durak
storage [sto:ric] depo
store [sto:] depo, mağaza, dükkan / depo etmek
storehouse [sto:haus] ardi-

ye, ambar
storey [sto:ri] evin katı
stork [sto:k] leylek
storm [sto:m] fırtına
stormy [sto:mi] fırtınalı
story [sto:ri] hikaye
stout [staut] sağlam / cesur / şişman
stove [stouv] soba
stow [stou] istif etmek
straight [streyt] doğru, dümdüz
straighten [streytın] düzeltmek / doğrulmak
straightforward [streytfo:wıd] dürüst
strain [streyn] germek, zorlamak / incitmek / elemek / germe, gerginlik / zorluk / nağme
strainer [streynı] süzgeç
strait [streyt] dar boğaz, geçit
strand [strend] sahil
strange [streync] tuhaf, acayip / yabancı
stranger [streyncı] yabancı
strangle [strengıl] (ip v.b. ile) boğmak
strap [strep] kayış
strategic [strıti:cik] stratejik
strategy [stretıci] strateji
straw [stro:] saman, hasırdan yapılmış
strawberry [stro:bıri] çilek
stray [strey] başıboş, serseri / tek tük
stream [stri:m] dere / akıntı / akmak
street [stri:t] sokak, cadde
strength [strengt] kuvvet
strenuous [strenyuıs] faal / çetin / yorucu
stress [stres] basınç / vurgu / basınç yapmak / basmak
stretch [streç] (yol, arazi) uzanmak, uzayıp gitmek / uzatmak / gerinmek / germek
stretcher [streçı] sedye
strict [strikt] sıkı, şiddetli / titiz / tam
strictly [striktli] tamamen / şiddetle
stride (strode, strode) [strayd, stroud, stroud] uzun adım / uzun adımlarla yürümek
strife [strayf] kavga
strike (struck, struck)

[strayk, strak, strak] grev / etkilemek / vurmak, çarpmak
striking [strayking] göze çarpan, dikkate değer
string [string] ip, sicim / dizi
strip [strip] şerit / soymak, soyunmak
stripe [strayp] çizgi, şerit, kumaş yolu
strive (strove, striven) [strayv, strouv, strivın] uğraşmak, çabalamak
strode, bak **stride**
stroke [strouk] darbe / okşamak
stroll [stroul] gezinmek / gezinti
strong [strong] kuvvetli / sağlam / dokunaklı
strove, bak **strive**
struck, bak **strike**
structure [strakçı] yapı, bünye
struggle [stragıl] uğraşmak, mücadele etmek / mücadele
stub [stab] kütük / izmarit
stubborn [stabın] inatçı
stuck, bak **stick**
student [stiu:dınt] öğrenci
studio [stiu:dyou] stüdyo
studious [stiu:dyıs] çalışkan
study [stadi] çalışma, inceleme / tahsil / (fikren) çalışmak / incelemek / çalışma odası
stuff [staf] madde, şey / kumaş / doldurmak / paketlemek
stumble [stambıl] sürçme / tökezlemek
stump [stamp] kütük, koçan
stun [stan] afallatmak
stung, bak **sting**
stupefy [stiupifay] sersemletmek
stupendous [stiupendıs] harikulade
stupid [stiupid] ahmak
stupidity [stiupiditi] ahmaklık
sturdy [stö:di] kuvvetli
stutter [statı] kekelemek
style [stayl] biçim / moda
suave [swa:v] [sweyv] nazik
sub— [sab] altında veya az anlamında önek

subconscious [sabkonşıs] şuuraltı, bilinçaltı
subdue [sabdiu:] itaat ettirmek / zaptetmek
subject [sabcekt] konu / (dilbilgisi) fail, özne / tebaa / tabi
subjunctive [sabcanktiv] dilek kipi
sublime [sıblaym] yüce
submarine [sabmıri:n] denizaltı
submerge [sabmö:c] suya batırmak, batmak
submission [sıbmişın] boyun eğme, teslim
submit [sıbmit] arzetmek / teslim etmek / boyun eğmek
subordinate [sıbo:dinit] tabi, bağlı
subscribe [sıbskrayb] abone olmak
subscription [sıbskripşın] abone / teberru
subsequent [sabsikwınt] müteakip, takip eden
subsequently [sabsikwıntli] netice olarak, müteakiben
subside [sıbsayd] çökmek, alçalmak
subsist [sıbsist] geçinmek / mevcut olmak
subsistence [sıbsistıns] geçim
substance [sabstıns] madde, öz, esas
substantial [sabstenşıl] sağlam / esaslı / varlıklı / hakiki
substantive [sabstıntiv] (gramerde) isim
substitute [sabstityu:t] vekil / yerine koymak
subtle [satıl] izahı güç / ince / kurnaz
subtract [sabtrekt] (matematikte) çıkarmak
suburb [sabö:b] civar mahalle, banliyö
subversive [sabvö:siv] yıkıcı
subway [sabwey] tünel, metro, yeraltı geçidi
succeed [sıksi:d] başarılı olmak / yerine geçmek / takip etmek, izlemek
success [sıkses] başarı
successful [sıksesfıl] başarılı
succession [sıkseşın] silsile
successive [sıksesiv] birbi-

rini takip eden
successor [sıksesı] halef, yerine geçen kimse
succumb [sıkam] yenilmek, dayanamamak
such [saç] öyle, böyle, bu derece
suck [sak] emmek
suckle [sakıl] emzirmek
sudden [sadın] ani
suddenly [sadınli] aniden
sue [siu:] dava etmek
suede [sweyd] süet
suffer [safı] katlanmak / çekmek, cefa çekmek / zarar görmek
suffice [sıfays] yetmek
sufficient [sıfişınt] yeterli
suffix [safiks] sonek
suffocate [safıkeyt] (dumandan) boğmak, nefes alamamak
sugar [şugı] şeker
suggest [sıcest] ima etmek / teklif etmek
suggestion [sıcesşın] teklif / ima
suicide [su:isayd] intihar
suit [siu:t] (elbise) takım / uygun gelmek / yakışmak
suitable [siu:tıbıl] uygun
suitcase [siu:tkeys] valiz
suite [swi:t] maiyet, takım / daire (otel)
suitor [siu:tı] davacı
sulk [salk] somurtmak
sulky [salki] somurtkan
sullen [salın] asık yüzlü
sulphur [salfı] kükürt
sultan [saltın] sultan
sum [sam] yekûn, toplam
summarize [samırayz] özetlemek
summary [samıri] özet
summer [samı] yaz
summit [samit] zirve
summon [samın] celp etmek, getirtmek
sun [san] güneş
Sunday [sandi] pazar (gün)
sundry [sandri] muhtelif
sunflower [sanflauı] ayçiçeği
sung, bak **sing**
sunk [sank] bak **sink**
sunlight [sanlayt] güneş ışığı
sunny [sani] güneşli
sunrise [sanrayz] gün doğuşu, şafak
sunset [sanset] gün batışı
sunshine [sanşayn] güneş

ışığı
super— [siu:pı] fevkinde, en âlâ anlamında önek
superb [siupö:b] enfes, fevkalade
supercharger [siu:pıça:cı] kompresör
superficial [siu:pıfişıl] sathi, üstünkörü
superintend [siupırintend] nezaret etmek, kontrol etmek
superintendent [siu:pırintendınt] müfettiş, şef
superior [siupiırii] üstün / üst, amir
superiority [siupiırioriti] üstünlük
superlative [siupö:lıtiv] en üstün
supermarket [siu:pıma:kit] self servis yapılan mağaza, süpermarket
supernatural [siu:pıneçırıl] doğaüstü
supersonic [siu:pısonik] sesten daha hızlı
superstition [siu:pıstişın] hurafe, batıl inanç
superstitious [siu:pıstişıs] hurafeye inanan
supervise [siu:pıvayz] denetlemek
supervisor [siu:pıvayzı] müfettiş, murakıp
supper [sapı] akşam yemeği
supple [sapıl] bükülüp eğilebilir / uysal
supplement [saplimınt] ek / eklemek
supplementary [saplimentıri] tamamlayıcı, ek
supply [sıplay] stok, mevcut / vermek, tedarik etmek
support [sıpo:t] destek, yardım / desteklemek
suppose [sıpouz] farzetmek / zannetmek
suppress [sıpres] bastırmak / örtbas etmek
suppression [sıpreşın] yoketme, bastırma
supremacy [siu:premısi] üstünlük, faikiyet
supreme [siu:pri:m] en yüksek, en üstün
sure [şuı] emin, sağlam
surely [şuıli] elbette
surety [şuıti] kefil / kefalet
surf [sö:f] kıyıdaki dalga köpükleri / dalga üzerinde gitmek

surface [sö:fis] yüzey
surge [sö:c] dalga / dalgalanmak
surgeon [sö:cın] operatör (hekim)
surgery [sö:cıri] operatörlük / doktor muayenehanesi
surmise [sö:mayz] tahmin / tahmin etmek, sonuç çıkarmak
surmount [sö:maunt] üstesinden gelmek
surname [sö:neym] soyadı
surpass [sö:pa:s] üstün olmak
surplus [sö:plıs] fazla
surprise [sıprayz] sürpriz / şaşırtmak
surrender [sırendı] teslim olmak, teslim etmek
surround [sıraund] kuşatmak, sarmak
surroundings [sıraundingz] çevre
survey [sö:vey] göz gezdirmek, kontrol etmek / kadastrosunu çıkarmak / göz gezdirme, teftiş
surveyor [sıveyı] müfettiş / toprak ölçen adam
survival [sıvayvıl] hayatta kalma
survive [sıvayv] sağ kalmak
susceptible [sıseptibıl] alıngan
suspect [sıspekt] şüphelenmek / [saspekt] sanık
suspend [sıspend] asmak / tehir etmek
suspenders [sıspendız] çorap askısı, jartiyer
suspense [sıspens] muallaklık, şüphede bırakma
suspension [sıspenşın] asma / erteleme
suspicion [sıspişın] kuşku
suspicious [sıspişıs] kuşkulanan, kuşkulu
sustenance [sastinıns] besin
swallow [swolou] yutmak / kırlangıç
swam, bak **swim**
swamp [swomp] bataklık
swan [swon] kuğu
swarm [swo:m] arı kümesi / kalabalık / kaynaşmak
swarthy [swo:di] esmer

swastika [swostikı] gamalı haç
sway [swey] sallanmak, sallamak
swear (swore, sworn) [sweı, swo:, swo:n] yemin etmek / küfretmek
sweat [swet] ter / terlemek
sweater [swetı] süveter
Swede [swi:d] İsveçli
Sweden [swi:dın] İsveç
Swedish [swi:diş] İsveçli / İsveççe
sweep (swept, swept) [swi:p, swept, swept] hızla ilerlemek / silip süpürmek / süpürmek
sweet [swi:t] tatlı, hoş
sweeten [swi:tın] tatlandırmak
sweetheart [swi:tha:t] sevgili
swell (swelled, swollen) [swel, sweld, swoulın] şişmek, kabarmak
swelling [sweling] şiş
swept, bak **sweep**
swerve [swö:v] sapmak
swift [swift] hızlı
swim (swam, swum) [swim, swem, swam] yüzmek
swimmer [swimı] yüzücü
swindler [swindlı] dolandırıcı
swine [swayn] domuz
swing (swung, swung) [swing, swang, swang] sallamak, sallanmak / sallanma / salıncak
swirl [swö:l] girdap
Swiss [swis] İsviçreli
switch [swiç] priz / elektrik düğmesi / çevirmek
switchboard [swiçbo:d] anahtar tablosu
Switzerland [switzılınd] İsviçre
swollen [swoulın] bak **swell**
swoon [swu:n] bayılmak
sword [so:d] kılıç
swore, sworn, bak **swear**
swum, bak **swing**
syllable [silıbıl] hece
syllabus [silıbıs] ders veya çalışma programı
symbol [simbıl] sembol
symmetry [simitri] simetri, bakışım
symmetrical [simetrikıl] simetrik
sympathy [simpıti] ilgi duyma / şefkat, sem-

pati
sympathetic [simpıtetik] ilgilenen, acıyan
symphony [simfıni] senfoni
symptom [simptım] belirti, alamet
synagogue [sinıgog] havra
synchronize [sinkrınayz] aynı hıza uydurmak
synonym [sinınim] eş anlamlı sözcük
syntax [sinteks] cümle kuruluşu (dilbilgisi)
synthesis [sintisis] sentez
synthetic [sintetik] yapay, sentetik, bireşimsel
Syria [siriı] Suriye
Syrian [siriın] Suriyeli
syringe [sirinc] şırınga
syrup [sirıp] şurup
system [sistım] sistem
systematic [sistımetik] sistemli

T

table [teybıl] masa / liste, tablo, cetvel
tablet [teblit] hap, komprime / levha
tabulate [tebyuleyt] tasnif etmek, sınıflamak
tacit [tesit] zımni, söylenmeden anlaşılan
taciturn [tesitö:n] ketum, az konuşan
tack [tek] teyel / teyellemek / raptiye
tackle [tekıl] takım, araç, düzen
tackle, uğraşmak, girişmek / yakalamak
tact [tekt] anlayış / diplomasi, taktik
tactics [tektiks] taktik
tactless [tektlis] beceriksiz, patavatsız, kaba
tag [teg] küçük etiket / eklemek, takmak
tail [teyl] kuyruk
tailor [teylı] terzi
taint [teynt] bozulma / bozmak

take (took, taken) [teyk, tuk, teykın] almak / götürmek
taken, bak **take**
tale [teyl] masal
talent [telınt] yetenek
talk [to:k] konuşmak / söz
tall [to:l] uzun boylu
tame [teym] ehli, evcil
tan [ten] meşe kabuğu / güneşten yanmak
tangerine [tenciri:n] mandalina
tangible [tencibıl] elle tutulur, mevcut
tangle [tengıl] karışıklık / karıştırmak
tank [tenk] sarnıç / tank
tanker [tenkı] tanker, petrol gemisi
tantalize [tentılayz] vermeyip işkence etmek, istetmek
tap [tep] musluk, tapa / hafif darbe / hafifçe vurmak
tape [teyp] kurdele, şerit, bant / teyp
tape recorder [teyp riko:dı] teyp
tar [ta:] katran / katranlamak
tare [teı] dara
target [ta:git] hedef
tariff [terif] tarife, gümrük (listesi)
tarnish [ta:niş] leke / lekelenmek / soldurmak
tart [ta:t] ekşi / turta
task [ta:sk] görev
tassel [tesıl] püskül
taste [teyst] lezzet / zevk / tatmak / tat vermek
tasteless [teystlis] lezzetsiz
tasty [teysti] lezzetli
tattered [tetıd] eski püskü / kılıksız
tattoo [tıtu:] (ten üzerine) dövme
taught, bak **teach**
taunt [to:nt] hakaret / sataşmak
tavern [tevın] meyhane
tax [teks] vergi / vergi koymak
taxi (cab) [teksi] [keb] taksi
tea [ti:] çay
teach (taught, taught) [ti:ç, to:t, to:t] öğretmek, ders vermek
teacher [ti:çı] öğretmen

teacup [ti:kap] çay fincanı
team [ti:m] takım, ekip
teapot [ti:pot] çaydanlık
tear (tore, torn) [teı, to:, to:n] yırtmak / yırtık
tear [tiı] gözyaşı
tease [ti:z] taciz etmek, kızdırmak, alay etmek
teat [ti:t] meme, emzik
technical [teknikıl] teknik
technician [teknişın] teknisyen
technique [tekni:k] teknik, yöntem
technology [teknolıci] teknoloji
tedious [ti:dyıs] sıkıcı
teenager [ti:neycı] on üç ile on dokuz arasındaki kız veya erkek
teens [ti:nz] on üçten on dokuza kadar yaş
teeth [ti:t] dişler (çoğul)
tele— [teli] uzağa, uzaklara anlamında önek
telegram [teligrem] telgraf / telgraf çekmek
telepathy [tılepıti] telepati, önsezi
telephone [telifoun] telefon / telefon etmek
telescope [teliskoup] teleskop
television [telivijın] televizyon
tell (told, told) [tel, tould, tould] anlatmak, söylemek / farketmek
teller [telı] veznedar
temper [tempı] huy, öfke / su verme (çeliğe)
temperament [tempırımınt] mizaç, huy
temperature [tempriçı] ısı, hararet
tempest [tempist] bora
temple [tempıl] tapınak / şafak
temporal [tempırıl] ölümlü, geçici
temporary [tempırıri] geçici, bir süre için
tempt [tempt] teşvik etmek, tahrik etmek, ayartmak
temptation [tempteyşın] teşvik, ayartma
ten [ten] on
tenacious [tineyşıs] inatçı, yapışkan
tenacity [tinesiti] yapışkanlık, inat
tenant [tenınt] kiracı

tend [tend] eğilim göstermek / yönelmek / gözetmek
tendency [tendınsi] eğilim
tender [tendı] yumuşak, hassas / müşfik / zayıf / bakıcı / teklif etmek / teklif
tenderness [tendınis] hassaslık, şefkat
tenement [tenımınt] kira evi, apartman
tenfold [tenfould] on katı, on misli
tennis [tenis] tenis
tenor [tenı] tenor
tense [tens] fiil kipi, fiil zamanı / gergin
tension [tenşın] gerginlik / gerilim
tent [tent] çadır
tentative [tentıtiv] deneme
tenth [tent] onuncu
tepid [tepid] ılık
term [tö:rn] sömestir, çalışma devresi / şart / terim / süre
terms [tö:mz] şartlar
terminal [tö:minıl] uçta bulunan, son durak, terminal
terminate [tö:mineyt] bitirmek, sona ermek
termination [tö:mineyşın] bitiş, hitam
terminus [tö:minıs] son durak
termite [tö:mayt] ağaç kurdu
terrace [terıs] taraça
terrible [teribıl] müthiş
terribly [teribli] müthiş bir şekilde
terrier [terii] küçük av köpeği
terrific [tırifik] korkunç
terrify [terifay] korkutmak
territory [teritıri] mıntıka, bölge
terror [terı] dehşet
terrorist [terırist] terörist
terse [tö:s] veciz, öz
test [test] tecrübe / tecrübe etmek, denemek / test yapmak
testament [testımınt] vasiyetname
New Testament İncil
Old Testament Tevrat
testify [testifay] şahitlik etmek, kanıtlamak
testimonial [testimouniıl]

bonservis, takdirname
testimony [testimını] şahadet, delil, belge
tetanus [tetınıs] tetanos
text [tekst] metin, okuma parçası
textbook, okuma kitabı
textile [tekstayl] mensucat
texture [teksçı] doku, örgü
than [den] ...den
thank [tenk] teşekkür etmek / teşekkür
thankful [tenkfıl] müteşekkir
thanks [tenks] teşekkür
that [det] şu, o / ki, ki o
thatch [teç] sazdan dam örtüsü
thaw [to:] (kar ve buz) erimek
the [dı:, di]harfi tarif, belirtme takısı
theatre [tiıtı] tiyatro
theft [teft] hırsızlık
their [deı] onların
theirs [deız] onlarınki
them [dem] onları, onlara
theme [ti:m] konu
themselves [demselvz] kendileri
then [den] o zaman / sonra / şu halde
theology [ti:olıci] teoloji, ilahiyat
theoretical [tiıretikıl] nazari, teorik
theory [ti:ıri] teori, nazariye, kuram
therapy [terıpi] tedavi
there [deı] orada, oraya
there is, (are) var
therefore [deıfo:] onun için, bu bakımdan
thermal [tö:mıl] ısıya ilişkin, termal / doğal sıcak
thermometer [tö:momitı] termometre
thermos [tö:mos] termos
these [di:z] bunlar
thesis [ti:sis] tez, dava
they [dey] onlar
thick [tik] kalın / sık / koyu
thicken [tikın] kalınlaştırmak / yoğunlaştırmak
thicket [tikit] çalılık
thickness [tiknis] kalınlık / yoğunluk
thife [ti:f] hırsız
thigh [tay] kalça

thimble [timbıl] yüksük
thin [tin] ince, zarif / seyrek / sulu / seyrekleştirmek, seyreltmek
thing [ting] şey, madde
things [tingz] eşya
think (thought, thought) [tink, **to**:t] düşünmek / sanmak
thinker [tinkı] mütefekkir, düşünür
thinking [tinking] düşünme
third [tö:d] üçüncü
thirst [tö:st] susuzluk
thirsty [tö:sti] susamış
thirteen [tö:ti:n] on üç
thirty [tö:ti] otuz
this [dis] bu
thorn [to:n] dikenli çalı
thorough [tarı] tam, baştan başa
thoroughly, adamakıllı
thoroughbred [tarıbred] safkan
thoroughfare [tarıfeı] büyük cadde
those [douz] onlar, şunlar
though [dou] her ne kadar, ...ise de, rağmen
thought, bak **think**
thought • [to:t] düşünce, fikir
thoughtful [to:tfıl] düşünceli / nazik
thoughtless [to:tlis] düşüncesiz
thousand [tauzınd] bin
thrash [treş] dövmek, mağlup etmek
thrashing, dayak, dövüş
thread [tred] iplik, tire
threadbare [tredbeı] aşınmış / yıpranmış
threat [tret] tehdit
threaten [tretın] tehdit etmek
threatening [tretining] tehditkâr
three [tri:] üç
thresh [treş] harman dövmek
thresher, harmancı, harman döven
threshold [treşould] eşik
threw, bak **throw**
thrift [trift] iktisat, tutum
thrifty [trifti] tutumlu
thrill [tril] heyecanlandırmak
thrilling, heyecan ve dehşet verici
thriller, dedektif romanı

thrive (throve, thriven) [trayv, trouv, trivın] iyi gitmek, gelişmek
thriving, müreffeh, başarılı
throat [trout] boğaz
throb [trob] (kalp) çarpmak, zonklamak
throne [troun] taht
throng [trong] kalabalık / tehacüm etmek, üşüşmek
throttle [trotıl] boğmak, kısmak
through [tru:] bir yandan öbür yana / içinden, arasından / vasıtasıyla
throughout [tru:aut] baştan başa
throw (threw, thrown) [trou, tru:, troun] atmak, fırlatmak / atma
thrust [trast] itmek, sokmak / hamle
thud [tad] tok ses
thumb [tamb] başparmak
thump [tamp] vurmak, çarpmak
thunder [tandı] gök gürültüsü / gürlemek
thunderous [tandırıs] gürleyen
Thursday [tö:zdi] perşembe
thus [das] böyle, böylece
thwart [two:t] işini bozmak / mukavemet etmek / engel olmak
tick [tik] tıkırdı / tıkırdamak / veresiye / kene / kontrol işareti
ticket [tikit] bilet
tickle [tikıl] gıdıklamak
tide [tayd] met ve cezir, gelgit
tidiness [taydinis] intizam, tertiplilik
tidy [taydi] muntazam, temiz, toplu
tie (tied, tied) [tay, tayd] bağlamak / bağ / boyunbağı, kravat
tiger [taygı] kaplan
tight [tayt] sıkı, dar / eli sıkı / sarhoş
tighten [taytın] sıkıştırmak, kısmak
tights [tayts] külotlu çorap
tigress [taygris] dişi kaplan
tile [tayl] kiremit / çini / kiremit döşemek

till [til] ...e kadar / kasa
tilt [tilt] meyil / yana yatırmak
timber [timbı] kereste
time [taym] vakit, zaman, süre, mühlet / kere, defa
timely [taymli] vakitli
timetable [taymteybıl] tarife
timid [timid] sıkılgan
timidity [timiditi] çekingenlik
timorous [timırıs] ürkek
tin [tin] kalay / teneke, teneke kutu / kalaylamak / kutuya konserve etmek
tinder [tindı] çıra, kav
ting [ting] çınlamak
tinge [tinc] renk / hafifçe boyamak
tinker [tinkı] tenekeci
tinkle [tinkıl] çınlamak
tinned [tind] kalaylı / kutuya konmuş (yiyecek), konserve
tinsmith [tinsmit] tenekeci
tint [tint] renk / renk vermek
tiny [tayni] ufacık
tip [tip] uç / bahşiş
tipsy [tıpsi] çakırkeyif
tiptoe [tiptou] parmakların ucunda yürümek
tire [tayı] yormak / usandırmak
tired [tayıd] yorgun
tiresome [tayısım] belalı, sıkıcı
tiring [tayıring] yorucu
tissue [tisyu:] nesiç, doku / ince kağıt
titbit [titbit] güzel yiyecek lokması / ilginç haber
title [taytıl] ünvan / kitap (resim, şiir) ismi
to [tu:, tu] ...ye, ...ya, **...e** / için / ...mek, ...mak
toad [toud] kurbağa
toast [toust] kızarmış ekmek / kadeh kaldırmak, sıhhatine içmek
tobacco [tıbekou] tütün
today [tıdey] bugün
toe [tou] ayak parmağı
together [tıgedı] beraber, birlikte
toil [toyl] pek zor iş, didinme / zahmet çekmek, didinmek
toilet [toylit] tuvalet

toilsome [toylsım] yorucu
token [toukın] alamet, işaret, belirti
told, bak **tell**
tolerable [tolırıbıl] dayanılabilir, fena değil, göz yumulur
tolerance [tolırıns] hoşgörü, tolerans
tolerant [tolırınt] hoşgörülü
tolerate [tolıreyt] müsamaha etmek, hoşgörmek
toll [toul] çan çalmak / geçit (yol) parası
tomahawk [tomıho:k] kızılderililerin savaş baltası
tomato [tıma:tou] domates
tomb [tu:m] kabir
tombstone [tu:mstoun] mezartaşı
tomorrow [tımorou] yarın
ton [tan] ton
tone [toun] ton, ses tonu / renk tonu, nüans
tongs [tongz] maşa
tongue [tang] dil, lisan
tonic [tonik] ilaç, tonik
tonight [tınayt] bu gece
tonnage [tanic] tonilato, tonaj
tonsil [tonsil] bademcik
too [tu:] de, da, dahi keza / çok, fazla
took, bak **take**
tool [tu:l] alet
tooth [tu:t] diş, çoğulu: **(teeth)** [ti:t]
toothache [tu:teyk] diş ağrısı
toothbrush [tu:tbraş] diş fırçası
toothpaste [tu:tpeyst] diş macunu
toothpick [tu:tpik] kürdan
top [top] tepe, baş, en üst / üst noktaya ulaşmak
topic [topik] konu
topple [topıl] devirmek
topography [tıpogrıfi] topografya
torch [to:ç] meşale, el feneri
tore, bak **tear**
toreador [toriıdo:] boğa güreşçisi
torment [to:mınt] eziyet / cefa etmek
tormentor [to:mentı] eziyet veren
torn, bak **tear**

ornado [to:neydou] kasırga

orpedo [to:pi:dou] torpil / torpillemek

orrent [to:rınt] sel

orrid [torid] sıcak

orso [to:sou] beden heykeli, büst

ortoise [to:tıs] kaplumbağa

orture [to:çı] işkence / işkence etmek

oss [tos] havaya fırlatmak

otal [toutıl] bütün, toplam, yekûn

otalitarian [touteliteıryın] tek partili hükümet

otally [toutıli] tamamen, büsbütün, tümüyle

otter [totı] sendelemek

ouch [taç] dokunmak, değmek / temas, dokunma

ough [taf] sert / zor / sağlam, metin

our [tu:ı] gezinti

ourist [tu:ırist] turist

ournament [tuınımınt] turnuva

w [tou] çekmek / cer

wards [tıwo:dz] ...e doğru

towel [tauıl] havlu

tower [tauı] kule

town [taun] kasaba, şehir

town hall, belediye dairesi

toxic [toksik] zehirli

toxin [toksin] toksin

toy [toy] oyuncak

trace [treys] iz, alamet, belirti / izini takip etmek

trachoma [trekouma] trahom

track [trek] patika / iz / izini takip etmek

trackt [trekt] mıntıka

traction [trekşın] çekme, cer

tractor [trektı] traktör

trade [treyd] ticaret, iş / ticaret yapmak

trader [treydı] tüccar

tradition [trıdişın] anane, adet, gelenek

traditional [trıdişınıl] ananevi, geleneksel

traffic [trefik] trafik

traffic jam [trefik cem] trafik sıkışıklığı

traffic light [trefik layt] trafik ışığı

tragedy [trecidi] trajedi, felaket

trail [treyl] iz / çiğneyerek açılan yol / izini takip etmek

trailer [treylı] treyler / filmin fragmanı / otomobile bağlanan kulübe, römork

train [treyn] tren / alıştırmak, terbiye etmek, idman etmek

trained, terbiye edilmiş yetiştirilmiş

training, talim, eğitim, antrenman

trainer [treynı] antrenör

traitor [treytı] hain

tram [trem] tramvay

tramp [tremp] serseri / ağır adımlarla yürümek

trample [trempıl] ayak altında çiğnemek

trance [tra:ns] kendinden geçme, vecit

tranquil [trenkwil] sakin, sessiz

trans— [tra:ns] bir yandan diğer yana, karşı tarafa anlamında önek

transact [trenzekt] (birisiyle) iş yapmak

transaction [trenzekşın] (işe ait) muamele

transfer [trensfö:] nakil / nakletmek, devretmek / havale etmek

transcribe [trenskrayb] kopyasını çıkarmak

transferable [trensfö:rıbıl] devredilebilir

transfix [trensfiks] delmek bir kimseyi kımıldama hale getirmek

transform [trensfo:m] değiştirmek, dönüştürme

transformation [trensfo:meyşın] değişim

transformer [trensfo:mı] transformatör

transgress [trensgres] sınırın ötesine geçmek, tecavüz etmek

transgression [trensgreşın] ihlal, tecavüz

transient [trenziınt] geçici

transistor [trensistı] transistor

transit [trensit] geçici, transit / geçiş

transitive [trensitiv] (dilbilgisi) geçişli

translate [trensleyt] tercüme etmek, çevirmek

translation [trensleyşın] tercüme, çeviri
translucent [trenzlu:sınt] yarı saydam
transmission [trenzmişın] nakil, ulaştırma
transmit [trenzmit] geçirmek, yaymak
transmitter, nakledici, verici cihaz
transparency [trenspeırınsi] saydamlık
transparent [trenspeırınt] saydam
transplant [trenspla:nt] bir yerden alıp başka yere dikmek, koymak
transport [trenspo:t] nakletmek / taşıma
transportation [trenspo:teyşın] nakil / araç
transverse [trensvö:s] eğri, çapraz
trap [trep] tuzak / tuzağa düşürmek
trash [treş] değersiz bir şey, saçma
travel [trevıl] seyahat etmek / hareket etmek / yolculuk
traveller's cheque [trevılıs çek] seyahat çeki
tray [trey] tepsi
treacherous [treçırıs] hain
treachery [treçıri] ihanet
tread (trod, trodden) [tred, trod, trodın] ayağını basmak / yürümek / yürüyüş
treadle [tredıl] pedal
treason [tri:zın] vatana ihanet
treasure [trejı] hazine
treasurer [trejırı] hazinedar
treasury [trejıri] devlet hazinesi
treat [tri:t] muamele etmek / ele almak / tedavi etmek / müzakere etmek / (içki, yemek) ısmarlamak
treatment [tri:tmınt] muamele, işlem / tedavi
treaty [tri:ti] antlaşma
treble [trebıl] üç katı
tree [tri:] ağaç
tremble [trembıl] titremek
tremendous [trimendıs] kocaman
tremor [tremı] titreme / zelzele
tremulous [tremyulıs] titrek,

ürkek

trench [trenç] hendek, siper

trend [trend] meyil, eğilim, yön

trespass [trespıs] başkasının arazisine girme / tecavüz etmek

tress [tres] bukle

trestle [tresıl] sehpa

tri— [tri] üçlü anlamında önek

trial [trayıl] tecrübe / yargılama

triangle [trayengıl] üçgen

triangular [trayengyulı] üç köşeli

tribe [trayb] kabile

tribunal [traybyu:nıl] mahkeme

tribute [tribyu:t] haraç / boyun borcu

trice [trays] bir an

trick [trik] hile / hüner

trickery [trikıri] hilekârlık

trickle [trikıl] damlamak

tricky [triki] hilekâr / zor, hileli

tricycle [traysikıl] üç tekerlekli bisiklet

tried, bak **try**

trifle [trayfıl] önemsiz şey

trifling [trayfling] cüzi, pek küçük, önemsiz

trigger [trigı] tetik

trigonometry [trigınomitri] trigonometri

trillion [trilyın] trilyon

trim [trim] düzenlemek / süslemek / uygunluk / temiz

trinket [trinkit] ucuz süs eşyası

trio [tri:ou] üçlü

trip [trip] (kısa) yolculuk, gezinti

tripe [trayp] işkembe

triple [tripıl] üç katı

triplet [triplit] üçüz

tripod [traypod] üç ayaklı sehpa

triumph [trayımf] zafer

trivet [trivit] sacayak

trivial [trivyıl] önemsiz, az, ufak tefek

trod, bak **tread**

trolley [troli] servis arabası

trombone [tromboun] trombon

troop [tru:p] takım, güruh / bölük

trophy [troufi] ganimet /

kupa
tropical [tropikıl] tropik
tropics [tropiks] sıcak ülkeler
trot [trot] tırıs gitmek
trouble [trabıl] dert, eziyet, tasa / bozukluk / zahmet vermek / eziyet vermek
troublesome, rahatsız edici, zahmetli / belalı
trough [trof] yalak
trousers [trauzız] pantolon
trousseau [tru:sou] çeyiz
trout [traut] alabalık
trowel [trauıl] inşaat v.b. malası
truce [tru:s] ateşkes
truck [trak] el arabası / kamyon / takas / sebze
truculent [trakyulınt] atılgan, kavgacı
trudge [trac] yorgun bir şekilde yürümek
true [tru:] doğru / gerçek / sadık
truly [tru:li] gerçekten, doğru olarak
trump [tramp] koz
trumpet [trampit] trompet / trompet çalmak
truncheon [trançın] cop
trunk [trank] ağaç gövdesi / beden / bavul
trunk call [trank ko:l] şehirler arası telefon
trunks [tranks] şort
trust [trast] güvenmek, inanmak, emniyet etmek / güven
trustee [trasti:] mutemet
trustworthy [trastwö:di] güvenilir
truth [tru:t] gerçek
try (tried, tried) [tray, trayd, trayd] gayret etmek / denemek, tecrübe etmek / tecrübe, deneme
trying [traying] güç / yorucu
tub [tab] tekne / leğen, küvet
tube [tiu:b] tüp / boru / tünel
tuberculosis [tiu:bö:kyulousis] verem
tuck [tak] kırma / kırma yapmak / tıkmak
Tuesday [tiu:zdi] salı
tuft [taft] bir tutam saç, saç kümesi
tug [tag] römorkör / yedeğe almak, çekmek

tuition [tiuişın] öğretim
tulip [tiu:lip] lale
tulle [tul, tiu:l] tül
tumble [tambıl] düşme / düşmek, yıkılmak
tumour [tiu:mı] şiş, ur
tumult [tiu:malt] gürültü, patırdı
tune [tiu:n] nağme, müzik / akort etmek
tuning [tiu:ning] akord etme
tunnel [tanıl] tünel
turban [tö:bın] sarık
turbid [tö:bid] çamurlu
turbine [tö:bayn, tö:bin] türbin
turbulence [tö:byulıns] çalkantı / bozuk hava
turbulent [tö:byulınt] çalkantılı, karmakarışık
turf [tö:f] çimenlik
Turk [tö:k] Türk
Turkey [tö:ki] Türkiye
turkey [tö:ki] hindi
Turkish [tö:kiş] Türk / Türkçe
Turkish delight [tö:kiş dilayt] lokum
turmoil [tö:moyl] hengâme, hercümerç
turn [tö:n] dönmek, sapmak, döndürmek /...haline sokmak / sıra / devir, dönüş / köşe
turner [tö:nı] tornacı
turning [tö:ning] dönen / dönemeç
turnip [tö:nip] şalgam
turn off [tö:n of] kapatmak, kesmek
turn on [tö:n on] açmak
turnstile [tö:nstayl] turnike
turret [tarit] taret, kule
turtle [tö:tıl] deniz kaplumbağası
tussle [tasıl] uğraşmak, cebelleşmek
tutor [tiu:tı] öğretmen / özel öğretmen
tweed [twi:d] (kumaş) tüvid
tweezers [twi:zız] cımbız
twelfth [twelft] on ikinci
twelve [twelv] on iki
twentieth [twenti:t] yirminci
twenty [twenti] yirmi
twice [tways] iki kere
twig [twig] ufak dal
twilight [twaylayt] alaca karanlık, şafak, gurup
twin [twin] ikiz

twine [twayn] sicim
twinge [twinc] sancı
twinkle [twinkıl] parıltı / parıldamak, yanıp sönmek
twirl [twö:l] kıvırmak, döndürmek
twist [twist] burmak, bükmek, kıvırmak / bükme, burma
twitch [twiç] irkilmek, oynatmak / seğirme
twitter [twitı] cıvıltı / cıvıldamak
two [tu:] iki
type [tayp] tip, cins / daktilo ile yazmak
typewriter [taypraytı] yazı makinesi
typhoid [tayfoyd] tifo
typhoon [tayfu:n] tayfun
typhus [tayfıs] tifüs
typical [tipikıl] tipik
tyranny [tirıni] müstebit idare / zulüm
tyrant [tayrınt] müstebit, gaddar, zalim
tyre [tayı] otomobil, lastiği

U

udder [adı] inek memesi
ugly [agli] çirkin
ulcer [alsı] yara, ülser
ultimate [altimit] son
ultimatum [altimeytım] ultimatom
ultra— [altrı] ötesinde anlamında önek
ultra-violet [altrıvayılit] ültraviyole, mor ötesi
umbrella [ambrelı] şemsiye
umpire [ampayı] hakem
un— [an] değil anlamında önek
unable [aneybıl] güçsüz
unacceptable [anıkseptıbıl] kabul edilemez
uneffected [anıfektid] samimi / etkilenmemiş
unambitious [anembişıs] ihtirası olmayan
unanimous [yunenimıs] aynı fikirde, ittifakla
unarmed [ana:md] silahsız
unassuming [anısyu:ming] alçak gönüllü

unattached [anıteçt] bağlı olmayan, serbest
unattainable [anıteynıbıl] elde edilemez
unaware [anıweı] habersiz
unbearable [anbeırıbıl] tahammül edilmez
unbelievable [anbili:vıbıl] inanılmaz
unbolt [anboult] sürgüsünü açmak
unborn [anbo:n] doğmamış
unbound [anbaund] çözülmüş / ciltlenmemiş
unbounded [anbaundid] hudutsuz, sınırsız
unbroken [anbroukın] fasılasız / kırılmamış
unbutton [anbatın] düğmelerini çözmek
uncalled-for [anko:ld fo:] beklenmedik, istenmeyen
uncanny [ankeni] esrarengiz
uncertain [ansö:tın] belirsiz, şüpheli
unchangeable [ançeyncıbıl] değişmez
uncivil [ansivıl] nezaketsiz
unclaimed [ankleymd] sahibi çıkmamış
uncle [ankıl] dayı, amca
unclothed [ankloudıd] çıplak
uncomfortable [ankamfıtıbıl] rahatsız
uncommon [ankomın] nadir
unconditional [ankındişınıl] şartsız
unconscious [ankonşıs] baygın, bihaber
uncontrollable [ankıntroulıbıl] zaptedilemez
unconventional [ankınvenşınıl] alışılmamış, göreneğe uymayan
uncouth [anku:t] kaba / çirkin / görgüsüz
uncover [ankavı] meydana çıkarmak
undecided [andisaydid] kararsız
undefined [andifaynd] belli olmayan, tanımlanmamış
undeniable [andinayıbıl] inkar olunamaz
under— [andı] altında
underclothes [andıkloudz]

iç çamaşırı
undercurrent [andıkarınt] dip akıntısı
underdo (underdid, underdone) [andıdu; andıdid, andıdan] az pişirmek
underfeed (underfed, underfed) [andıfi:d, —fed, fed] az gıda vermek
undergo (underwent, undergone) [andıgou, —went, —gon] katlanmak / duçar olmak
undergraduate [andıgrecuit] üniversite öğrencisi
underground [andıgraund] yeraltı, metro
undergrown [andıgroun] büyümemiş, sıska
underline [andılayn] satırın altını çizmek
undermine [andımayn] baltalamak, sabote etmek
undermost [andımoust] en alttaki
underneath [andıni:t] aşağısında
undersell [andısel] diğerlerinden daha düşük fiyata vermek
undersized [andısayzd] cılız
understand (understood, understood) [andıstend, —stud, —stud] anlamak, kavramak
understandable [andıstendıbıl] anlaşılabilir
understood, bak **understand**
undertake (undertook, undertaken) [andıteyk, andıtuk, andıteykın] üzerine almak, üstlenmek
undertaker [andıteykı] cenaze kaldırıcısı
undertaking [andıteyking] taahhüt, üzerine alma / teşebbüs
undertook, bak **undertake**
undervalue [andıvelyu] az değer biçmek, küçümsemek
underwear [andıweı] iç çamaşırı
underwent, bak **undergo**
underworld [andıwö:ld] caniler alemi, yer altı dünyası
undesirable [andızayrıbıl]

hoşa gitmeyen
undeveloped [andivelıpt] gelişmemiş
undid, bak **undo**
undistinguished [andistingwişt] mümtaz olmayan, alelade
undisturbed [andistö:bd] sakin, istifi bozulmamış
undivided [andivaydid] tam, bütün
undo (undid, undone) [andu, andid, andan] çözmek, bozmak
undoubted [andautid] şüphesiz, kuşkusuz
undress [andres] soyunmak, soymak
undue [andyu:] fazla aşırı derecede
undulate [andyuleyt] dalgalanmak
unduly [andyu:li] gereğinden fazla
undying [andaying] ölmez
uneasy [ani:zi] rahatsız, huzursuz
unemployed [anemployd] işsiz
unemployment [anemploymınt] işsizlik
unending [anending] bitmez, sonsuz
unequal [anikwıl] eşit olmayan
unerring [anö:ring] şaşmaz, hata yapmayan
uneven [ani:vın] düz olmayan, pürüzlü
unexampled [angiza:mpıld] emsalsiz
unexcelled [anekseld] emsalsiz, daha iyisi olmayan
unexpected [anekspektid] umulmadık
unexplored [aneksplo:d] keşfedilmemiş
unfading [anfeyding] ebedi, solmayan
unfailing [anfeyling] şaşmaz
unfair [anfeı] haksız, hileli
unfamiliar [anfımilyı] garip, yabancı
unfashionable [anfeşınıbıl] modaya uygun olmayan
unfasten [anfa:sın] çözmek
unfit [anfit] uygun olmayan, işe yaramaz, sağlığı bozuk

unfix [anfiks] sökmek
unfold [anfould] açmak, yaymak
unforeseen [anfo:sin] tahmin edilmeyen
unforgettable [anfıgetıbıl] unutulmaz
unfortunate [anfo:çınit] talihsiz, aksi
unfortunately [anfo:çınitli] maalesef, yazık ki
unfounded [anfaundid] sebepsiz, asılsız
unfriendly [anfrendli] hasmane, düşmanca
ungainly [angeynli] hantal, biçimsiz
ungracious [angreyşıs] nezaketsiz
ungrateful [angreytful] nankör
ungrounded [angraundid] asılsız
unguarded [anga:did] muhafaza edilmemiş / dikkatsiz
unhappy [anhepi] mutsuz
unhealthy [anhelti] hastalıklı
unheard [anhö:d] işitilmemiş
unhook [anhuk] kopçalarını çözmek
unidentified [anaydentifayd] kimliği saptanmamış
unification [yu:nifikeyşın] birleştirme
uniform [yu:nifo:m] üniforma / muntazam / tek cins
uniformity [yu:nifo:miti] yeknesaklık
unify [yu:nifay] birleştirmek
unimaginable [animecinıbıl] akıl ermez
uninformed [aninfo:md] malumatsız, bilgisiz
uninterested [anintristid] alakasız, ilgisiz
uninteresting [unintresting] ilginç olmayan
union [yu:nyın] birlik, sendika
unique [yu:ni:k] yegâne, eşsiz
unit [yu:nit] birim
unite [yu:nayt] birleşmek
United Kingdom [yu:naytid kingdım] Britanya krallığı
United States [yu:naytid

steyts] Birleşik Devletler (Amerika)
unity [yu:niti] birlik
universal [yu:nivö:sıl] evrensel
universe [yu:nivö:s] kainat, evren
university [yu:nivö:siti] üniversite
unjust [ancast] haksız, adaletsiz
unkempt [ankempt] taranmamış
unkind [ankaynd] kaba, haşin
unknown [announ] bilinmeyen, meçhul
unlawful [anlo:fıl] kanuna aykırı
unless [anles] meğer ki, ...medikçe, ta ki
unlike [anlayk] benzemez
unlikely [anlaykli] umulmaz, ihtimal dışı
unlimited [anlimitid] hadsiz, sınırsız
unload [anloud] yükü boşaltmak
unlock [anlok] kilidini açmak
unlucky [anlaki] talihsiz
unmask [anma:sk] meydana çıkarmak, foyasını çıkarmak
unmatched [anmeçt] emsalsiz
unmeasured [anmejıd] ölçüsüz
unmerciful [anmö:sifıl] gaddar, merhametsiz
unmistakable [anmisteykıbıl] yanılmaz, aşikar
unnatural [anneçırıl] gayri tabi
unnecessary [annesisıri] gereksiz
unnerve [annö:v] cesaretini kırmak
unnoticed [annoutist] görülmemiş, gözden kaçmış
unobjectionable [anobcekşınıbıl] itiraz edilemez
unobserved [anobzö:vd] farkedilmemiş
unpack [anpek] (bavuldan) çıkarmak, bohça açmak
unpaid [anpeyd] ödenmemiş
unparalleled [anperıleld] eşsiz, emsalsiz
unperturbed [anpıtö:bd] fü-

tursuz, umursamaz
unpleasant [anplezınt] hoş olmayan, nahoş
unpopular [anpopyulı] sevilmeyen, popüler olmayan
unpopulated [anpopyuleytid] iskan edilmemiş boş yer
unpractical [anprektikıl] kullanışlı olmayan / beceriksiz
unprecedented [anpri:sidentid] evveli emsali yok
unprepared [anpripeıd] hazırlıksız
unpretentious [anpritenşıs] iddiasız, mütevazi
unprotected [anprıtektid] muhafazasız, korunmayan
unpunctual [anpankçuıl] geç kalan, dakik olmayan
unqualified [ankwolifayd] ehliyetsiz, yeteneksiz
unquestionable [ankwesçınıbıl] şüphesiz, kuşkusuz
unravel [anrevıl] halletmek, çözmek
unreal [anriıl] hayali
unreasonable [anri:zınıbıl] makul olmayan
unrest [anrest] huzursuzluk
unrestricted [anristriktid] serbest, tahditsiz, sınırsız
unrivalled [anrayvıld] rakipsiz
unruffled [anrafıld] aldırış etmeyen
unruly [anru:li] ele avuca sığmaz, asi
unsafe [anseyf] emin olmayan, tehlikeli
unsatisfactory [ansetisfektıri] tatminkar olmayan / uygun olmayan
unsatisfied [ansetisfayd] tatmin olmamış / doymamış
unscrew [anskru:] vidalarını sökmek
unscrupulous [anskru:piulıs] vicdansız
unseasonable [ansi:zınıbıl] mevsimsiz
unsecured [ansikyuıd] temin edilmemiş
unseemly [ansi:mli] yakışıksız

unseen [ansi:n] görülmemiş, gizli
unsettle [ansetıl] bulandırmak, karıştırmak
unskilful [anskilfıl] hünersiz, beceriksiz
unsound [ansaund] çürük, kusurlu / batıl
unspeakable [anspi:kıbıl] ağıza alınmaz / sözle anlatılamaz
unspoiled [anspoyld] bozulmamış, şımarmamış
unspoken [anspoukın] açığa vurulmamış
unsteady [anstedi] sağlam olmayan
unstitch [anstiç] dikişini sökmek
unsurpassed [ansö:pa:st] emsalsiz
unsuspected [ansıspektid] şüphe edilmeyen
unswerving [answö:ving] sapmaz, şaşmaz
unthinkable [antinkıbıl] düşünülemeyen
untidy [antaydi] dağınık, düzensiz
until [antil] ...kadar
untimely [antaymli] mevsimsiz, yersiz
untouchable [antaçıbıl] dokunulmaz
untrodden [antrodın] ayak basılmamış
untroubled [antrabıld] rahat, kaygısız
untrue [antru:] yalan / vefasız
unusable [anyu:zıbıl] faydasız, kullanılmaz
unusual [anyu:juıl] nadir, fevkalade, alışılmamış
unutterable [anatrıbıl] ağıza alınmaz
unvaried [anveırid] değişmez
unvarying [anveıriying] değişmez
unwary [anweıri] gafil
unwell [anwel] keyifsiz, hasta
unwilling [anwiling] isteksiz
unwise [anwayz] makul olmayan, akılsız
unworthy [anwö:di] layık olmayan
unyielding [anyi:lding] boyun eğmez, teslim olmayan
up— [ap] yukarıya doğru anlamında önek

up [ap] yukarı, yukarıya

upbringing [apbringing] çocuk terbiyesi

uphold (upheld, upheld) [aphould, —held, —held] tutmak, idame etmek, devam ettirmek

upholster [aphoulstı] döşemek / kaplamak

upholsterer, döşemeci

upholstery, döşeme

upkeep [apki:p] idame, bakım

uplands [aplends] yayla

uplift [aplift] yükselme / yükseltmek

upon [ıpon] üzerine, üzerinde

upper [apı] üst

upright [aprayt] dik

uprising [aprayzing] isyan

uproar [apro:] şamata, kargaşalık

uproot [apru:t] köklemek, köküyle birlikte çıkarmak

upset [apset] altüst etmek, bozmak / karışıklık

upsidedown [apsayddaun] altüst

upstairs [apsteız] üst kat, yukarı

upstart [apsta:t] yeni zengin

upstream [apstri:m] nehrin akıntısının ters yönünde, akıntıya karşı

up-to-date [aptudeyt] şimdiki, en yeni, modern

upwards [apwıdz] yukarıya doğru

uranium [yu:reynyım] uranyum madeni

urban [ö:bın] şehre mensup, şehirle ilgili

urbane [ö:beyn] nazik

urchin [ö:çin] afacan

urge [ö:c] zorlamak / ısrar etmek

urgency [ö:cınsi] acele, zorunluk

urgent [ö:cınt] acil, zorunlu

urine [yuırin] idrar

us [as] bizi, bize

U.S.A (The United States of America) Amerika Birleşik Devletleri

usage [yu:zic] kullanış, yarar / görenek

use [yu:z] kullanmak

used [yu:zd] kullanılmış

useful [yu:sfıl] yararlı
useless [yu:slis] yararsız
usher [aşı] mübaşir / yol göstermek
usual [yu:juıl] olağan, her zamanki
usually [yu:juıli] çoğunlukla, ekseriya
usurer [yu:jırı] tefeci
utensils [yu:tensils] mutfak v.b. takımı
utilitarian [yu:tiliteıriyın] faydacı
utilize [yu:tilayz] kullanmak, yararlanmak
utmost [atmoust] son derece
utter [atı] tam, son derece
utter [atı] ses çıkarmak

V

vacancy [veykınsi] boşluk, münhal yer
vacant [veykınt] boş, münhal
vacation [vıkeyşın] tatil
vaccinate [veksineyt] aşılamak (ilaç)
vaccination [veksineyşın] aşı, aşılama
vacuum [vekyuım] vakum, boşluk
vacuum cleaner [vekyuım kli:nı] elektrik süpürgesi
vagabond [vegıbond] derbeder, külhanbeyi
vagrant [veygrınt] serseri, avare
vague [veyg] müphem, belli belirsiz
vain [veyn] beyhude, boşuna / kendini beğenmiş
valet [velit] uşak
valiant [velyınt] yiğit
valid [velid] geçerli
validity [veliditi] geçerlilik
valise [vıli:z] valiz
valley [veli] vadi
valour [velı] yiğitlik, cesaret
valuable [velyuıb:l] değerli
valuation [velyueyşın] değer biçme
value [velyu] değer / değer biçmek
valve [velv] supap, valf /

(radyo) lamba, tüp
vamp [vemp] seks kadını
vampire [vempayı] vampir
van [ven] yük vagonu / yük arabası / ordu veya donanmanın ön kısmı / öncü
vanguard [venga:d] öncü, ön cephe
vanilla [vınilı] vanilya
vanish [veniş] gözden kaybolmak, yok olmak
vanity [veniti] hiçlik, beyhudelik / kibir
vanquish [venkwiş] yenmek
vapour [veypı] buhar / buhar çıkarmak
vaporize [veypırayz] buharlaşmak
vaporous [veypırıs] buharlı
variable [veıriıbıl] değişken
variance [veıriıns] fark
variation [veırieyşın] değişme
varied [veırid] çeşitli türlü
variety [vırayıti] çeşitlenme, nevi, çeşit, cins
various [veıriıs] çeşitli, türlü
varnish [va:niş] vernik
vary [veıri] değişmek
vase [va:z] vazo
vaseline [vesıli:n] vazelin
vast [va:st] geniş, engin
vault [vo:lt] atlamak / kubbe
veal [vi:l] dana eti
vegetable [vecitıbıl] sebze
vegetarian [veciteıriın] et yemeyen kimse
vehemence [vi:imıns] hiddet, sertlik
vehicle [vi:ikıl] taşıt, araç, vasıta
veil [veyl] peçe / örtmek
vein [veyn] damar
velocity [vılositi] sürat
velvet [velvit] kadife
vendor [vendı] satıcı
venerable [venrıbıl] muhterem, saygıdeğer
venerate [venıreyt] hürmet etmek, saymak
veneration [venireyşın] hürmet, saygı
vengeance [vencıns] intikam
venom [venım] zehir

vent [vent] delik
ventilate [ventileyt] havalandırmak
ventilation [ventileyşın] havalandırma
ventilator [ventileytı] vantilatör
ventriloquist [ventrilokwist] vantrilok, karnından konuşan
venture [vençı] kalkışmak, cüret etmek / teşebbüs
veracity [vıresiti] doğru sözlülük
veranda [vırendı] veranda
verb [vö:b] (dilbilgisinde) fiil, eylem
verbose [vö:bous] çok konuşan
verdict [vö:dikt] hüküm, karar, yargı
verge [vö:c] kenar, sınır / karar, yargı
verify [verifay] tasdik etmek, doğrulamak / kontrol etmek
vermin [vö:min] haşarat, zararlı hayvan
vermouth [vö:mu:t] vermut
versatile [vö:sıtayl] verimli, her işi beceren
verse [vö:s] şiir
version [vö:şın] terçüme / nüsha, yorum
vertical [vö:tikıl] dikey
very [veri] pek, çok / tam, tıpkı, ta kendisi
vessel [vesıl] gemi, tekne / kap
vest [vest] (yetki) vermek / yelek
vestibule [vestibyu:l] dehliz, hol
veteran [vetırın] emekli asker / pişmiş, emektar
veterinary [vetırinıri] baytarlık
veto [vitou] veto
vex [veks] canını sıkmak
via [vayı] yolu ile
vibrate [vaybreyt] titremek, sallanmak
vibration [vaybreyşın] ihtizaz, titreşim
vicar [vikı] mahalle papazı
vice [vays] kusur, kötülük / mengene
vice— [vays] yerinde, muavin anlamında ö-

nek
vice versa [vaysivö:sı] bilmukabele, karşılık olarak
vicinity [visiniti] civar, etraf, çevre
vicious [vişıs] kötü, zalim, tehlikeli
victim [viktim] kurban
victor [viktı] fatih
victorious [vikto:ryıs] muzaffer, galip
victory [viktıri] zafer
view [viu:] fikir, görüş / görünüş, manzara
vigil [vicil] gece nöbeti
vigour [vigı] kuvvet, güç
vigorous [vigırıs] kuvvetli
vile [vayl] kötü, alçak
villa [vilı] villa
village [vilic] köy
villain [vilın] habis, kötü insan
vindicate [vindikeyt] hakkını savunmak
vindictive [vindiktiv] öç alıcı
vine [vayn] asma
vineyard [vinyıd] üzüm bağı
vinegar [vinigı] sirke
vintage [vintic] bağbozumu
violate [vayıleyt] bozmak, tecavüz etmek
violation [vayıleyşın] ihlal, bozma
violence [vayılıns] şiddet, zorbalık
violent [vayılınt] şiddetli, zorlu, sert
violet [vayılit] menekşe
violin [vayılin] keman
violinist [vayılınist] kemancı
viper [vaypı] engerek
virgin [vö:cin] bakire
virile [virayl] kuvvetli, kudretli, iktidarlı
virtue [vö:çu:] meziyet, fazilet, erdem
virtuous [vö:çuıs] faziletli, erdemli
virulence [viryulıns] şiddet, keskinlik
virulent [viryulınt] şiddetli, sert, zehirli
virus [vayrıs] virüs
visa [vi:zı] vize
vise [vays] mengene
visibility [vizibiliti] görünürlük, görüş alanı
visible [vizibıl] görülen
vision [vijın] görüş / ha-

yal
visit [vizit] ziyaret / ziyaret etmek
visitor [vizitı] ziyaretçi
visor [vayzı] kasket siperliği, vizör
visual [vijuıl] görmeğe ait, görüşle ilgili
vital [vaytıl] hayati
vitamin [vaytımin] vitamin
vivacious [vayveyşıs] canlı, şakrak
vivacity [vayvesiti] canlılık
vivid [vivid] canlı
viz [viz] (Latince) mesela, yani, örneğin
vocabulary [vıkebyulıri] kısa sözlük / bir kimsenin kullandığı sözcükler, sözcük dağarcığı
vocal [voukıl] sese ait, vokal
vocation [voukeyşın] meslek
vogue [voug] moda
voice [voys] ses (insan)
void [voyd] boş / beyhude / boşluk / boşaltmak
volatile [volıtayl] uçucu
volcanic [volkenik] volkanik
volcano [volkeynou] volkan
volley [voli] yaylım ateş / top yere değmeden vurma
volt [voult] volt
voluble [volyu:bıl] çenebaz / rahat konuşan
volume [volyu:m] cilt / hacim
voluntary [volıntıri] isteyerek, ihtiyari, gönüllü
voluptuous [vılapçuıs] şehvete düşkün, şehvani
vomit [vomit] kusmak
voracious [vıreyşıs] obur
vote [vout] oy / oy vermek
vouch [vauç] tasdik etmek, onaylamak / üstüne almak, garanti etmek
voucher [vauçı] para yerine geçen fiş, belge
vow [vau] adak / adamak / yemin etmek
vowel [vauıl] sesli harf
voyage [voyic] deniz yolculuğu
vulgar [valgı] kaba, bayağı
vulnerable [valnırıbıl] yaralanır, kolay incinir

vulture [valçı] akbaba

W

wad [wod] tapa, tıkaç
wade [weyd] su içinde yürümek
wag [weg] sallamak
wage [weyc] ücret / haftalık
wager [weycı] bahis (at yarışı v.b.)
wagon [wegın] yük arabası / eşya vagonu
wail [weyl] haykırarak ağlayış / ağlamak
waist [weyst] bel
waistcoat [weystkout] yelek
wait [weyt] beklemek
waiter [weytı] garson
waitress [weytris] kadın garson
wake (woke, woken) [weyk, wouk, woukın] uyandırmak, uyanmak
walk [wo:k] yürümek / yürüyüş / gezinti
wall [wo:l] duvar
wallet [wolit] cüzdan
wallflower [wo:lflauı] şebboy
wallow [wolou] çamurda yuvarlanmak
walnut [wolnat] ceviz
waltz [wols] vals / vals yapmak
wan [woռ] soluk, donuk
wand [wond] ince çubuk
wander [wondı] amaçsız gezmek, yoldan ayrılmak
wane [weyn] küçülmek, azalmak
want [wont] istemek / yokluk, zaruret
wanton [wontın] amaçsız / havai, aşifte
war [wo:] savaş
warble [wo:bıl] şakımak
ward [wo:d] muhafaza, koruma / koğuş, hücre
warden [wo:dın] muhafız, gardiyan
warder [wo:dı] muhafız, nöbetçi, gardiyan
wardrobe [wo:droub] elbise dolabı, gardrop
ware [weı] mal
warehouse [weıhaus] antrepo, depo

warfare [wo:feı] savaş hali
warlike [wo:layk] savaşçı
warm [wo:m] ılık / ısıtmak, ılındırmak
warmly [wo:mli] hararetle
warmth [wo:mt] hararet, sıcaklık
warn [wo:n] uyarmak, ihtar etmek, ikaz etmek
warning [wo:ning] ihtar, ihbarname
warrant [worınt] tutuklama emri / berat / ruhsat vermek
warranty [worınti] kefalet
warrior [woryı] savaşçı
warship [wo:şip] savaş gemisi
wart [wo:t] siğil
wary [weıri] uyanık, ihtiyatlı
was [woz, wız] bak **be,** idi, oldu
wash [woş] yıkamak, yıkanmak / yıkanma
washable [woşıbıl] yıkanabilir, yıkanınca çıkar
washbasin [woşbeysin] lavabo
washerwoman [woşıwumın] çamaşırcı kadın
wasp [wosp] eşek arısı
wastage [weystic] israf, fire
waste [weyst] israf, ziyan / israf etmek
wasteful [weystfıl] tutumsuz, müsrif
watch [woç] seyretmek, gözetlemek, bakmak / cep veya kol saati / nöbet, vardiya
watcher [woçı] bekçi
watchful [woçfıl] tetikte, dikkatli
watchman [woçmın] bekçi, gözcü
watchword [woçwö:d] parola
water [wo:tı] su / sulamak
W. C. (water-closet) [dabılyu:si (wo:tı klozit)] hela, tuvalet
water-bottle [wo:tıbotıl] matara
water closet [wo:tıklozit] hela, tuvalet
watercourse [wo:tıko:s] mecra, ark
waterfall [wo:tıfo:l] çağlayan

watering [wo:tıring] sulama
waterless [wo:tılis] çorak, susuz
waterproof [wo:tıpru:f] su geçirmez
watery [wo:tıri] sulu
watt [wot] wat (elektrik)
wave [weyv] dalga / dalgalanmak / (mendil v.b.) sallamak
waver [weyvı] kararsızlık göstermek
wavering, kararsız
wavy [weyvi] dalgalı
wax [weks] balmumu / mumlamak
way [wey] yol / taraf / tarz
wayside [weysayd] yol kenarı
wayward [weywıd] dik başlı
we [wi: wi] biz
weak [wi:k] zayıf, halsiz, aciz
weaken [wi:kın] zayıflatmak
wealth [welt] servet
wealthy [welti] zengin
weapon [wepın] silah
wear (wore, worn) [weı, wo: wo:n] giymek, takmak / eskitmek, aşındırmak / giyim / eskime / dayanıklılık
wearisome [wiırisım] usandırıcı
weary [wiıri] yorgun
weather [wedı] hava
weather beaten [wedı bi:tın] güneşten yanmış
weather forecast [wedı fo:ka:st] hava raporu
weave (wove, woven) [wi:v, wouv, wouvın] dokumak
weaver [wi:vı] dokumacı
weaving [wi:ving] dokumacılık
web [web] ağ / doku
wed [wed] evlenmek, evlendirmek
wedding [weding] düğün
wedge [wec] oduncu kaması, takoz
wedlock [wedlok] evlilik
Wednesday [wenzdi] çarşamba
weed [wi:d] işe yaramaz ot, ayrık otu / otlarını temizlemek
week [wi:k] hafta
weekday [wi:kdey] iş günü

weekend, hafta sonu
weekly [wi:kli] haftalık
weep [wi:p] ağlamak
weeping [wi:ping] ağlayan
weigh [wey] tartmak
weight [weyt] ağırlık
weighty [weyti] ağır
welcome [welkım] hoş geldin / makbul / "hoş geldin" demek / iyi karşılamak
weld [weld] kaynak / kaynakla birleştirmek
welfare [welfeı] refah, sıhhat
well [wel] iyi bir şekilde, iyi olarak / tamamen / sıhhatte / şu halde / kuyu
went, bak **go**
wept, bak **weep**
were, bak **be**
west [west] batı
western [westın] batıya ait
westward [westwıd] batıya doğru
wet [wet] ıslak / ıslatmak
whale [weyl] balina
wharf [wo:f] rıhtım, iskele
what [wot] ne / ne ki
whatever [wotevı] herhangi, her ne
wheat [wi:t] buğday
wheel [wi:l] tekerlek / direksiyon
wheeze [wi:z] hışırtı
when [wen] ne zaman / ne zaman ki / iken
whenever [wenevı] her ne zaman
where [weı] nerede, nereye / ki orada
whereabouts [weırıbauts] yaklaşık olarak nerede
whereas [weırez] halbuki
wherever [weırevı] nerede olursa, her nerede
whether [wedı] acaba, ...mi
whichever [wiçevı] hangisi / ki o, ki onu
whiff [wif] püf, (hava, duman v.b.) dalgası
while [wayl] iken, müddetçe / müddet, süre
whilst [waylst] iken
whim [wim] ani ve geçici istek, heves, kapris
whimper [wimpı] inilti
whine [wayn] sızlanmak
whip [wip] kırbaç / kamçıla-

mak, dayak almak

whirl [wö:l] savrulmak / dönmek

whisker [wiskı] hayvan bıyığı

whisky [wiski] viski

whisper [wispı] fısıltı / fısıldamak

whistle [wisıl] ıslık, düdük / ıslık çalmak

whit [wit] zerre, hiç

white [wayt] beyaz

whiten [waytın] beyazlatmak

whiteness [waytnis] beyazlık

whitewash [waytwoş] badana / badanalamak

whizz [wiz] vızıltı / vızıldamak

who [hu:] kim / ki o

whoever [hu:evı] kim olursa, her kim ise

whole [houl] bütün, tam, toptan

wholesale [houlseyl] toptan

wholesome [houlsım] sağlam, besleyici

wholly [houli] tamamiyle

whom [hu:m] kimi, kime / ki onu

whoop [hu:p] haykırmak / öksürmek

whooping cough [hu:ping kof] boğmaca öksürüğü

whore [ho:] orospu

whose [hu:z] kimin / ki onun

why [way] niçin

wick [wik] fitil

wicked [wikid] kötü, hain

wide [wayd] geniş

widely [waydli] geniş ölçüde, çok

widen [waydın] genişletmek

widespread, yaygın

widow [widou] dul (kadın)

widower, dul (erkek)

width [widt] genişlik

wife (çoğulu **wifes**) [wayf, wayvz] eş, karı

wig [wig] peruka

wild [wayld] vahşi, yabani / fırtınalı

wildness [wayldnis] yabanilik / şiddet / delilik

wilderness [wildınis] çöl, boş arazi

wile [wayl] oyun, hile
wilful [wilfıl] inatçı
will [wil] gelecek zaman kipini teşkil için kullanılan yardımcı fiil, ...ecek, ...acak / istek / vasiyatname
willing [wiling] istekli
willingly [wilingli] istekle
willow [wilou] söğüt
willy-nilly [wilinili] ister istemez
win (won, won) [win, wan, wan] (oyunda, savaşta, kumarda) kazanmak, yenmek
wince [wins] ürkmek / sakınmak
winch [winş] vinç, çıkrık
wind [wind] rüzgar
wind (wound, wound) [waynd, waund] dolaşmak, dolaştırmak, dolanmak / sarmak / (saat v.s.) kurmak
windfall [windfo:l] devlet kuşu, talih / yere düşmüş meyva
winding [waynding] dolambaçlı, dönemeç
windlass [windlıs] kuyu çıkrığı
windmill [windmil] yel değirmeni
window [windou] pencere, vitrin
windpipe [windpayp] nefes borusu
windscreen [windskri:n] otomobil ön camı
windy [windi] rüzgârlı
wine [wayn] şarap
wing [wing] kanat / (otomobilde) çamurluk
wink [wink] göz kırpma / göz kırpmak
winner [winı] kazanan, galip, yenen
winter [wintı] kış / kışlamak
wipe [wayp] silmek, temizlemek
wire [wayı} tel / telgraf / telgraf çekmek
wireless [wayılis] telsiz / radyo
wiring [wayring] elektrik tesisatı
wiry [wayri] tel gibi sırım
wisdom [wizdım] akıl
wise [wayz] akıllı
wish [wiş] arzu etmek, dilemek / arzu, dilek

wishbone [wişboun] lades kemiği
wistful [wistfıl] arzulu
wit [wit] akıl, nükte / nüktedan
witch [wiç] büyücü, cadı
with [wid] ile, birlikte / ...lı
withdraw (—drew, —drawn) [widdro:, —dru:, —dro:n] geri çekilmek
withdrawal [widdro:ıl] rücu, geri çekilme
wither [widı] kurumak, kurutmak / solmak
withhold (—held, —held) [widhould, —held, —held] esirgemek, alıkoymak
within [widin] içinde / zarfında
without [widaut] ...siz, olmaksızın / dışta
withstand (stood, stood) [widstend, —stud, —stud] karşı koymak, direnmek
witless [witlis] akılsız
witness [witnis] tanık, şahit / kanıt / tanık olmak
witty [witi] nükteli
wizard [wizıd] sihirbaz
wizened [wizınd] kurumuş, buruşmuş
woe [wou] elem, dert
woke, bak **wake**
wolf (çoğulu: **wolves)** [wulf, wulvz] kurt
woman (çoğulu: **women)** [wumın, wimin] kadın
womb [wu:m] rahim
won, bak **win**
wonder [wandı] acaba demek, hayret etmek / hayret / harika
I wonder, acaba
wonderful [wandıfıl] olağanüstü, fevkalade
woo [wu:] kur yapmak
wood [wud] odun, tahta / küçük orman
woodcock [wudkok] çulluk
wooden [wudın] tahtadan yapılmış, ahşap
woodpecker [wudpekı] ağaçkakan
wool [wul] yün
woollen [wulın] yünlü
word [wö:d] sözcük, söz
wore, bak **wear**
work [wö:k] iş / çalışma /

eser / çalışmak / işletmek
worker [wö:kı] işçi, çalışan
workman [wö:kmın] işçi
workshop [wö:kşop] atölye
world [wö:ld] dünya
worldly, dünyevi
worldwide [wö:ldwayd] dünya çapında, yaygın
worm [wö:m] (ağaç v.b.de) kurt, solucan
worn [wo:n] bak **wear,** yıpranmış
worn out, bitkin, eskimiş
worry [wari] tasalanmak, üzülmek, üzmek, canını sıkmak / üzüntü
worse [wö:s] daha fena
worship [wö:şip] tapmak, ibadet etmek
worst [wö:st] en kötü
worth [wö:t] değer / değerinde olmak, etmek
worthy [wö:di] değerli
would [wud] **will**'in geçmiş şekli
wound [wu:nd] yara
wove, bak **weave**
wrap [rep] sarmak, örtmek
wrapper [repı] paket sargısı, kitap ceketi
wrath [ro:t] öfke
wreath [ri:t] çelenk
wreck [rek] (gemiyi, uçağı) kazaya uğratmak / parçalamak / bozmak / mahvetmek / kazazede gemi veya uçak / kaza / enkaz
wreckage [rekic] enkaz
wren [ren] çalıkuşu
wrench [renç] burkulma / İngiliz anahtarı / burkmak
wrest [rest] bükmek, zorlamak
wrestle [resıl] güreşmek
wrestler [reslı] güreşçi
wretched [reçid] biçare, sefil
wriggle [rigıl] kıvrılmak, kıvrıla kıvrıla yürümek
wring (wrung, wrung) [ring, rang, rang] kıvırmak, bükmek
wrinkle [rinkıl] buruşuk, buruşturmak
wrist [rist] bilek
write (wrote, written) [rayt, rout, ritın]

yazmak
writer [raytı] yazar
writhe [rayd] kıvranmak
writing [rayting] yazma
written, bak **write,** yazılı
wrong [rong] yanlış / haksız / haksızlık
wrongdoer [rongdu:ı] kabahat işleyen, suçlu
wrongdoing [rongdu:ing] kabahat, suç
wrote, bak **write**
wrought [ro:t] işlenmiş
wrung, bak **wring** bükük
wry [ray] çarpık

X

Xmas (Christmas) [krismıs] noel
X-ray [eksrey] röntgen ışını
xylonite [zaylınayt] sellüloit

Y

yacht [yot] yat
yachting [yoting] yatçılık
Yankee (U.S.A.) [yenki] kuzeyli (Amerikalı)
yard [ya:d] yarda / avlu, alan / tersane
yarn [ya:n] olmayacak hikaye / iplik
yawn [yo:n] esnemek
year [yiı] yıl, sene
yearling [yiıling] bir yaşında yavru
yearly [yiıli] yıllık
yearn [yö:n] arzu etmek, özlemek
yeast [yi:st] maya
yell [yel] bağırmak / feryat
yellow [yelou] sarı
yelp [yelp] köpeğin bağırması, uluması
yes [yes] evet
yesterday [yestıdi] dün
yet [yet] henüz / lakin
yield [yi:ld] ürün vermek / teslim olmak / teslim etmek / çökmek

yoke [youk] boyunduruk
yolk [youk] yumurta sarısı
yonder [yondı] şurada, orada, oraya, ilerde
you [yu:, yu] sen, siz, seni, sizi, sana, size
young [yang] genç / yavru
youngster [yangstı] çocuk
your [yo:] senin, sizin
yours [yo:z] seninki, sizinki
yourself [yıself] kendiniz
youth [yu:t] gençlik / delikanlı
youthful [yu:tfıl] genç, genç gibi
youth hostel [yu:t hostıl] gençler için ucuz otel
Yugoslav [yugousla:v] Yugoslav
Yugoslavia [yugousla:vyı] Yugoslavya

Z

zeal [zi:l] gayret, büyük istek
zealous [zelıs] gayretli
zebra [zi:brı] yaban eşeği. zebra
zephyr [zefı] hafif rüzgar, meltem
zero [ziırou] sıfır
zest [zest] lezzet / şevk, büyük ilgi
zigzag [zigzeg] zikzak
zinc [zink] çinko
zip [zip] fermuar
zip fastener [zip fa:snı] fermuar
zipper [zipı] fermuar
zone [zoun] mıntıka, bölge
zoo [zu:] hayvanat bahçesi
zoology [zouolıcı] zooloji, hayvanbilim